The End of White World Supremacy

Roderick D. Bush

The End of White World Supremacy

*Black Internationalism and
the Problem of the Color Line*

TEMPLE UNIVERSITY PRESS
Philadelphia

Roderick D. Bush is an Associate Professor of Sociology and Anthropology at St. John's University in New York City. Long an activist in the Black Power and radical movements of the 1960s through the 1980s, Bush returned to the academy in 1988 to obtain a Ph.D. He is the author of *We Are Not What We Seem: Black Nationalism and Class Struggle in the American Century* and editor of *The New Black Vote: Politics and Power in Four American Cities.*

Temple University Press
1601 North Broad Street
Philadelphia PA 19122
www.temple.edu/tempress

∞ The paper used in this publication meets the requirements of the American National Standard for Information Sciences—Permanence of Paper for Printed Library Materials, ANSI Z39.48-1992

Library of Congress Cataloging-in-Publication Data

Bush, Roderick D.
   The end of white world supremacy : black internationalism and the problem of the color line / Roderick D. Bush.
      p. cm.
   Includes bibliographical references and index.
   ISBN 978-1-59213-572-1 (cloth : alk. paper) – ISBN 978-1-59213-573-8 (pbk. : alk. paper)
   1. African Americans–Politics and government.   2. Black nationalism–United States–History.
   3. United States–Race relations.   4. Internationalism.   I. Title.
   E185.61.B975 2009
   305.896'073—dc22   2008047833

Printed in the United States of America

2   4   6   8   9   7   5   3   1

Contents

Introduction

"The Handwriting on the Wall"

Many young people with whom I have conversed over the past twenty years have seen the 1960s as a golden age in the United States, when African Americans completed the last stage of their long march from slavery to freedom by building a noble and courageous movement that captured the hearts and minds of the people of the United States and the sympathy of many throughout the world. It was a time when young Americans (including soldiers) opposed the militarism of the U.S. government, ultimately convincing most Americans that the U.S. intervention in Vietnam was not in the interest of the people of the United States or the people of Vietnam. It was a time when African Americans marched to center stage in American society and forced the walls of Jim Crow segregation to come tumbling down. It was a time when Malcolm X, Stokely Carmichael, and the Black Panther Party raised high the banners of Black Liberation.

These young people often wanted to know what it was about my generation that enabled us to have such an impact on the country, which they saw as sorely lacking in their own generation. My response was always that there was nothing so special about my generation; we were products of our time. Sometimes I point out that a key intellectual failing of our popular discourse is a lack of appreciation of temporalities, but before my listeners' eyes glaze over in that "here comes another professorial lecture" expression, I move quickly to my main point about the 1960s: It was not merely the achievement of youth in the United States (as important as that was); the 1960s was a period of world revolution. All over the world the emancipatory designs of the common people tempered the corrosive and socially degrading power of corporate capitalism, and people of color boldly challenged the presumptions of a global geoculture rooted in the assumptions of a white world supremacy. People of color all over the globe rose to claim their place in the human family as full and respected members of the world community. These movements in Africa, Latin America, and Asia inspired people of African descent, Puerto Ricans, Mexican Americans, Native Americans, Asians, and whites in the United States to believe that a democratic, just, and egalitarian world was indeed possible and that they could and should contribute to the building of such a world.

The rise of what was called the dark world was heralded by Malcolm X as the end of white world supremacy. Malcolm pointed out that the black revolution in the United States was not the rebellion of a minority but a part of the worldwide struggle of the oppressed against the oppressor. The great Chinese revolutionary Mao Zedong agreed. He argued that the evil system of imperialism began with the enslavement of the Black people and would surely come to an end with their complete liberation. While people often associate this period of militancy beyond the civil rights movement with Malcolm X's comment that we will achieve our freedom "by any means necessary" and the Black Panther Party's rhetoric about picking up the gun, the more enduring legacy of Malcolm X and the Black Panther Party was their contribution to a larger movement: They illuminated the landscape with their fresh understanding of the world and a vision that ordinary people who had been victims of the most ruthless exploitation and degradation could collectively create a world that was egalitarian, democratic, and just. However, the tension between the heroic act of the oppressed and the larger and more democratic vision that Malcolm X and the Black Panther Party articulated created a juncture at which federal and local law enforcement agencies could implicitly justify acting as occupying armies not only to bring these dangerous organizations under control but also to monitor and undermine the efforts of all who were involved in the movement as a whole. It is only in this context that we can understand how the FBI's war against Dr. Martin Luther King, Jr., could gain such wide support among liberals, who in theory supported the program of the civil rights movement.

While it is often difficult for the actors in these dramas to operate at a remove that allows them to see both sides of this story, it is much simpler to locate one's own assessment on the basis of whom one trusts. Can Black folks trust whites, who have so seldom risen above self-justifying discourse in their relationship to Black people? Can whites trust Blacks, whose judgments are so often refracted through the memory of past wrongs that they cannot appreciate that there has been a sea change in the racial attitudes of white Americans? Is it simply that there can be no trust from their very different locations within the racial order of U.S. society?

Intellectually and practically, this seemed to be a dead end, but maybe that is the reality. Derrick Bell (1992) and Molefi Asante's (1999) argument about the intractability of the racial divide may have won the day after all.[1] One cannot argue for a position simply because one does not wish to feed cynicism about the possibilities for social change or because one wants only one type of intellectual position to hold. This is clearly not my position. My first response to a simple linear understanding of race relations is that one cannot fully understand the differences that separate liberal intellectuals, activists, and citizens unless one looks at the phenomenon over a long time frame. This, of course, takes us back to the issue of temporalities, or social time.

Like many who have argued for what has recently emerged as the study of the "long civil rights movement," I argue that we may understand the actions of these three entities better if we position the dilemma in the context of the rise to prominence of a liberal internationalism that Henry Luce referred to as the American century. It was through this worldview that powerful forces within the United States sought dominion over the earth. It consisted of a mature global liberalism promising the spread of the good and then the great society to all Americans and eventually to everyone in the world who followed America's example and *direction*. Though it was a frankly hegemonic project that was global in scope, it differed in form from the colonialism practiced by the European powers. It seemed to be of a piece with the civil rights movement, which sounded the central themes of democratization, equal rights, and social justice. Dr. Martin Luther King , Jr., a young Baptist minister who had led the Montgomery Bus Boycott came to symbolize the spirit of the civil rights movement and the promise of America. He skillfully articulated a vision of the American dream that captured the imaginations of tens of millions of Americans of all colors and creeds. King's challenge that America live up to the true meaning of that dream was viewed as the final push that would inspire the people of the United States to complete the great unfinished American revolution. But Malcolm X was skeptical; he had listened carefully to the voices of millions of Black people who lived outside the Jim Crow South yet who were more deeply marginalized from the U.S. white mainstream. Malcolm X helped call the attention of the nation to these marginalized masses by speaking in their voice and helping them to speak in their own voice. Ultimately the eloquence of these voices plus the voices of "the barefoot people in the jungles of Vietnam" (King 1967) drew King closer to Malcolm's view, and King began to say that the operations of U.S. power were a nightmarish ordeal for the world's have-nots and for many of the most disadvantaged people of color within America's borders. During the early 1960s, the most idealistic period of America's global liberalism, the youthful rebels of Students for a Democratic Society argued for a radical democratization of U.S. society, but the rebellion against U.S. hegemony manifested in the struggles in Vietnam, Algeria, Cuba, China, Ghana, Guinea, and other parts of Africa, Asia, and North America combined with the struggle of oppressed strata within the national borders of the United States undermined the largesse of the liberal state. The *rapports de force* had shifted decisively in favor of the colonized, semicolonized, dependent zones of the world-economy occupied in the main by people of color. Malcolm X, the Student Nonviolent Coordinating Committee, Students for a Democratic Society, the Congress of Racial Equality, King, and a host of others called not only for solidarity with the revolutionaries of the three continents but also for the people of the United States to become a part of this elemental rebellion. The world revolutionary trend was global in scope, arrayed against the global power of the U.S. hegemon.[2]

In the conservative atmosphere of neoliberal globalization and the Project for the New American Century, it may be easy to forget or difficult to comprehend a time when third world elites allied with the American hegemon all over the world were under challenge, and many people felt that victory was in sight. What was truly remarkable about this period was the depth of support within the United States for these movements in opposition to the power of the country's own ruling class. This kind of internationalism had been a regular feature of large sections of the Black freedom struggle and of the world socialist movement, but now it was the dominant position of large sections of the population of the hegemonic power, with a majority of young blacks and 40 percent of college students arguing that a revolution was necessary in the United States.

During the late 1960s and early 1970s "all society was a battleground," argues Max Elbaum in the opening pages of his book *Revolution in the Air* (Elbaum 2002:2). Elbaum captures the essence of this period by pointing out that the radicalization of large segments of U.S. youth stemmed in part from their all-important recognition "that the power of the oppressed was on the rise and the strength of the status quo was on the wane" (Elbaum 2002:2). Increasingly revolution seemed to be on the agenda for significant numbers of young people (Elbaum 2002:2).

By the fall of 1968, he points out, 1 million students saw themselves as part of the Left, and 368,000 people agreed on the need for a mass revolutionary party. Among African Americans, he argues, revolutionary sentiments contended not just for influence but for preeminence, especially among those under thirty, as more than three hundred rebellions flared up among inner-city Blacks from 1964 to 1968.

He reminds us that Nixon's brutal invasion of Cambodia in May 1970 led to the largest explosion of protest on U.S. college campuses in the country's history. Four of ten college students, nearly 3 million people, thought that a revolution was necessary in the United States. (Elbaum 2002:18–19). *Business Week* lamented, "The invasion of Cambodia and the senseless shooting of four students at Kent State University in Ohio have consolidated the academic community against the war, against business, and against government. This is a dangerous situation. It threatens the whole economic and social structure of the nation" (*Business Week* 1970:140). This, then, is one level of explanation if we pay attention to the issue of social time, or temporalities. If there is a lesson in this short story, then persons who are involved in this discussion with me often conclude that indeed it is true that there is something special about the sixties as a time but that the key to understanding it is the coincidence between the times and the people who acted in it. This conclusion generally increases the discussion's intensity and complexity. I then argue that the next level of discussion relates to how we articulate an emphasis on social time with the actions of subjects. There are three trajectories that we should pay attention to if we are to understand where the 1960s fit within U.S. and world history. Careful attention to such a framework might enable us to see a history that we missed when we were focusing on that particular moment in time. First, there is the time frame of our historical system—the modern world-system, a capitalist world-economy—which came into existence during the sixteenth century. We should be able to locate the civil rights movement within the trajectory of our historical social system. How does the U.S. civil rights movement relate to the conquest of America, the enslavement of Africans, and the naturalization of the relations of the conquerors to the conquered in the concept of race? Second, there is the time frame of the rise and expansion of Europe, the progenitor of the capitalist world economy, which articulated its dominance of the non-European world via an ideology of Pan-European racism, or white supremacy. Third, there is the shorter time frame of global hegemonic states, of which there have been three: the United Provinces, the United Kingdom, and the United States. Unlike the formal empire of the era of British hegemony, the era of U.S. hegemony is marked by informal empire, or what some refer to as neocolonialism, thus U.S. support for formal decolonization with its clear implications for Jim Crow segregation in the United States.

While the emphasis of this work is on how Black internationalism articulated with the inexorable rise of the dark world during the nineteenth, twentieth, and twenty-first centuries, it does not exclude that portion of the story that has to do with the rise, reign, and decline of the American century and with the workings of our historical social system, the capitalist world economy.

Maybe we can position ourselves best by examining Anibal Quijano's (2000) provocative notion about globalization, a term used as a deus ex machina in today's world, a stand-in for Margaret Thatcher's notion that there is no alternative but the current system. On the contrary, Quijano argues that what we call globalization is the culmination of a process that began with the constitution of the Americas and colonial-modern Eurocentric capitalism as a new global power. Fundamental to this new model of power, he argues, is the social classification of the world's population around the idea of race. While this concept is said to have originated with the origin of what Immanuel Wallerstein calls the modern world-system, Quijano points out that the racial axis of the modern world-system has proved to be more durable than its origin in the colonial situation. This is the basis of Quijano's notion that the model of power that is today hegemonic presupposes an element of coloniality.

My emphasis on the last five hundred to seven hundred years of Pan-European hegemony does not at all deny the fact that civilizations were recognized as distinct constellations of sociocultural formations for thousands of years prior to the rise of the modern, colonial, capitalist, Eurocentric world-system, which is the subject of this book, and of intellectual and public discourse, which is my focus here. Most relatively informed people know something of the parallel existence of such major civilizations as Egypt, Persia, China, the Aztec, the Maya, and the Incas long before the creation of the sociocultural formations in Europe that were united under Rome. At the time of the Roman Empire, there existed four major constellations, according to Anouar Abdel-Malek (2000):

(a) China, maintaining its continuity since its formation, twenty-five centuries B.C. to this day.

(b) The central area of Islam, in South-West Asia and North Africa, around the Arab caliphates and shi'ah Iran.

(c) The Indian sub-continent with a predominant Hindu culture while power was mainly the domain of Muslim rulers.

(d) The Mongol Asian and Eurasian world, which came under Muslim rule during recent times. (Abdel-Malek 2000:565)

As John Henrik Clarke (1996) points out in his historical studies of the African world, by this historical period Africa had had its long walk in the sun—and it was indeed a great and mighty walk—but the great African empires were in decline.

Abdel-Malek argues that from the eleventh century onward, the rising European power waged protracted warfare against Islam in the Arab world. Abdel-Malek is highly skeptical of the religious-civilizational banner under which the Crusades were launched, seeing them instead as a matter of plunder and subjugation. From the end of the fifteenth century to our time, according to Abdel-Malek, successive waves of colonialism, classical imperialism, and hegemonic imperialism were viewed as the spread of civilization (now identified exclusively with Pan-European civilization) to the rest of the world (Abdel-Malek 2005:564-566).

With the global expansion of European hegemony, this pattern spread to the rest of the world, along with the imposition of a Eurocentric perspective on knowledge and the use of a concept of race to naturalize the colonial relation between Europeans and non-Europeans. Race as the means to justify the distribution of the world population into ranks, places, and roles in the world's structure of power outlasted the system of formal colonialism. This history calls on us to look at racism from a world-historic perspective (Fernand Braudel's (1972) longue duree)[3] using Michael Omi and Howard Winant's (1994) idea of racial formation and the rearticulation of race over the middle run as a component of this longer-term trajectory.

Despite the significance of the enslavement of Africans and the struggles of people of African descent in the United States and the larger world to the struggle against racism, it should be clear that this is a global rather than a local issue. I do not see Black-White dynamics as a defining issue; rather, the issue is one of Pan-European racism, or white supremacy. I object to the facile and flattering notion that the United States of America is a nation of immigrants, which, except for African Americans, has been a city on a hill, a shining light that has attracted people from every corner of the world to its welcoming shores. Modern North America began not as a nation of immigrants, as is often claimed, but as a settler colony: British North America. This is clearer to no group more than the Native Americans, who were the first victims of this colonial expansion. The advancing frontier, so celebrated in North American folklore, is predicated on the dispossession of Native American lands and the elimination of the Native Americans themselves. I agree with Stephen Steinberg's (1989:5) insistence that the fabled diversity of the United States is based on the conquest, enslavement, and exploitation of foreign labor. The expansion of the United States entailed a process of imperial conquest that extended to Mexico, the Philippines, Puerto Rico, and Cuba, and a neocolonial policy of domination of all of the Americas (the Monroe Doctrine), which during the American century spread to the whole world.

The incorporation of the Americas was the constitutive act of the formation of the modern world-system, which was a capitalist world-economy. It involved, first, the subordination of the Americas as a periphery to the Western European core states. The political subordination of additional peripheries included the colonization of Africa, Southeast Asia, and the Pacific and the incorporation of East Asia.

The war against Mexico reflected the U.S. quest for a passage to India in obeisance to the "divine command to subdue and replenish the earth" (Takaki 1993:191). In doing so, the United States would finally bring civilization to the "Yellow" race, including the Chinese, who would be imported as cheap labor to build the transcontinental railroad. Railroad owners viewed them as quiet, peaceful, industrious, and economical but also wanted them to be permanently degraded caste labor, forced to be foreigners forever (the first were so designated via the Chinese Exclusion Act of 1882). In the white imagination, the Chinese took on racial qualities that had been assigned to Blacks: dark skin, thick lips, morally inferiority, childlikeness, savageness, lustfulness—only "a slight remove from the African race." (Takaki 1993:205). Amalgamation with the Chinese would lead to "a mongrel of the most detestable sort that has ever afflicted the earth" (Takaki 1993:205). The Chinese Exclusion Act set the precedent for the National Origins Act of 1924, which prohibited Japanese immigration. The mass imprisonment of Japanese Americans during World War II was a continuation of more than a hundred years of racial aggression against people of Asian descent in the United States and in their homelands (Rhea 1997:40). Soon, however, the nineteenth-century expansion of an imperial and racist enterprise in the United States would join the rest of the Pan-European world in a fight to maintain white world supremacy in the face of a counterhegemonic force among the residents of the dark world.

The rise of the dark world had a number of fronts. I mention only a few elements of this arc of struggle here: the creation of the Indian National Congress in 1886; the Ethiopian defeat of Italy in 1896; the Japanese defeat of Russia in 1905; the founding of the NAACP in 1909; the Mexican Revolution of 1910; the Chinese Revolution of 1911; the founding of the South African Native National Congress in 1912 (later to become the African National Congress); and a succession of revolutions in the Ottoman Empire (Turkey, Persia, Afghanistan, and the Arab world) in the early part of the twentieth century.

I am attempting here to restore an angle of vision that was much more common during the early twentieth century so that we may better understand how Black people it in the international arena. "History is not everything," John Henrik Clarke once wrote, "but it is the starting point. History is a clock that people use to tell their time of day. It is a compass they use to find themselves on the map of human geography. It tells them where they are, but more importantly, what they must be" (Clarke 1987:3). With regard to the need for Africana history, Dr. Clarke pointed out that the Europeans not only colonized most of the world; "they began to colonize information about the world and its people,"

(Clarke 1994:2) forgetting or pretending to forget much that they had already known about the Africans.

It is because of this historiographical obfuscation that I have made this rather extended preface. While there are a variety of angles one might take to understand the history of African Americans—and there are some who would acknowledge the peculiar internationalism of Black social thought and praxis—I wish here to relate the trajectories of various manifestations of Black radicalism to the increasing social power of the dark world and the decline of white Western hegemony over the course of the twentieth and twenty-first centuries.

There can be little question that the domination of the white world over the dark world has declined in the last 150 years. Although the hierarchical relationship between the white world and the dark world continues, the white world has made adjustments to the changes in *rapports de force* between the two worlds. The sense of self-assurance that once marked the persona of the Pan-European population is no more, although some have sought to overcompensate for the changes in *rapport de force* by assuming a more strident assertive stance. Hegemony does not require macho assertiveness, though, and thus the strident assertion of moral superiority among large sections of the Pan-European world, most decisively in the United States, is a sign not of strength but of a loss of confidence. The cultural options of the dominated people in the world-system include courting or imitating the dominant people to win their favor or allay their antagonisms, and distancing themselves from the dominant people to build their strength. In the 1950s Sekou Touré spoke of the need to overcome the complex of the colonized (Wallerstein 1966, 1958, Toure 1959, 1972).[4] Touré called for African peoples to overcome their identification with the oppressor, echoed in Malcolm X's mocking comments about the house Negro identifying with the master so much that when the master was sick, the house Negro asked, "Boss, we sick?" The distancing option is represented by the stance of Malcolm X's field Negro, what William Sales (1994) deems the tradition of field Negro revolt. Within the United States there has been a long and continuing debate about integration versus separation (Black Nationalism), codified in the work of Harold Cruse (1967), among others. But the two positions are seldom as diametrically opposed as indicated in political debates. Some nationalist approaches are aimed at pluralist integration on a group basis into the dominant society, and some integrationist-assimilationist approaches seek to use the best principles of the dominant group to compel them to recognize the entitlement of all to fair treatment, or as a means of creating space for more options by "putting on ole massa."

Some have joked that it requires a good deal of optimism to undertake a project about the end of white world supremacy, especially at a time when racism seems to be increasing in intensity not only in the United States but on a world scale. But this has not always been very funny over the past hundred years or so, and it is increasingly less funny some thirty-five years after the end of the period of unquestioned U.S. hegemony in the world-system, which lasted from 1945 to 1970. The rise of East Asia, the terrorist attack on U.S. territory by al Qaeda, and what Samuel Huntington sees as the Hispanic (mostly Mexican) challenge to the United States' Anglo-Protestant culture are all signs of growing

concern about both the decline of U.S. hegemony and the decline of the hegemonic status of the Pan-European world.

This is not the first time since the dawn of European hegemony five hundred years ago that such fears have assumed significance in the nation's discourse. World War I certainly shook the confidence of the Pan-European world
and was reflected in Lothrop Stoddard's classic, *The Rising Tide of Color against
White World-Supremacy* (1920), and Madison Grant's *The Passing of the Great
Race or the Racial Basis of European History* (1916). While W.E.B. Du Bois's
commentary in *The Souls of Black Folk* is often given credit for predicting that
the problem of the twentieth century would be the problem of the color line, Du
Bois's position at the time of that writing was much more optimistic, anticipating
that a rational appeal would vindicate the race in the eyes of a significant section
of a rational but ill-informed white public.

The social thought of people of African descent have long included the idea
of the eventual rise of the dark world—from the Christianized Africans at the
time of the American Revolution, who saw themselves as people of the New
Covenant (Moses 1998:44), to ordinary field hands, who underwent a Pan-
Africanization with religious men at the center (Stuckey 1975). The notion of
the rising of the dark world is part and parcel of the culture of resistance that
animated people of African descent in slave and postslavery societies. It is a logical consequence of the widespread notion that the United States is a white nation, as is discussed in the work of numerous scholars (M. Bush 2004; Alexander
Saxton 1990). Hubert Harrison's *When Africa Awakes* (1997) and George Wells
Parker's *The Children of the Sun* (1981) are early examples of the manner in
which the early New Negro intellectuals embodied this outlook.

While many scholars have a passing familiarity with the work of Winthrop
Stoddard and Madison Grant, the more general reading public might benefit
from a short review of their work. In June 1914 Stoddard argued, "The worldwide struggle between the primary races of mankind—the 'conflict of color,' as
it has been happily termed—bids fair to be the fundamental problem of the
twentieth century" (quoted in Stoddard 1921:v). In the introduction to the Stoddard classic, Madison Grant focuses on Eurasia as the main theater of world
history, a conflict between three races found in the western part of Eurasia and
their Asiatic challenger. The races that are the focus of Grant's introduction to
the Stoddard classic and the subjects of his *Passing of the Great Race* are "the
great" Nordic race in the northwestern peninsula of Eurasia, the Mediterranean
race (which has been Nordicized), the Alpine (or Slavic) race, and the Asiatic
Mongols. Grant is alarmed by the retreat of the Nordic race westward from the
grasslands of western Asia and eastern Europe to the borders of the Atlantic but
takes comfort in the Nordicizing of the Mediterranean race north of the sea and
the Nordicizing of some of the Slavic populations in central Europe, Austria,
and the Balkans. But the establishment of a chain of alpine states from the
Baltic to the Adriatic at the end of World War I at the expense of the Nordic
ruling classes is said to take us back to the days of Charlemagne, whose succes-
sors took a thousand years to push the frontiers of Europe eastward (Stoddard
1921).

Grant concludes his introduction as follows: "Now that Asia, in the guise of Bolshevism with Semitic leadership and Chinese executioners, is organizing an assault upon western Europe, the new states—Slavic-Alpine in race, with little Nordic blood—may prove to be not frontier guards of western Europe but vanguards of Asia in central Europe." Grant doubts that the Alpine states can hold firm against Asian incursion "now that they have been deprived of Nordic ruling classes through democratic institutions" (Stoddard 1921:xxxii). For Grant, democratic ideals are fine as long as we are dealing with a homogenous population of Nordic blood, as in England or the United States, but it is "suicide pure and simple" for the white man to share his blood with or entrust his ideals to brown, yellow, black, or red men.

Stoddard echoes Grant's condemnation of Bolshevism as the archenemy of civilization and of the Nordic race: "To the Bolshevik mind, with its furious hatred of constructive ability and its fanatical determination to enforce leveling, proletarian equality, the very existence of superior biological values is a crime. Bolshevism has vowed the proletarianization of the world, beginning with the white peoples." Every political grievance, every act of discrimination, every nationalist aspiration is fuel for the Bolsheviks' incitement of race and class warfare. Stoddard sees the Bolshevik menace in "China, Japan, Afghanistan, India, Java, Persia, Turkey, Egypt, Brazil, Chile, Peru, Mexico, and the 'black belts' of our own United States" (Stoddard 1921:220).

Stoddard concludes that "Bolshevism is the renegade, the traitor within the gates who would betray the citadel, degrade the very fiber of our being, and ultimately hurl a rebarbarized, racially impoverished world into the most debased and hopeless of mogrelizations" (Stoddard 1921:221). It is for this reason that Bolshevism must be crushed, no matter what the cause, *not in defense of democracy*, as would later be claimed, but in order *to oppose the democracy*, leveling, and egalitarianism that Stoddard and Grant considered to be Bolshevik ideals. For Stoddard, there is no "imprescriptable right" to independence or to empire. One has to deal with the realities of each case in terms of the logic of the overall defense of the system of white world supremacy. Stoddard argues that the period of white expansion took two forms: areas of white settlement such as North America, which has become an integral part of the white world, and regions of political control such as India. Those areas of white settlement are called the "inner dikes" of white civilization and must be defended at all costs. Future generations are said to have "a right to demand of us that they be born white in a white man's land" (Stoddard 1921:226). This, Stoddard contends, is an elemental "call of the blood," which must be heard lest the white world heed the writing on the wall.

At the same time, Stoddard argues, the practically absolute world dominion that the white man enjoyed during the nineteenth century can no longer be maintained, since the "life conserving nature of white rule everywhere has favored colored multiplication." Therefore, in those areas of political control, such as Asia, where the populations are capable of self-governance, the white world should be governed by pragmatic considerations rather than by the overheated passions of "doctrinaire imperialists." In these areas whites should cede control by evolutionary and peaceful means and thus retain the capacity of cooperative relationships with the newly independent regimes. The alternative to this pragmatic concession, Stoddard cautions, is the opening up of violent shortcuts that would be mutually disastrous, especially because the weakening of the white world during World War I evoked in "bellicose and fanatical minds the vision of a 'Pan Colored' alliance for the overthrow of white hegemony at a single stroke" (Stoddard 1921:229).

Not only would such a prospect make World War I seem like child's play, but also the fanning of the flames of needless antagonism would only increase the hostility of Asians toward the white world and could have dire geopolitical ramifications for the white world in the long run. Stoddard argues that causing such festering hatred might poison the attitudes of people in other colored lands and even reverberate among some in the white world as well. This kind and level of hostility could ultimately result in the formation of a "Pan-Colored" or "Colored-Bolshevist alliance" (Stoddard 1921:233). Therefore, taking a conciliatory attitude toward the aspirations of Asians for independence would enable the white world more effectively to defend what Stoddard considers the true "outer dikes" of the white world in Black Africa and "mongrel-ruled" Latin America, which could not stand alone (Stoddard 1921:232-233).

The danger to the "inner dikes" of the white world is constituted by allowing immigration to overwhelm the process of natural selection that had enabled America to amass an unprecedented racial treasure by the beginning of the nineteenth century. Stoddard argues that the colonial stock was perhaps the finest that nature had evolved since the classic Greeks, the pick of the Nordics of the British Isles and adjacent areas in Europe. Since the very process of migration was so difficult, only persons of courage, initiative, and strong willpower would face the difficult journey to "an untamed land haunted by ferocious savages" (Stoddard 1921:262). This magnificent stock was undermined, however, by the opening of the country to a deluge of immigrants, allowing for the dilution and supplanting of superior stock by inferior stock.

Stoddard laments the "impossibility of any advanced and prosperous community maintaining its social standards and handing down to its posterity" *in those days* of cheap and rapid transportation. The only solution to this dilemma, Stoddard argues, was restrictions on immigration. The entire logic of civilizational progress was undermined by the way that the modern world was proceeding. Why practice prudence if hungry strangers can crowd in at your table at places reserved for your children (Stoddard 1921:261)? The great accomplishments of the white man in abolishing distance have destroyed the protection that nature once conferred. The white world will be swamped by the triumphant colored races and will finally perish (Stoddard 1921:303).

Since the time of Stoddard's and Grant's classics, the twentieth century has been dotted with revolutionary challengers to the capitalist system and to the system of white Western hegemony. It was only in the 1960s, though, that the magnitude of the challenge in the United States assumed such proportions that scholars such as Maurice Isserman and Michael Kazin began to refer to that period as the "civil war of the 1960s." Indeed, their conceptually bold *America*

Divided: The Civil War of the 1960s (2000) captures the scope of the transformation attempted but suffers from its short time frame and thus its inadequate periodization. Since Black internationalism has been one of the most consistent and persistent challengers to the problem of the color line and its more modern ideological analog the notion of liberal universalism and has constantly rebuked the United States for its grossly exaggerated democratic claims, I think an examination of Black internationalism is a necessary element for a thorough examination of the social tensions and contradictions in U.S. society and the larger social world in which it is embedded.

What I attempt to do in this project is to locate the New Negro, civil rights, and Black Power phases of the Black freedom struggle in a larger tradition with sites in the United States, the Caribbean, and Africa and among the social and national movements of the Three Continents. This study seeks to determine the overall impact of these movements, their impact on other social forces, and the resultant transitions in U.S. society as a whole. While this work is not a detailed history of these movements, it attempts a serious estimate of the significance and impact of the movements. Some may caution that a more modest scope is needed; this may be the case for some investigators, but I do not hesitate to locate myself in a long tradition of Black radical scholars, Black scholar activists,* and radical scholars from a variety of traditions who have consistently attempted to contextualize social research within the framework of large-scale, long-term social change. Indeed, the use by Manning Marable (1984) and others of the term *Second Reconstruction* to describe the 1960s is an indication that other scholars feel the need for a broader conceptualization of these elements of social movement theory.

The origins of this study are in part positive, from my study of Black Nationalism and class struggle in the twentieth-century United States, and in part negative, from the practice of counterinsurgency forces operated by the state. Former FBI director J. Edgar Hoover argued during the early 1960s that the nation was in the midst of a social revolution, with the racial factor at its core (O'Reilly 1989:355). Hoover sought to prevent the rise of a messiah to unify the Black militant forces (Churchill and Vander Wall 1988, 1990), but Malcolm X and King were not only charismatic leaders who together commanded the attention of most of those at the bottom of the economic ladder and a substantial section of those in the middle; they were also visionary intellectuals who viewed America and its oppressed within a world context. They both called for siding with the barefoot people of the earth. King followed Malcolm X, and then the Black Panther Party followed both men, though it claimed only Malcolm X. The ruthless repression of this populist Left by the state's security forces in allegiance with conservative nonstate organizations led to the cadrefication of large segments of the New Left, which is noted in this study but the details of which are the subject of a subsequent research project.

The societal convulsions caused by this uprising affected not only the lower orders but the centers of governance as well, who in attempting to settle the grievances being raised crafted far-reaching policies that redefined and expanded notions of equality, justice, and democracy. This in turn had an impact on scholars, including sociologists, and the public's understanding of race, class, and poverty. This shows that the public's ideas and their capacity for creative conceptualization is not static but responds to the agency of human subjects. Here we note some elements of the societal transformation that justified the use of the term the *Second Reconstruction*, but the details of that story will be the work of a subsequent research project.

The research undertaken here is intended to deepen the insights from my recent book, *We Are Not What We Seem: Black Nationalism and Class Struggle in the American Century* (Bush 1999), and to broaden my focus on the trajectory of opposing ideologies and movements. The most urgent corrective to my previous work must involve a more sophisticated use of the concept of social time. Much of my elaboration about the trajectory of the Black Liberation movement in the twentieth century focused on the middle run. This was an important corrective to the focus on the short term that one finds in many works of historical analysis, but the work lacked all but a very cursory perspective on the long term.

In subsequent work I have attempted to correct this oversight. I follow the Working Group on Coloniality at the State University of New York at Binghamton (Binghamton University), which has argued that the modern capitalist world that unfolded over the last five hundred to seven hundred years had as a fundamental element processes of racial formation and domination that have been central to its expansion and organization. These processes have been the focus of social movements that have organized against the multiple forms of this global structure of racial formation and domination. Quijano argues that the formation of the Americas was constituted by two fundamental historical processes: (1) the codification of the differences between conquerors and conquered in the idea of "race," assumed to be a biological category that naturalized the hierarchical relationship between the conquerors and the conquered on the basis of the superiority of the conquerors and the inferiority of the conquered, and (2) the articulation of all known forms of labor control (slavery, serfdom, small-commodity production, and reciprocity) on the basis of capital and the world market. The population of the new world and later the entire world was ordered along these axes. Terms that had heretofore referred to geographical designations, such as *European, Spanish, Portuguese*, now referred to a putative racial designation. In the Americas, the idea of race was a way of granting legitimacy to the relations of domination imposed by the conquest. After the colonization of America, Quijano argues, the expansion of European colonialism to the rest of the world and the subsequent constitution of Europe as a new identity required the elaboration of a Eurocentric perspective of knowledge, what Quijano views as "a theoretical perspective on the idea of race as a naturalization of colonial relations between Europeans and non-Europeans" (Quijano 2000:534–535).

Of course social domination was not new, but the use of the concept of race as a means of legitimizing this domination was indeed new and (with the important exception of gender) has proved to be the most effective and long-lasting instrument of universal social domination. Race became the fundamental criterion for the distribution of the world population into ranks, places, and roles in the new society's structure of power. Within the Pan-European world, race re-placed religion as a means of ordering the world's people. In a presentation about cultures in conflict at the Hong Kong University of Science and Technology, Wallerstein pointed out that it was in the course of a revolt against the domi-nance of religion that Enlightenment humanism-scientism staked its claim to a true universalism, one that could in theory be accessed by all via verifiable ratio-nal analysis. However, since people still came to different conclusions about truths, there was a need to resolve this quest for a universal truth. Enlighten-ment humanism-scientism was forced to create a hierarchy of human beings according to their degree of rationality. So if the course of things were to be or-dered in the most useful way, then priority should be given to the more rational. This is of course the usefulness of the concept of race, because human popula-tions are ordered on the basis of who is more rational, which of course always turns out to be groups to which the dominant strata belong.

This new structure of power included a new articulation of a variety of forms of labor control deliberately established to produce commodities for the world mar-ket. These forms of labor control, which included slavery, serfdom, petty commod-ity production, reciprocity, and wage labor, were not mere extensions of their his-torical antecedents, because of the manner in which they were tied and articulated under a system of commodity production for the world market.

In Anglo-America the indigenous people were not colonized but were for-mally recognized as nations, with formal international commercial and military relations. Colonial-racial relations existed only between Blacks and whites. When the nation began to expand, it dispossessed the Native Americans of their land and almost exterminated them. The survivors were then imprisoned within North American society as a colonized race (Quijano 2000:560), but "the use of race as the means of justifying the distribution of the world population into ranks, places, and roles in the world's structure of power outlasted the system of formal colo-nialism" (Bush 2006:345).

The fact that racism is so deeply encrustated in the social structures, the super-egoes, and the institutional and ideological structures of the pan-European world; the fact that racism is what defines a European (white) identity means that many racialized practices pass under the radar of the non-racialized populations. They are simply normal and there is no need to take account of these practices.[5] It is therefore not a variable easily susceptible to liberal reformism (and its some-times good intentions) or conservative color blindness (a much more defensive orientation often with eyes wide shut). While the rearticulation of racial dis-course may alter the expression of this pillar of our historical system, it remains as firmly in place as ever.[6] Racism is not simply a divide-and-conquer strategy among capitalists; it is constitutive of the class system within historical capital-ism, which has taken the form of a capitalist world-economy. So the radical im-pulse that insists that racism will be with us as long as we live in a capitalist sys-tem is fundamentally correct, even if we cannot accept the old line of the U.S. Socialist Party, based on the "class first" idea, that we must wait for socialism, which will abolish the "exploitation of man by man" and thus the basis of "natu-ral" competition among workers, which most of the Socialist Party leadership viewed as the foundation of racism within the capitalist system. Harrison's assertion that the Socialist Party militants saw this competition as natural is key here and is similar to the critique that Anibal Quijano and others have made of the Marxist revolutionary and intellectual tradition.

The old idea that capitalism began in Europe and later expanded to incorporate other parts of the world as colonial zones is an imprecise formulation. The capitalist world-economy was born as a European core *and* an American periphery. Racism was a part of that birth; it did not come later as a strategy of divide and conquer used by capital. It was part of the stratifying processes that were constitutive of historical capitalism, which was a capitalist world-economy.[7] The formation of a world working class performing different types of labor (wage labor, slave labor, petty commodity production, etc.) at different levels of remuneration was constitutive of the capitalist world-economy. Sections of the world worker's movement, particularly those outside the core zones, would eventually seek to explain such inequalities within the working classes in terms of the emergence of a labor aristocracy or a bourgeois stratum of the working class.

If the cultural hegemony of a European-based world-economy relied in part on the social glue of Pan-European racial solidarity as moral justification for and defense of Euro–North American world hegemony, then the subordinate populations of the non-European world and their descendents experienced this outlook as a system of oppressive humiliation that denied their humanity, intelligence, and dignity. People of African descent, who were at the bottom of the world status and social hierarchy, were actively engaged in constructing dreams of freedom and liberation, which in the postslavery twentieth century were often captured by the slogan "The Rise of the Dark World." This then became a central component of African American radical thought. Since radical Black Nationalism had little hope of a strictly "nationalist" solution, it has long pegged its hopes on an internationalist solution. The logic of Ida B. Wells's appeals against lynch-mob violence at the end of the nineteenth century; Du Bois at the turn of the century speaking at the Pan-African Congress; the New Negro Movement; Du Bois, Graham, and Robeson during the popular-front period; and Malcolm X, King, the Student Nonviolent Coordinating Committee, Angela Davis, and the Black Panther Party during the 1960s and 1970s all followed this trend.[8]

The twentieth century had witnessed the dramatic rise of the dark world but not "the end of white world supremacy," which really seemed an accurate observation and not merely wishful thinking on the part of Nation of Islam leader Malcolm X in 1963 (Malcolm X 1971). While I argued in *We Are Not What We Seem* that Malcolm's judgment was premature but that it was indeed a sign of the times that we must continue to take seriously, it would benefit us to look at the logic of Malcolm X's argument in more detail. First let us look at a snapshot of Malcolm's comments, which in my view summarized Malcolm's reflections on the spirit of Bandung,[9] so salient to the times in which he spoke:

> The time is past when the white world can exercise unilateral authority and control over the dark world. The independence and power of the dark world is on the increase; the dark world is rising in wealth, power,

prestige, and influence. It is the rise of the dark world that is causing the fall of the white world.

As the white man loses his power to oppress and exploit the dark world, the white man's own wealth (power or "world") decreases. . . . You and I were born at this turning point in history; we are witnessing the fulfillment of prophecy. Our present generation is witnessing the end of colonialism, Europeanism, Westernism, or "White-ism" . . . the end of white supremacy, the end of the evil white man's unjust rule. (Malcolm X 1971:130)[10]

The period during which Malcolm X spoke was the era of decolonization in Africa, a time when the spirit of Bandung was the framework for what Malcolm referred to as a worldwide revolution. For those who accepted the authority of the white world as a given, these were troubled times. Unlike a time when nothing could happen without the approval of the United States, the Soviet Union, or France, the people and nations of the dark world came together at the Bandung Conference in Indonesia in 1955 and agreed to submerge their differences and present a united front against the common enemy, the colonizing authorities of the European world. It was in the context of this unity of the African-Asian-Arab bloc, Malcolm argues, that African nations were able to obtain independence and join the United Nations.

Now the members of the dark world had a voice, a vote, in the United Nations and were soon able to outvote the white man, who had formerly been their colonial authority. By being able to outvote the colonial powers, they were able to force the people of Europe to "turn loose the Black man in Tanganyika, the Black man in the Congo, and the Black man in what we know today as the former French West African territories" (Malcolm X 1971:97). While Malcolm was certainly not deceived by the real power of the United Nations, he viewed it as a forum in which international debates and discussions about issues of world power and justice could be aired. For Malcolm the new arithmetic of the United Nations was an opportunity to exert pressure for more democracy on the hegemonic powers of the white world, who had long exercised unilateral and dictatorial powers over the peoples and nations of the dark world. The new arithmetic of the United Nations was the handwriting on the wall, and Malcolm X was a master at showcasing this handwriting so that it was plain for all to see. Malcolm would not allow the world to miss the significance of British prime minister Harold McMillan's remarks and those of others "crying the blues" because of the passing of the famed British Empire, on which the sun had finally set. Like no one else, Malcolm was able to provide a narrative that explained in the clearest terms the implications of the French defeat in Indochina and the impact of the loss of its colonial possessions there on its economy and consequently on its inability to maintain an army sufficient to control its large West African colonies, leading ultimately to the collapse of French colonial power in Algeria under the weight of another fierce war of national liberation.

Malcolm turned the spotlight on the Netherlands' loss of Indonesia and the Belgian loss of the Congo. Malcolm taunted the former colonial powers, chiding

Belgium, which, he argued, had been a power on this earth as long as it controlled the mineral wealth the Belgian Congo. But once it lost control of its central African colony, the economy was so traumatized that the Belgian government collapsed.

Malcolm called out to both the Black, Brown, Yellow, and Red victims of Euro–North American hegemony and the residents of the Pan-European world themselves to read the handwriting on the wall. He called on them all to recognize the fundamental fact of that historical moment, in which the rise of the dark world was the occasion for the decrease in power of the white world over the dark world. It was his recognition of this change in the constellation of world power that gave Malcolm X such remarkable insight and that led him to make the correct call following the Kennedy assassination that this was a case of the chickens coming home to roost. If Dr. King's August 1963 speech represented the most articulate statement of the American dream and represented the height of the mature global liberalism that was the signpost of the American century, then it was Malcolm who most clearly understood and articulated the other side—or the underside—of this phenomenon. Malcolm X was a master teacher without peer (see Malcolm X 1971:81–120, 121–148; Sales 1994).

Power in defense of freedom, Malcolm argued, is greater than power on behalf of tyranny and oppression. For Malcolm the latter inevitably lacks the kind and degree of conviction of the former because the mentality of most who would implement power on behalf of tyranny and oppression is that of an employee.[11] However, there is a sense in which white supremacy has the capacity to produce a certain derangement and degrading of mentality that can be passionate in a negative and hateful sense. Malcolm clearly believes in the power of a life-affirming passion that can produce uncompromising and hopeful action (see, for example, Malcolm X 1965:150).

Malcolm X taught that this was a period of worldwide revolution far beyond the bounds of Mississippi, Alabama, and Harlem. The revolutionary forces coming to the fore were to oppose not simply the U.S., French, or English power structure but an international Western power structure consisting of U.S., French, English, Belgian, and other European interests. These former colonizers of the dark world had formed an international combine, but Malcolm called for unity among 22 million Black people in the United States and urged them to unite with 700 million of their Muslim sisters and brothers in Africa and Asia and with the revolutionary people in Africa, Asia, and the Americas (Malcolm X 1992:106–126). Malcolm reestablished in the 1960s what other people of African descent had known in the past—that the struggles of Black people in the United States were not just an American problem but a world problem.

Malcolm restored the sense of internationalism that had long been a part of the imagination of people of African descent—of its leaders and intellectuals and among the common people. Fanon Wilkins (2001) has most effectively navigated the break in this Black internationalism by the "liberal compromise" among sections of the civil rights leadership during the cold war period of the late 1940s to the late 1960s.[12] While Wilkins focuses on the continuity of Black internationalism breached by the liberal compromise, William Jelani

Cobb (2006) focuses on the history of Black anticommunism in the United States.

Malcolm clearly thought that the end had come for the dominant strata of the white world. He was of course not alone. "What time is it?" was a common refrain during the period from 1965 to 1975, when the cumulative strength of a variety of liberation movements seemed to signal the death knell of Pan-European domination.

Having established the convincing case made for Black internationalism by Malcolm X, I would like to look back at the social, economic, political, and spiritual forces that have been the foundation of my own analysis of this issue.

Articulating the International Dimensions
of the Black Experience

While this view comes preeminently from reflections on Malcolm X's remarks about the end of white world supremacy, my sense of Black internationalism was powerfully reinforced by an essay published in the mid-1980s by Bernard Magubane, a South African scholar and member of the African National Congress, then an anthropology professor at the University of Connecticut speaking at the tenth anniversary of the Africana Studies and Research Center at Cornell University, which focused on theoretical and research issues in Africana studies. The task that these scholars set for themselves was to understand the theoretical and research issues to be focused on in Africana studies during the next decade. The organizers of the conference could have hardly chosen a better person than Magubane to conceptualize the political economy of the Black world. The title of Magubane's presentation was "The Political Economy of the Black World—Origins of the Present Crisis."

I was impressed by his manner of addressing the conference. He cautioned his audience about viewing history as nostalgia and gently chastised some for their tendency to reify the past, as if Black history consists of simply identifying and enumerating "dead mummies" (Magubane 1984:283). The past, Magubane argued, is very much a part of the present, and Black poverty could not be understood without viewing it through the lens of a world perspective. In historical perspective, then, the economic plight of the black world is rooted in the exploitation that resulted from the rise and expansion of the world capitalist system.

The African slave trade not only integrated the Black world into the world capitalist system; it was the major source of primitive accumulation for European and American capitalists.[13] The overall consequence of this pattern of social and economic integration of Africans into the world-economy is that Black skin continues to be associated with genetic inferiority. One could thus conclude a system of structural and ideological racism turned on the historical incorporation of Africans into the capitalist world-economy as involuntary servants. This manner of incorporation of Africans into the emerging world-economy also had implications for the determination of agency. Thus, a very important consequence of the forced dispersal of African people as involuntary servants within the capitalist world-economy made of Africans the first truly international proletariat and, moreover, made the fortunes of capitalism inseparable from the misfortunes of Blacks (Magubane 1984:285–286).

In describing the place of slavery in the capitalist world, Magubane quotes directly from a letter from Marx to P. V. Annenkov in 1846:[14]

> Direct slavery is just as much the pivot of bourgeois industry as machinery, credits, etc. Without slavery you have no cotton; without cotton you have no modern industry. It is slavery that has given the colonies their value; it is the colonies that have created world trade, and it is world trade that is the pre-condition of large scale industry. Thus slavery is an economic category of the greatest importance.
>
> Without slavery North America, the most progressive of countries, would be transformed into a patriarchal country. Wipe out North America from the map of the world, and you will have anarchy—the complete decay of modern commerce and civilization. Cause slavery to disappear and you will have wiped America off the map of nations.
>
> Thus slavery, because it is an economic category, has always existed among the institutions of the people. Modern nations have been able only to disguise slavery in their own countries, but they have imposed it without disguise upon the New World [Marx, 1971, 94–95].[15] (Magubane 1984:284)

For Magubane, Black people are held to be outcasts from civilization. Slavery not only shattered the fabric of African society; it is the foundation of Africa's underdevelopment. Moreover, the enslaved Africans were the first proletarians to suffer the full weight of capitalist exploitation and dehumanization (Magubane 1984:287). Despite the particularities of people of African descent, Magubane echoes Du Bois's call that we should never lose sight of our commonality with "that dark and vast sea of human labor in China and India, the South Seas . . . in Central America . . . that great majority of mankind on whose bent and broken backs rest the founding stones of modern industry" (Magubane 1984:286).

There is a fertile intellectual tradition, Magubane informs us, that should assist us in overcoming this reified historical consciousness, consisting of intellectuals from various locations within the Black diaspora: Dr. Du Bois, C.L.R. James, Aimé Césaire, Frantz Fanon, Walter Rodney, and Lerone Bennett, Jr. On the whole, Magubane suggests, the Black professional managerial strata everywhere have become accessories in the enslavement of their own masses. The counter to the status quo universalizing of the intermediate strata is that the class position of the overwhelming majority of the Black world, as an international proletariat, has been the foundation of much more enduring social aspirations located in much of the Pan-African and Garvey movements (Magubane 1984:293). I would only add that Magubane also might have mentioned the National Negro Congress and the Council on African Affairs of the 1930–1950 period, the 1960s radicals, such as the Student Nonviolent Coordinating Committee, the Revolutionary Action Movement, the Nation of Islam, and the Black

Panther Party; and the 1970s radicals from organizations such as the League of Revolutionary Black Workers, the Congress of African Peoples, Malcolm X Liberation University, Peoples College, the Youth Organization for Black Unity, the Republic of New Africa, the African Peoples Party, the African People's Socialist Party, and many others.

There is an irony here that is not at all subtle. In contrast to the civilizational rhetoric of the enlightenment of which Marx and the European workers' movement were a part, the idea and practice of Black Liberation by the enslaved Africans and those at risk of enslavement in Africa itself were examples for the rise of the socialist and workers' movements of a later time.[16]

While Magubane recognizes the commonality of the Black experience and others despoiled by a rapacious system, he views the black experience as unique. Imperialism negated the historical process of African people in Africa and throughout the world. Yet despite the nominal independence of most African countries and the increasing electoral gains made by blacks in the United States, the Black world remains in the grips of hunger, poverty, and disease. For the most part Magubane attributes this political weakness to the ideological weakness of the black leadership, consisting in the main of a comprador bourgeoisie that voluntarily chooses capitalist solutions to the problems of poverty both for personal expediency and because they have been conditioned to believe in such solutions.[17]

Even this class is often on the margins of the power elite of the world-system, though, given their proximity to a group that is central to the pariah classes of the world-system. Despite the gains of some members of the African world, it is undoubtedly true that Pan-European racism is the Achilles' heel of the modern world-system, and the demographic situation of the United States, with its large, strategically located populations of color, is a key locus of struggle for a more just, democratic, and egalitarian world order.

Clearly Magubane articulates a class-based understanding of the international dimensions of the Black experience, focusing on processes of capitalist development and class formation in the context of capitalism as a world-system. He locates the cultural expression of Black internationalism in a structural context, in contrast to an approach that places greater emphasis on the evolution of a global African culture as an expression of what Eddie Glaude, Jr., calls "a specific form of life which binds Black people together in the United States and throughout the world" (2000:12). Glaude is much more evenhanded in this analysis and avoids the extremism of what I would call radical antiessentialists such as Paul Gilroy (2000). I too wish to avoid a misdirected and one-sided criticism of cultural nationalist or Afrocentric scholars and activists.

Instead I would like to review briefly an analysis of Black internationalism that I believe is much more sophisticated, that of Tiffany Patterson and Robin D. G. Kelley (2000). Patterson and Kelley take the position that dating back at least to the sixteenth and seventeenth centuries, Black writers and activists (such as Juan Latino, Ottobah Cuagano, Olaudah Equiano, and Jose Manuel Valdes) have described themselves as part of an international Black community. While some assume that this international Black consciousness was a consequence of the dispersal of Africans away from the motherland, others argue that it was the context of the dispersal as much as internal developments in Africa that gave rise to this sense of community, or peoplehood, among people of African descent. In other words, racial capitalism, imperialism, colonialism, and the slave trade are integral to the formation of what some call the African, or Black, diaspora, not simply as a counterculture but as integral to the formation and continuing functioning of the modern world-system. This takes the form of a counterculture only because of the manner in which a hegemonic Pan-European world has exorcised Blackness in order to create its own myths of racial purity, white supremacy, and Black inferiority (Patterson and Kelley 2000).

While Patterson and Kelley briefly review the work of those who assert that much of West and central African culture, in the form of music, dance, religion, and linguistic patterns, survived in the Americas (for example, Melville Herskovits, Sterling Stuckey, and Joseph Holloway), they seem to lean in the direction of scholars such as Sidney Mintz and Richard Price, who argue that what survived was a consequence of the process of cultural syncretism shaped by the context of the "cultural contact" (Patterson and Kelley 2000:16). Unlike E. Franklin Frazier and Charles Johnson, who in an earlier generation argued quite forcefully that there were no cultural retentions after the first generation, Mintz and Price do not outright reject all forms of cultural continuity between Old World and New World Africans but reject the notion of a single African culture, placing great emphasis on the emergence of new, dynamic cultures.

Patterson and Kelley point out that forced labor, racial oppression, colonial conditions, and capitalist exploitation were global processes that incorporated Black people into what I would call (following Wallerstein 1979) the modern world-system, or, more expansively (following Quijano and others), the modern, colonial, capitalist world-system (Grosfoguel and Cervantes-Rodriguez 2002). These processes did not always operate in the same manner, according to Patterson and Kelley, but they did create systems that were sometimes tightly coordinated across oceans and national borders. For Patterson and Kelley this raises the question of whether the so-called cultural survivors were the most effective cultural baggage Africans used throughout the world in their struggle for survival or whether they were created by the very conditions under which Africans were forced to live.

One of the most valuable insights that we get from Patterson and Kelley's exploration of the concept of the African diaspora is that diaspora is both a process and a condition. It is a process, they argue, that constantly is being remade through movement, migration, and travel, as well as imagined through thought, cultural productions, and political struggles.

While we can see the usefulness of the term *diaspora*, in reality Black labor migration is a product of the same processes that induce other populations to migrate. So how do we position Chinese and Indian migration to the Caribbean, Africa, and the U.S. South in relation to the African diaspora? The patterns of these various populations of overlapping migration and systems of subordination have led to patterns of collective identity, such as Afro-Asian and Black and Latino solidarity and competition, and thus to the use of the term

Black internationalism. The Black world can be understood only in the context of the wider world and vice versa. Black internationalism, then, is related not only to Pan-Africanism but also to other international movements: socialism, communism, feminism, surrealism, Islam, and so on (Patterson and Kelley 2000:27).

Like Patterson and Kelley, Michelle Stephens (1998, 1999) articulates a version of Black internationalism that transcends Pan-Africanism, which she calls Black transnationalism. She views this as a specific process of group formation that takes place in the context of U.S.-based ethnic communities.

Stephens points out that social scientists in the 1990s increasingly came to refer to a set of processes by which immigrants became "transmigrants," with allegiances, loyalties, and networks beyond the nation-state (Basch, Schiller, and Blanc 1994:27). While most nonscholars may find this term awkward, it describes a reality that long predates the 1990s and can be readily identified in many communities in the African diaspora. Stephens locates the origins of scholarly research and commentary on this issue in Randolph Bourne's 1918 essay titled "Trans-national America." In this essay Bourne held that World War I had revealed the failure of the melting-pot theory of U.S. culture by instigating vigorous feelings of nationalistic and ethnic loyalty among European immigrants in the United States.

It was also during this period that nationalism and the nation-state were becoming normative features of the modern world-system. In 1919 the Treaty of Versailles and the League of Nations were vehicles through which the principle of democratic national self-determination became a model of political organization. Stephens contrasts this new norm to the idea of proletarian internationalism promulgated by the Communist International, which was formed in the wake of the Bolshevik Revolution of 1917 in Russia (James 1993).

According to Stephens, the failure of the melting pot led Bourne to recast the American nation in a form that borrows from the internationalist rhetoric of the Russian Revolution (Stephens 1998:596). Since the intellectual contradictions of European nationalism were being played out in the ethnic body politic of the United States, Bourne envisioned a resolution that would combine both the dream of nationalism and the dream of internationalism. The tension of the nationalist currents in the mother country exerted great pressure on European immigrants, but this was not true, in Stephens's view, of the immigrants from the Caribbean, where home was still a colony. At the same time, these immigrants tended to assimilate into what Hanchard (1990) calls the U.S. African American group, which at that time was decidedly a second-class citizen of the United States. Given this double exclusion, Stephens argues that Caribbean American intellectuals such as Cyril Briggs, Marcus Garvey, and Claude McKay became central figures in articulating a Black transnational vision that transcended the nationalist vision of the European nations and the contradictory ethnic and national sensibilities of white Americans.

Briggs, an editor of the *New York Amsterdam News*, engaged in a public interrogation of President Woodrow Wilson's rhetoric on democracy and the self-determination of nations. As early as 1917 Briggs argued that if Wilson wanted to guarantee freedom and self-determination for Poles and Serbs, why not for colored Americans as well? Briggs also wanted to know what Wilson and the European nations intended to do about the European colonial empire in Africa. The League of Nations refused to include any but free states as members, so those who most needed self-determination and international protection from imperialism were excluded from the organization, leading Briggs to deem it "The League of Some Nations" (Stephens 1998:598).

Given the utter failure of Wilsonian internationalism to address the needs of Black people, Briggs turned to the alternative, the internationalism of the Bolsheviks and the Third International. Consistent with the norms of the Third International revolutionaries, Briggs formed a clandestine organization in 1919, which he called the African Blood Brotherhood (ABB).[18] Stephens describes it as a "secret revolutionary army, . . . the black arm of the international revolution" (Stephens 1998:598). In the October 1921 edition of *The Crusader*, the Supreme Council of the ABB offered a new program "for the Guidance of the Negro Race in the Great Liberation Struggle" (*The Crusader*, 1249, in Hill 1987).[19] In this program the Supreme Council of the ABB called for the creation of "A Great Negro Federation," which would include representatives from all Negro organizations. Stephens argues that the notion of the federation had been conceived at a meeting of the ABB membership attended by Claude McKay, editor of the white Left magazine *The Liberator*, who had just returned from England. The council decided that they would take this plan aboveground through the international convention of Marcus Garvey's Universal Negro Improvement Association.

Stephens argues that Briggs's vision of a transnational federation as a stateless entity for organizing the proletariat of the darker races was based on an analysis of the position of Black people in the contemporary world that was similar to Garvey's, but Garvey's proposed solution of a Black empire differed fundamentally from that of the ABB, and sensing that the ABB members were seeking to co-opt the Universal Negro Improvement Association, Garvey expelled them from the 1921 international convention. The "Black Empire urge" that was championed by the Garveyites embodied a notion of Black freedom grounded not in self-determination or social revolution but in imperial political and cultural conquest of Africa by Western Negroes (Stephens 1998:600).

For Stephens it was Claude McKay who had the greatest understanding of what the coming together of the ABB and the Universal Negro Improvement Association would have meant for a radical vision and movement of Black self-determination. Stephens cites McKay's role in the Second Congress of the Communist International, where he argued for a Communist definition of self-determined Blackness, which Stephens argues was in the Black Belt South in the United States.[20] As McKay moved away from the political activities of both the New Negro Movement and the Communist International, he expressed his notion of Black transnationalism in the less-well-known sequel to *Home to Harlem*, the novel *Banjo: The Story without a Plot*. In this book McKay takes us through a world of denationalized colonial immigrants in the French seaport of Marseilles, who use their marginalization in Europe and their exclusion from the League of Nations as the basis for a transnationally imagined community.

This frees them to form relations with others across national borders for reasons that have noting to do with raison d'état (Stephens 1998:603).

Stephens makes the important point that the New Negro intellectuals and activists could not be simply dismissed as having resorted to a "disengaged cosmopolitanism" or having resigned themselves to a "state of exile"; instead, Stephens says, they represented the hope for an engaged Black internationalism that could generate new conceptions of citizenship and the meaning of a national community (Stephens 1998:604).

We should not miss that Stephens's focus on the "Masculine Global Imaginary of Caribbean Intellectus in the United States 1914–1962" is framed almost entirely within the New Negro Manhood Rights Movement (Stephens 2005:46). The New Negro movement was about manliness and militariness, a sharp rejection of the subordinate and "feminized" status of Black men prior to this period. If Black male mobility is the trademark of the Black internationalism of the New Negro intellectuals portrayed by Stephens, the Black woman is the site of domesticity and nationalism (as in McKay's *Home to Harlem*). This new worldly sense of Black collectivity and subjectivity assumes specifically gendered and masculinist terms (Stephens 2005:48).

The turn-of-the-century notion of manhood into which the New Negro generation came to the fore was intimately connected to the idea of dominance. For Stephens the manliness and militariness of the New Negro Manhood Rights Movement was a response to white imperial domination. Stephens follows Carole Boyce Davies's notion that the woman of color appears at first to be invisible in narratives of nationalism and postcolonialism, but this is because she is doing something else somewhere else, in less territorial transnational spaces. The Africana women intellectuals and activists embody a less triumphalist vision of home, nation, and empire and an often vulnerable mobile subjectivity (Stephens 2005:17). Thus, the race's hybridity is mapped onto the body of the woman of color, and the masculine vision of the race's transnationalism is projected onto the Black male body (Stephens 2005:18).

Angela Davis has recalled her first encounter with Malcolm X as one of four or five Black undergraduates at Brandeis University in the early 1960s. The meeting evoked in her a sense of Black Nationalism and pride in those components of her persona that she associated with Blackness (her hair, her speech patterns, her musical proclivities). While this feeling did not imply any action for her, she feels that she needed the sense of pride as much as she would "later need the appeal of the image of the leather-jacketed, black-bereted warriors standing with guns at the entrance of the California legislature" (an image that she glimpsed in a German newspaper while studying with Theodor Adorno in Frankfurt) (Davis 1998:290). It was this image of the Black Panther Party members that called her home and directed her into an organizing frenzy in the streets of South Central Los Angeles, during which she worked with the Student Nonviolent Coordinating Committee, the Black Panther Party, and the Che-Lumumba Club of the Communist Party of the United States of America (Davis 1998:290–291).

During the 1960s Davis expressed her nationalism in practice in progressive, politicized Black communities. This form of nationalist consciousness was a call to transformative action, but she strenuously avoided forms of nationalism rooted in the masculinist notions and practice of male dominance, violence against women, and conservative essentialist racialization. During the Black Nationalist revival of the 1990s, the masculinist dimensions of Black Nationalism criticized by Angela Davis absorbed the cultural sentiment that it generated among young Blacks into depoliticized consumption, negative personal practices and attitudes toward women and gays and lesbians, and a tendency to move away from collective political practices.

Unlike the pronouncements of a Malcolm X, which made most Blacks feel good about themselves in the 1960s (and later), Angela Davis sought quite explicitly to avoid the pitfalls of Black Nationalism elaborated by Frantz Fanon, which she further elaborated. She did so against a backdrop of white Left antinationalism (the Communist Party of the USA), however, which made it somewhat difficult to separate her voice from those of her Communist Party comrades. Many of those from the left wing of the Black Power generation, whose views were closer to Davis's than they realized, did not listen closely enough to detect that she was indeed singing a different tune. This is not to deny that there was an element of patriarchy and heteronormativity involved in the dialogue of the deaf here.

Clearly Black scholars and activists have thought deeply about these issues and have fully investigated and articulated their analyses and conclusions from a variety of angles. While Magubane's address may have been intended to speak to an ascendant Afrocentric school of thought within the academy-based Africana studies movement, which he cautioned about a reified historical consciousness focusing on "dead mummies," as I have indicated above, I do not wish to engage in a one-sided and dogmatic debate against positions that we would today say are culturalist.

This project reviews the evolution of this worldview among people of African descent and integrates it into the internal dynamics of the evolution of American democracy. This study is a contribution to our understanding of the social world in two ways. There continues to be a need for the contextualization of the Black freedom struggle within the larger social world of which it is a part. Moreover, most analyses of race and class attempt to determine which is the primary determinant of social stratification, whereas in my account race and class are inextricably intertwined, though race occupies a fundamental position in the stratifying processes of historical capitalism.

The race-first versus the class-first debate among Black radicals at the turn of the century was an early expression of the ideological tension that sometimes split Black radicals and at other times was understood as a consequence of the contradictory social position that people of African descent occupied within the United States specifically and within the Pan-European world more generally.

W.E.B. Du Bois authored an early formulation with which many are already familiar. At the dawn of the twentieth century, on July 23, 24, and 25, 1900, the Pan-African Conference addressed the "nations of the world" regarding the "present situation and outlook of the darker races of mankind" (Lewis 1995:639). The young African American scholar W.E.B. Du Bois in his keynote address argued, "The problem of the twentieth century is the problem of the colour line, the question as to how far differences of race . . . are going to be made, hereafter, the basis of denying to over half the world the right of sharing to their utmost ability the opportunities and privileges of modern civilization" (Lewis 1995:639). This is not just an American problem, as Malcolm X would dramatically drive home later. Here it is the young Du Bois who argued that "the Negro problem in America is but a local phase of a world problem" (Lewis 1995:42).

Later Du Bois would author a text on the African origins of World War I, a position supported by most Black radicals of that time, both those who held to a class-first strategy and those who held to a race-first strategy. In practice there is a great deal of overlap between the two strategies. Hubert Harrison is acknowledged by all of the New Negro Manhood Rights Movement as the father of New Negro radicalism (Perry 2001). Harrison had been a member of the Socialist Party but was expelled because he would not accept the simplicities of how white members of the Socialist Party articulated a class-first position. Notice how Harrison expresses the manner in which race and class are intertwined in a system of racial capitalism:

> The Nineteenth Christian Century saw the international expansion of capitalism—the economic system of the white peoples of Western Europe and America—and its establishment by force and fraud over the lands of the colored races, black, brown, and yellow. The opening years of the Twentieth Century present us with the sorry spectacle of those same white nations cutting each other's throats to determine which of them shall enjoy the property which has been acquired. For this is the real sum and substance of the original "war aims" of the belligerents; although in conformity with Christian cunning, this is one which is never frankly avowed. Instead we are fed with the information that they are fighting for "Kultur" and "on behalf of small nationalities." (Harrison, 1918, subsequently published in *When Africa Awakes*, 1920:116)

There is some public awareness about the impact of the political psychology of the anticolonial movements on groups located within the core states of the world-economy, especially people of African descent in the United States. While Professor Darryl Thomas's (2001) recent work about the politics of third world solidarity is exemplary, there is today a dearth of scholarly work outside of the Pan-African traditions that has attempted to comprehend the structural and ideological components of this change in world and internal *rapports de force* in the manner that I have tried to do in this work. This is a far cry from the status of third world movements and thinkers from the time when Malcolm X, Dr. King, and a host of others seemed to think that the epoch of white world supremacy was in its terminal phase. In the 1960s and 1970s it was the very challenges to white Western hegemony mounted by social movements and the intellectuals with whom they were allied that gave rise to a vibrant intellectual tradition within the social movements and among intellectuals sympathetic to those movements. In the social sciences, the influence of these social movements was the primary factor that gave birth to dependency theory and world-systems analysis as intellectual movements, which to some extent transformed the landscape of the world of social knowledge. Intellectuals and social movements in the core were inspired by the movements in the periphery of the world-system and by leaders and thinkers such as Frantz Fanon, Kwame Nkrumah, Mao Zedong, Che Guevara, Fidel Castro, Aimé Césaire, Amílcar Cabral, Malcolm X, Ella Baker, Fannie Lou Hamer, Dr. Martin Luther King, Jr., Angela Davis, Mohandas Gandhi, and Ho Chi Minh.

By the dawn of the twenty-first century, intellectuals in the United States and parts of the Pan-European world had been on the defensive for twenty years against a withering ideological offensive by the conservative and neoconservative carriers of the tradition of Madison Grant and Lothrop Stoddard, who now peddle their ideological harangue in the guise of color blindness. While this has enabled these conservatives to co-opt a considerable number of the liberal integrationists who up to this point were opposed to them, the increasing weight of the "third world within," both in the United States and in the Pan-European world as a whole, particularly in a world that is widely seen as increasingly subject to the dictates of a globalized capitalism, increasingly brings to the fore the issue of not only solidarity against white world supremacy but also global solidarity.

Such solidarity has long been a concern of intellectuals in the movements for racial and social justice among people of African descent and among movements for social justice in all lands. The interplay of feminism and antiracism has introduced notions that have dramatically altered the angle of vision of social movements and the intellectuals allied with them. Black feminist thought contains powerful criticism not only of racism, patriarchy, capitalism, and Eurocentrism but also of patriarchal notions within Black nationalism, while often offering a corrective Black feminist nationalism (or Afrocentrism) oriented not solely toward nation building per se but also toward reconceptualizing race, class, and gender as interlocking systems of oppression. The work of Patricia Hill Collins (1991) and other Black feminists is used here to attempt to transcend the search for a counterhegemonic ideology such as traditional Afrocentrism and to a form of knowledge that involves dialogue between partial perspectives in which there is no need to decenter the experience of others (except for the dominant group, which by definition must be decentered). In this dialogue everyone has a voice, but everyone must listen and respond to others in order to remain in the community. Collins argues that sharing a common cause fosters dialogue and encourages groups to transcend their differences. As I have argued in previous work (Bush 1999), this kind of perspective seems central to the project of overcoming the contradictions among the people, which is in turn central to the overall project of social transformation to which all of these groups aspire. This project attempts to draw on the peoples' understanding and experience and weave them together with a comprehension of the structural forces and the larger social and historical system. I hope that this larger project (with sections focusing on theory, radical social movements, and radicalism in the twenty-first century) makes a modest contribution to the literature on Black Liberation, U.S. society, and related social struggles on a world scale.

The twentieth century was indeed the American century; about that there can be little disagreement. The likelihood of a new American century may exist in the imaginations of a lunatic fringe that has attached itself to state power in the United States, but their actions are doing more than any other factor to hasten the decline of U.S. hegemony. The twentieth century has no less been the site of the slow but steady reassertion of the power of the extra-European world. W.E.B. Du Bois had already sounded the alarm about the problem of the twentieth century. Even before World War I there were revolutions in Mexico, Afghanistan, Persia, and China, and the Japanese had defeated the Russians. Indeed, Wallerstein argues that the Russian Revolution was not really a proletarian revolution, but the most successful and spectacular of the rebellions against Pan-European dominance, even if the Bolsheviks leaned to the side of the Westernizers against the Slavophiles. But the debate about Westernization did not occur only among the Russian revolutionaries; it was a sign of the central ambivalence of the movements, which sought both to separate from and to integrate into the existing world-system as a means of obtaining social equality. When the German revolution did not rescue them and establish the proletarian revolution, though, they realized that their survival depended on their link to the world anti-imperialist struggle. Wallerstein argues that this was the meaning of the Baku congress in 1920, the First Congress of the Peoples of the East, held in the city of Baku from September 1 to September 8, 1920 (Wallerstein 2000:4).

While the First Congress of the Peoples of the East is said to have marked a decisive break with the neglect of the national and colonial question by the Second International, based almost exclusively in the Pan-European world, in the first years of the existence of the Soviet Union the leadership felt that the imminent victory of the revolutionary forces in Western Europe was certain. Only in England and the United States was there a possibility that capitalism might survive another year or so (White 1974:493–494). The most vociferous opposition to this Eurocentric approach came from M. Sultan-Galiev (1982), who argued in 1919 that the leaders of the October Revolution had erred in directing their attention almost entirely to the West because of their sense that class antagonisms were sharpest there. "But the East, with its population of one and a half billion enslaved to the western European Bourgeoisie, is forgotten" (Sultan-Galiev 1982:7).

Sultan-Galiev was one of the early theoreticians to see clearly the centrality of imperial domination to the capitalist world-system. He argued that the might and force of the bourgeois culture and civilization of Europe and America is derived from their exploitation of the peoples of the East. The "lion's share of all the material and spiritual wealth of the 'whites' is stolen from the East, and built at the expense of the blood and sweat of hundreds of millions of laboring masses of 'natives' of all colors and races" (Sultan-Galiev 1982:9). How contemporary are his words as he continues: "It was necessary for up to ten million aborigines of America and Africa to perish, and to extinguish completely from the face of the earth the entire rich culture of the 'Incas' in order that contemporary 'freedom-loving' America, with her 'cosmopolitan culture' of 'progress and technology' might be formed. The proud skyscrapers of Chicago, New York and other cities are on the bones of the 'redskins' and Negroes tortured by inhuman planters and on the smoking ruins of the destroyed cities of the 'Incas'"(Sultan-Galiev 1982:9).

Wallerstein argues that in comparison with the twentieth century, the nineteenth century was the century of progress, a time in which the capitalist system seemed to deliver a new and better world. The liberal geoculture seemed to sweep away all signs of the ancien régime. The citizen dethroned the crown as the bearer of sovereignty. It was the century of Pax Britannica in the core zones but also the century of the final imperialist conquest of the extra-European zones. In this world, to be bourgeois, white, male, Christian, and skilled were proof of civilization and a guarantee of progress. It was the progressive aura of this century that made the outbreak of World War I in 1914 such a shock in the Pan-European zones. While the twentieth century continued on something of a progressive road, the changes in *rapports de force* listed above forced Wallerstein to raise the question of whether the twentieth century is darkness at noon or bright sun at midnight.

It was of course during the nineteenth century that the liberal geoculture was formed and the Eurocentric nature of the modern world-system was locked solidly in place and adhered to across the political spectrum. Even Friedrich Engels was to argue, quite unambiguously, according to Abdel-Malek (1981:81), that the 1847 war between the United States and Mexico had a positive character, with the expansion of the U.S. territory into Mexico seen as the expansion of advanced capitalist civilization. The European Left had embraced the civilizing mission.

What, then, after all is said and done, is the problem of the color line that Dr. Du Bois famously raised at the opening of the twentieth century? Is it not that the dangerous classes of the extra-European world, including those descendents of the extra-European world within the political boundaries of the Pan-European world, had in fact not been tamed, not even by a long shot? The implication of this social fact is that they constituted a fundamental problem of the social order of the world-system, for which even today there is no simple resolution. M. Sultan-Galiev's words from nearly one hundred years ago ring just as true today, with barely a shift in the cast of characters. Gerald Horne notes that the collapse of the Soviet Union loosened the ties of Asian anticommunist conservatives to the United States, such that in a recent book Mahatir Mohamad and Shintaro Isihara cite Lenin to show that European prosperity was based on exploiting the cheap labor and abundant resources of the colonies, and thus that European hegemony is based on plunder and exploitation. "If the United States can get away with . . . peddling arms throughout the Middle East, intervening militarily to protect its supply of oil, and arm twisting Japan to pay the bill— then the white race still rules the world" (Horne 1999:460). I would like here to underline Gerald Horne's contention that what has gone unnoticed in the wake of the decline of the Communist parties is the concomitant "general crisis of white supremacy" (Horne 1999:440). Black internationalism is one route that opens up this vast arena of potential for social transformation to a more comprehensive collective investigation.

Here I would like to insist on an element of caution regarding much of the discourse of the past twenty years or so about "the disuniting of America" from the center (Schlesinger 1991) and "the twilight of our common dreams" from the Left (Gitlin 1995). The turn to identity-based groups is not a consequence of the ultramilitant tactics of oppressed groups within the United States and elsewhere; it is a refuge from the very real disintegration of the state structures of the modern world-system as a locus of social reform that can better the lot of the world's peoples. While it is true that the traditional antisystemic movements have reached the end of their rope, what this implies is a new strategy that we think has to start from a sense of international solidarity and international social justice, which is the reality of the world in which we now live. The confrontation with North-South polarization is essential to any such strategy. Black internationalism is one locus from which this strategy can be developed, to the extent that it reflects the outlook of a community and not just intellectuals and cadres.

Organization of the Book

In Part I of the book I deal with the issue of theory as it developed historically. First, in Chapter 1, "The Peculiar Internationalism of Black Nationalism," I try to articulate an understanding of Black Nationalism based on the development of nationalist consciousness rather than a strict adherence to any ideological notion of nationalism.[21] Use of such a flexible approach to the study of Black Nationalism enables us to study a range of phenomena, which include both self-proclaimed nationalists and those for whom racial solidarity is key to their political psychology. This enables us also to focus on some of the peculiarities of Black Nationalism, especially its internationalism. Once I have established my own understanding of Black Nationalism I move in Chapter 2, "The Sociology of the Color Line: W.E.B. Du Bois and the End of White World Supremacy," to the most sustained critique of the color line in the history of African American social thought. In reviewing the contribution of Dr. Du Bois to the study of the color line and the debates that surround his work, I hope to provide a framework that will take us through the remainder of the book. In Chapter 3, "The Class First/Race First Debate: The Contradictions of Nationalism and Internationalism and the Stratification of the World-system," we find the first revolutionary challenge to the status quo in the modern United States in the form of the New Negro Movement and follow that debate as it manifested itself during the 1960s. While this debate is central to the evolution of Black radicalism in the United States and on the world stage, it should be noted that the target of this debate was the world Left, especially the white Left in the United States, and large sections of the European Left.

As Rose Brewer (2003) argues, the focus on race and class in Black radical theory has long obscured the gender dimension of Black subordination and the central role of gender in the construction of social resistance in the African American sector of society. Chapter 4, "Black Feminism, Intersectionality, and the Critique of Masculinist Models of Liberation," focuses on the unique role of

Black women in the Black freedom struggle and how the leadership of Black women gave a certain character to the movement that needed much more attention from all of us.[22]

Part II focuses on radical social movements, demonstrates the legacy of Black Internationalism rooted in the New Negro period and beyond, and shows how it was manifested from the 1960s to the present in the civil rights movement, the Black Power Movement, the Afrocentric movement, the multicultural movement, and the Black feminist movement. Chapter 5, "The Civil Rights Movement and the Continuing Struggle for the Redemption of America," demonstrates that the civil rights movement shared the Black radical and internationalist tradition and shows why FBI director J. Edgar Hoover viewed the civil rights movement as the center of a social revolution under way in the United States. Chapter 6, "Black Power, the American Dream, and the Spirit of Bandung: Malcolm X and Dr. Martin Luther King, Jr., in the Age of World Revolution," situates the Black Power Movement of the 1960s and 1970s and the trajectories of Malcolm X and Dr. King in a long global context. This includes an interrogation of the notion that Dr. King's dream and Malcolm X's nightmare (Malcolm X 1966) were polar opposite views of the United States and thus represented opposing views of strategy for the Black freedom struggle. This reexamination of the legacies of these two giants of African American, U.S., and world leadership finds and details a convergence of views between Dr. King and Malcolm X, as well as a movement toward a common front, as I discussed in an earlier work (Bush 1999). A key issue in Chapters 5 and 6 is to locate these manifestations of the Black freedom struggle more clearly in the center of the international strategy of the U.S. elites and to demonstrate not only how the war against Vietnam undermined the war on poverty but how the U.S. right wing perceived people of color within our borders as in the same social category as our putative "enemies" of color outside our borders. Indeed, the failure of liberals to grasp the international dimensions of the struggle for social justice neutralized their often very sincere desire for social justice within our borders. This was something of a "dialogue of the deaf." One could conclude, though, that the stakes became clearer and some opted for a defense of what they felt the United States had contributed to the world, while others opted for living out the true meaning of our creed, or linking the American dream to the aspirations of all humanity. Increasingly radicals attempted to follow Malcolm X's advice that our struggle should be for human rights since civil rights were no longer an issue. The success of the civil rights movement in defeating Jim Crow had clarified the deeper nature of the contradictions in U.S. society, and the war in Vietnam had clarified the international dimensions of the struggle even more clearly.[23]

The U.S. defeat in Vietnam seemed to stay the hand of the United States in international affairs, but the conservative Right, which had mobilized against egalitarianism, racial liberalism, and libertarianism at the same time as the civil rights movement, continued to build despite the temporary setback of Watergate. The conservative setback of Watergate blinded the Left, which saw the conservative backlash to civil rights and the cutback of the war on poverty as attacks on the civil rights movement in a narrow sense instead of an attack on the legacy of the New Deal, the welfare state, and the social democratic compromise. The victory of Ronald Reagan in 1980 brought all of these things into focus. During the 1970s the Black Left had moved in two directions—one that affirmed its revolutionary nationalist legacy, the others still under the influence of the world revolutionary current, which started in the late 1960s to move toward merging elements of their organizations with the mostly white organizations that had come out of the New Left to create a multiracial or (in the language of the time) multinational form of organization.

I

Theory

The Peculiar Internationalism
of Black Nationalism

Nationalism is an ideology that asserts the right of nationhood of a particular group, affirms the cultural similarities of members of the nation,
and draws boundaries for that group vis-à-vis others who are deemed
outsiders. The central contention of nationalists is that political boundaries
should be coterminous with cultural boundaries. Thus, the concept of the nation has always seemed to be inextricably bound to the concept of the state.

But how does one define a nation? Scholars and movements have used various criteria, including language, ethnicity, common territory, common history,
and cultural traits. One influential definition conceptualized during the course
of the mobilization of diverse populations in revolutionary struggles against the
Russian Empire holds that a nation is "a historically evolved, stable community
of language, territory, economic life and psychological make-up manifested in a
common culture" (Davis 1967:163).

This definition, rendered by the Georgian Communist J. V. Stalin in 1913,
though widely quoted without attribution, adds to previous definitions, that
there be a community not only of language and culture but also of territory. The
intent of this definitional dispute is to refute the principle of national-cultural
autonomy articulated by the Austrian Marxist Otto Bauer. According to Bauer,
the nation is defined by the totality of people who are united by a common fate
(history) so that they possess a common national character (Davis 1967:150).
Bauer's definition clearly implies that a nation exists whenever a people believe
that they are a nation.

While Stalin's "Marxism and the National Question" had V. I. Lenin's bless-
ing as the Bolshevik position on the national question, in practice Lenin's stance
was much more conciliatory than Stalin's. After Lenin came to view imperialism

as the framework for revolutionary struggle, his understanding of the national question evolved in tandem. If indeed imperialism is the highest stage of capitalism, if it is moribund capitalism, and if it is a world-system of colonial oppression and the financial strangulation of the great majority of the world's people located in oppressed countries by a handful of advanced (oppressor) countries, then the issue of anti-imperialism is central to the revolutionary struggle. This becomes much clearer in the founding of the Third International (see Chapter 3 for elaboration of this issue). The founding of the Third International elevated the national question to the top of the agenda of the radical workers' movements and relocated the center of those movements on the margins of the advanced capitalist countries of that time (the Eurasian land mass occupied by the Russian Empire, China, India, and much of the Muslim world). The strongest appeal of the radicals was to the colonial slaves of the capitalist world. The intellectuals and revolutionaries from the dark world (including people of African descent) were attracted to communism precisely because of the Bolsheviks' nationalities policy. In Chapter 5 we will see how E. Franklin Frazier discusses the Bolshevik nationalities policy in his book *Race and Cultural Contacts in the Modern World*.

As we can see in the above discussion, there is a great deal of definitional ambiguity in the debate about the national question. Nonetheless, most of us tend to assume that we know what constitutes a nation, which of course is the strength of the Bauer position. Later scholarly investigations of the concept of the nation tend to show that the notion is not self-evident. Scholars mostly agree, however, that a nation is not a God-given way of classifying people; nor is it an inherent political destiny. While many people assume that nationalism is an ideology that develops logically among members of a nation, many scholars of nationalism hold that, historically speaking, nationalism comes before nations. Nationalists are said to construct nations by fashioning preexisting cultures into a nation, by inventing cultures, or by obliterating preexisting cultures.

Like all nationalism, Black Nationalism can be viewed as the reaction of formerly disparate groups of African descent to a sense of mutual oppression and humiliation. Prior to the African slave trade, African people, like their European counterparts, were organized around local cultural loyalties and traditions. In such societies, tradition as embodied in the wisdom of living elders or revered ancestors is sacred. In the slave states of the United States, where enslaved Africans were a minority of the population expressions of African culture were stringently prohibited. Some scholars argue that such practices destroyed the traditions of the enslaved population within a generation or two. Other scholars argue that the traditions were driven underground, giving rise to a kind of surreptitious Pan-Africanization of the culture of the ordinary field hands, which persisted despite the formal adoption of Christianity by the overwhelming majority of Africans within the United States. Both narratives recognize that this experience endowed them with a sense of common experience and identity, the root of nationalist consciousness.

The identity developed in the seventeenth century between Africans and slavery was the edifice upon which a racial division of labor was constructed.

This near-absolute correlation between Blackness and this most sordid social rank played havoc with the social psychology of whites, who dreaded falling into this unenviable social status themselves. For this reason the lines were starkly drawn and reinforced with all of the power that racial myths could muster. Following slavery, many whites fought to maintain the prerogatives of racial privilege with respect to the Black population. These practices led to the restriction of Black people from certain desirable jobs, neighborhoods, social activities, and so forth. The dehumanization of Blacks became the preoccupation of scientists and scholars following the precepts of social Darwinism to a coherent explanation and justification of the relegation of Black people to a subordinate status.

Black Nationalism as an ideology has long been an element in the structuring of political action and cultural standpoint. It was both an affirmation of the humanity, strength, and dignity of Black people and an opposition to the degrading myths fashioned by whites. It is generally believed to have emerged during the eighteenth century as a challenge to racist ideology that sought to justify the enslavement of people of African descent within the labor force of a presumably democratic country. Until the establishment of the American Colonization Society in 1816, free blacks in the North were called Africans and regarded themselves as Africans (despite the fact that educated blacks were quite distinct culturally from Africans on the continent). Uneducated blacks, in contrast, because of their isolation from whites and their contact with slaves from the West Indies and new saltwater slaves (directly from Africa), were substantially African. Free blacks felt that the American Colonization Society was a scheme to strengthen slavery by sending free blacks back to Africa.

By the 1850s, emigration appeals were echoed by several black leaders: Martin Delaney, Henry Highland Garnett, and Alexander Crummell. The desire to establish an independent nation outside of the control of the United States was a consequence of the belief of large numbers of free Black people that their experience outside of the slave states was marked by racist treatment, almost tantamount to the treatment of their enslaved brethren. Slavery required the integration of the enslaved Africans with the white slave owners, but it was the nonslave North that took the lead in the establishment of segregated institutions. These institutions existed in practically every sphere, including schools, churches, hospitals, jails, hotels, and public conveyances. Blacks in the North were also subject to pogroms, not to mention the possibility of being enslaved because of the stipulations of the 1850 Fugitive Slave Act.

The Negro Convention Movement was the most effective forum for Afro-American protest in the antebellum period, and the debates within the convention reflected the shifting tides of the black struggle. Until the 1850s, the advocates of moral suasion and the absorption of blacks into the larger society predominated within the convention movement. With the Fugitive Slave Act of 1850, the Kansas-Nebraska bill of 1854, the Dred Scott decision of 1857, and the general proliferation of scientific racist theories, the attitude of blacks about strategies and tactics for liberation from North American racist oppression were transformed. Frederick Douglass, who had opposed Henry Highland Garnett's call for insurrection in

1843, by the 1850s began to believe that liberation could be obtained only by resorting to violence.

Underneath these debates, however, was the resistance of the slaves themselves, ranging from the Denmark Vesey conspiracy of 1822 to the Nat Turner rebellion of 1831, and the resistance exemplified by thousands of runaway slaves. Such resistance ultimately inspired John Brown's bold assault on Harpers Ferry in 1859, which indicated that the die had been cast; North American civil society could no longer live with the contradiction of enslavement.

With the defeat of Reconstruction, the promise of a nonracial democracy was buried beneath a system of racist terror institutionalized throughout the South. It was in this context that Booker T. Washington emerged as the most distinguished black leader of this period (1895–1915). Washington did not mount a frontal attack on white supremacy but counseled blacks to learn the value of manual labor, hard work, and thrift and to practice the Christian virtues of being clean and quiet. These values rather than empty rhetoric and flashy protest would enable blacks to win acceptance. Although Washington's strategy is commonly referred to as accommodationist, many scholars and militants in the Black freedom struggle recognize a nationalist component in his emphasis on self-help and his promotion of Black businesses and economic development.

While Ida B. Wells-Barnett, W.E.B. Du Bois, and William Monroe Trotter championed a militant protest movement in opposition to Washington's accommodationist approach, World War I brought new radical actors on the scene known generically as the New Negro Movement. The New Negro Movement was part of the revolutionary anticolonial and socialist movements that shook the capitalist world. Most members of this movement upheld the race-first viewpoint, that race must be the first concern of people of African descent. The numerous betrayals at the hands of white allies had taught them that race was the first principle of White America and was thus their most important challenge. Race was not merely an expression of class relations; it was the main stratifying process of U.S. society. This is not to say that there cannot be principled alliances, but such alliances had to be constructed on the basis of independent Black leadership and the insistence that opposition to racism be a fundamental principle of all members of the alliance. For the most radical among the New Negro militants, represented by the African Blood Brotherhood, Cyril Briggs, Richard Moore, and Hubert Harrison, race first made sense in the context of an anticapitalist and socialist perspective because they understood that the class structure was constructed on the basis of race. That is, the subordinate status of Black people and white supremacy were inextricably intertwined with the formation and consolidation of capitalist civilization, and no progress was possible unless antiracism and respect for the self-determination of Black people were central to the grievances of all the movements.

During World War I and its aftermath, the New Negro Movement fueled the flame of revolt. In 1921 a State Department official by the name of Charles Latham argued that Marcus Garvey's movement was considered dangerous because its agitation would find a more fertile field of class divergence than Bolshevism would likely find in the United States. Garvey's organization, the Universal

Negro Improvement Association, is the largest organization in the history of the Black freedom struggle.

The African Blood Brotherhood had been the most sophisticated organizational expression of New Negro radicalism, but its leaders liquidated the issue of independent Black leadership by joining the Communist Party of the United States and allowing it to disband the African Blood Brotherhood. Yet the former members of the African Blood Brotherhood leadership were instrumental in pushing the Communist Party of the United States toward a revolutionary perspective and enrolling it in the fight for racial justice to a degree unmatched by any other predominantly white organization.

In the 1930s the Moorish American Science Temple was prominent on the streets of many Black communities, providing a milieu from which much of the leadership of the early Nation of Islam emerged. Later the Nation of Islam would become the largest of the Black Nationalist organizations after the Universal Negro Improvement Association. During the 1930s the movement to stop Benito Mussolini's invasion of Ethiopia was one of the broadest manifestations of nationalism in the African diaspora. W.E.B. Du Bois was ousted from his position in the National Association for the Advancement of Colored People (NAACP) because he advocated the development of Black economic power within Black communities, taking advantage of the existing racial solidarity and sense of common destiny. During this period Du Bois also wrote his masterpiece, *Black Reconstruction in America*, which took the revolutionary nationalism of the New Negro militants to a new level and articulated the most sophisticated class analysis of the world-system to be known until the 1970s.

Student Revolutionaries: Nationalist in Form, Internationalist in Scope

In February 1968 police opened fire on a Black student demonstration against a segregated bowling alley in Orangeburg, South Carolina, killing three students from South Carolina State College, in what has come to be known as the Orangeburg Massacre. Owusu Sadaukai (Howard Fuller), who was an organizer for the Foundation for Community Development, called a meeting in Durham, attended by representatives from sixteen different colleges, including Nelson Johnson, a student at North Carolina A&T State University and a protégé of Sadaukai's. All of the representatives who attended the meeting were given the responsibility of using their own creative resources to organize a demonstration on each of their campuses. It was this event that brought Nelson Johnson's leadership capabilities to the attention of the general public. In the wake of this demonstration, Johnson would emerge as the most influential leader of radical forces in the historic Greensboro community and at the historic North Carolina A&T State University. He would also emerge as the leader of the soon-to-be-formed Student Organization for Black Unity.

In March 1968 students at the historically Black Howard University staged a sit-in at the university's administration building, and the sit-in became a takeover, introducing to a new generation a tactic that was repeated at many campuses across the nation. By 1969 Black students had staged such takeovers on fifty campuses over a variety of issues focused on their need for a relevant education (most often Black studies), more Black professors, and a variety of student rights. In April 1968 the Students' Afro-American Society and the Students for a Democratic Society at Columbia University formed an alliance in opposition to the university's plan to take over land in the adjoining Black community to build a gym and the university's support of the war in Vietnam via its Institute for Defense Analysis and other institutions. They staged a takeover of several buildings at the university, demonstrating the confluence of multiple movements on the liberal university: the movement for minority rights, which started as a quest for inclusion and wound up with an ambition to transform society; the movement against U.S. hegemony over the world-system by military and other means; and the movement for a culturally liberated society (Wallerstein and Starr 1971).

It began to dawn on the elites of liberal U.S. society that in fact they were in the first stages of a new kind of war that they had not anticipated, a revolution in the midst of the liberal university, which was the representation of what was most ideal about U.S. society, and especially at a time when they had thought that they were on the way to meeting the challenge posed by Gunnar Myrdal in his famous 1944 book, *An American Dilemma*.

In late May 1968 the Third World Liberation Front (which included the Black Student Union), in alliance with the Progressive Labor Party and the Students for a Democratic Society, occupied the administration building at San Francisco State University, demanding preferential admissions for minority students, the rehiring of a Chicano professor who was being fired, and the removal of an air force ROTC program (Ex-PL Cadre 1979). In 1969 the Third World Liberation Front began a strike at the University of California, Berkeley, demanding an autonomous Third World College.

These snapshots provide only a glimpse of what was going on during that time. What is important here for those who are familiar with the dynamics of social movements and the social groups that often come to the fore is that the peculiar position of African Americans, based mostly in the working class and belonging to internally colonized strata, gave them the social distance of the colonized world without but also the geographic and personal proximity to the levers of power, which greatly magnified their social location in the world configuration of the struggles between the powerful and the powerless. Given their social location in the configuration of power in U.S. society at that time as mostly residents of marginalized working-class communities with a sense of collective solidarity across U.S. society, they combined class, national, and racial solidarities in a manner that made them the ideal candidates not for simple inclusion in U.S. society but for radical transformation of that society in a manner that was democratic, egalitarian, and just.

I focus first on the interactions of some of the known organizations situated in or derived from the Black student movement. I begin by looking at the history of the Revolutionary Action Movement (RAM).

What little public image there is of RAM tends to be that of inner-city militants plotting urban guerrilla warfare on the white world. It is important that RAM came very much out of the student movement, as did its more moderate older cousin, the Student Nonviolent Coordinating Committee (SNCC), and one of its offshoots, the Black Panther Party for Self-Defense. According to Maxwell Stanford (2003), RAM evolved out of the southern civil rights movement and the Black Nationalist movements in northern cities. While he was a student at Case Western Reserve University, Don Freeman of Cleveland, Ohio, became involved in the civil rights movement in February 1960 in support of the sit-in at Woolworth in Greensboro, North Carolina. Two months later Freeman attended a socialist conference at the University of Michigan, which led him to enlist in the ranks of socialists for the rest of his life.

In the summer of 1961, at the end of the Freedom Rides, Robert Williams called for Blacks to arm for self-defense and come to Monroe, North Carolina, for a showdown with the Ku Klux Klan. During that same summer, the League for Industrial Democracy had planned to form a student branch to be called Students for a Democratic Society (SDS). SDS had planned to hold a conference on the New Left during the conference of the National Student Association. Since the news of Williams's flight into exile reached movement circles during the conference, SDS's Black cadre met to discuss developing a radical Black movement that would help to create conditions that would make it favorable to bring Williams back into the country.[1] Freeman became the coordinator of this group, which included a student from Central State College in Wilberforce, Ohio, where Max Stanford (aka Muhammad Ahmad) was a student.

During the fall of 1961 an off-campus chapter of SDS called Challenge was created at Central State (Stanford 2003:142). The members of Challenge included students who had been expelled from southern colleges for sit-in demonstrations, some who had been involved in Freedom Rides, and students from the North who had been members of the Nation of Islam and other Black Nationalist organizations. Freeman, who was a teacher in Cleveland, was a mentor to this group. While the group did not have a particular ideology, they became radicalized during a year of conflicts with the Central State administration over students' rights.

In the spring of 1962 the journal *Studies on the Left* published Harold Cruse's article "Revolutionary Nationalism and the Afro-American," which described African Americans as an oppressed nation within a nation, a domestic or internal colony. Freeman wrote a letter to Challenge members encouraging them to read the article, which was being studied by Black radicals elsewhere, who were also contemplating establishing a movement in the North similar to the Nation of Islam, using the tactics of the SNCC, but outside of the Congress of Racial Equality (CORE) and the NAACP (Stanford 2003:144).

This then was the impetus for the formation of RAM, after which two of the cadres, Wanda Marshall and Max Stanford, returned to their communities to organize. In Philadelphia, Stanford worked with the SNCC and met with the leader of a Black Marxist group called Organization Alert, who invited him to join. But when Freeman came to Philadelphia and met with the Organization Alert leader, he found the group to be too bourgeois intellectual and insufficiently activist. Stanford was not convinced but later had a fierce disagreement with the Organization Alert leader, who harshly criticized the SNCC and argued that it would never change (Stanford 2003:146).

In November 1962 Max Stanford and Wanda Marshall met with Malcolm X at the Shabazz Restaurant of Temple No. 7 in Harlem. When Stanford asked Malcolm X if he should join the Nation of Islam, Malcolm replied that he could do more for the Honorable Elijah Muhammad by organizing outside of the Nation of Islam.

Soon after this meeting, Stanford drafted a position paper entitled "Orientation to a Black Mass Movement, Part One," and circulated it among much of the Black Left in Philadelphia. The document called for a focus on Black working-class youth who had the sustained resentment, wrath, and frustration toward the present social order that if properly channeled could revolutionize black America and make it the vanguard of the world's black revolution (Stanford 2003:146–147).

As the tempo of white resistance to the southern movement increased with the bombing of a Birmingham church, killing four young girls in the fall of 1963, the concept of nonviolence suffered a setback in the eyes of SNCC workers (Ahmad 1978:5). RAM organized a student wing called the Afro-American Student Movement, which organized chapters in Nashville (Fisk University), Detroit, and Los Angeles. The movement called for a student conference on Black Nationalism in May 1964, hoping to expand the horizons of the southern movement beyond liberal integrationism, which RAM saw as limited, even in the militant practices of the SNCC.

Ahmad argues that the convening of this conference was the catalyst that eventually led some sections of the civil rights movement to take up the struggle for Black Power. Through the summer after the conference, RAM was able to get the permission of SNCC chair John Lewis to work with the SNCC in Mississippi. During this period RAM militants encountered the hostility of white SNCC workers who opposed the idea of an all-Black organization and the idea of armed self-defense.

In the fall 1964 edition of RAM's journal, *Black America*, Don Freeman explained that the first session of the conference evaluated "bourgeois reformism, as articulated by the integrationist civil rights movement," which for him included CORE, the Southern Christian Leadership Conference (SCLC), the SNCC, and the NAACP. For Freeman this session substantiated Du Bois's conviction that "capitalism cannot reform itself, a system that enslaves you, cannot free you" (Freeman 1964:15). But the conferees were also critical of white Marxists who sought to lead a white working class who wanted to reform capitalism and not "revolutionize the social order." The only revolutionary force in the United States, they agreed, was embodied in the Afro-American struggle, and thus would be led by Black radicals rather than "opportunistic white Marxists."

On the whole, the conferees supported Malcolm X's position that the struggle of African Americans should be for human rights and not civil rights. The refusal of the U.S. government to enforce the Thirteenth and Fourteenth amendments rendered Afro-Americans slaves a colonized nation within the United States, not U.S. citizens. Their position was said to be analogous to that of the Afro-Asian and Latin American nations under Western imperialism (Freeman 1964:16).

Finally the conferees argued that the prerequisite for a Black revolution in the United States was a fundamental cultural revolution, a re-Africanization of Black people in the United States, which would renounce bourgeois materialistic values, pathological egoism, individualism, and the rat race. Black people must know their own history in order to demolish the inferiority instilled by "American" indoctrination (Freeman 1964:16).

Greenwood, Mississippi, became the base for revolutionary Black Nationalist activity. Ahmad himself and Askia Touré (aka Ronald Snellings) were leading RAM cadres in Greenwood. They spoke with Black SNCC workers about the necessity to control their own organization. Both Ahmad and Touré argue that SNCC field staff were increasingly won over to the cause of Black Nationalism. Askia Touré affirms the good intentions of many of the white activists in the SNCC as dedicated to the liberation of Black people but points out that they realized that eventually they would have to organize white working people to change this country. Touré contrasts the humility of many of the white SNCC workers with the arrogance of Saundra "Casey" Hayden.[2] Touré would later join the Atlanta Project in 1966 and participate in the drafting of what has been called the SNCC's Black Power Position Paper.

The Atlanta Project under the leadership of Bill Ware was constituted in the wake of violent uprisings in the Black communities of Atlanta known as Vine City and Summerhill. The intent of the Atlanta Project was to increase black community "control over the public decisions which affect" their lives, a position that by then was part of the apparatus of the federal government's antipoverty programs. The eminent historian of the Black freedom struggle Clayborne Carson argues that the project emphasized racial identity as a means to eliminate racial inferiority and political impotence. Although Stokely Carmichael initially opposed the position of Atlanta Project staff for political, not ideological, reasons, he became greatly influenced by many of their positions. Indeed, the debate clarified his ideas and made him believe that it was time to challenge John Lewis as chair, whose soft-spoken commitment to nonviolence, continuing participation in the planning of the White House Conference on Civil Rights, and relationship with the SCLC made him seem out of step with the mood of most of the other SNCC staff (Carson 1981:202–203).

Carmichael emerged the victor in the contest with Lewis, since his views were more representative of the majority of the SNCC staff. But Carmichael's subsequent announcement of the Black Power concept created a furor within the civil rights movement. At a meeting with the SCLC, the SNCC, and CORE at Yazoo City, Mississippi, Floyd McKissick spoke out in favor of the Black Power concept. Dr. Martin Luther King, Jr. attempted to convince Carmichael and others that they should not use a slogan that would "confuse our allies, isolate the Negro community and give many prejudiced whites, who might otherwise be ashamed of their anti-Negro feelings, a ready excuse for self-justification" (Carson 1981:210). Carmichael and McKissick responded that there was nothing wrong with the concept of Black Power since it was the same kind of group power other ethnic groups had sought.

My attention has long been riveted on this debate. As I have said elsewhere (Bush 1999), this discussion must have clarified in the minds of the discussants that the civil rights era had come to an end. "The utter desperation signaled in King's remarks, who himself had come to symbolize the moral high ground which the civil rights movement had so long commanded, spoke volumes about Black people's dependence on liberal 'allies' and the naked power relations behind it. Carmichael and McKissick could do little more here than state the obvious, but the very obviousness of their statement only confirmed the verdict that we might have reached if we had heard only King's remarks. It was time on all sides for a reassessment of direction" (Bush 1999:168–169).

The Black freedom struggle at this point was entering the revolutionary whirlwind that encompassed almost all areas of the world in the late 1960s and early 1970s, what Wallerstein refers to as the world revolution of 1968. While this revolution was not about the seizure of state power, which is the image that we normally have of revolutions, it was a revolution because it broke the back of the reformist co-opting liberal geoculture, which had been the basis of stability of historical capitalism since 1848. Malcolm X had been the prime mover in this transformation, but at this point Dr. Martin Luther King, Jr., himself could no longer deny the obvious and henceforth moved rapidly into this whirlwind. I cover this process in more detail in Chapter 6, "Black Power, the American Dream, and the Spirit of Bandung: Malcolm X and Dr. Martin Luther King, Jr., in the Age of World Revolution."

The Example of the Student Organization for Black Unity

In 1969 the post-SNCC Black student movement began to take shape with the creation of the Student Organization for Black Unity (SOBU), formed in May 1969 at a meeting at North Carolina A&T State University in Greensboro. SOBU held its first national convention in October 1969 at North Carolina Central University in Durham. The group's focus was Pan-Africanist, but its self-description claimed a wider sphere in the sense that it claimed to be nationalist in form, internationalist in scope, and scientific in principle. The designation *scientific* here, of course, refers to the *scientific* in *scientific socialism*. The focus of SOBU's mass work included African Solidarity Day, South Africa, the Pan-Africanism of Malcolm X, and a report on the United Nations. In August 1972, SOBU changed its name to Youth Organization for Black Unity (YOBU) to reflect its movement toward the wider world, which it sought to organize as part of the desired revolutionary transformation.

The leadership of SOBU had viewed the SNCC in 1966 as a synthesis of the ideas and approaches of Dr. King and Malcolm X. While they noted the simultaneous emergence of eruptions in inner-city areas inhabited by Black folk and confrontation politics on campuses, they did not initially use their analytic framework to understand and contextualize these phenomena. Confrontation politics escalated on campuses to the point that at Cornell University, Black students with guns took over buildings.

These were tense times; everywhere Black folk were in struggle against forces who wanted to maintain the status quo, including Black guardians of the existing social order. On May 21, 1969, a student by the name of Willie Grimes was shot to death at North Carolina A&T State University when university students came to the assistance of students at Dudley High School who were struggling against an extremely authoritarian administration supported by local authorities with brutal measures. Only weeks before, the university had been the scene of the founding meeting of SOBU, but the proceedings were interrupted when students from Dudley High School walked out of their school to get support from the college students for their struggles. The conferees took leave from the conference to assist the high school students, but the situation was of long standing and led to continued struggles until the shooting occurred (Bermanzohn 2003:100–101; Waller 2002:48–49).

In the late 1960s the community activist Owusu Sadaukai became a confidant of SNCC activists Cleve Sellers and Stokely Carmichael and was a major player in the development of SOBU and the Malcolm X Liberation University (Johnson 2003:484; Belvin 2004). During May 1969, many Black students were calling for the formation of Black studies programs at historically white universities and colleges. There was a second tendency among other Black students, who focused on the need for independent educational institutions. The Center for Black Education was established by students at Federal City College in Washington, D.C., and Malcolm X Liberation University was established by students at Duke University. The latter took hard-line positions against Black studies programs that were not really under the control of Black people and against people in the social sciences. Technical skills were stressed because those are the skills needed for nation building and for the construction of Africa with the departure of the colonial powers. SOBU had been part of this network of organizations spawned by what Peniel Joseph calls the SNCC diaspora (Joseph 2006:260).

Both SOBU and the National Association of Black Students (NABS) were formed by students who had been active within the National Student Association. SOBU cadres broke from the National Student Association in May 1969, and NABS broke from the National Student Association in October 1969 (SOBU National Assembly 1972). According to SOBU cadres speaking at the 1972 SOBU National Assembly in Epps, Alabama, NABS was more service oriented than SOBU but was also troubled by conflicts between Gwen Patton and Willie Ricks and Cleve Sellers (SOBU National Assembly 1972).[3]

In the beginning, the SOBU program was very Pan-Africanist in its emphasis, oriented toward the process of nation building in Africa. Militants were encouraged to develop technical skills so they could move to Africa and use those skills to build African countries. But Samora Machel cautioned Owusu Sadaukai, of SO-BU's sister organization Malcolm X Liberation University, that they did not need more people; they needed someone to intervene with the U.S. government who was central to both the still-existing colonial structures in some African countries and the neocolonial structures that existed almost everywhere else in Africa (Waller 2002:54–55).[4]

This discussion led to the convening of African American radicals to plan African Liberation Day in support of the liberation movements in Africa and eventually to form the African Liberation Support Committee, which consisted of Black organizations from a number of perspectives who united around the need to support the African liberation movements. Despite the discarding of the "Back to Africa" emphasis at the insistence of the representatives of the African liberation movements, SOBU continued to emphasize their African identity above all else in their program. According to Nelson Johnson, the chairman of SOBU, Pan-Africanism meant that the liberation of Blacks in the United States was impossible without first liberating Africa. This conception of Pan-Africanism held, further, that "Black people are a world community without national or class differences, and that the enemy is white people, all white people" (Bermanzohn 2003:105).

However, it was Amilcar Cabral, the leader of the liberation movement in Guinea-Bissau, who argued that sending support to the liberation movements should be a secondary task for them, that their primary responsibility should be to unite with other people within the United States to overthrow U.S. imperialism, including white people (Waller 2002:55). In debate with comrades from the continent in the Pan-African Student Organization in the Americas (PASOA), the leadership of SOBU/YOBU learned the inadequacies of what they termed their own "infantile" Pan-Africanism. Despite the intellectual heavyweights from around the country who were associated with SOBU/YOBU, they could not hold their own in the debates with the Marxist-inspired militants of PASOA. After the debates, the SOBU/YOBU leadership was struck by the analytic power of Marxism and in 1971 began their own study of Marxism, which opened them to the larger world in unanticipated ways. They found Marxism to provide an insight into the structure of the entire society, the economic system, the relationships among social groups (race, class, nations, parties, and to a lesser extent gender), an understanding of social transformation or revolution, and so on (Bermanzohn 2003:121–122).

Similar paths would be taken by a variety of militant Black Nationalist organizations whose origins were in that tumultuous period in U.S. and world history from the late 1960s to the early 1970s. Some of the organizations traversed this ground carefully and enhanced their analytic and practical capacities through creative use and development of the forms of knowledge that have been produced within the world antisystemic movements. However, since these movements were all involved in efforts to change the world, they ran the same risks as any organization with such a risky vocation, from repression to disillusionment.

In the early 1970s many of the Black student revolutionaries departed the campuses to work in communities and factories. Some became full-time cadres in the political organizations that were formed during that period. The movement toward a more orthodox Marxist formulation among some part of the Black Left meant for the most part a departure from the academy.

This led to an alteration of the relations of force within the universities such that they were less the terrain of struggle than they had been during the period from 1967 to 1973. Those intellectuals who remained in the universities strove to get intellectuals to use their knowledge to serve the Black Liberation movement. One of the key figures in this very small stratum was Abdul Alkalimat, founder of a revolutionary think tank known as Peoples College, a central organizer of the Black studies movement, and author of the popular textbook *Introduction to Afro-American Studies: A Peoples College Primer.*

In a proposal to Black intellectuals to serve the Black Liberation movement through a year of study and struggle in 1974–1975, Alkalimat declared that Black intellectuals had not lived up to their historic responsibilities of intellectual seriousness and social responsibility. "Instead, as Brother E. Franklin Frazier has stated, 'most Negro intellectuals simply repeat the propaganda which is put out by people who have large economic and political interests to protect. They have failed to study the problems of the Negro in America in a manner which would place the fate of the Negro in the broad framework of man's experience in the world'" (Alkalimat 1974:3). Alkalimat continued:

> Comrade Mao Tse-Tung in a 1941 report to a cadres' meeting summed up a situation which existed then in China in a way which speaks to many of the problems facing us: ". . . we have not done systematic and thorough work in collecting and studying materials on [our conditions], and we are lacking in a climate of investigation and study of objective reality. . . . To be crude and careless, to indulge in verbiage, to rest content with a smattering of knowledge—such is the extremely bad style of work that still exists among many comrades. . . ." To correct these shortcomings Mao proposed in this essay called "Reform Our Study," that extensive study of current conditions, study of history, and the study of international revolutionary experience be undertaken. It was here that Mao's famous dictum "no investigation, no right to speak" was invoked. (1974:3–4)

Alkalimat has long argued that radical ideology is a Black tradition. Moreover, it was the moral power of Black religion—what E. Franklin Frazier called a nation within a nation—and the collective strength of Black Nationalism that held the tradition together, while Pan-Africanism and socialism have been the central ideological notions underlying the debate about self-determination and which way forward. So for Alkalimat it is no mystery that Black intellectuals and activists were so central to the intellectual and political uprising of the 1960s.

As the mass mobilization that was the foundation of 1960s radicalism subsided, however, or as the seawater receded, the fish with much less water to
swim in underwent an involution, which, as Max Elbaum and others have argued, focused on the internals of party building.[5]

What is positive about this internal focus is the development of a theory that
broadened the perspectives of the militants but that, under the influence of a
centralized top-down organizational apparatus, limited the ability of the militants
to act upon what they increasingly came to understand. While such an involution fostered the formation of dogmatic approaches, throughout the movement
there was also an increasing awareness of the significance not only of class but
also of race and gender. While there was still much wrangling about the priority
of class analysis over race and gender, which were often viewed as secondary
contradictions in which the possibility of bourgeois interests were being concealed in the guise of race and gender grievances, one of the most important
consequences of this period of revolutionary struggle is that at least these issues
were now on the table in all of these organizations. It would be only a matter of
time before the unquestioned adherence to the class first would no longer be
hegemonic within the antisystemic movements of the United States and core
states.

The Reemergence of the Black
Women's Movement

Linda Burnham, cofounder of the Women of Color Resource Center at Memphis State University, and member of a family with a long history in the Black
Liberation, working-class, and world revolutionary movements, has argued that
"the idea that race, class and gender are interrelated dynamics of power and oppression has gained sufficient currency in the academic world to go by the short-
hand 'intersectionality'" (Burnham 2001:2). Such impeccable academic pedigree
is testimony to the power of a cadre of Black feminist scholars who have acted
against the grain of scholarly knowledge. Black feminist thought has a long pedigree in the political work of Black women, however, as Patricia Hill Collins insistently argues.[6]

Here I wish to follow Burnham's exploration of the evolution of Black feminist thought during the 1960s and 1970s as a critique of the masculinist norms
of the Black Power and civil rights movement of that period, though this was not
a new phenomenon. Indeed, we should note that Ida B. Wells's activism predated all of the male heroes that we have historically lionized (more on this topic
in Chapter 4, "Black Feminism, Intersectionality, and the Critique of Masculinist Models of Liberation").

Burnham traces the Black feminism of the current era to the Black Women's
Liberation Committee of the SNCC. Black women in the SNCC who had been
central to the fight against racism began to rally around the minimizing of their
talents, skills, and contributions by the men with whom they had been working

so intently. These women had been central to the elaboration of the struggle against racism as deeply structured institutional arrangements that required collective political action to challenge both the institutional structure within the white world and the mental and social-psychological structures within the Black world.

It was thus in the course of struggle that they learned important lessons about how to mobilize people, run meetings, and engage in a collective process of reflection and decision making. These collective processes enabled women in the SNCC not only to contribute significantly to the transformation of the struggle against racism, in which the SNCC was central, but also to view their work in the SNCC as a site from which they could identify sexism as a major factor in their lives.

Attempts to raise this issue within the SNCC met the resistance of those who argued that "women's liberation" was a divisive issue that would distract the organization from its main goal of combating racism. Black women who persisted in raising this issue were deemed saboteurs and had to find an autonomous setting "in which Black women could develop their ideas, their politics and their methods of struggle" (Burnham 2001:5). This was the context within which the Black Women's Liberation Committee of the SNCC became the Black Women's Alliance, under the leadership of Fran Beal, author of an important text called "Double Jeopardy: To Be Black and Female." The concept of "Double Jeopardy" was that Black women's femaleness was not divisible from their Blackness (Burnham 2001:5). Beal argued that it was not so much that the identification of sexism within the Black community was divisive but that the real divisiveness stemmed from the suppression of Black women's initiative in the political arena.

The internationalism of the struggle via the influence of the anticolonial movements of this period brought the issue of class and capitalism before the entire movement, so that the Black Women's Alliance transitioned into the Third World Women's Alliance and included Latinas and Asian American women in its membership.

The articulation of race, class, and gender as a triad became a fundamental component of the political assertion of the Third World Women's Alliance to establish its relationship with and its distinction from the middle-class white women's movement.

In 1977 the Combahee River Collective, a Boston-based group of Black feminists, published a manifesto that argued, "The most general statement of our politics at the present time would be that we are actively committed to struggling against racial, sexual, heterosexual, and class oppression and see as our particular task the development of integrated analysis and practice based upon the fact that the major systems of oppression are interlocking" (quoted in Burnham 2001:7).

Authored by collective members Barbara Smith, Beverly Smith, and Demita Frazier, the manifesto traced the development of the group's thinking from a focus on racism and sexism to an increasing focus on heterosexism and economic exploitation. The Combahee River Collective argued for a central role for lesbians in the elaboration of feminist theory and practice since heterosexism is such a significant form of social oppression (Burnham 2001:6–7).

The issues covered in the last two sections of this chapter are covered in greater detail in Chapter 3, "The Class First/Race First Debate: The Contradictions of Nationalism and Internationalism and the Stratification of the World-system," and Chapter 4, "Black Feminism, Intersectionality, and the Critique of Masculinist Models of Liberation."

2

The Sociology of the Color Line:
W.E.B. Du Bois and the End
of White World Supremacy

W.E.B. Du Bois's long struggle against white world supremacy is well-known by all who cite his famous turn-of-the-century declaration that the problem of the twentieth century is the problem of the color line. Though Du Bois would also analyze in great detail the souls of Black folk, the souls of white folk, and the autobiography of a race in the United States and in the modern world, his key contribution is illuminating the vast scope of the problem of the color line in class analysis; the history of social stratification in the United States and the world-system; the politics of the United States, people of African descent, and the world-system; and the quest for a democratic, just, and egalitarian world order. His development of social thought and his political practice constitute the most persistent and penetrating critique and challenge to social justice and social inequality mounted by twentieth-century intellectuals and political activists. It was Du Bois who built on the revolutionary tradition of Karl Marx and the nineteenth-century revolutionaries whose praxis Marx attempted to frame and articulate and who indeed surpassed this tradition with even deeper analysis of the social world that had evolved over the previous five hundred years.

The idea for this book was concieved during the commemoration of the centennial of *The Souls of Black Folk*, since I wished to locate this commemoration in the context of Du Bois's larger contribution to clarifying the nature of the modern world, the color line, and the possibilities for human emancipation. By the 1930s Du Bois was not only arguing for the humanity of Black people and the peoples of the dark world but also seeking to transform our intellectual landscape by a dramatic reshaping of our understanding of the social world. Du Bois illuminated the world-scale scope of racism as central and not incidental to our historical system in a manner that is not only dimly understood by most scholars of the social world but seldom even glimpsed by them.

So it was on the centennial of W.E.B. Du Bois's great classic, *The Souls of Black Folk*, that I set out to explore two of its central themes: (1) the critique of the accommodationist stance of Booker T. Washington in favor of a militant fight for political inclusion of Black people in a truly democratic nation and (2) the elaboration of the duality of the African American people and the significance of their monumental battle to transform or transcend the color line. Although this itself was a daunting task, it is not possible to justify a singular focus on *The Souls of Black Folk*, for Dr. Du Bois's later writings constitute the most elegant attempt ever not only to navigate the contours of the world color line but also to abolish it. During his long intellectual and activist life, Du Bois inhabited, complicated, and discarded a variety of ideological stances, mixed idealism and pragmatism, and pushed the barriers of the possible in his profound exploration of the far reaches of a collectivized vision for the advancement of Black people and for all humanity.

In the process of seeking to change first race relations in the United States and then power relations in the world-system, Du Bois worked, fought, and allied with a dizzying number of individuals, organizations, institutions, movements, and states. That Du Bois was so intensely involved in the process of thinking through and implementing so many strategies is not only a testament to this giant of a figure in our history but also a testament to all who have been involved. It is no wonder that Du Bois's Pulitzer Prize–winning biographer, David Levering Lewis, titled the first volume of Du Bois's biography *W.E.B. Du Bois: Biography of a Race, 1868–1919*, and the second volume *W.E.B. Du Bois: The Fight for Equality and the American Century, 1919–1963*. This is a testament not merely to Dr. Du Bois as an individual who was so strongly identified with the life of a people, of oppressed strata, and finally of humanity ourselves, but also to all of those social strata to whom he dedicated his life.

My point is that even such fulsome praise greatly oversimplifies not only a complex human being and his interactions with a complex set of actors but also the struggles with which he is so closely identified: the struggle against capitalist exploitation and the social dominations of race, class, and gender; the hegemony of the United States of America over the world-system; the system of white world supremacy; and the rise of the dark world. Over the course of these struggles, he could be classified variously as a bourgeois democrat, a Pan-African nationalist, a Fabian socialist, a revolutionary internationalist, a revolutionary nationalist, and a Marxist revolutionary. During this long period of struggle and writing he engaged in fights with any number of ideological foes and learned lessons from all of these fights that gradually were incorporated into his overall worldview.

Since the sociology of the color line is the focus of this chapter, I focus on that component of Du Bois's contribution to this issue, though it is not always easy to compartmentalize his views given the awesome scope of the preoccupations of the man that Dr. Martin Luther King, Jr., honored as one of the most remarkable men of our time, an intellectual giant exploring the frontiers of knowledge and a dedicated teacher who gave his life to teaching all of us about our tasks of emanci-pation (King 1968:1).

Cheryl Townsend Gilkes (1996) has provided us with an astounding and in-sightful analysis of how Du Bois perceived the expansion of democracy in the United States and the role of Blacks in the democratization of the United States and quite literally in the making of America. Gilkes holds that Du Bois heralded "three great revolutions" in the making of the United States, those of "women, labor, and Black folk" (Gilkes 1996:112). Black women embodied all three revo-lutions "in their historical roles in the family, the community, and the labor force" (Gilkes 1996:112). Du Bois held furthermore that a decisive consequence of the positioning of Black women at the intersection of race, class, and gender has been their development of a critical perspective or standpoint. In order, then, to understand the overall breadth of the Du Boisian perspective Gilkes argues, one must first grasp that Du Bois believed that the expansion of democ-racy in the United States and the role of Blacks in this democratization *is* the making of America.

Gilkes locates the origins of sociological theory in the attempts of students of political economy to explain the massive changes in European society fueled by the industrial and political revolutions of the eighteenth and nineteenth cen-turies. Marx, Max Weber, and Émile Durkheim focused on the issues of class, social order, and industrialization. Du Bois, located in the United States, saw clearly how the issues of race, class, and gender impacted the making of Amer-ica. He viewed Black women as the intellectual leadership of the race (Gilkes 1996:128). Black women, he argued, exercised a higher morality in their political behavior, a higher morality rooted in religious faith. Du Bois thought Black women to be role models for human emancipation.

The Black Women's Club Movement had a profound influence on Du Bois and nurtured what Gilkes refers to as his feminism and his overall social analysis. Du Bois is also said to have exercised influence among the Black Women's Club movements. Gilkes's framing of Du Bois's contribution through the lens of Black feminist theory explains in part what is unique in Du Bois as a critical intellec-tual theorizing the making of America. I review here Du Bois's role in the intel-lectual debates and the practical politics on the United States, but I also attempt to articulate his role in analyzing the social contradictions of the modern world-system, which continue to be of enormous importance to scholars, the exploited classes, the oppressed people of color, women, and all interested in the construc-tion of a just, democratic, and egalitarian world. Du Bois's analysis speaks to a comprehensive analysis of the capitalist world and its social and political contra-dictions and most importantly to its relations of rule.[1] His understanding of the relation of the color line to relations of rule is key to grasping the significance of his work. His work helps us to understand not only the social and class structure of the capitalist world economy but also its relations of rule. Du Bois's analysis of the first Reconstruction and its aftermath is key to our analysis.

The Republican Party's political abandonment of the freedmen in the 1870s, the strength of the counterrevolution in the South, and the reversal of the alliance with the southern populists enormously undermined the belief among African Americans and their leaders about the possibility of the race being able to advance by utilizing conventional political means. In this context there occurred a revival of the ideas that had been popular in the 1850s concerning the importance of African American racial solidarity and Negro support of Negro businesses (see Meier 1962:256).

The end of radical Reconstruction marked the end of the system of class alliances most central to the relations of rule of that period and the inauguration of a new ruling coalition that would serve in part to reassert authority over the freedmen. This was important because the democratic thrust of the freedmen posed an example for other groups and involved an attempt to coalesce with other groups against a fundamentally undemocratic social system. Radical Reconstruction posed a democratic model for the people of the United States, one that gave voice to the least among us, thus establishing a precedent for broad inclusiveness and rectification of injustice for the United States. The choice was whether this would be a model for the growth of the nation or whether it would seek the continuation of a privileged existence for certain sections of the population.

Those who opposed the establishment of a multiracial democracy sought to achieve their objectives by gaining control over the freedmen—disenfranchising them, controlling their schools, and, most important, controlling their leadership. Southern whites and northern philanthropists wanted a Negro leader who would symbolize the end of Reconstruction and represent moderate solutions to the race problem.

One of the main ideologists of the New South, Henry Grady, advocated a policy by which there would be industrial cooperation between the North and the South, but in which the South's customs in race relations would prevail because the white people of the South knew best what would benefit the Negro. Grady argued that whites and Negroes in the South were the best of friends and that Negroes were as much opposed as whites to outside interference.

Grady pointed out that although the South stood for economic cooperation between the races, it emphatically did not believe in social equality. Grady even argued that the Southern white elites were prepared to use the "best" Negroes, the most gifted of them, to forestall the political aspirations of their own people. "We have no fear of [the Negro's gaining control in the South]; already we are attaching to us the best elements of that race, and as we proceed our alliance will broaden" (quoted in Cox 1950:238).

It is in this context that we should assess Booker T. Washington's speech at the Atlanta Cotton States and International Exposition on September 18, 1895 (the year of Frederick Douglass's death). In the 1890s liberal arts colleges were temporarily eclipsed by growing support for industrial education, including manual training, home economics, preparation for farming, and trades such as shoemaking, printing, carpentry, and bricklaying. Washington was president of one of the nation's best industrial schools for Blacks, Tuskegee Institute.

Industrial education among Blacks was widely believed to lead eventually to a class of self-sufficient artisan-entrepreneurs. It was on behalf of this vision that Washington spoke. He argued that Negroes should cultivate their relations with their southern neighbors instead of moving to a "foreign land." "Cast down your bucket where you are," he implored (Washington 1971:5). The South offered opportunities in agriculture, mechanics, commerce, domestic service, and the professions; it is in the world of business, Washington felt, that the Negro has the best chance. However, "our greatest danger is that in the great leap from slavery to freedom we may overlook that the masses of us are to live by the production of our hands" (Washington 1971:5).

To white employers who were trying to make decisions about their labor force and wondering about the utilization of immigrant labor, Washington argued,

> Cast down your buckets where you are. Cast it down among the eight million Negroes whose habits you know, whose fidelity and love you have tested. . . . Cast down your bucket among those people who have, without strikes and labor wars, tilled your fields, cleared your forests, builded your railroads and cities, and brought forth the treasures from the bowels of the earth, and helped make possible this magnificent representation of the progress of the South. . . .
>
> In all things that are purely social we can be as separate as the fingers, yet one as the hand in all things essential to mutual progress. (Washington 1971:5, 6)

Agitation about social equality is the extremest folly, Washington concluded; political progress will come to us as a result of the service we render. "No race that has anything to contribute to the markets of the world is long in any degree ostracized" (Washington 1971:7).[2]

The next day the *Atlanta Constitution* remarked that Washington's whole speech had been "a platform upon which blacks and whites can stand and do justice to one another" (quoted in Cox 1950:239). "The speech stamps Booker T. Washington as a wise counselor and safe leader" (quoted in Marable 1986:42). James Creelman, a famous war correspondent, sent a story to the *New York World* that described Booker T. Washington as a "Negro Moses" who had delivered an oration that marks "a new epoch in the history of the South" (see Washington 1965:157).

Initially Black people's response to Washington was mixed. T. Thomas Fortune, editor of the *New York Age*, called Washington the new Frederick Douglass. W. Calvin Chase, editor of the *Washington Bee*, described Washington's speech as death to Blacks and uplifting to whites. African Methodist Episcopal Zion Bishop Henry McNeal Turner thought it would be a long time before Blacks would be able to undo the harm done by Washington's speech. The *Atlanta Advocate* condemned Washington's "sycophantic attitude" (see Marable 1986:42).

Washington's strength is that he blended an emphasis on self-help and racial solidarity designed to build a strong class of Negro landowners and businessmen with an ability to appeal to the best sentiments among the southern upper class and the northern philanthropists.[3] In Du Bois's estimate, the "striking . . . ascendancy" of Booker T. Washington was due to his mastery of the "speech and

thought of triumphant commercialism" (Du Bois 1961:42–43). Despite his public and studied role as an accommodator, however, behind the scenes Washington used his resources to fight for civil rights. In 1900 he obtained funds from
white philanthropists to lobby against a racist election provision in the Louisiana
constitution. From 1903 to 1904 he privately fought Alabama's disenfranchisement laws in the federal courts, and in 1903–1904 he spent at least $4,000 to
promote the struggle against Jim Crow (see Marable 1986:43).

Booker T. Washington was not only the most distinguished Black leader of
this period (1895-1915); he was also the most powerful. His authority derived
from his political influence and from his popularity with philanthropists. No
Black schools received donations from Andrew Carnegie, John D. Rockefeller,
and various other donors without Washington's approval.[4] He served as a political adviser to Presidents Roosevelt and Taft, and recommended all of the Black
appointees made by President Theodore Roosevelt and most of the Black ap-
pointments made by President Taft (see Meier and Rudwick 1976:222).

Although Du Bois had previously been a supporter of Washington, he took
strong exception to Washington's condoning of the caste system and his according to Black people the major responsibility for racial prejudice.[5] He was also
concerned about the extent to which Washington was able to silence his critics
through intimidation and revengeful acts.[6] Black intellectuals by and large dis-
sented from Washington's program. The Afro-American Council, the forum for
the radical protest tradition from 1890 to 1908, began to level severe criticism at
Washington toward the end of the century. In 1902, however, Washington supporters took over the council, removed Ida Wells-Barnett from her position as
secretary, and replaced African Methodist Episcopal Zion Bishop Alexander
Walters with T. Thomas Fortune as council president. William Monroe Trotter
accused Du Bois of not standing up to the Tuskegee takeover and of showing
evidence of jumping on the Washington bandwagon.[7]

In 1903, Trotter and three other "radicals" disrupted a meeting at which
Washington spoke; they were arrested, and Trotter spent a month in jail. Du
Bois had not known about the plans to disrupt the meeting but agreed with Trotter's criticisms. This marked the definitive split between Washington and Du
Bois. It was from this point that Du Bois began to articulate the notion of a "Talented Tenth," which would be the vehicle of uplift for the Black masses. Unlike
the Tuskegee Machine, which was composed of businessmen, ministers, and
politicians seeking to feather their own nests with appeals to racial solidarity,
Du Bois's theory of the "Talented Tenth" held that the Black professionals and
intellectuals should transcend their narrow self-interest for the common good of
all Black people.[8]

In 1905 Du Bois wrote an article for the Atlanta-based *Voice of the People* in
which he charged that the Tuskegee Machine had been funneling hush money
to several Black newspapers, which meant that they were being dominated by
Washington for political purposes. In the ensuing controversy, Du Bois concluded that there was no longer a basis for cooperation with Washington since
"by means of downright bribery and intimidation" Washington was "influencing
men to do his will . . . he was seeking not the welfare of the Negro race but

personal power" (quoted in Marable 1986:55). In 1905 Du Bois formed the Niagara Movement with the support of Trotter, Walters, and educator John Hope. The membership of the new organization represented diverse ideological strands. Some had previously been associated with the Tuskegee Machine, some might be called Trotterites, and others were socialists. Overall the Niagara Movement consisted of the most progressive fraction of the middle class, those willing to sacrifice their material and political security for the sake of advancing the general interests of Black people at all levels.

The new organization might have emblazoned on its banners Du Bois's words from "Of Mr. Booker T. Washington and Others:" "Manly self-respect is worth more than land and houses, and . . . a people who voluntarily surrender such respect, or cease striving for it, are not worth civilizing" (Du Bois 1961:48). This group followed in the tradition of Frederick Douglass and based themselves on the tenet "Persistent manly agitation is the way to liberty" (quoted in Robert Allen 1970:96).

In sharp and vigorous language the Niagara Movement placed the blame for the race problem squarely on the shoulders of whites. The organization drafted a statement of principles, calling among other things for universal manhood suffrage, equal treatment in public places, equal opportunities in economic life, equal treatment in the court system, an end to the use of Negroes as strikebreakers, an end to discrimination against Negroes by trade unions, an end to racial discrimination, and an end to segregated churches.[9] The statement concluded in typical spirited fashion, declaring that "on the above grievances we do not hesitate to complain, and to complain loudly and insistently. To ignore . . . these wrongs is to prove ourselves unworthy of freedom. Persistent manly agitation is the way to liberty" (Grant 1968:209).

Although Niagara Movement members were actively engaged in fighting for various local reforms, they did not build up a large membership. The organization's publication, *The Horizon*, consistently lost money, and the organization's fund-raising capabilities were negligible, having raised less than $1,300 in its first two years. In addition members were often behind in their dues. Tensions developed between members and within the leadership, including a sharp conflict between Trotter and Du Bois in 1907. By 1908 many of the branches had ceased to have regular meetings (Marable 1986:68).

The Tuskegee Machine had set out to destroy the new organization from the beginning. One of Washington's lieutenants was able to get the Associated Press bureau in Buffalo to halt its coverage of the group's activities there. Washington's secretary, Emmett Scott, ordered the National Negro Press Bureau to suppress any information about the group (according to Marable 1986:56). Moreover, Washington also used the more vicious tactic of getting his enemies removed from jobs through the use of his political clout. This method also was used to intimidate actual and potential supporters of Du Bois (see Marable 1986:58–59).

Although the Niagara Movement failed organizationally, it clearly prefigured the rise of an alternative model to the accommodationist program of Booker T. Washington. Tuskegee's power was able to undermine the new organization, but its power was clearly on the wane. Niagara's focus on the legal redress of

grievances prefigured the approach of the National Association for the Advancement of Colored People (NAACP), which was founded in 1909 when after a
race riot in Springfield, Illinois, the white socialist William English Walling
challenged white liberals to form a new movement for racial equality. Mary
White Ovington then contacted Walling and Dr. Henry Moscowitz, who decided to organize a conference. Oswald Garrison Villard was called into the
discussion and asked to issue a conference call.[10]

The call was finally issued by a who's who of socialists and liberal reformers,
including pioneer social workers Jane Addams and Florence Kelley, writer William Dean Howells, and educator John Dewey (Marable 1986:72). Although
Villard, who had worked closely with Washington, requested the involvement of
the Tuskegee Machine, Washington and his group quickly recognized a threat
and called on Carnegie and other white philanthropists to boycott the new organization. During the course of the conference, however, Du Bois was able to win
over some of the persons who had previously supported the Washington position
in the Niagara-Tuskegee debate, especially Villard (Marable 1986:72).

Within a year a consensus had been reached to form a permanent organization to be called the National Association for the Advancement of Colored People. Most of the members of the Niagara Movement joined the new organization,
although William Monroe Trotter, among others, played a lesser role because he
feared white control of the organization. The Niagara constituency, however,
made up the majority of the black membership of the new organization.

Washington proceeded with a full-fledged attack on the new organization.
He ordered the *New York Age* to attack Walling in an editorial. Tuskegee Machine lieutenants were ordered to criticize Blacks who were joining the NAACP
or creating new local chapters (see Marable 1986:72–73).

In contrast to the all-Black Niagara Movement, however, the NAACP was
interracial in composition, although Du Bois was the only Black person among
the national leadership. Du Bois was named director of publicity and research,
the post from which he founded the NAACP journal *The Crisis*.

The official purpose of the new organization, as indicated in its incorporation
papers, was "to promote equality of rights and eradicate caste and race prejudice
among citizens of the United States; to advance the interests of colored citizens;
to secure for them impartial suffrage; and to increase their opportunities for
securing justice in the courts, education for their children, employment according to their ability, and complete equality before the law" (quoted in Hughes
1968:212).

The new organization got off to a strong start. Within the first three months
it had opened its first local office in Chicago and filed a petition of pardon for a
South Carolina sharecropper who had been sentenced to the death penalty for
slaying a constable who had burst into his cabin after midnight to charge him with
breech of contract. In November 1910 the first issue of *The Crisis* was published.
In this issue Du Bois stated that *The Crisis* would stand for "the highest ideals of
American democracy, and for reasonable but earnest and persistent attempts
to gain these rights and realize these ideals." *The Crisis* attained a readership of

twelve thousand in its first year, eventually growing to one hundred thousand (Hughes 1968:213).

Within two years the NAACP had grown to twenty-four chapters, but violence and racial discrimination were increasing, not decreasing. The number of lynchings increased from sixty-three to seventy-nine. Within another year the number of chapters had more than doubled to fifty, but the organization still faced the enmity of wealthy philanthropists who gave no aid and conservative whites (and even some Blacks) who attacked the NAACP as being too radical. These groups took the position that the NAACP's demand for complete equality was impractical if not downright utopian (Hughes 1968:213–214).

In *The Crisis* Du Bois had already begun to cast about for potential members of an alliance for racial equality. He called in the pages of *The Crisis* for a Black-Jewish alliance, repeatedly denounced anti-Semitism, and praised Jewish Americans as a tremendous force for good and uplift in this country. However, Du Bois also argued that the abolition of lynching and opposition to political disenfranchisement and Jim Crow required a race-conscious policy and thus demanded a certain degree of Black unity (see Marable 1986:79).

Throughout this early period, Du Bois had had an uneasy relationship with NAACP disbursing treasurer Oswald Garrison Villard, who tended to be paternalistic toward Blacks. Villard saw his role as curbing the radical currents inside the NAACP and thus distrusted Du Bois's militancy. Over the year 1913 there were a number of conflicts between Du Bois and Villard, and Villard, who by this time had become chairman of the board of the NAACP finally resigned as chairman of the board but remained as a board member. When he subsequently attempted to curb Du Bois's editorial independence in *The Crisis*, the majority of the board sided with Du Bois (see Marable 1986:80–81).

Despite this, the organization lived in an uneasy tension with an editorial policy that was independent of the organization but dependent on the congruence between the organization and a particular editor. This tension gnawed at the entrails of the organization, eventually leading to a split between Du Bois and the leadership of the NAACP.

Although the tensions in the NAACP to some extent took the form of tension between Du Bois and the remainder of the leadership (all white), accompanying this was the tension between radical and liberal tendencies in the organization and across the broader movement for racial equality. The increasing weight of radical and liberal tensions in the Black freedom struggle is an indication of a larger shift that was reflected in the strategies of the contending forces.

The Rise of the Dark World Within

With the birth of the NAACP there came a dramatic shift in relations of force toward what Washington refers to as "the man farthest down" (Washington and Park 1913). This was not only a shift in the political culture of the United States but a shift of world-scale proportions. Du Bois's Pan-African Congress involvement was a preview of this evolution. While I elaborate on the details of this shift in the next chapter, we must grasp that this change in world relations of force was something that Washington was forced to address, given that his rise to prominence was based in part on a broad political calculation that his strategy would help to end the political turmoil of the first Reconstruction, which the nation needed to take its proper place in the world. This involved strengthening the United States in relationship to other nations, a process that had started in the 1870s with the decline of British hegemony and the reassertion of authority over the freedmen whose social practices had unleashed a much broader yearning for social change among others in the lower strata of U.S. society. During this same period, which extended from 1870 to 1914, the social world witnessed a prodigious growth and expansion of the workers' movement not only in the United States but throughout the Pan-European world, which some refer to as the heyday of the Second International (Wallerstein 1991:22). The urgency of Washington's study of the "man farthest down" must be situated within the context of these changes in relations of force.

The Washington program had sought to assimilate the previously enslaved strata into U.S. society on terms that were most favorable to the capitalist elites and the higher (white) strata of the United States. By 1910, however, the conservative forces that Washington represented were losing ground to the rise of the progressive movement and a variety of socialist currents, both of which were represented in the NAACP.

This was the context for Washington's European trip with Robert Park. As documented in *The Man Farthest Down*, Booker T. Washington, assisted by Robert Park, traveled to Europe to find out about the conditions of the poorer and working classes there, especially in those regions from which increasing numbers of immigrants were coming to the United States. Washington was particularly concerned about efforts to divert a portion of those immigrants to the southern states to substitute for Black labor, which some saw as a potential solution to the South's "race problem" (Washington and Park 1913:3–4).

Washington was of the opinion that there was a distinctive European race problem, though, and that it was different from the U.S. problem. The value in exploring the dimensions of the European race problem for him was to demonstrate that other societies had their own distinctive problems in this area and to illustrate that all societies contained a bottom strata who were severely stigmatized, the subject of stereotypical views, and subject to prejudicial treatment. Washington felt that these bottom strata in European countries were similar in social position to Black people in the southern United States.

Though there was some concern that Washington was seeing the worst of Europe and not all the glories that visitors should see, Washington offered that "the man who is interested in living things must seek them in the grime and dirt of everyday life. To be sure, the things one sees there are not always pleasant, but the people one meets are interesting, and if they are sometimes among the worst they are also frequently among the best people in the world. At any rate, *wherever there is struggle and effort there is life*" (Washington and Park 1913:13; my emphasis).

Washington conceived of a class of people in the bottom strata who had moved to the city from the agricultural zones of their respective nations, but there were some who had sunk to the bottom from a higher social position, some of whom he characterized as degenerate. This presumably was a characteristic of social strata in the most developed countries, such as England. This, of course, sounds very much like the characterization of the much-reviled lumpen proletariat. Washington held that Black folk were never without hope or a sense of joy in life (Washington and Park 1913:26).

Interestingly, while there was a campaign to limit the birth rate of this bottom rung of English society, what Theodore Roosevelt called "race suicide," (Washington and Park 1913:27) "thousands of immigrants from the south of Europe were pouring into London every year to take the places left vacant by the recession of the native Anglo-Saxon" (Washington and Park 1913:27). Despite Washington's implicit recognition of the international scope of the economic arena in this case, he attributed the differences in the depth of poverty in England, with its starving and destitute people, and the United States as a special or exceptional characteristic of the United States.

What was the solution that Washington would modestly recommend to the English on how they might deal with their destitute populations? Give them the same opportunity for constant and steady work that the Negro had in the South and establish schools to provide industrial education that would enable them to enter a trade, similar to what Washington was doing at Tuskegee Institute (Washington and Park 1913:36).

Another problem with England, according to Washington, was that the proportion of its population dedicated to agriculture was smaller than anywhere else in the world. As opposed to Hungary, with an agricultural population that comprised 68 percent of its total; Italy, with 59 percent; Denmark, with 48 percent; and the United States, with 37.5 percent, England and Wales in 1901 had only 8 percent of their populations engaged in agriculture (Washington and Park 1913:49–50).

Despite discoveries that Washington felt were practices unique to European societies, he also discovered some commonalities. He was surprised when he saw women in Vienna, Austria, walking the streets barefoot, as did many in the countryside of southern Europe. On asking a native Austrian about this practice, Washington was told, "Oh, well . . . they are Slovaks." This sounded to Washington very much like a familiar refrain: "Oh, well, they are Negroes!" (Washington and Park 1913:56).

Everywhere he went in Austria and Hungary he found the people to be divided by race, but what was common to all of these areas was that it was the Slavs (of which there were five or six branches) who occupied the bottom rung of the economic ladder. The story of this "inferior species" was the same everywhere: "They were lazy and would not work; . . . they had no initiative; . . . they were immoral and not fitted to govern themselves." For all these attributions, Washington found that it was these groups who did "nearly all of the really hard, disagreeable, and ill-paid labour" (Washington and Park 1913:57).

Washington argues that it was the situation of the Slavs in the Austro-Hungarian Empire that was most similar to that of the Negro in the southern United States. They were an agricultural people who had lived on and worked the land for centuries, but they were viewed as an inferior race, distinguished by the language that they spoke rather than the color of their skin (Washington and Park 1913:65).

Washington takes some pains to describe the socialist movement in Hungary and Italy in terms of its representation of the masses at the bottom of life in Europe (Washington and Park 1913:100). It was through this party that the millions of people who had had no voice in and no ideas with respect to government were learning to think and give voice to their grievances and aspirations. For the most part, Washington argues, there was little awareness of the extent to which the immigrants who came to the United States from these sections of Europe had been influenced by socialist ideas.

Washington details his impression of the socialists he met in Denmark and Italy, where the most patriotic and brilliant men were writers, students, and teachers. In Poland he met socialists who were an active part of the revolution in Russia. Wherever the masses of the people were oppressed, where the people on the bottom were being crushed by the people above them, the meaning of socialism was revolution. Where governments showed a liberal spirit, however, socialists showed a spirit of cooperation instead of seeking to overturn the government by means of revolution.

Washington denied any sympathy for socialism, especially given his location in the southern United States. He believed that change should be brought about through education, which changes the individual from within rather than by government decree. In this way the individual is made fit for life but is still free (Washington and Park 1913:102).

When the serfs were freed in Hungary, Italy, and other parts of Europe, they were given land but denied political privileges. Within a short time the peasant owners were wiped out and their lands absorbed into the large estates. In contrast, when the Negroes were emancipated from slavery in the United States, they were given the franchise but did not know how to use it. For Washington these two instances proved his long-held position that it is hard for a man to make use of anything that he is given without effort and without the proper education (Washington and Park 1913:104).

As we have seen, despite his eminence as a public figure, Washington retained his sympathy for and commitment to the man farthest down, given his own origins as a slave in the southern United States. Even though this European trip was a personal tour to acquaint himself with the lives of the man farthest down in Europe, he was also interested in the methods they used to better their lives, that is, the socialist movement and socialist ideas. So it is not surprising that he sought an audience with John Burns, who had lived the life of a casual laborer and had organized the great dock strike in 1889, which brought together into the labor unions one hundred thousand starving and disorganized laborers who had previously been shut out of organized labor's protection. Burns was an agitator, a socialist, and was referred to as "the man with the red flag" (Washington and Park 1913:361). He had been arrested many times for making speeches and had served three months on the charge of rioting.

In 1889 he was elected to the London County Council and in 1890 to Parliament. As a member of the London County Council, Burns was instrumental in enacting a series of projects that resulted in dramatic increases in the living circumstances of the working people of the area of London for which he was responsible. In response to one thirty-eight-acre estate planned down to the minutest detail to accommodate some five thousand inhabitants, Washington expressed a skeptical note in his own mind, but not to Burns: "In the building of this little paradise all of the architectural and engineering problems had indeed been solved. There, remained, however, the problem of human nature, and the question that I asked myself was: Will these people be able to live up to their surroundings?" (Washington and Park 1913:375). Even so, for Washington these folk are fortunate that they have a leader who speaks to them of their faults as well as their virtues, so that they can be inspired toward the better life that is open to them.

Washington concluded from his travels that the position of Black people in the United States whether in slavery or in freedom was not as exceptional as it had frequently seemed. The man farthest down in the United States had much in common with the man farthest down in Europe. They had both been subject people in slavery and in serfdom. They had both gained their freedom in the course of the previous century, and they both found that their emancipation from bondage was a first step, not the full realization of freedom.

The socialist advocates of the laboring people in Europe felt that the growth of factories and city life undermined the independence of the laboring classes, but Washington did not think that the socialists were united around a common program; far from it. He was quite skeptical of what he referred to as the old-fashioned socialists, who believed that a social catastrophe would bring an end to the present regime and thus enable the political power of the masses to reorganize society in a way that would give every individual an economic opportunity equal to every other. Given the differences among individuals, Washington did not see how this state of equality would be obtained (Washington and Park 1913:381–382).

Washington did see, however, a great silent revolution already in progress, a revolution that was touching and changing the lives of those at the bottom, especially in remote farming communities. In contrast to the social order of feudalism, which was determined entirely from the top, the new social order of the nineteenth and twentieth centuries was preoccupied not with holding down the man farthest down but with lifting him up, making him more efficient in his labor, and giving him a more intelligent share and interest in the life of the community and polity. The great medium for achieving these ends was the school.

This revolution was seeking not to "tear down or level up" in order to bring about what Washington viewed as an artificial equality, but to give every individual a chance to make good, to determine her or his own place or position in the community by the character and quality of the service she or he was able to perform.

Washington wanted to convey finally that in all the movements that affected the masses of the people (socialism, nationalism, emigration, the movements for the reorganization of urban or rural life), there was always the man farthest down, groping for a path upward. The upward-seeking efforts of the man farthest down generated responses in the larger society, the collective effect of which was to raise the level of everyone above him. One cannot, Washington concludes, hold another down in the ditch unless one is down in the ditch oneself. In helping the man farthest down, one is freeing oneself of the burden that would drag all to the same level.

Washington reports that the overall impact of his trip throughout the lower strata of European society was to push himself to look at the world from their perspective and to discover that "the world looks more interesting, more hopeful, and more filled with God's providence, when you are at the bottom looking up that when you are at the top looking down" (Washington and Park 1913:389).

Despite the skepticism of the militants who had long opposed the accommodationism of Washington and his followers, I think that Washington had of necessity moved to a different political position, a movement that was a sign of the times. The strong accommodationist position that he had taken was fast losing credibility among any but the truly hard-core. To truly oppose the party of movement, the party of the status quo had to give ground so that they could maintain the essentials of the social order. This means they had to move to a more liberal position to establish a new equilibrium in which the dominant strata maintained the upper hand. The oppressed strata were about to shake the foundations of the old order and stability required that the elite give some ground.

By 1915, when Booker T. Washington died, the conservatives were largely in retreat. It was now a different world. Black people were moving in increasingly larger numbers from the farms to the cities and from South to North. With Blacks increasingly concentrated in the large cities in the North, the strength of their numbers and the right to vote became powerful weapons in their defense. However, in 1911 the National Urban League was founded by an interracial group ideologically close to Booker T. Washington to deal principally with the problems migrant Blacks, mostly from rural areas, encountered in their increasingly urban life. The National Urban League was strictly a service organization, not at all involved in protest or popular political action.

By 1915 the mantle of leadership was passing slowly from the conservatives associated with the Tuskegee Machine to the radicals connected with the NAACP, who in the Black world were represented by W.E.B. Du Bois. Shortly after Washington's death, the NAACP called a Negro leadership conference, which included all views, ranging from Trotter to Emmett Scott (formerly Washington's secretary), to try to reach a consensus on the principal goals for racial equality (Broderick 1969:366–372). The Amenia Conference resolutions held that

> all forms of education were desirable for the Negro and should be encouraged, that political freedom was necessary to achieve highest development, that Negro advancement needed an organization and the practical working understanding of Negro leaders, and that old controversies were

best forgotten. Finally, the conference "realizes the peculiar difficulties . . . in the South and the special need of understanding between leaders of the race who live in the South and those who live in the North. It has learned to understand and respect the good faith, methods and ideals of those who are working for the solution of the problem in various sections of the country." (Broderick 1969:371-372)[11]

Despite the power of his intellect and the force of his determination, Du Bois was ultimately expelled from the NAACP in the 1930s because of his radicalism. Why did this happen?

Despite Du Bois's dramatic announcement that the problem of the twentieth century was the problem of the color line, the conjuncture at which he produced *The Souls of Black Folk* was one of relative optimism about the chances of forcing a breach in the color line. The Talented Tenth social bloc sought to demonstrate their dignity, intelligence, commitment, and patriotism to whites. This social bloc was militant but culturally subordinate to the white upper strata of the United States. This strategy was a measure of their level of understanding of the social forces with which they were confronted and thus the condition for a measure of medium-run optimism about the possibility for a national solution brokered by such appeals.

While Du Bois had been criticized by the young militants of the New Negro Movement during World War I, by the 1920s his engagements and fights with these young radicals and, his observations of the increased horrors of U.S. society and of the Pan-European world would push him to seek broader solutions to the problems of race, now following the paths blazed by the New Negro radicals.

These deliberations and debates led him toward an embrace with the radicals of the Three Continents (Asia, Africa, and Latin America), including an intense study of Marx and the Marxist-influenced intellectuals around the world. This meant that he deepened his understanding of the relationship between the fight for racial justice in the United States and the fight against imperialism, capitalism, colonialism, and white Western world hegemony.

The tone of Du Bois's 1920 book, *Darkwater: Voices from Within the Veil* (Du Bois 1999), differs dramatically from that of *The Souls of Black Folk*. In *Darkwater* he interprets the "Negro Problem" in the United States and the color problem between the dark world and the white world in light of the great social problems of the day. In his prepublication commentary on *Darkwater*, Du Bois notes that the "nation and the world tend to think of their problems of work and wage, domestic service, government, sex, and education, and then envisage the race problem as apart and beyond these, to be considered by itself, if at all, and after more pressing problems." But the analysis presented in *Darkwater* is intended to show that "the color line shows itself not as a separate problem, but directly as a problem of work, rule, sex, and training" (Du Bois 1975:9).

Written during the same period as Madison Grant's *The Passing of the Great Race* (1920) and Lothrop Stoddard's *The Rising Tide of Color against White World-Supremacy* (1921) (see the introduction for a summary of these works), *Darkwater* shows Du Bois at his finest in combat with inequalities of race and color in a world perspective. In the chapter titled "The Souls of White Folk," he casts a withering and critical gaze on the racial arrogance of the white world and takes white folks to task in no uncertain terms. The context that Du Bois sets for this of the racial arrogance of the white world is laid out below, and he invites the objects of these criticisms to open their eyes and read the handwriting on the wall.

Here Du Bois seeks to theorize the souls of white folks to the residents of the dark world and to white folks themselves. He hopes that these voices from behind the veil will bring a shock of recognition to all those he invites to listen in: "In the awful cataclysm of World War, where from beating, slandering, and murdering us the white world turned temporarily aside to kill each other, we of the Darker People looked on in mild amaze" (Du Bois 1999:20).

Dr. Du Bois declares that "here is a civilization that has boasted much. Neither Roman nor Arab, Greek nor Egyptian, Persian nor Mongol ever took himself and his own perfection with such disconcerting seriousness as the modern white man. We whose shame, humiliation and deep insult his aggrandizement so often involved were never deceived" (Du Bois 1999:20). But the white demigods would not listen to our lowly voice even as we pointed silently to their feet of clay (Du Bois 1999:20).

Was it that the Great War indicated that Europe and the white world had somehow gone mad? Du Bois does not allow for any such wiggle room. No, he asserts quite emphatically. "This is neither aberration nor insanity; this *is* Europe; this seeming Terrible is the real soul of white culture—back of all culture,—stripped and visible today. This is where the world has arrived,—these dark and awful depths and not the shining and ineffable heights of which it is boasted" (Dubois 1999:22; emphasis in original).

While the white world was using the women and men of the dark world in all of the ways known by the holders of social advantages, slowly there began to evolve a theory that the women and men of the dark world were not women and men in the same way as the residents of the white world, but were born beasts of burden for white folk. "How could we have thought otherwise?" Du Bois has them utter in this mock dialogue. "Their voices grow stronger and shriller in accord. The supporting arguments grow and twist themselves in the mouths of merchant, scientist, soldier, traveler, writer, and missionary." It is the task of the civilized world to raise them insofar as their shallow capacities allow for any kind of elevation so that they can at least perform useful tasks in the world that we have made: "raise cotton, gather rubber, fetch ivory, dig diamonds" (Du Bois 1999:24). None of this is new, Du Bois tells us. One of the age-old follies of humankind has been to explain how the victim was different from the victors "in soul and blood, in strength and cunning, and in race and lineage" (Du Bois 1999:24). What the white world has given us is a single means of making such a distinction: color! Du Bois locates the consolidation of this ideology in Boxer times, when the European powers responded to the 1895 Japanese defeat of China with a policy that they referred to as carving up the Chinese melon. This was, of course, ten years after the partitioning of Africa among the European powers. White supremacy was all but worldwide, he tells us. "Africa was dead,

India conquered, Japan isolated, and China prostrate, while white America whetted her sword for mongrel Mexico and mulatto South America, lynching her own Negroes all the while" (Du Bois 1999:24). What was new about this business in Du Bois's eyes was its "imperial width" and "heaven defying audacity." This is a response to the writing on the wall of the rich people of the white nations, whose room for maneuver was being more and more limited by the growth in the social power of the working people of those nations. There was a loophole, though, which according to Dr. Du Bois was an opportunity for exploitation on a grand scale—for inordinate profits—not only for the very rich but for the middle classes and laborers as well. This chance is the exploitation of the people of the dark world on a global scale. This would allow free reign, with no labor unions, no right to vote, and no onlookers asking inconvenient questions (Du Bois 1999:25).

For Du Bois the main cause of the Great War is all too obvious. In the practical world, there is jealousy and strife for the possession of the labor and the raw materials of the dark world. It was this competition for the labor of yellow, brown, and black folks, Du Bois asserts, that was the cause of World War I. Whatever other causes may have contributed to the conflict, they were decidedly subsidiary to "this vast quest for the dark world's wealth and toil" (Du Bois 1999:25).

These colonies belt the earth," but they cluster in tropical zones inhabited by darkened people in Hong Kong, Sierra Leone, Nigeria, Havana, and Panama." Du Bois holds that "these are the El Dorado's towards which the world powers stretch itching palms" (Du Bois 1999:26). Germany hoped to rival the other European powers but did not have a source of massive and fast wealth via access to the wealth and toil of the dark world. She turned to China, to Africa, to Asia Minor "like a hound quivering on the leash, impatient, irritable, with blood-shot eyes and dripping fangs" (Du Bois 1999:26). "England and France crouched watchfully over their bones, growling and wary, but gnawing industriously, while the blood of the dark world whetted their greedy appetites" (Du Bois 1999:26).

So when finally the tinder is lit and the world plunges into war, guarding their national interests, their "right to colonies, the chance to levy endless tribute on the darker world—on coolies in China, on starving peasants in India, on black savages in Africa, on dying South Seas Islanders, on Indians of the Amazon" (Du Bois 1999:27). Even those who had pledged themselves to the brotherhood of labor did not envision the working women and men of the dark world as members of their ranks. There is no doubt, Du Bois argues, that there was one unanimity among the contending powers in Germany and England: that they maintain white prestige in Africa. Du Bois is quite blunt when he says that this amounts to "the doctrine of the divine right of white people to steal" (Du Bois 1999:27).

But matters will not end here, says a Dr. Du Bois whose very tone here is embedded in an overarching analysis of the social dynamics of that period from the underside of the modern world-system and the pretensions of modernity. This tone which I feel to be appropriate is too seldom appropriated by the intellectuals of the pan-European world in our time faced with similar attrocities. He holds this war is just a prelude to the "armed and indignant protests of these despised and raped peoples. Today Japan is hammering on the door of justice, China is raising her half-manacled hands to knock next, India is writhing for the freedom to knock, Egypt is sullenly muttering, the Negroes of South and West Africa, of the West Indies, and of the United States are just awakening to their shameful slavery" (Du Bois 1999:28). The white world should not be deceived. This is not indeed the end of all wars, but the beginning of a very terrible struggle that the greed and avarice of the white world will have brought on itself.

Alys Eve Weinbaum (2001) argues that for Du Bois during the 1920s whiteness came to signify class as much as race. In *Dark Princess* he presents an organization called the Darker Peoples of the World. While this organization seems to derive its name from the International League of the Darker People, formed by A. Philip Randolph, Marcus Garvey, C. J. Walker, and Japanese representatives, it reflects Du Bois's attempt to think through the possibilities and contradictions of elaborating this kind of organizational structure. This clearly represents an attempt to explore the idea of a Pan-African and Pan-Asian joint solidarity. He is attempting to connect the world's darker people into a single world-shaping force. Here we can see an example of an author who has already taken the cautionary note of Giovanni Arrighi, Terence Hopkins, and Immanuel Wallerstein (1989) about resisting the temptation to reify groups.

In the pages of *Dark Princess* we see evidence of Du Bois's awareness of the debates swirling around him about the African American nation animating Lenin, M. N. Roy (See chapter 3), and the Communist International. Du Bois has Kautilya and Matthew debate this position, where Du Bois agrees that African Americans constitute a nation within a nation but also transcends that position by arguing that it merges with all the oppressed nations that together comprise the Land of the Blacks (Weinbaum 2001:35).[12] It is here that we see the clearest enunciation of the concept of a racialized internationalism that is similar to a later notion of what has been variously deemed Black internationalism, Pan-African internationalism, and African internationalism.

In an important article in a special issue of *Positions* titled "The Afro-Asian Century," Bill V. Mullen argues that *Dark Princess* represents Du Bois's engagement with three central movements and events of the interwar period: "the Indian home rule and national movements, the emergence of black radicalism in the United States, and the role of black and Asian radicals in revising Soviet policy on both 'Negro' and Asian liberation during the formation of the third international after 1919 and the crucial 1922 and 1928 Cominterns in Moscow" (Mullen 2003:218). Mullen hails *Dark Princess* as a central text representing African American engagement with the American, Asian, and international Left during the twentieth century, which furthermore demonstrated how resistance to Eurocentric discourses of race led to the radical recasting of Afro-Asian relationships as central to twentieth-century world revolutionary struggle (Mullen 2003:219).

After his February 1937 visit to China in the midst of civil war, Du Bois would write in the *Pittsburgh Courier* that China is inconceivable, that after only four days there he is absolutely dazed: "Any attempt to explain the world, without giving a place of extraordinary prominence to China, is futile." He went on to conclude that "perhaps the riddle of the universe will be solved in China; and if not, in no part of the world that ignores China" (Mullen 2004:3).

For Mullen this statement indicates an expansion of Du Bois's Pan-African internationalism (my term) to a broader internationalism that holds that Afro-Asian mutuality and recognition are the cornerstones of global liberation against white Western racism and capitalism. Du Bois, however, had a much larger scope than many social scientists of that time (and of more recent times) since he straddled what even at that time was a rigid divide between the two cultures (the social sciences and the humanities). Du Bois thought that a sense of mutuality and recognition between these two broad groupings of peoples would be central to the struggle binding and bridging the ancient and contemporary colored worlds. Du Bois's worldview is said to consist of a welding of quasi-mythic renderings of colored empires in antiquity to a secular, though idealized, social comprehension of the major political movements of the twentieth century (Mullen 2004:3). Wilson Moses has dubbed the worldview produced by this synthetic and syncretic fusion "Afrocentric Marxism" (Moses 1998:96).

Du Bois had abandoned the liberal nationalism and the bourgeois democratic ideological stance in no uncertain terms with the publication of *Darkwater* in 1920. The tone of *Darkwater* differed dramatically from that of *The Souls of Black Folk*, and *The Negro*, which fell between the two. *Darkwater* sparked strong reactions from a variety of reviewers. The *Times Literary Supplement* of London said that *Darkwater* revealed the "dark depths of a passionate and fanatical mind." The Paris edition of the *New York Herald* featured an editorial on the book titled "Black Bolshevism." The reviewer held that Du Bois was intoxicated by colonial self-determination, which "partakes of the frenzy" and "represents the spread of the Bolshevist madness" (Mullen 2004:12). Indeed, Mullen argues that the events between 1917 and 1928 highlighted in *Dark Princess* reconfigured Du Bois's ideas about Afro-Asia as well as the color of his own political ideas.

In 1925 Du Bois is said to have indicated his turn in the December *Crisis* column that noted the formation of the Brotherhood of Sleeping Car Porters and the American Negro Labor Congress. In response to being questioned about the 1925 meeting of the American Negro Labor Congress in Chicago, Du Bois was noncommittal, according to Earl Ofari Hutchinson, since he did not know who had organized the conference, but he did defend the right of Black people to investigate and sympathize with any industrial reform whether it sprang from Russia, China, or the South Seas (Hutchinson 1995:32–33).

Du Bois's 1926 visit to the Soviet Union overlapped with Harry Haywood's arrival for training at the Moscow University of the Toilers of the East (opened with the support of M.N. Roy in 1926).[13] Du Bois would spend six weeks in the Soviet Union while working on *Dark Princess*.

Despite the poverty and the signs of war that he could still clearly see, Du Bois felt that Russia was the most hopeful land in the modern world. Although the Russian people seemed as ignorant, poor, and superstitious as the Blacks in the United States at the time, Du Bois also sensed a new feeling of hope and determination among the workers and peasants of Russia (Du Bois 1968:290):

> I did not believe that the communism of the Russians was the program for America; least of all for a minority group like the Negroes; I saw that the program of the American Communist party was inadequate for our plight. But I did believe that a people where the differentiation in classes because of wealth had only begun, could be so guided by intelligent leaders that they would develop into a consumer conscious people, producing for use and not primarily for profit and working into the surrounding industrial organization so as to-reinforce the economic revolution bound to develop in the United States and all over Europe and Asia sooner or later. I believed that revolution in the production and distribution of wealth could be a slow, reasoned development and not necessarily a bloodbath. I believed that 13 millions of people, increasing albeit slowly in intelligence, could so concentrate their thought and action on the abolition of their poverty, as to work in conjunction with the most intelligent body of American thought; and that in the future as in the past, out of the mass of American Negroes would arise a far-seeing leadership in lines of economic reform. (Du Bois 1968:290–291)

For Du Bois the Pan-African congresses he called in 1919, 1921, and 1923 were memorable for the excitement they caused among the colonial powers. The prominent newspapers of the colonial world used them to call on their governments to clamp down on colonial unrest. Still Du Bois was going too fast for the board of the NAACP, which had no interest in Africa. Their maximum program was to make Blacks into citizens of the United States. They had no sense that if Europe persisted in upholding and strengthening the color bar, then the United States would follow suit (Du Bois 1968:291).

But as Du Bois himself tells us, his racial politics from the 1930s onward derived from analytic concepts that he derived from Marxism and from the manner that such concepts were interpreted and implemented in the Soviet Union. As we shall see, I agree only partially with this assertion. I think the influence of Marxism in Du Bois's thought does stem in part from his analysis of the Soviet experience, but it seems he initially pursued an independent path before deciding to become aligned with official communism. I will look first at the reasoning that held during the period in which he was aligned with communism and then return to the revolutionary internationalism that he articulated during the 1930s since this stream of his social thought has had so much influence in the social thought of world antisystemic forces since the 1960s.

Kate Baldwin (2002:153) cautions those who would use the corruption and the final failure of the Soviet regime to dismiss Du Bois's vision, since Du Bois himself had argued explicitly that in the final analysis the success or failure of Russian communism was less important than whether "the ideals of human uplift as conceived by Marx and Lenin are ideals that should be realized" (Baldwin 2002:153).

Olga Peters Hasty (2006), professor of Slavic Languages and Literatures at Princeton University, explains that in the nineteenth century, Russian intellectuals often regarded the United States as a potential political model but were confounded by the common issue of human bondage in both societies. These intellectuals condemned slavery in the United States in order to register their opposition to the serfdom that plagued their own society. If the image of the enslaved African figured large in the Russian liberal imagination, after the abolition of slavery and serfdom, it remained a point of linkage between the disenfranchised African Americans and a new Soviet state that valorized the downtrodden and presented itself as the arbiter of a new world-system that sought to abolish the inequalities of race and social class.

In her analysis of Du Bois's unpublished manuscript, *Russia and America: An Interpretation*, in *Beyond the Color Line and the Iron Curtain*, Kate Baldwin's exploration of the dynamics of the relationship between Blacks and Russians allows us a new insight into the logic of how Du Bois rearticulated his understanding of the color line through his thinking about and renegotiating the relationship with the new Soviet power. I start on what is familiar ground to some with his comments about his 1926 visit to the Soviet Union:

> What amazed and uplifted me in 1926 was to see a nation stoutly facing a problem which most other modern nations did not dare even to admit was real. Taking inspiration directly out of the mouths and dreams of the world's savants and prophets . . . this new Russia led by Lenin and inspired by Marx proposed to build a socialist state with production for use and not for private profit; with ownership of land and capital goods by the state and state control of public services including education and health. It was enough for me to see this mighty attempt. It might fail, I knew; but the effort in itself was social progress and neither foolishness nor crime. (Baldwin 2002:154)

Ten years earlier, in *Dusk of Dawn*, Du Bois explained how he had come to embrace a Marxian analytic framework and its influence on his strategy for social transformation after his 1926 trip to Russia (see Du Bois 1970). He had been profoundly influenced by his observations of the impact of the invasion by the Western powers (the United States, England, France, and the Czechs had left the Soviet people hungry and their cities in ruins but with an unforgettable spirit in the face of the contempt and chicanery of the "civilized world"). In the face of all these difficulties, they were determined to go forward to establish a government of men such as the world had never seen (Du Bois 1968:287). After a struggle with the world and famine, the Soviets had made up their minds to face a set of problems that no other nation was willing to face: the problem of poverty and the maldistribution of wealth.

Their solution was to place control over society and the state in the hands of the people who did the work so they could run society in the interests of the people as a whole. Unlike those who argued that only those with long experience in running society or those with special expertise could run society, the revolutionaries held that in the mass of working people existed the ability and character to run society truly in a democratic way.

Du Bois believed passionately in this dictum and held that this had long been the basis of his fight for Black folk. He experienced this as a flight of insight that explained his life in a way that he had not heretofore conceptualized clearly. How does one achieve this, though, without a violent and destructive revolution, which he could not contemplate? The oppressed must build their own organization and power, which would then be a resource as they fought to transform society. With regard to the situation of Black folk, he realized now that the fight against racial prejudice was a fight against not only the rational and conscious intent of white people to oppress Black people but also "age-long complexes sunk now largely to unconscious habit and irrational urge, which demanded on our part not only the patience to wait, but the power to entrench ourselves for a long siege against the strongholds of color caste" (Du Bois 1968:296).

The strategy of the NAACP, which sought unimpeded entry into the political life of the country, was only a preliminary to the establishment of democracy, which would replace the tyranny that now dominated industrial life.

This position found no traction with the members of the NAACP board, however, who declared that this was simply the same segregation that they had been fighting for some twenty years. Du Bois finally realized that he was touching on an old and bleeding sore in Negro thought:

> From the eighteenth century down the Negro intelligentsia has regarded segregation as the visible badge of *their* servitude and as the object of their unceasing attack. The upper class Negro has almost never been nationalistic. He has never planned or thought of a Negro state or a Negro church or a Negro school. This solution has always bee a thought up-surging from the mass, because of pressure which they could not withstand and which compelled a racial institution or chaos. Continually such institutions were founded and developed, but this took place against the advice and best thought of the intelligentsia. (Du Bois 1968:305; my emphasis)

What sense can one make of the stance of the NAACP board? Du Bois cautions that common sense contradicts any such absolute stance. When the NAACP was formed, a great mass of Black people attended Black schools, were members of Black churches, lived in Black neighborhoods, voted in a block for particular political parties and candidates, and cooperated with other Black people to fight the further extension of segregation. Even that position could not be absolute, though, for wherever an increase in segregation benefited the mass of Black people, then such action was taken.

In the midst of this great ideological struggle in the NAACP, the organization was beset by the contention from the Russian and American Communists, who wished to foment revolution in the United States by organizing a campaign to defend a group of Black youths who had been accused of raping two white women in Scottsboro, Alabama. The intervention of the Russian Communists in this case, Du Bois argues, was based on an abysmal ignorance of patterns of race prejudice in the United States. They made the whole issue turn on property rights and race, and they spread propaganda about the issue over the whole world. Though they may have been right about the merits of the case, Du Bois argues, they were wrong in the methods they used if they were seeking to free the victims.

Du Bois saw the path of violent revolution as a disaster for Black people. He was opposed not so much to the goals of socialist struggle as to the methods of revolutionary violence, which may have been the only method possible against the Russian Empire; he did not think this the case in the United States.

This was especially true because the United States was not a society with a class structure based on the exploitation of the overwhelming majority of the population (workers) by a small minority of capitalists. Du Bois held that the color line in the U.S. working class was more significant than the division between white workers and capitalists. This, he argued, was an incontrovertible fact that Russian Communists ignored. "American Negroes were asked to accept a complete dogma without question or alteration. It was first of all emphasized that all racial thought and racial segregation must go and that Negroes must put themselves blindly under the dictatorship of the Communist Party" (Du Bois 1968:205).

Du Bois Confronts the Praxis of Official Communism

During the period of the Great Migration and the Great War, Du Bois confronted the criticism of a younger generation of intellectual activists who came to be known as the New Negro radicals. These young radicals were mostly organic intellectuals who readily grasped the need for an internationalist approach to the oppression of the race. While I discuss the impact of the New Negro radicals in the next chapter, I should indicate here that by the 1920s Du Bois had passed most of these intellectuals on the Left, becoming in the process the new standard bearer of the race-first Black radicals. During the 1930s a number of academically based intellectuals found themselves in the realm of the Communist Party (E. Franklin Frazier, Abram Harris, and Ralph Bunche) and criticized Du Bois for his alleged petit bourgeois nationalism.

The manner in which Du Bois moved to the Left eventually illuminated the entire landscape of historical capitalism in a way no one had before. In this sense Du Bois differed from a number of younger Black intellectuals among the New Negro radicals of the post–World War I period (such as Hubert Harrison, Cyril Briggs, Richard Moore, and A. Philip Randolph) and the 1930s intellectuals who became members of the National Negro Congress (John Davis, E. Franklin Frazier, Ralph Bunche, and Abram Harris).

John Davis, who was a classmate of Ralph Bunche's at Harvard University, founded the Negro Industrial League with Robert Weaver as a critic of the discriminatory practices of Roosevelt's National Recovery Administration. After the Negro Industrial League was disbanded, Davis persuaded the NAACP to fund the Joint Council for National Recovery. Because of his connection with

Bunche, who headed Howard University's Division of the Social Sciences (which had been the brainchild of Bunche, Frazier, and Harris), Mordecai Johnson, president of Howard University, offered a conference hall on Howard's campus to John Davis for a National Conference of the Economic Crisis and the Negro. A variety of positions were put forward at this conference. James Ford spoke about the Communist Party's position; Norman Thomas discussed the Socialist Party's position; A. Philip Randolph spoke about the Negro and the trade union movement; Ralph Bunche presented a critique of New Deal social planning as it affected the Negro; John Davis spoke about the overall plight of the Negro under the New Deal; Emmett Dorsey spoke about the Negro and social planning; and Du Bois spoke about social planning for the Negro past and present. There was a consensus that the New Deal was failing Blacks and that something drastic had to be done. Hutchinson (1995) holds that Du Bois proposed a mixture of nationalist, Black capitalist, and socialist economic solutions to attack the crisis. Du Bois cautioned the participants that there was no automatic power in socialism to override and suppress racial prejudice (Hutchinson 1995:160). Du Bois (1936) held that: "one of the worst things that Negroes could do today would be to join the American Communist Party or one of its branches. The Communists of America have become dogmatic exponents of the inspired word of Karl Marx as they read it. They believe, apparently, in immediate, violent and bloody revolution, and are willing to try any and all means of raising hell anywhere and under any circumstances. This is a silly program even for white men. For American colored men, it is suicide." Du Bois agreed that the world-wrenching changes needed for the abolition of capitalist exploitation would call for revolution as Marx had argued, but he did not think such revolution required violence and bloodshed (Du Bois 1936:123–124). After the conference, according to Hutchinson, Du Bois quietly withdrew his support for the congress movement. Also after the conference, some of the conveners met at Ralph Bunche's campus house to sketch out plans for the National Negro Congress (Holloway 2002:75).

Du Bois had resigned from the board of the NAACP and from his position as the editor of *The Crisis*, having been unable to convince the organization that its criticism of his so-called segregationist position was wrong. Now he was faced with a similar but distinct criticism from the Left. It is important to understand the substance of these criticisms because they still carry some weight among some of the Leftist intelligentsia even today, though some of these criticisms are now muted since Du Bois would later join forces with the Communist Party. It is important to note, however, that his membership also had internationalist context, in much the same way as that of an earlier group of New Negro radicals who joined the Communist Party of the United States.

While Communist Party spokesman James Ford (1936) agreed with Du Bois that the Black upper class was not by and large an exploiter of Black labor, Ford was concerned that this bourgeoisie obtained its existence via the existence of segregation and that it was in the interest of this class to maintain segregation or the very basis of Negro businesses would be destroyed. However, segregation was the worst feature of the oppression of the Negro masses. Segregation was thus the enemy of the Negro masses.

According to Ford, Du Bois is said also to have argued that it was the Negro upper class that bore the brunt of color prejudice and were the leaders of the Negro people toward a better future. Along with Kelly Miller, Du Bois is said to have favored "race solidarity" and opposed the solidarity of Negro and white labor.[14]

Du Bois is further said to have attributed the exploitation of the Black working class not to the white capitalist but to white labor, whose racial attitudes were said to be inborn and not subject to change. To accept such a position meant for Ford that there was no hope of liberation (Ford 1936).

Ralph Bunche likewise declared his opposition to certain Black Nationalist ideologies, racially inspired boycotts that he argued widened the already deplorable gap between white and Black working classes by placing competition for jobs on a strictly racial basis. "Black separatist schemes, such as those proposed by individuals like W.E.B. Du Bois, were even more futile" because by marginalizing Black workers from full participation in American life, they would set them "up in a black political and economic outhouse" (Kirby 1974:131).

Anthony Platt's reconsideration of E. Franklin Frazer provides us with a wonderful snapshot of how Frazier responded to what Platt refers to as Du Bois's dramatic shift to the right in the 1930s. In May 1934, just prior to Du Bois's resignation from the NAACP, Frazier wrote a long letter to NAACP chair Walter White about his disagreements with Du Bois and the NAACP and clarified how his own nationalism differed from the nationalism expressed by Du Bois.

The root of Frazier's disagreement with Du Bois seems to have been in a formulation about human agency that Frazier's own rendition does not entirely clarify. While Frazier accused Du Bois of giving an analysis that stressed the futility of the fight against segregation, he also concedes that "this may be so. It is conceivable that institutions and social arrangements cannot be affected by human effort. But even the Communist, with his materialistic conception of history, does not believe it" (Platt 1991:188).

Here Frazier himself seems to evade the very real tension between agency, ideology, and structure which seems to have bracketed Dr. Du Bois' hesitance toward the Communists during this period. Travel to the USSR and China during that period seems to have broadened his view and widened the scope of his praxis, that praxis, as well as analysis could be internationalized.

In "The Failure of the Negro Intellectual" published in the February 1962 issue of *Negro Digest*, Frazier looking wistfully back on the heady days of the 1930s and 1940s had somewhat of a more appreciative stance on Du Bois. He was deeply disappointed about the "current crop of Negro intellectuals who "have accepted supinely as heroes the negroes whom white people have given us and told us to revere. Even today they run away from Du Bois and Paul Robeson" (Frazier 1962).

But during the 1930s, when the masses were on the move, things looked different to Frazier: now was the time to act, and such action required an alliance with the Communist movement. Platt focuses on Frazier's contention that the time to act is now. He points out that the heart of Frazier's critique of Du Bois's position was that "Du Bois was taking refuge in a tame and harmless racialism, because he was 'too old or is afraid to risk his livelihood in coming out in favor of Communism or the destruction of competitive capitalist society as the only solution to the Negro's problem.' He told [Walter] White that it was a mistake to confuse Du Bois's 'racial separateness' with Frazier's advocacy of the development of group morale and solidarity, a position that he had taken at the Amenia Conference" (Platt 1991:188).

Frazier held that he "did not envisage a Negro ghetto, stratified to bourgeois society." Unlike Du Bois, Frazier claimed to be "advocating "revolutionary nationalism," which Frazier defined as the development of racial solidarity as a cohesive force among a people who were exploited by the white master class in this country" (Platt 1991:188).

Later, in the first issue of the journal *Race*, which had invited Frazier to its editorial board, Frazier penned a devastating attack on Du Bois.

> Du Bois remains an intellectual who toys with the idea of the Negro as a separate cultural group. He has only an occasional romantic interest in the Negro as a distinct race. Nothing could be more unendurable for him than to live within a Black Ghetto or within a Black nation—unless perhaps he were king, and then probably he would attempt to unite the whites and blacks through marriage of the royal families. . . . If a fascist movement should develop in America, Du Bois would play into the hands of its leaders through his program for the development of Negro racialism. . . .
>
> Since Du Bois is an intellectual who loves to play with ideas but shuns reality, whether it be in the form of black masses or revolution, he likes to display a familiarity with Marxian ideology. In an article in the *Crisis* he demonstrated, in a few hundred words, the error of applying Marxian conceptions to the economic conditions of the Negro in America. Later in *Black Reconstruction in America* he played with Marxian terminology as a literary device. This is all as it should be, for Du Bois has said that there shall be no revolution and that economic justice and the abolition of poverty shall come through reason (the intellectual speaks), sacrifice (the romanticist speaks), and the intelligent use of the ballot (in the end he remains a liberal), and like Douglass and Washington before him he does not provide the kind of social criticism which is needed for Blacks to achieve an appropriate orientation in the present state of American capitalism. (Platt 1991:189)

Frazier's criticism intersects with a much later critique of the extent to which Du Bois's mature revolutionary phase, from the mid-1930s onward, even including his post–World War II embrace of Bolshevism, continued to be a manifestation of Fabian socialism, as is argued by Adolph Reed (1997). Reed contends that Lenin's fascination with scientific management indicates that even the most revolutionary trend in Marxism can be considered a more politically aggressive and successful version of collectivism.

Reed notes that Lenin defined the revolutionary Social Democrat as a "Jacobin who totally identifies himself with the organization of the proletariat, a proletariat *conscious* of its class interests." For Reed, Bolshevism is thus distinguished precisely by "its Jacobinist radicalism, its political aggressiveness and willing to force its program of rationalist homogenization on society through rupture." In this sense Reed argues "Bolshevism joins other collectivist stances as a realization under contemporary historical circumstances of a central strain of the telos of the bourgeois Enlightenment, the domination of the concept over its object" (Reed 1997:22).

For Reed this distinction means that it diminishes the significance of our need to distinguish when or whether Du Bois actually became a revolutionary Marxist. The organizing principle of Du Bois's thought remains pretty much the same throughout his long career, according to Reed, a fact particularly evident in his attitude about the importance of science in social affairs and the proper organization of the African American population and even in his political concerns about Pan-Africanism and socialism (Reed 1997:22). Reed argues that Du Bois's intellectual and political evolution embracing collectivism, the cooperative commonwealth, and antimodernism represented a set of responses manifest in the intelligentsia of this period to the cultural crises of the late nineteenth century, which I have designated variously as the onset of the rise of the United States to a hegemonic position in the world-system, the beginning of the worldwide challenge of the extra-European world to Pan-European supremacy, and the organization of the laboring classes against the exploitation and rationalization of the capitalist organization of societies (the capitalist world-economy).

In the post–World War II period, Du Bois would change his position and explain it in the context of the appeal of the Soviet Union to a range of Black radicals from the 1920s through the 1940s. Du Bois wrote *Russia and America* to situate the growing attraction of Soviet communism in the context of the manner in which the Soviet Revolution dealt with the minority nationalities within the Russian borders and the 1936 constitutional amendment outlawing racism. Viewing the possibility of new forms of egalitarian communities arising in such an environment, Du Bois set out in *Russia and America* to "unhinge the prevailing misconception that communism was an antidemocratic conspiracy posturing as a peace movement. In the aftermath of the second world war Du Bois was convinced that the Soviet Union promised a democratic and egalitarian society more so than any Western nation" (Baldwin 2002:155).

Indeed, Baldwin argues that Du Bois had increasingly interpreted the Soviet experience through his own experience as an African American and thus increasingly came to understand that racial and cultural differentiation were transnationally oriented. The systematic violence of industrial capitalism seemed to weld various populations together as common foes of an oppressive social system. The Russians had been marked as nonhistoric people by Western philosophers of identity and thus like African Americans were excluded from the Hegelian Geist of historical progress. "Du Bois was keenly aware of these historical resonances between 'Slavs' and 'Africans,' and found in Russia a nonoppositional counter to

Western European constructs of selfhood. Du Bois elaborates the similarities between enslavement and serfdom, and concludes that what the U.S. has actually done in the post World War II period is to reformulate the color line in the face of 'the Soviet Union's refusal to be white'" (Baldwin 2002:158–159).

Du Bois's publisher, Robert Giroux, declined to publish *Russia and America* because he thought it an uncritical apologia for the Soviet Union and unduly critical of the United States. Although Du Bois cautions the reader throughout that the Soviet Union is not a utopia or a fairyland of joy and plenty and that his reason may be strained (Baldwin 2002:170), Baldwin thinks that the sections of the manuscript on enforced collectivization and liquidation of the kulaks by Stalin are a bit more than strained (Baldwin 2002:170). Du Bois's Pulitzer Prize–winning biographer, David Levering Lewis, points out that Du Bois justified the corruption of the Soviet revolution manifested in such practices by adjusting "the Russian casualty tables in the light of the Atlantic slave trade, the scramble for Africa, the needless First World War, Nazi death camps, and the color coded poverty and wage-slavery raging in and beyond North America. To Du Bois, the degradation of the communist ideal was philosophically irrelevant to the expiation of the sins of American democracy, whose very possibility he now doubted" (Lewis 2000:557).

While significant political forces that have been aligned with official communism counted themselves comrades of Du Bois, the New Left and intellectuals associated with the New Left, including anticolonial revolutionaries who came to prominence in the 1950s and 1960s, are also the intellectual and political progeny of Du Bois. In my view, this stream derives from the independent position that Du Bois staked out in the 1930s. I try here to trace the trajectory of this stream and its challenge to white world supremacy.

First we should underline that *Black Reconstruction in America* was written during the period when Du Bois was in the process of developing a new analysis of the world and the place of Black people in it, inspired by Marxism and the world socialist movement. In addition he was advocating a new strategy for social change on the basis of reconceptualizing the lessons of the past strategy of the NAACP. Second, it should be noted that the original title of the work according to Lewis was "Black Reconstruction of Democracy in America" (Lewis 2000:361). This gives a sense of the scope that Du Bois had for the work that we have come to know as *Black Reconstruction in America*, in which Du Bois (1979) presents his task as arguing against the intellectual apologists for slavery for the humanity of Black people. In effect, however, he is undertaking a much more radical transformation of the intellectual landscape by a dramatic reshaping of our intellectual understanding of the shape of the social world and the place of Black people in it, both as objects of racial capitalism and as subjects of revolutionary transformation.

I argue in what follows that *Black Reconstruction in America* reflects the most sophisticated analysis of the world capitalist system as a historical social system until the time of its publication and for the next forty years, when intellectuals associated with the national liberation movements in the periphery and with the New Left in the core states began to assimilate the lessons that Du

Bois had articulated in *Black Reconstruction*. The analysis in *Black Reconstruction* is also significant because it captures that particular moment in time like no other work at that time in terms of the beginning of the quest of the United States for hegemonic status in the world-system and the implications of that strategy for democracy in the U.S. and world racial order. A third issue that *Black Reconstruction* addresses is the revolutionary agency of the southern rural strata, which contradicts both the Marxist dogma about the industrial proletariat against a so-called rural peasantry and the Leninist dogma about the revolutionary party as the necessary transmitter of revolutionary ideas and methods of organization to the working class.

From the history of the struggle between the industrial North and the slave South, Du Bois learned important lessons that enabled him to make this important contribution. When the South decided to strike out on its own because of the political power it held because of slavery and the disenfranchisement of poor whites, it did not reckon on the weakness of its social fabric, related specifically to its failure to incorporate the working strata into any kind of partnership or perceived partnership with the ruling strata.

When the South went to war with the North, its entire labor class, Black and white, went into economic revolt. "The breach could only have been healed by making the same concessions to labor that France, England, and Germany and the North had made. There was no time for such change in the midst of war. Northern industry must, therefore, after the war, make the adjustment with labor which Southern agriculture refused to make. But the loss which agriculture sustained though the stubbornness of the planters led to the degradation of agriculture throughout the modern world" (Du Bois 1979:47).

> The abolition of American slavery started the transportation of capital from white to Black countries where slavery prevailed, with the same tremendous and awful consequences upon the laboring classes of the world which we see about us today. When raw materials cannot be raised in a country like the United States, it could be raised in the tropics and semitropics under a dictatorship of industry, commerce and manufacture and with no free farming class. . . .
>
> The competition of a slave-directed agriculture in the West Indies and South America, in Africa and Asia, eventually ruined the economic efficiency of agriculture in the United States and in Europe and precipitated the modern economic degradation of the white farmer, while it put in the hands of the owners of the machine such a monopoly of raw material that their domination of white labor was more and more complete. (Du Bois 1979:48)

The slaveholding class of the South sharply objected to what they deemed to be the hypocrisy of the North and liberal Europe, who in their opposition to slavery failed to comprehend that it was a system of work that was not different in essence from the system of labor in the North and Europe. They were all exploiting labor. The so-called free laborers of the North and liberal Europe were only free to starve if they did not work on terms dictated by the employers, while slave laborers were the responsibility of the slaveholding classes from birth to death.

Du Bois thought this was a credible argument in solely economic terms, but even in these terms this system was illogical. It enforced a system of cheap and degraded labor that undermined the possibility of modernization and the consequent upgrading of the worker's standard of living and quality of life. It thus enforced a backwardness that precluded the internal growth of the system, which could grow only by the expansion of its land base, which of course would quickly come up against its limits.

Even more important was the untenability of the human consequences of the system, in terms of both the labor, which could not forever be repressed, and the employers, whose humanity was constantly degraded by this system. Frederick Douglass summed up the issue as well as anyone: "I understand this policy to comprehend five cardinal objects. They are these: 1st, The complete suppression of all anti-slavery discussion. 2d, The expatriation of the entire free people of color from the United States. 3d, the unending perpetuation of slavery in this republic. 4th, The nationalization of slavery to the extent of making slavery respected in every state of the Union. 5th, The extension of slavery over Mexico and the entire South American states" (Du Bois 1979:53).

Du Bois argued that this was a system of industry so humanly unjust and economically inefficient that if it had not committed suicide in civil war, it would have disintegrated of its own weight. In the end, however, the system could not endure and resulted in civil war as a means to extend its life. The final death of the system exacted its own revenge as it stalled the ability of the working classes to gain any hegemony over the resulting society to prevent it from imposing a compromise such as that established and built on in Europe and the North. It did so by demonizing Black labor.

The slaveholding South feared the success of their former property more so than their own failure. They were angry, vengeful, and hysterical. They held up Black people to ridicule. They said, "Look at these niggers: they are black and poor and ignorant. How can they rule those of us who are white and who have been rich and have at our command all wisdom and skill? Back to slavery with the dumb brutes!" (Du Bois 1979:633).

Du Bois points how the former slaveholding class lied about Black people, accused them of theft, crimes, moral enormities, and laughable grotesqueries. They appealed to the fear and hatred of white labor, offering them alliances, the pleasures of the pillage of Black bodies, the hands of their daughters in marriage, and the achievement of a solid South: an ignorant, intolerant, and ruthless land impervious to reason, justice, or fact. They encouraged white labor to indulge their hatred (Du Bois 1979:633).

On the other side of the coin was a North that had developed as a counterpoint opposed to the expansion of slavery, not so much because it offended their sense of morality, but because of the threat that such expansion posed to them. Indeed morality is was a dead issue since the profitability of some northern industries were built in part on the slave system. In an attempt to balance the oppositions among northern white labor, free Africans, and idealists, they were forced to refuse more land to slavery, refuse to catch and return slaves, and, finally, fight for freedom since this preserved cotton, tobacco, sugar, and the southern market. This contradictory situation led to the glimpse in the North of a degree of concentrated wealth unprecedented in the history of the world, which gave rise in 1876 to a new capitalism and a new enslavement of labor, including a relatively high-wage section of whites and a low-wage section of people with white, brown, yellow, and black skin, without legal recourse. What Du Bois had called the dictatorship of the proletariat during the period 1867–1876 had been defeated, and with it the possibility of the steady rise of the working classes and the casting of the entire world-system into a racial capitalism that operated in ways that had to be understood to be challenged. This was the context in which Du Bois sought to reconstruct the strategy of social transformation of the world-system.

Du Bois argues in contrast to the Communist Party of the United States of America and most other Marxists in the United States and Europe that what is unique about the white working class in the United States is that despite their history as laboring people in the lands from which they emigrated, once they reached the United States they did not regard themselves as a permanent laboring class. Du Bois argues that because of its property, the successful, well-paid American working class formed a petite bourgeoisie always ready to join capital in exploiting common labor, black or white, foreign or native.

In contrast to the European working-class notion of a collective struggle to elevate the whole class, in the United States the ideology of the working class was individual upward mobility. This exacerbated the competition for jobs, which is the lot of any working class that denies the existence of a class community.

Even the early Marxists among the English and German émigrés were infected by the availability of free land in the U.S. West. Because of the land monopoly in Europe, immigrant workers grasped the significance of abundant land more quickly. They thus viewed more clearly the divergent trajectories they might take in the new land: gravitating toward the degraded status of the enslaved African or moving upward into the petite bourgeoisie. This hardened the contention between wage labor and free labor.

An example is the position taken in 1846 by Hermann Kriege, a German immigrant who had worked very closely with Marx and Engels. Originally a trade union organizer and socialist, by 1846 he was preaching land reform and free soil:

> We see in the slavery question a property question which cannot be settled by itself alone. That we should declare ourselves in favor of the abolitionist movement if it were our intention to throw the Republic into a state of anarchy, to extend the competition of the "free workingmen" beyond all measure, and to depress labor itself to the last extremity. That we could not improve the lot of our "black brothers" by abolition under the conditions prevailing in modern society, but make infinitely worse the lot of our "white brothers." That we believe is in the peaceable

development of society in the Untied States and do not, therefore, here at least see our only hope in condition of the extremist degradation. That we feel constrained, therefore, to oppose Abolition with all of our might, despite all the importunities of sentimental philistines and despite all the poetical effusions of liberty-intoxicated ladies. (Quoted in Du Bois 1979:23)

For these early Marxists in the United States, abolition represented capital. Thus they made no attempt to bring the antislavery movement into an alliance with the trade union movement, much less view the antislavery movement as part of the workers' movement. On a much larger scale, scholars, journalists, public officials, and the white public in the South chose to discredit the efforts of the formerly enslaved Africans in an unprecedented manner involving universities, history, science, social life, and religion.

Du Bois provides a panoramic view of these efforts that speaks volumes about these efforts of historical distortion:

The most magnificent drama in the last thousand years of human history is the transportation of ten million human beings out of the dark beauty of their mother continent into the new-found Eldorado of the West. They descended into Hell; and in the Third Century they arose from the dead, in the finest effort to achieve democracy for the working millions that the world has ever seen. It was a tragedy that beggared the Greeks; it was an upheaval of humanity like the Reformation and the French Revolution. Yet we are blind and led by the blind. We discern in it no part of our labor movement; no part of our industrial triumph; no part of our religious experience. Before the dumb eyes of ten generations of ten million children, it is made mockery of and spit upon; a degradation of the eternal mother; a sneer at human effort; with aspiration and art deliberately and elaborately distorted. And why? Because in a day when the human mind aspired to a science of human action, a history and psychology of the mighty effort of the mightiest century, we fell under the leadership of those who would compromise with truth in the past in order to make peace in the present and guide policy in the future. (Du Bois 1979:727)

Du Bois argues that the plight of the white working class throughout the world was traceable to Black slavery in the United States, the foundation of modern commerce and industry. Because slavery was deemed a threat to free labor, "it was partially overthrown in 1863. The resulting color caste founded and retained by capitalism was adopted, forwarded, and approved by white labor and resulted in the subordination of colored labor to white profits the world over. Thus, the majority of the world's laborers, by the insistence of white labor, became the basis of a system of industry that ruined democracy and showed its perfect fruit in World War and Depression" (Du Bois, 1979, p. 30).

Du Bois's class analysis of the slave system is at once elegant and insightful. He argues that the planters were a bourgeoisie who refused to act like a bourgeoisie. By focusing on consumption of their profits and by refusing to invest in the workforce, use machinery, and adopt modern methods, they allowed northern and European capital to set the prices for the goods they produced.

The planter justified the slave system by arguing that the Black people were not capable of higher intelligence and increased efficiency. Religious leaders reverted to the curse of Canaan, men of science gathered and supplemented all available doctrines of race inferiority, and educators and scholars repeated these ideas. The planter's propaganda was based on his angle of vision on his enslaved laborers. "He saw ignorant and sullen labor deliberately reducing his profits" (Du Bois 1979:40). The enslaved Africans might be made to work continuously, but there was no power the slaveholders could wield that would make them work well.

In contrast to some Marxist arguments about a so-called false consciousness among the white working class, who identified their interests with their own ruling class instead of their class brothers and sisters across national borders and ethnic lines, Du Bois argues that the problem of the times was not that the white workers were ignorant. "William Green and Matthew Wolf of the A.F. of L. have no excuse of illiteracy or religion to veil their deliberate intention to keep Negroes and Mexicans and other elements of common labor, in a lower proletariat as subservient to their interests as theirs are to the interests of capital" (Du Bois 1973:210–216). In the capitalist world economy of the twentieth century, the white working class no longer occupied an unambiguous proletarian position in the social structure. Since capitalistic production had now gained worldwide organization, there developed in the American working class a large petite bourgeoisie. According to Du Bois:

> A new class of technical engineers and managers has arisen forming a working class aristocracy between the older proletariat and the absentee owners of capital. . . .
>
> [They] form a new petty bourgeois class, whose interests are bound up with those of the capitalists and antagonistic to those of common labor. . . . Common labor in America and white Europe far from being motivated by any vision of revolt against capitalism, has been blinded by the American vision of the possibility of layer after layer of the workers escaping into the wealthy class and becoming managers and employers of labor. (Du Bois 1971:213–214)

This new class structure of the capitalist world economy meant that in the United States there was a "wild and ruthless scramble" of labor groups seeking to obtain greater wealth on the backs of Black and immigrant labor. However, immigrant labor adopted the same stance toward Black labor, eventually resulting, in my view, in the creation of a "white working class" that by 1945 occupied an essentially intermediate status in the capitalist world economy.

On the one hand, this arrangement has spawned a "new proletariat" world-wide of colored workers toiling under conditions equivalent to those of nineteenth-century capitalism. On the other hand, "capitalists have consolidated their economic power, nullified universal suffrage, and bribed the white workers by high wages, visions of wealth, and the opportunity to drive 'niggers'" (Du Bois 1971:213–214). "Soldiers and sailors from the white workers are used to keep 'darkies' in their 'places' and white foremen and engineers have been established as irresponsible satraps in China, India, Africa, and the West Indies, backed by the organized and centralized ownership of machines, raw materials, finished commodities and land monopoly over the whole world" (Du Bois 1971:214).

While this same process has given rise to a petite bourgeoisie among Blacks in the United States, West Africa, South America, and the West Indies, the opportunity for upward mobility of the petite bourgeoisie in these different locales varies. The group in the United States is particularly weak, having little opportunity or no ability to exploit the labor power of Black workers. Furthermore, any significant hope of enlarging this group is an idle dream, because, as Braverman (1974) points out, those individuals who in earlier times might have become small-business persons for the most part have opportunities only to become employees of capital, that is, a part of the *new petite bourgeoisie* (Braverman 1974:403–409).

As Du Bois argues, the period of radical Reconstruction was the only time that there was an opportunity for the United States to eliminate race instead of class as the principal stratifying process. As the United States became a contender for the hegemonic position in the capitalist world, as capital expanded to incorporate the African, Asian, and Latin American peripheries more securely under its control, and as the core ruling classes consolidated their rule through a social democratic alliance with sections of the organized working class, racism became pervasively integral to the structures of authority (as an open or tacit form of legitimation) and to the structures of rule (to which matters of legitimacy are strictly incidental). These relations of rule and authority are complemented in the world-scale social system of production by the intensification of core-periphery polarization, itself a reflection of the ordinary working of the capitalist world economy. Wage structures followed suit everywhere; white workers received higher wages and people of color lower wages. In the core during this period the United States was the only principal locale of nonwhite workers. Since inequality was a given, this racial distinction anchored the principal social arrangements of structures of rule (by both government and organizations) and structures of production (as administered and developed by increasingly large-scale—that is, centralized, concentrated—capital).

The world-scale scope of racism, as fundamental to rule and to the determination of wage scales, made equality a historical impossibility in the United States. No matter what the Communist Party of the USA did, inequality between white workers and people of color would have remained a central feature of the society. Only a successful revolution, which would have to have been a world revolution, could have changed this situation.

Nonetheless, an American Communist Party made up disproportionately (not necessarily predominantly) of Black and Latino workers and intellectuals would have seriously altered the relations of force between capital and labor in the United States and would have been a much more serious obstacle to the consolidation of a white-dominated and exclusionary social democratic alliance in the United States.

The social democratic alliance accepts both the hegemony of capital and implicitly a racially structured capitalist world economy, which allows white workers to assume an intermediate position in the social division of labor. From the perspective of the dominant strata of the United States, the second reconstruction simply sought to assimilate Blacks, Puerto Ricans, Mexican Americans, and other historically disadvantaged groups to the subaltern intermediate strata, whose job it was to manage the subordinate classes in the United States and in the world capitalist division of labor. This was not responsive to Dr. King's 1963 challenge that the United States live out the true meaning of its creed, movement toward a truly collective commonwealth which he later envisioned would unite with the barefoot people of the world.

The world-system's relations of rule cut two ways. The mobilization of these subaltern strata did not simply serve the aims of the ruling classes of the United States and the capitalist world. Never are the class alliances of the world-system so unidimensional. As in most cases, these subaltern strata, despite their embeddedness in the capitalist world economy, had a historical consciousness that sought to make arrangements on their own terms. These classes were of course also embedded in oppressed communities whose lives manifested a phenomenon close in some ways to the colonial experience, though in some ways more intense in terms of political psychology. The complexities of what could be called an instance of domestic colonialism gave rise to an alternative to the capitalist project among those who were more closely related to the lower strata in these communities. This alternative was manifest in various oppositional or counterhegemonic ideologies: Black Power, cultural nationalism, Afrocentrism, revolutionary nationalism, social democracy, Marxism, womanism, Black Liberation theology, and so on. The proportion of the Black intelligentsia who supported one or another of these counterhegemonic ideologies tended at various times to hold sway over this social group.

This was true during the New Negro movement of the post–World War I period and during the various movements that came to the fore during the nationalist movements of the 1930s, the movements associated with the popular front during the 1930s and 1940s, and the movements of the 1960s and 1970s. This is a very broad swath of time and a quite remarkable occurrence for a group that has lived in the core of the capitalist world for more than a century and that is still politically associated with the radicals on the periphery of the capitalist world economy. Thus, in the 1960s, when Malcolm X argued that African Americans and other oppressed groups in the United States were not a minority but a part of the majority of the have-nots of the capitalist world, he captured the key point of what Du Bois had argued for most of the century. Malcolm articulated a sense of self that had long existed in the deepest recesses of the Black imagination and had been suggested by the most visionary Black leaders since the time of Henry Highland Garnet and David Walker. When Du Bois argued at the turn of the century that the problem of the twentieth century would be the problem of the color line, he was bringing forward a vision with deep roots. Dr. Du Bois would ultimately do the deep theoretical formulation that revealed the power of this vision, but it was like a part of the collective unconscious of the Black population.[15] When able to give expression to this sense, the people became infused with a transcendent spirit that gave them exceptional spiritual power. When King called for unity with the barefoot people of the world against the biggest purveyor of violence, inequality, and oppression on the face of the earth, the U.S. government, the stage was set for the final showdown between the rulers of the capitalist world and their subaltern allies, and the overwhelming majority of the people of the world. This staging had to be undone in no uncertain terms. The murders of Malcolm X, King, Fred Hampton, Bunchy Carter, George Jackson, and dozens of members of the Black Panther Party were deliberate actions of a counterinsurgency designed to destroy this movement in its tracks. There is a tendency in the movement itself to view revolution in cataclysmic terms and therefore to view what the movement was doing as prerevolutionary. The state had a clearer appreciation of the problem posed to the fundamental inequalities of the status quo. They moved aggressively to stop this movement.

W.E.B. Du Bois had himself been a victim of such repression, regardless of his assiduous avoidance of the language of violent revolution and his vocation as a Fabian socialist, a Pan-African nationalist, a Pan-African internationalist, and a revolutionary Marxist over the course of his life. His attempt to simultaneously engage the African world inside U.S. borders, the African world outside U.S. borders, the dark world, and progressive people everywhere was clear to the defenders of the existing power relations of the world-system. Again, Black particularisms were the crucible of a position that was truly internationalist and revolutionary. This was the lesson that many millions of people took from the teachings, writings, and practices of the great African American intellectual and activist W.E.B. Du Bois.

3

The Class-First, Race-First Debate: The Contradictions of Nationalism and Internationalism and the Stratification of the World-System

As we saw in Chapter 2, Dr.W.E.B. Du Bois's monumental struggle against white world supremacy took its radical turn initially from the push given him by the New Negro Movement, which formed during the period of World War I and the Great Migration of the African American and Afro-Caribbean people to the cities of the United States. The New Negro radicals of that period were embroiled in a fierce debate about the merits of a race-first versus a class-first strategy. The details of this debate are little known today, but the substance of the debate remains an ongoing feature of contention about strategies for the advancement of Black people in the United States and throughout the world. As I have argued elsewhere (Bush 1999), the New Negro radicals transformed the *rapport de force* of the relationship between the dominant and subordinate strata in U.S. society and influenced the rise of radical and revolutionary sentiment in other parts of the African diaspora.

By the 1960s the Black freedom struggle had placed these issues before the U.S. American public in such a powerful manner that the entire society began to open up to the voices of the oppressed in an unprecedented fashion, as I describe in Chapters 4 and 5. While many saw the civil rights movement as an attempt to complete the program of social democracy introduced by the New Deal (or more grandiosely as an attempt to complete the "Great American Revolution"), the civil rights revolution and the movements that emerged in its wake eventually came to be seen by many whites (under the leadership of an intelligentsia that was now concerned about the stability of U.S. power in the wider world) as a movement of special interests that defected from the alleged universal programs of the New Deal.

Within this context, many now argue that the conservative realignment that took place during the post–civil rights period was a justified response of the beleaguered white working and middle classes to the narrow agenda of the civil rights movement and its allied movements. Charles Krauthammer (1990), A. M. Rosenthal (1995), and Jim Sleeper (1991) have articulated this position most clearly. Thomas Byrne Edsall and Mary Edsall (1992) have written extensively about this phenomenon.

The nature of these responses was influenced by changes in *rapports de force* in U.S. society and on a world scale. Because of these changes in *rapports de force* against the hegemonic U.S. strata, a small but important section of the liberal intelligentsia (many of whom had been on the left during the 1930s and 1940s) were upset at the instability of U.S. power, which they saw as a positive force in world affairs, and dramatically defected from the great society. These intellectuals came to be called neoconservatives, and they provided a sophisticated intellectual agenda for the Right. With its rise during the 1980s, the Right built its program on the basis of the legitimating the ideas of the neoconservative intelligentsia: color blindness, family values, the meritocracy, individualism. The ideological transformations of this period would finally undermine liberalism as the hegemonic ideology in the world-system.

While the response of intellectuals more partial to the "truly disadvantaged" has varied from outraged on the part of Adolph Reed, Jr., Julian Bond (1991), Stephen Steinberg (1995), and Robin D.G. Kelley (1997) to defensive and measured on the part of William Julius Wilson (1979, 1987), I want to point out that we are essentially replaying a form of the class-first/race-first debate from the early twentieth century, and we would do well to reexamine that debate so that we can position our current debate in an understanding of the *longue durée* of our historical social system.

Race, Class, and Agency

I would thus like to take a longer view on this debate by going back to the historical grounding of the class-first/race-first debate. My position is somewhat unorthodox to be sure, but I think it certainly merits a hearing.

In the nineteenth century there existed two antisystemic movements that speak to the issues of racial conflict and social class conflict that we address today. Karl Marx and Friedrich Engels described the specter that haunted Europe, the specter of communism.[1] The logic of the workers' movement seemed inexorable. Marx and Engels analyzed how capitalism concentrated workers in urban areas, formed the context in which social production was to evolve, and described with remarkable elegance the contradictions of capitalism. They elaborated a powerful analysis of how capitalism would produce its own grave diggers, would disgrace itself in its degradation of workers, and would undermine our humanity by reducing everything to the cash nexus.

Marx and Engels could not analyze the full scope of the capitalist incorporation of the noncapitalist world, however, because this did not happen during their lifetimes. While some Marxists have not gone far beyond their original account of primitive accumulation, others have ascertained more fully the impact of capitalism's worldwide impact as it leveled the noncapitalist world, bending it to its own aims and in the process destroying much of value in those societies. The historical formation of Western hegemony involved an incalculable attack on the non-Western world.

Anouar Abdel-Malek (1981:72–73) provides a precise reading of this phenomenon:

1. The first wave of invasions, looting, penetration, occupation was to hit the Islamic-Arab . . . area, from the ninth century, from the crusades to Zionist militarism.

2. The second, more humanely murderous wave reached for the African continent, with the subsequent hemorrhage caused by the slave trade, which has so deeply influenced the potential of contemporary Africa.

3. The third wave was to destroy the Indian civilizations and societies in central and South America, subjugated by the Hispanic and Portuguese seaborne empires.

4. The last and final wave reached for south Asia, mainly the Indian subcontinent, and then south-east and, in the last instance East Asia.

The rising bourgeoisies of the West thus succeeded in destroying the centers of power of the three continents and in accumulating in their zones their material wealth and cultural potential. This is much more than primitive accumulation; it is a brutal assault, a criminal assault by an oppressive social system whose logic twisted the humanity of those who prosecuted it to a cold-blooded bottom-line mentality to which all else—all else—was subjected.

What a contrast. Marx and Engels were implacable critics and opponents of the capitalist world, yet they presented it as a progressive system that transformed the precapitalist world for the better. The view of Egyptian intellectual Anouar Abdel-Malek could not be more different. He is critical of the Eurocentrism of the Pan-European world. Rather than progress, could we say that there is a particular sense of evil embedded in the capitalistic system? I would like to preface our detailed history of the class-first perspective with two perspectives on Eurocentrism: one from the non-European world, from the Peruvian scholar Anibal Quijano, and one from the Pan-European world, from the U.S. scholar Immanuel Wallerstein.

Quijano points out that capitalism integrates and exploits workers under all forms of labor (wage labor, slave labor, commodity production, etc.), utilizing gender and race as mechanisms of domination. Prior to the advent of global capitalism, gender, age, and labor power were clearly the oldest of the attributes used in the process of the social classification that constructed and maintained power relations. With the foundation of the Americas, phenotype was added, which became the social classification on which the concept of race was based.

It would be difficult, Quijano emphasizes, to exaggerate the importance of the meaning of the category of race for the modern, colonial, Eurocentric capitalist model of global power, for this process enabled the production and elaboration of new social identities, and their distribution in global capitalist power relations was established and reproduced as the basic form of societal classification and as the foundation for new geocultural identities and their power relations in the world. Race came also to serve as the foundation for the production of intersubjective relations of domination and a new epistemological perspective that was imposed throughout the world as the only source of rationality.

The racialization of power relations between these new social and geocultural identities was the foundation of the Eurocentrism of this model of material and intersubjective power and pervaded all other areas of social existence in that model of power (Quijano 2006:23). As a consequence of this particular structuring of power, Quijano argues, although race and social class are conceptually separate and viewed as external to each other, social classes under capitalism have always been differentially distributed among the populations of the earth on the basis of the coloniality of power (capitalists, wage labor, middle classes, and independent peasants in the Euro-core, and tributary capitalists, dependent associates, slaves, serfs, small independent mercantile producers, reciprocal workers, wage workers, middle classes, and peasants in the colonial periphery). It is precisely this set of power relations that has allowed the capitalists to shape and finance the loyalty of the exploited or dominated whites against the other "races" (Quijano 2006:26–27).

Wallerstein's assessment of Eurocentrism involves an extended debate about precisely what constitutes Eurocentrism. He opposes those who say that whatever Europe did, others were also doing up to the moment when Europe used its geopolitical power to interrupt the process in other parts of the world. He also opposes those who say that what Europe did is nothing more than a continuation of what others had already been doing for a long time, with the Europeans temporarily achieving hegemony for a limited time—a relatively short time in the long history of the world, which they consider to have been a capitalist world for thousands of years. He calls these two conceptions of Eurocentrism Eurocentric anti-Eurocentrism (Wallerstein 1999:177–178).

Wallerstein agrees, however, with the third argument, which holds that whatever Europe did, it has been analyzed incorrectly and subjected to inappropriate extrapolations, which have dangerous consequences for both science and the political world (Wallerstein 1999:178). His position is that Europe's achievement is indeed different from what others were doing and that there were societal limitations in these civilizations that prevented them from launching modernity and capitalism and going on to conquer the world and exploit resources and people. Whereas there have always been some people who were involved in commercial activities and thus sought profits in the marketplace, in none of these worlds were the capitalist ethos and practice dominant. Other loci of power and values were always able to rein in the power of the capitalists and thus of the market economy. Why did this change in Europe?

Wallerstein attributes the change to the development of the structures of knowledge in Europe that were different from previous structures of knowledge, structures that gave priority to a particular kind of scientific thought. Scientific thought antedates the modern world and is present in all major civilizations.

What is specific about the structures of knowledge in the modern world-system is the concept of *two cultures*" the divorce between science and philosophy/ humanities, or what Wallerstein refers to as the separation of the true from the good and the beautiful. We have thus in the West the figure of the scientist, a value-neutral specialist whose objective assessment of reality forms the basis not only of engineering decisions but also of sociopolitical decisions. The affect of the two cultures was to remove the major underlying social decisions we have been taking for the past five hundred years from substantive (as opposed to tech- nical) scientific debate. Here Wallerstein formulates the impact of Western "ra- tionality" in a way that completely exposes the manner in which it has concealed its secrets from the world and from the general public in the West as well. Our inability to treat simultaneously the true and the good has undercut our ability to think with any degree of social intelligence, because such questions have no standing in the scientific canon of the forms of knowledge that prevail in the Pan-European world and the world where its views prevail.

It is for that reason that I argue in what may seem a reckless or shocking fashion that a cold-blooded bottom-line mentality has been written onto the su- peregos of the populations of the core states. This is despite the fact that we see ourselves as virtuous and good and at least good-intentioned, even if our leaders make mistakes and blunders in their policy formulation and implementation. We can learn from those outside the cultural blinders that imprison our mentali- ties and from those whom Patricia Hill Collins (1991:11-13) calls "the outsiders within."

This again emphasizes the significance of our need to learn the lessons of the struggle for social equality from the perspective of the enslaved Africans who produced this other great movement, a captive people locked in a stolen land who articulated an internationalist and egalitarian vision that did not stem from the Euro–North American workers movement but that had its own logic. That they constituted the most dynamic and militant wing of the world proletariat should be noted, but their captivity and their status as an internal colony in the bowels of the capitalist metropolis, ultimately the center of metropolitan capital- ism, is of enormous import here.

We all know the story of the European workers' movement: the theoretical commitment to internationalism, the rise of imperialism, the entering of the work- ers into a social democratic compromise, the resulting pro-imperialist and procapi- talist stance among white workers, all resulting in what we call the taming of the dangerous classes. V. I. Lenin and the Bolsheviks attacked the fat-cat working classes of Western Europe and split with the Second (socialist) International to form the Third (Communist) International, a revolutionary socialist movement dedicated to destroying capitalism by any means necessary.

The Bolsheviks seized power in a semiperipheral zone of the capitalist econ- omy and declared that they would hold on until the proletariat came to power in the advanced industrial countries in which the potential to build a proletarian socialist society was strongest. The proletariats of the advanced industrial zones rose in revolt but were everywhere crushed. The Bolsheviks were forced to go it alone, giving rise to the doctrine of socialism in one country.

In the meantime, the petit bourgeois socialists of Western Europe had abandoned their internationalist pretensions for a pro-imperialist line reinforced by an ideology of Pan-European racism that reasserted the superiority of white, Western civilization. This was, of course, consistent with the positions of Marx and Engels.

Enslaved Africans underwent a Pan-African evolution, however, because of the conditions of their captivity, having a variety of African peoples thrown together and at least in the North experiencing an attempt to suppress all expressions of their African cultures. Scholars differ in their interpretation of these phenomena, that is, whether these expressions were effectively suppressed or whether they merely went underground. There is agreement, though, that these conditions of captivity led to the development of a common culture, a quite extraordinary achievement that in my view reinforced the already existing tendencies toward Pan-Africanism.

The tradition of field Negro revolt that emerged was an alternative and more vigorous expression of proletarian revolt than all of the European workers' movements. We know the stories of some of the actors here: Denmark Vesey, Henry Highland Garnet, David Walker, and Nat Turner. We need not look at the details of all these stories.

At the turn of the century the Trinidadian barrister Sylvester Williams called for the first Pan-African Congress, at which Du Bois first articulated his notion that the problem of the twentieth century is the problem of the color line.

World War I created conditions that loosened the chains of social control throughout the world, making way for rebellions. One of the most significant groups that emerged out of these postwar conditions was the New Negro Movement. Du Bois even said this movement had left him far behind. During the 1920s, as we have seen, Du Bois moved dramatically away from the Fabian socialism of his earlier years. By the 1930s he had caught up with the race-first radicals of the New Negro Movement. We can better understand what this means if we review some details of the history of that movement.

The class-first position was articulated by militants and leaders of the Socialist Party. In response to a question about how they would deal with racism in the United States, the Socialist Party argued that they were the party of the proletariat and had no special program for any part of the class. Negroes, they held, were simply members of the working class. Racism would disappear with the establishment of a socialist society and the cessation of the exploitation of man by man. The basis of racism, they argued, was the divide-and-conquer tactics of capitalists who were seeking to pit one set of workers against another. Thus, any attempt to deal with the issue of racism before the establishment of a socialist society was divisive and played into the capitalists' divide-and-conquer tactics. A. Philip Randolph and Chandler Owen of the *Messenger* Group were the main proponents of the class-first position among Black people.[2] When they later organized the Brotherhood of Sleeping Car Porters and the March on Washington Movement (both all Black), they declared a tactical retreat from that position.

The race-first position was supported by a large section of the leadership of the New Negro Movement. Hubert Harrison, Cyril Briggs, W. A. Domingo, Richard Moore, W.E.B. Du Bois, and Marcus Mosiah Garvey were well-known proponents of this position. With the exception of Garvey, these men were Black nationalists and socialists. Garvey could be called a social democrat. Those who took the race-first position held that Blacks were first and foremost victims of racial oppression, but they did not deny the importance of class. They argued that the class structure of U.S. society and of the capitalist world more generally can be understood only in terms of the impact of race and racial oppression. W.E.B. Du Bois's writings of the 1930s articulated this position clearly. He argued that the workers of color were the true proletariat of the world-system, while white workers occupied an intermediate position in the world division of labor. The psychological sop of racism undermined the commitment to equality among white workers, who instead guarded their position of relative privilege, acting as police over "niggers." Du Bois's very clear position of the 1930s came in the wake of a powerful body of literature reflecting the political thought of the New Negro Movement.

New Negro Radicalism and Race First

Winston James (1998) tells us that Hubert Harrison was a prodigious intellectual who devoted himself to the study of African and African American history, the social sciences, literature, and the natural sciences. After being fired from the post office because of his criticism of Booker T. Washington in a letter to the editor of the *New York Sun*, Harrison was employed full-time by the Socialist Party. A member of the Socialist Party since 1909, Harrison resigned in 1914 because of the party's lack of commitment to Black workers and their racist treatment of him. One of the chief architects of the race-first position of the New Negro radicals, Harrison was called the father of Harlem radicalism by none other than A. Philip Randolph, the main voice of the class-first position among the New Negro radicals. Winston James argues that Harrison was an inspiration for "two powerful and seemingly incompatible currents of black radicalism in Harlem: revolutionary socialism . . . and radical black nationalism" (James 1998:126). James divides Harrison's legacy into an early Socialist Party and Industrial Workers of the World phase, which inspired Randolph, and a later Black Nationalist phase of the Liberty League of Negro Americans, during which Harrison was closer to Marcus Garvey.

Such a distinction has to be made with a great deal of care, however, for as James points out, Harrison remained a socialist from the time that he discovered Marx to the end of his life. Harrison kept the socialist faith, but American socialism did not keep faith with Harrison, according to Winston James. Despite his fierce criticism of the Socialist Party and his tense relations with the party's New York City leadership, Harrison was not mystified by the failure of the Socialist Party to adequately address the special situation of the Black workers. They succumbed to the racist corruption of the American environment. The Socialist Party of America, like so many others, capitulated to "southernism."

Following are a few telling examples: There was no official condemnation of the white members of the Socialist Party in Tennessee who prevented a leading member of the party from lecturing to black people on socialism. The national office would not route Eugene Debs through the South during the presidential year because he let it be known that he would not remain silent on the race question while in the South. Harrison criticized a report by a leading party member that argued that race feelings were a consequence of biological evolution and not social circumstances. The writer of the report argued that "class-consciousness must be learned, but race consciousness is inborn and cannot be wholly unlearned" (quoted in James 1998:127).

The report went on to say that "where races struggle for the means of life, racial animosities cannot be avoided. Where working people struggle for jobs, self-preservation enforces its decrees. Economic and political considerations lead to racial fights and legislation restricting the invasion of the white man's domain by other races."

Harrison was clear that it was the Socialist Party itself that was responsible for the alignment along racial lines of the overall radical movement. A section of the Black radicals then decided that it was necessary for Blacks to respond with their own sense of racial solidarity since the socialists were acting on the basis of the naturalness and desirability of white solidarity. Once support for the Socialist Party had shrunk among the white population, they began to go to Black folks with their hats in their hands, calling for a doctrine of class first. Harrison concluded, "We say Race First, because you have all along insisted on Race First and class after when you didn't need our help" (Harrison 1997:81).

James holds that Harrison was a reluctant Black nationalist, the last resort of a Black socialist in a racist land. Harrison had long waited for a better day, when the white socialists would truly open their arms to their class sisters and brothers in the Black world, but feared that such a day would never come. In the meantime, Black people had to defend themselves, and the standard defensive ideology in a racist land is an ideology of racial nationalism for one's own race.

Any man today who aspires to lead the Negro race must set squarely before his face the idea of "Race First." Just as the white men of these and other lands are white men before they are Christians, Anglo-Saxons, or Republicans; so the Negroes of this and other lands are intent upon being Negroes before they are Christians, Englishmen, or Republicans. . . .

Sauce for the goose is sauce for the gander. Charity begins at home, and our first duty is to ourselves. It is not what we wish but what we must, that we are concerned with. The world as it ought to be, is still for us, as for others, the world that does not exist. The world as it is, is the real world, and it is to that real world that we address ourselves. Striving to be men, and finding no effective aid in government or in politics, the Negro of the Western world must follow the path of the Swadesha movement of India and the Sinn Fein movement of Ireland. The meaning of both these terms is "ourselves first." (Harrison 1997:40)

Like Winston James, Clifton Hawkins (2000) dates Harrison's conversion to the race-first position to his experiences in the Socialist Party and the white Left milieu of that time. These experiences, Hawkins argues, disillusioned Harrison with cross-race organizing not only because of the pervasive racism of whites but also because of the defensive race consciousness of Blacks. Hawkins quotes Harrison as follows: "'Behind the color line,' Harrison sadly acknowledged, 'one has to think perpetually of the color line, and most of those who grow up behind it can think of nothing else.' . . . Race, not class, was the organizing principle of American life" (Hawkins 2000:51). By 1916, Hawkins argues, Harrison had embraced the *American* doctrine of race first (Hawkins, 2000:51; my emphasis).

Clifton Hawkins is blunt about how the New Negro radicals filled a void that had been vacated by the dubious tactics of the "old crowd" radicals. Of Dr. W.E.B. Du Bois's "close ranks" period, Hawkins argues, "Du Bois' self-interested accommodationism undermined his reputation and crippled his leadership among Afro-Americans of many persuasions, not merely the radicals. For decades afterwards, Du Bois extenuated, justified, agonized over, and apologized for his wartime stance. Although he resumed a militant stance in 1919, his temporary lapse no doubt facilitated the rise of new generation of militant, uncompromising Afro-Americans, represented in part by A. Philip Randolph, Chandler Owen, Wilfred A. Domingo, and other radicals associated with the *Messenger*" (Hawkins 2000:95–96).

Hawkins views the *Messenger* Group as a counterhegemonic enterprise. Randolph located the social base for his activities and aspirations in the working class (both Black and white) rather than in the Talented Tenth. For Randolph the role of intellectuals should have been in overcoming the hegemony that the master class and the master race exercised over the working class of all races, but this was not at all an unproblematic position, for it put him at odds with the major underpinnings of Afro-American culture and identity (Hawkins, 2000:163). Hawkins argues that Randolph was scathingly critical of all prominent civil rights organizations and educational institutions, holding that none of them were controlled in any considerable degree by Negroes. If not in the Talented Tenth, then where was the agency for the transformation of the United States in the first decades of the twentieth century? Hawkins notes that Randolph looked to the working class (Black and white) but sadly felt that they were victims of capitalist and white supremacist hegemony, both Black and white. Hawkins notes this statement of Randolph's: "As a group we are too sentimental and credulous. We are loath to judge Negroes by universal standards. We want to change the multiplication tables for the benefit of Negro incompetents" (quoted in Hawkins 2000:187). For Randolph the agents of working-class revolution needed the guidance of an organ of worker-intellectuals such as those in the ranks of the *Messenger* Group. But how would an intellectual vanguard such as the *Messenger* Group, given its own ambivalence about the relative merits of cultivated Blacks and working-class

Blacks, "inspire and mobilize a constituency so unlike themselves?" (Hawkins 2000:189).

Randolph had argued that the struggle against the ruling class was not simply a struggle in the workplace or at the ballot box; it was a struggle for the soul of humanity in the social order. It was in this context that the *Messenger* Group criticized every aspect of Afro-American life and called for Afro-Americans to "remake themselves, their culture, and their institutions in the very process of their liberation struggle" (Hawkins 2000:190). Hawkins does an excellent job of pointing out the contradictions and tensions in the *Messenger* Group. He clearly does not think such demands could be a realistic basis for a mass, working-class insurgency.

Hawkins's logic is clear here, but is it really true, historically speaking, that it is not possible for someone who is critical of the masses to organize an insurgency of these same masses? I would invite Hawkins to look at the example of Malcolm X, but this is merely a suggestion to which we will return for serious analysis later in this narrative. For now we might think about how Malcolm X (a clearly race-first leader and a member of an organization with a presence on the streets of most Black communities) differed from A. Philip Randolph and the *Messenger* Group (class-first radicals with a much smaller organizational footprint on the streets).

Hawkins argues that until 1919–1920 the New Negro Movement was ecumenical. Garvey had been introduced to Harlem by Socialist Party member Hubert Harrison. He had spoken at a rally with Randolph in 1916. In 1918 he helped Randolph, Owen, Monroe Trotter, and others form the International League of the Darker Races, whose goal was securing justice for Africans at the Paris Peace Conference. When Garvey felt so discouraged by infighting in the Universal Negro Improvement Association (UNIA) that he contemplated returning to Jamaica in the spring of 1917, he was encouraged to stay in the United States by Harrison and Domingo, who, along with Briggs and McKay, worked in the UNIA.[3] In fact, Garvey had appointed Domingo, a prominent socialist, to the position of editor of the UNIA's weekly newspaper, *The Negro World*.

In the tumultuous years 1919–1920 Hawkins argues, the state launched fierce attacks on militants in the Socialist Party and the Industrial Workers of the World. It was in this context, Hawkins argues, that Garvey distanced himself from the socialist-oriented members of the New Negro radicals. This entailed the dismissal of Domingo from his post as editor of *The Negro World* because of his inclusion of articles from the socialist press and because his socialist-oriented editorials conflicted with Garvey's race-first orientation. On June 21, 1919, agents of the Lusk Committee raided the Socialist Party–affiliated Rand School, where they found a document by Domingo arguing that the Achilles' heel of the socialist movement in the United States was its failure to attend to the need to effectively organize 12 million Negroes.[4] The discovery of this pamphlet caused a public sensation. On August 5 the district attorney summoned Garvey and grilled him on his connections to the Socialist Party, the Industrial Workers of the World, and the anarchists. Garvey, who as an immigrant was vulnerable in this area, replaced Domingo as editor of *The Negro World* with Hubert Harrison, a former member of the Socialist Party who maintained key aspects of his socialist class-based ideology but framed it in the context of a race-first political practice. Harrison argued that Blacks resented "not the exploitation of laborers by capitalists; but the social, political, and economic subjection of colored persons by white" (quoted in Hawkins 2000:239). The color line had trumped the class line.

Hawkins argues that the African Blood Brotherhood (ABB), *The Crusader*, and Cyril Briggs "propounded a coherent and wide-ranging ideology that cogently united Garvey's 'race first' and Randolph's 'class first' philosophies" (Hawkins 2000:336–337).[5] For Hawkins there were three attempts to inject class consciousness into the UNIA. Harrison, McKay, and Domingo worked within the UNIA, hoping to persuade its members to embrace socialist ideas and analysis. Randolph and Owen (and Domingo after his forced exit) criticized the UNIA from outside. The ABB, a parallel organization, sought to gather enough recruits, publicity, and power to negotiate with the UNIA on equal terms, thus securing a hearing for a position that sought to combine race and class.

While James and Hawkins view Harrison's evolution from a member of the Socialist Party to a Black nationalist as a tactical maneuver by a socialist who in a racist society both advocates and unites with the defensive Black nationalism of the Black masses, James views the trajectory of the ABB quite differently. Cyril Briggs, the founder of the ABB, started out as a Black nationalist and, combining elements of Black nationalism and revolutionary socialism, evolved more and more in the direction of revolutionary socialism until the ABB was finally merged into the Workers Party (Communist Party of the United States of America [CPUSA]) sometime after most of its national leadership had become party members.[6]

While James presents his investigation of this process in the form of an interrogation of the reason for the ABB leadership's move to the CPUSA, he really seems clear about the reasoning. Indeed, for all his detailed analysis seeking to prove or understand the relationship between the ABB and the CPUSA, Winston James seems clearer than any other scholar who has published substantial commentary on this issue.

The year 1919 was a tumultuous one. White mobs rioted against Blacks in twenty-six U.S. cities and were confronted with Blacks fighting back, resulting in considerable bloodshed on both sides. For this reason it has come to be known as the "Red Summer." In the December 1919 edition, The *Messenger* issued an editorial titled "Thanksgiving Homily to Revolution." They called the Russian Revolution the greatest achievement of the twentieth century. They gave thanks for "the German Revolution, the Austrian Revolution, the Hungarian Revolution, and the Bulgarian Revolution" (quoted in Vincent 1973:46). They gave thanks for the unrest that swept so much of the world, manifested in "titanic strikes . . . sweeping Great Britain, France, Italy, the United States, Japan, and every country of the world." They gave thanks for the solidarity of labor, the growth of industrial unionism, the growing radicalism of the U.S. working class, the general strike in Seattle, the growth of the New Negro Movement and its involvement in socialist politics, and what they called "the speedy oncoming of the new order of society" (quoted in Vincent 1973:47).[7]

The Founding Congress of the Communist International announced, "The epoch of the final, decisive struggle has come later than the apostles of the socialist revolution [Marx and Engels] expected and hoped. But it has come." The CPUSA argued that "Europe is in revolt. The masses of Asia are stirring uneasily. Capitalism is in collapse. The workers of the world are seeing a new life and securing new courage. Out of the night of war is coming a new day." Even the American Socialist Party declared that "[t]he Capitalist class is now making its last stand in history" (quoted in James 1998:164).

In addition to the sense that the hour of the proletarian revolution was at hand, Black radicals were attracted to Bolshevism because of the nationalities policies of the Soviet Union, especially toward Jews; its uncompromising rhetoric of anticolonialism, anti-imperialism, and the right of nations to self-determination; and the policies, practices, and proclamations of the Communist International. As far as Briggs and the Black radicals associated with the ABB were concerned, the Bolsheviks were the deadly enemies of the very same people who were the most trenchant enemies of Black people around the world. So despite their sincere adherence to the race-first position emphatically reasserted at this time in the pages of *The Crusader*, the embrace of the revolutionary socialist tradition adhered to by the Bolsheviks and the Communist International made perfect sense in the minds of the ABB radicals. Thus, when members of the leadership of the ABB joined the Workers Party of America (CPUSA), this was the only means by which they could join the Communist International, to which they gave their primary allegiance.[8] They felt that even if the white members of the Workers Party were hypocrites with feet of clay, the Comintern would force them to follow the right policy.

Race First and Internationalism

Keith Griffler (1993) disputes the assertion that the U.S. Communist movement inherited the pure-class approach of the Socialist Party out of which the class-first notion associated with the *Messenger* Group in African American parlance is assumed to have derived. Griffler argues that an alternative to the pure-class view developed simultaneously in the United States and in the Soviet Union. This view originated in the United States with the leading theoreticians of Black radicalism and in the Soviet Union with the leading theoreticians of Russian Marxism.

Both Marx and Engels had commented on the centrality of the "Negro question" to the issue of class and social struggle in the United States. Marx argued that liberation of labor in white skin could not happen as long as it was branded in Black skin. Engels argued that "race privilege" had trumped class privilege from the inception of the republic. By the turn of the century, these insights would be abandoned by the leading light of the Socialist Party, Eugene Debs. Griffler cites an article in the socialist periodical *New Solidarity* titled "There Is

No Race Problem": "The problem of the workers is not a race problem. There is [sic] no white or brown races. All have but one problem to solve, and that is the problem of how to overthrow the system of slavery under which all are bound to the employing class. When this problem is solved there will be no race problems" (quoted in Griffler 1993:40).

Griffler also quotes W.E.B. Du Bois, who he says gave up on the Socialist Party as a vehicle for transforming the social position of Black folks. Du Bois held that the Socialist Party lacked the "political courage" to face up to the race problem, and for that reason he did not foresee any substantial Black support for or openness to a socialist program without some wrenching changes in circumstances. How wrenching? Griffler argues that nothing short of a social revolution forced a change in the attitude of Black people in the United States toward socialism.

What made for the change? Griffler cites the elevation of the national and colonial question by Lenin and Leon Trotsky.[9] As is well-known, Lenin showed an interest in African Americans, arguing that their social position in the American South was equivalent to that of the Russian serf except that in addition to the grinding class oppression, they were burdened by an all-pervasive racial oppression. In 1916 he argued that the American Negro should be classified as an oppressed nation and in 1920 took this position to the Second Congress of the Communist International, where he made it part of a special commission he headed, which produced "Theses on the National and Colonial Question." It was at this congress that Lenin made the acquaintance of Otto Huiswood, a member of the ABB and a charter member of the CPUSA.

Leon Trotsky, the second-ranking member of the Communist International had lived in the United States. He wrote the "Manifesto of the Communist International to the Workers of the World," in which he argued that the most important consequence of World War I was that it called attention to "the infamy of capitalist rule in the colonies" and highlighted "the problem of colonial slavery" like never before. It was Trotsky who authored the famous statement referred to over and over by again by the New Negro radicals: "Colonial slaves of Africa and Asia! The hour of proletarian dictatorship in Europe will strike for you as the hour of your own emancipation" (quoted in Griffler 1993:43). Later Trotsky made contact with Claude McKay during his stay in the Soviet Union and commissioned him to write a treatise on the Negro question; it was later reissued in English as *The Negroes in America.*

ABB founder Cyril Briggs, who had refused to join the Socialist Party because it did not recognize the special character of Negro oppression in the United States, was so impressed by the solution to the national problem in the Soviet Union that he joined the CPUSA, confident that the American party would in time follow the lead of the Soviet party.[10] Griffler shows that W. A. Domingo and Otto Hall shared Briggs's sentiments.[11]

Griffler holds that Briggs was the earliest and most original of the Black radical intellectuals of this period. While Briggs was a member of both the ABB and the CPUSA, he held to the race-first position, which placed race consciousness at the forefront of Black radicalism. He argued that race consciousness was a weapon that Blacks could not dispense of since it lay at the heart of the rise and fall of nations and races and was constantly utilized by other people. The ABB, according to Griffler, "explicitly linked the destiny of African American workers to that of all people of African descent" not simply as a part of the U.S. working class but as representatives of a people dispersed throughout Africa, Latin America, and North America. They constituted not so much a peculiarly "American problem" but part of a much larger question that could be understood only in a world context (Griffler 1993:61–62). McKay also insisted that Blacks the world over could not afford to ignore the Negro question but had to insist on its resolution over and above the class question. He argued that for the Left the Negro question demanded attention on its own terms but also that its correct resolution was required before the resolution of the class question.

Richard Moore would add the proviso that large sections of the white working class of Europe, North America, and Africa "are bribed with a share of the imperialist spoils drawn out of the toil and degradation of the Negro masses, and are filled with white imperialist propaganda against these workers" (quoted in Griffler 1993:70). This meant that the labor problem could not be solved unless the race problem was solved. If white workers and their Communist Party did not renounce caste privilege, they were not only not revolutionaries but enemies of the revolution.

By 1925, Griffler argues, Black radicals had divided into three camps, one group associated with the Communist Party, another with the Socialist Party, and a third made up of independents such as the veteran W.E.B. Du Bois and the young Abram Harris.12 The socialists clung to the Debsian position, allying themselves with the racist American Federation of Labor. The Black Communists attempted to put their internationalist line into practice. Griffler argues that under the leadership of Du Bois, the independent group articulated a middle-class nationalist program that refused any contact with white workers. This group, according to Griffler, shared the racial chauvinism of the Black Communists but had nothing but disdain for the masses of Black people.

While the leadership of the ABB had effectively merged with the CPUSA, the ABB program was not at all accepted by the white members and leadership of the CPUSA. ABB founder Cyril Briggs pointed out that most of the Negro work of the CPUSA from 1919 to 1929 was of a sporadic nature, intended as a gesture to impress the Comintern. Briggs understood white chauvinism in the CPUSA as a general underestimation of the importance of the Black masses to the overall revolutionary struggle. The CPUSA, Briggs pointed out, had even opposed the spontaneous migration of southern Blacks to the industrial North on the basis that they would hurt the economic position of northern white workers, a position that Briggs equated to Social Democracy and the American Federation of Labor. The CPUSA not only failed to consult the senior Black cadre in the party's Negro work; they "utilized the old bourgeois trick" of assigning the least militant of the oppressed race to the work among the oppressed races (Briggs 1929).

According to ABB leader W. A. Domingo, the Negro question was the touchstone, the measure of sincerity of white radicals in the United States. Domingo held that the strategic position of Black workers in the industrial arena gave them a power out of proportion to their numbers (McKay 1979:40).

Further, Griffler points out, the Black Communists had to carry their case to the Communist International, which they did beginning with the Second Congress in 1920, at which ABB and CPUSA member Otto Huiswood met Lenin. In his report to the CPUSA, Huiswood presented the conclusions of the Comintern's Negro Commission, in which he placed the Negro question in the domain of the colonial question. It was indeed Lenin who argued that the Communist parties of the imperialist countries had a special obligation toward the oppressed nations and colonial peoples, especially those oppressed by their own imperialists. Since Lenin had included American Negroes in this special category, Huiswood was able to say that an adjustment of CPUSA policy was required. The CPUSA had argued in 1920 that the class war knew only the capitalist class and the working class. Later the party's trade union wing would argue that the idea that white workers were relatively privileged was employer-inspired propaganda (Griffler 1993:76). Senior Black cadre such as Otto Huiswood and Richard Moore were criticized by the party leadership for speaking out against instances of white chauvinism in some party organizations.

In 1925, when Lovett Fort-Whiteman wrote an article in the Comintern's international organ, *The Communist International*, criticizing the failure of the CPUSA to recognize or implement the Comintern's understanding of the Negro question, the Comintern leadership took the unusual step of appending editorial comments supporting Fort-Whiteman's criticism.[13] The CPUSA was effectively held up for ridicule before the world Communist movement. Fort-Whiteman had characterized them as Social Democrats, who were viewed by Communists as decidedly reformist and not revolutionary.

In 1917–1918, A. Philip Randolph of the *Messenger* Group enjoyed positive relations with the radicals who would later become members of the ABB and the CPUSA. During this period, according to Griffler, Randolph was as critical of the AFL as any, calling it "a machine for the propagation of race prejudice" (Griffler 1993:95). It might be useful to recall that Randolph and Chandler Owen were often known during those days as the Lenin and Trotsky of Harlem. Even in 1919 Randolph differed from most of the New Negro radicals, whose emphases were invariably on the Negro question. Randolph argued that the "Negro question" was a red herring introduced not by Black radicals but by the employing classes. For Randolph as for most of the members of the Socialist Party, this was a divide-and-conquer scheme. Griffler attributes the hardening of Randolph's position to his election to the head of the Brotherhood of Sleeping Car Porters in 1925, at which time the AFL was transformed in Randolph's eyes from a machine for the propagation of race prejudice to the champion of the African American people.

After Lenin's death and the expulsion of Trotsky from the Comintern, Stalin's ascension allowed, in Griffler's terms, for the transformation of the old internationalism of the Comintern into neo-Debsianism. This, according to Griffler, started with the Sixth Congress of the Communist International. Whereas Lenin had emphasized the distinction between oppressor nations and oppressed nations and the duty of Communists to support those oppressed by their own imperialism, the new class-against-class position of the third period of the Comintern exhorted Black Communists to impress on the mass of the Negro people that despite white workers' Negrophobia, the U.S. working class was the only revolutionary class that would be the mainstay of Negro liberation. Furthermore, the Comintern argued that the Black working class must be taught that the first rule of proletarian morality is that no worker who wants to be an equal member of his class must ever serve as a strikebreaker. This was apparently a break from the substance of the position previously advocated by the Comintern. Further, the Comintern dropped its criticism of the CPUSA, which was subsequently left to make its own way on the Negro question (Griffler 1993:126–127). As we shall see, this was consistent with the struggle against Mir Sayit Sultan-Galiev in the Communist Party of the Soviet Union.[14]

Griffler criticizes James Allen's formulation that the crisis in the Black Belt might have led the farmers to choose revolution before the urban proletariat did.[15] This could have led, in Allen's view, to uncontrollable race warfare. To avoid this possibility, it was of the utmost importance to ensure the hegemony of the working class in order to combat chauvinistic expressions.[16] The cure for Black chauvinism was an interracial movement for Black self-determination led by the Communist Party. Griffler is astounded that Allen does not even seem to notice that this formulation does away with the notion of self-determination of the Negro people altogether. The treatment of white chauvinism and Black Nationalism as twin (but not quite equal) dangers requiring the leadership of a predominantly white political party meant that the internationalist positions advocated by the former members of the ABB and the Comintern under Lenin were set aside.

Minkah Makalani (2004) lifts the debate about the relationship between the CPUSA and the ABB above the level of Communist conspiracy that is so often the foundation of the scholarship on the ABB. Makalani argues that the larger significance of the relationship between the ABB and international communism can be glimpsed in the debate between Lenin and M. N. Roy at the Second Congress of the Communist International.[17] Some will be familiar with this debate.

According to Makalani, Lenin transcended the more doctrinaire class-first position associated with most socialists in the Pan-European world. He opposed the dismissal of national liberation in the "backward" colonies because whatever the limitations of this movement from the perspective of socialist transformation, it was more important for "the working class in the oppressor nations to build an internationalism that opposed their own nationalism and material interests of their own ruling classes" (Makalani 2004:133–134). In this way the proletarian revolutionaries would demonstrate a genuine commitment to democracy, not one that asked the oppressed nations to put their grievances aside until they were liberated by the coming to power of the socialist movement. For Lenin this strategy applied foremost to Negroes in the United States who he regarded as an oppressed nation. The representative of the CPUSA, John Reed, disagreed with Lenin. He argued that U.S. Blacks merely sought social equality and, since they were concentrated mostly in the rural South, did not understand their op-pression as an extension of the class struggle. The duty of the U.S. Communists should be to redirect the racial consciousness of the Negro people into class consciousness.

Roy was much less sanguine about the social character of the national bour-geoisie in oppressed nations, which in his view tended to be reactionary. More important, Roy argued for a different relationship between the national libera-tion and the class struggle than was generally accepted in international commu-nism and socialism.

Makalani points out that Roy had developed this position long before the Second Congress. It was from Mexico in 1914 that he pointed out "that the na-tional liberation of India was central to breaking down the British Empire and capitalism" (Makalani 2004:137). In contrast to the notion that socialist revolu-tion would lead automatically to the liberation of the colonies as Engels had ar-gued in 1882, Roy held that it was the existence of the colonies in Asia and Af-rica that allowed the imperialist bourgeoisie to maintain social control over workers in the metropole, and that it would not therefore be possible to over-throw the capitalist system in Europe without the breaking up of the colonial empire (Makalani 2004:138). Lenin's position prevailed in the deliberations at the Second Congress of the Comintern, but from the perspective of the Black radicals it broke ranks with the previous practice of the Western Left by arguing that "communist parties must give direct support to the revolutionaries in the dependent countries and those without equal rights (e.g. Ireland, and among the American Negroes), and in the colonies" (Makalani 2004:139). Makalani argues that Roy's position would have placed the liberation of Africa and Asia (and I would add Blacks in the United States) at the center of the world socialist revolution. I think this is the more appropriate framework for understanding the significance of the ABB's approach to the Communist International and the CPUSA.

The final issue of *The Crusader* reported on the founding convention of the Workers Party (CPUSA), to which Briggs reported the ABB had sent delegates. This association would help to weaken white supremacy and would provide sup-port for the Black Liberation movement in the form of access to multiple publi-cations and printing presses, a large membership, and international connections, the most important of which he felt to be Soviet Russia. Makalani argues, as have others, that the ABB militants felt that they were joining an international revolutionary organization of which the CPUSA was a part, and that as members of an international organization they were free to put pressure on the CPUSA to follow the directives of the parent organization, particularly the "Theses on the National and Colonial Question," developed as the Second Congress of the Communist International. In the longer run, Makalani shows that the ABB moved the Communist International toward its own theoretical formula-tions. The "Theses of the Fourth Comintern on the Negro Question," written in 1922, outlined four areas of organizational activity among Blacks in the United States that directly reflected the ABB'S organizational program (Maka-lani 2004:152).

When the CPUSA finally began to respond to the pressure from the Comintern after the Fourth Congress, Black radicals, including ABB members, began to join the CPUSA. The CPUSA had actually altered its practice among Black people, had agreed to abide by the Comintern's "Theses of the Fourth Comintern on the Negro Question" (which was taken from the views of the ABB), and had agreed to help meet some of the needs of the ABB. While the relationship between the ABB and the CPUSA is portrayed as a symbiotic one, as Briggs indicated, Makalani argues quite forcefully that "the ABB never integrated into the Workers Party [the CPUSA] or relinquished organizational autonomy" (Makalani 2004:157). It was their own problems running the ABB that prompted the leadership to make a formal relationship with the Harlem branch of the Workers Party, especially given that most of the members of the ABB leadership were active members of the Harlem branch. Nonetheless, the Workers Party increasingly constrained the activities of its Black members, and the dissolution of the ABB itself meant that the Black radicals in the CPUSA were not able to promote an independent agenda that differed from the agenda of the leadership of the CPUSA.

Winston James is more to the point on this issue. He argues that the Black radicals, including the members of the ABB, did not see themselves as simply having joined the CPUSA. In their view, they were joining the American division of Lenin's multinational army of revolutionaries. For it was the Comintern who stated at their 1919 founding congress, "Colonial slaves of Africa and Asia! The hour of the proletarian dictatorship in Europe will strike for you as the hour of your own emancipation" (quoted in Winston 1998.180). The only way to join the Comintern was through one of its national branches, and that is what they did (Winston 1998:180–181).

The Road to Unity

Mark Solomon's treatment of the New Negro radicals varies in its angle from that of some of the other scholars we have discussed; Solomon views them through the prism of the Communist movement, which means that Solomon's focus is on the ABB more than on the other New Negro radicals, on the race-first position espoused especially by Cyril Briggs, and on Briggs's efforts at developing a synthesis of Black Nationalism and revolutionary socialism. Solomon shows a convergence of Briggs's views with those of the Communist International and the development of a strategy of working-class unity that sought not so much assimilation of the Black working class into the white working class but a strategy that would prevent an interclass alliance between white workers and white capitalists.

Because of his nationalist credentials, Solomon viewed Briggs as unique among the New Negro radicals in "introducing the twentieth-century revolutionary tide to black America" (Solomon 1998:7). Solomon views the March 1919 formation of the Communist International as a defining event whose hostility to the veiled colonialism of the League of Nations paralleled Briggs's view of the organization, described in the "League of Thieves," an article published in the March 12, 1919, edition of the *New York Amsterdam News*.

During and after the Red Summer of 1919, according to Solomon, Briggs forged an ideological link among national, race, and class consciousness that provided a basis for Blacks to join the Communist movement. Briggs reaffirmed the race-first position, saying that he was first, last, and always a Negro, that if he was ever deported (the nation was in the midst of a deportation hysteria) it should be to a free Africa. If the Polish and Jewish people sought a national existence, why shouldn't the Negro? At the same time, Briggs called for class unity between Black and white workers as the only means by which to break the power of capital over U.S. society and the power of imperialism and colonialism over people of African descent and of the dark world everywhere. The Soviets were viewed as allies of Black people's global aspirations, and anti-Bolshevism was viewed as a hypocritical cover for those who wished to undermine the ability of Black people to fight the racists who would deprive them of their rights. This line is not dissimilar from Stoddard's position in *The Rising Tide of Color* (see the introduction, "The Handwriting on the Wall").

What better company for Blacks than whites who stood up for the rights of Black people in a manner similar to the antislavery abolitionists? The connections between the ABB and the CPUSA during its formative years influenced the evolving character of the ABB and the degree to which Blacks themselves influenced Communist involvement in African American life. The ABB was based on "the themes of race patriotism, anticapitalism, anticolonialism, and organized defense against racist assault" (Solomon 1998:9–10). In addition, Briggs sought to fuse his own sense of African identity with Leninist internationalism, arguing, for example, that the destruction of capitalism and the creation of a socialist cooperative commonwealth was along the lines of "our own race genius as evidenced by the existence of Communist States in Central Africa and our leaning toward Communism wherever the race genius has free play" (Solomon 1998:13).

Could Blacks reject statehood and accept the "point of view of humanity"? (Briggs 2005:209) Here Briggs tread carefully. It might have been preferable to accept the socialist cooperative commonwealth, but the Negro had been so mistreated by the rest of humanity that he might be pardoned for looking at this issue from the perspective of a Negro rather than from the perspective of a humanity that has not always treated him humanely. Therefore, part of the strategy of liberation, from the perspective of the Negro, should involve the creation of a strong, stable, independent Negro state in Africa or elsewhere for the salvation of all Negroes. The socialist commonwealth would be the protective framework for Black national independence. The nature of the involvement of the Black world with the world and U.S. socialist movement would be that of an alliance in which a distinct Black agenda would be maintained (Solomon 1998:14).

Garvey was critical of the ABB's alliance with the Workers Party, arguing that the Communists might be worthy of sympathy but as white pariahs they could do nothing for their own cause, not to mention for Negroes. Briggs argued that the alliance with the Workers Party created international connections and a place for Black radicals on the stage of the world revolution. It forged links with two hundred thousand souls in groups tied to the Workers Party. This was quite different, Briggs argued, from Garvey's pathetic and useless groveling before presidents and monarchs who had engaged in ruthless exploitation and oppression of Black folks for centuries. Despite this criticism, the ABB radicals attempted to win Garvey and the UNIA to a more radical position, but they were ultimately ousted from the roster of the UNIA by Garvey. Though some prominent UNIA members who were frustrated with Garvey (Bishop George Alexander McGuire, James D. Brooks, and Cyril A. Critchlow) switched their allegiance to the ABB, the ABB was unable to win any substantial number of the UNIA rank and file to the ABB. In the meantime, the revolutionary tide in Europe began to recede with the collapse of uprisings in Germany and Hungary. Gradually the world capitalist system, widely thought by the revolutionary forces, as well as many others, to be on the brink of collapse, began to consolidate and re-stabilize itself. Mark Solomon points out that in the context of the conservative realignment, the accumulation of Blacks in the urban ghettos outside the South provided a degree of insularity from a hostile white society that they did not wish to engage. Without dangerously confronting the bourgeois order, Garvey's vibrant expressions of outrage had more appeal to these ghettoized communities than did the far more active confrontation urged by the ABB (Solomon 1998:27–28).

Solomon's verdict here seems plausible, but it is far from the only conclusion that one can draw from the contention between the two organizations and between their leaders, Marcus Garvey and Cyril Briggs. One approach to further investigation of this issue, which tends to be polarized along ideological lines, is to look more closely at the age-old issue of class consciousness versus status consciousness, whether in this case the latter be called racial or national.

We are indebted to Solomon for his close presentation of the debate on the Negro national question at the Sixth Congress of the Communist International. We already know some of the details of this from Harry Haywood's classic, *Black Bolshevik: Autobiography of an Afro-American Communist*. The Siberian Communist Charles Nasanov, who had served in the United States as a member of the Young Communist International and had known Heywood Hall during his stay in Chicago, renewed contact with Hall, who was studying at the Lenin School in the Soviet Union and who had changed his name to Harry Haywood.[18] Haywood tells us that Nasanov had a strong interest in the national and colonial questions and during his stay in the United States had reached the conclusion that Blacks in the South constituted an oppressed nation who should be entitled to the right of self-determination (Haywood 1978:218–219).

The details of the debate over the issue reveal a bewildering set of agendas and considerations that the members of the international and U.S. Communist movements sought to address. One is impressed with the subtleties of the dialectical imagination revealed in these debates and astonished at the statements of self-assured arrogance that presumed to proscribe the lives and destiny of an entire people on a decidedly mechanical application of Marxian historical materialism.

Solomon's presentation of the debate and the outcome is all the more interesting because he is one who is committed to the need for unity. His understanding is quite in the classical prescription of Lenin and others, however, who argue that true unity can only be the basis of an alliance of equals. This indeed is the line of one of the most embittered but still radical members of the former Communist theoreticians, Harold Cruse.

Solomon points out that those who argue against the idea that Blacks were an oppressed nation on grounds of lack of a common territory, economic system, language, and culture "neglect the bonds of memory, culture, and spirit in black American life, where the name 'Africa' adorned churches and civic and fraternal organizations." He notes in passing the attacks by Communists on "the sensitive barometers of Black longing (like Du Bois) as self-serving dilettantes seeking to monopolize the Negro market" (Solomon 1998:83). While Solomon understands such positions as a "grievous weakness in the great debate of 1928," he does not seem to comprehend the very degree to which Communists were walking on thin ice in their fierce critiques of Blacks as politically underdeveloped and lacking in class and political consciousness.

While he cites Nasanov's statement that "a people's sacred right to choose their own political life was a confirmation of their equality," he does not seem to see the proscriptions against separatism and the very attempt to define a nation in terms that would restrict someone's right to self-determination as inherently undemocratic.

Whether the term *race* or *nation* is used in this discussion the race-first versus class-first controversy is central to the debate in the U.S. Communist movement and the Communist International about the nature and solution to the oppression of the African American people. As Hubert Harrison and Cyril Briggs pointed out during the 1910s, the race-first position was a defensive reflex among Blacks against the depredations of a racist society. Indeed Winston James (1998:286) notes that correspondence between Briggs and Haywood during the 1960s reveals that they saw themselves as allies in the party debates about the nature of the Negro national question. James argues that "they stuck to the old line—even though at times they seemed overwhelmed by their own questioning." Briggs writes, "With Negro nationalism even then on the increase, as witness the Garvey movement, why did our Negro nation analysis have such little appeal to the Negro people?" (quoted in James 1998:286). Briggs thought that many of the thousands who passed through the party did not accept or understand that analysis.

While Solomon really seems to capture the extent to which the Communist movement's articulation of the Negro as a "nation within a nation" in the United States was key to the real democratization of the Communist movement and of the United States, in the last analysis the Left's attempt to grapple with Black Nationalism and the nationalism of other oppressed people has been grievously weak.

What, then, made Garvey so popular? Solomon is not the first to suggest that it is because his approach was less dangerous than that of his contemporaries.[19] In 1921 the class appeal of the Garvey movement was recognized by

Charles Latham, a State Department official who considered Garveyism more dangerous than communism. In one memo he wrote, "Though he is certainly not an intellectual his particular propaganda and agitation is considered dangerous in that it will find a more fertile field of class divergence than Bolshevism would be likely to find in the United States" (Martin 1976:232).

The Left (including the radical Left, which often takes strong antiracist positions) is frequently resistant to the idea that Garvey's ideas achieved such a wide audience among African peoples everywhere precisely because of his insistence on Black control of Black institutions and the need to reinforce the solidarity of the Black community against the white world. This is inevitably related to the class-first position of most of the Left, which feels that an emphasis on racism evades the subtleties of capitalist domination of the institutions of the modern world, and that therefore antiracist strategy must be mediated through approaches that include an implicit anticapitalist component.

What if antiracist strategies are anticapitalist by definition? This is certainly an overstatement, but if we look at the evolution of the struggle against Eurocentric Marxism, we may be able to shift our stance somewhat from the Eurocentric position that is often found in the literature of the world socialist movement.

Rethinking Race First versus Class First: African Americans in the Whirlwind

Having traversed some distance along the trajectory of an old debate about race, class, and nation in U.S. and world social movements, I would like now to try to establish where this debate has taken us. This will require an examination of the origins of the class-first stance in the history of the European workers' movement, the changing meaning of class over the history of the capitalist world-system and in the anticapitalist forces, the changing relations of force with the coming to power of the movements of the old Left in various zones of the world-system, and the relations of antiracist movements to the configuration of world-system power in the twentieth and twenty-first centuries.

The European Workers' Movement and the Origins of the Class-First Stance

The centrality of class in the discourse of the modern world-system originated in the interstices of the original core of the capitalist world economy in Europe. The social movements of the late nineteenth and early twentieth centuries were shaped by the social structures of the nineteenth century. These structures have been totally transformed in the course of the twentieth century and have given rise to their own social movements.

According to Arrighi, Hopkins, and Wallerstein (1989a), a variety of social groups found their traditional ways of life threatened by widening and deepening proletarianization. The groups included craftsmen, low-status professionals, servants, peasants, shopkeepers, and small traders. The effectiveness of the social movements initiated by these groups stemmed from the very changes brought about by the processes against which their struggles were directed: "the capitalist centralization and rationalization of economic activities" (Arrighi, Hopkins, and Wallerstein 1989a:78).

While earlier struggles, even those at the point of production, were essentially localized disturbances, the broadening and deepening of the capitalist process mentioned above transformed isolated laborers into a society-wide social stratum. This meant that their struggles became a social problem of significant social import. However, the main weakness of the labor movement of this period was precisely that the process of centralization and rationalization of capital had not gone far enough. In the main, wage workers of this period played a limited role in production and were the majority of the population in only a few countries.

The earliest attacks on industrial capitalism predated socialist thought. John Gurley (1982) explained that they stemmed from the wrenching changes that capitalism wrought on the precapitalist world—a world that was simpler, more rural and agricultural, and more religious. The massive inequalities and competitiveness of capitalist society were shocking in their impact. Furthermore, the change from a rural agricultural society to an urban industrial society disrupted family structures in its incorporation of child labor into a labor force mired in miserable living and working conditions. The initial critics of capitalism were the followers of Jean-Jacques Rousseau who sought a return to the simpler, uncorrupted life of the precapitalist period.[20] Thus, strong movements arose for the religious regeneration of humankind or the formation of utopian communities in which humankind could recreate conditions which favored their more optimal development. In the early period of industrial capitalism, it was easier for the critics of capitalism to visualize a step or two backward into a better life than to see it through the continued progress of existing society.

Although socialism was initially elaborated in 1827 in the work of Robert Owen (1827), these socialists were strongly influenced by Rousseau's theories of humankind and society. The early socialists favored a system of mutual cooperation, collective organization, social and economic planning, and common ownership of capital goods. The utopian socialists who flourished from roughly 1820 to 1860 believed that the evils of capitalism could be avoided and eventually eliminated through example. They advocated the construction of model communities in which cooperation and scientific order would produce economic abundance and harmony for all their members. Although some of the utopian communities (mostly religious ones) sought to escape from the world, for the most part they sought to influence and change the world.

Accounts of the European workers' movement often trace the definitive entry of the working class itself as a social force to Chartism, which was a movement in Great Britain to extend the franchise and to reform Parliament, with the aim of an immediate increase in the political power and the long run increase in the economic welfare of workers and other disadvantaged groups. Despite the economic aims at the basis of the Chartists' political demands, the movement itself was limited to the political plane because it did not have a definite economic program. Although the demands of the Chartist movement were repeatedly rejected by Parliament, the mobilizations the Chartists led eventually resulted in the establishment of the Ten Hour Bill, which for Marx was the first great victory for the political economy of the workers over the bourgeoisie.[21]

Marx and Engels were born in Prussia about thirty years after the outbreak of the French Revolution, in the midst of the Industrial Revolution. Engels was later to say that modern socialism was the direct product of the Enlightenment— the eighteenth-century intellectual movement in Europe that expressed confidence in human reason and thus in a rational and scientific approach to all problems. This movement fostered belief in inevitability of progress and the possibility of perfectibility from humankinds own efforts and attacked the dogmatism, spiritual authority, intolerance, and all other magisterial pronouncements of existing authorities. It advanced the notion that the people themselves, acting in harmony with the universal order, could bring about rational progress. Through its attacks on religion and absolutism and its advocacy of economic reforms and constitutionalism, the Enlightenment is thought to have figured prominently in bringing about the French Revolution.

The development of Marxism, specifically envisioned as a tool of combat for the working class and as a methodology for the analysis of society from the point of view of the working class, and the rise of a Marxist political movement have been central to the socialist movement of the last 150 years. As the Marxist system of theory and praxis grew, it absorbed the philosophies of three countries (French socialism, British Political Economy, and German Philosophy), the ideas of the working classes and the cultured strata, and the fruits of many areas of thought. The Marxist system of theory and praxis summed up an immense accumulation of knowledge, combined many streams of speculation, and endowed a new point of view with a more vivid and compelling life, specifically animated by its advocacy of a working class standpoint and scientific viewpoint in its analysis of capitalism.

Marx and Engels differed from other nineteenth-century socialists in the comprehensiveness and systematization of their thought, but the key political difference was that they did not imagine that socialism would be imposed on society from above by disinterested members of the ruling class. They believed that the bourgeoisie as a class could not be convinced to go against their interests. The key to the politics of revolutionary Marxism was the centrality of the class struggle, and the standpoint of the working class.

Marxism is not simply about class struggle, however. The power of Marxism is that it combines an analysis of humankind as the agent of its own emancipation (via the propertyless proletariat) with an analysis of the "laws of motion" of capitalist society and with the possibilities that might emerge from human intervention. To those who felt that it was enough merely to agitate among the people and allow the revolution to follow their wrath, Marx responded "that it was simple fraud to arouse the people without any sound and considered basis for their activity. The awakening of fantastic hopes . . . would never lead to the salvation of those who suffered, but on the contrary to their undoing" (quoted in Wilson 1972).

Marx had been a member of the League of the Just, which was renamed the Communist League in the spring of 1847. The rapid building of the European railroad during 1846 and 1847 had been followed by a severe depression in which some fifty thousand men were thrown out of work and 10 percent of the population of Berlin was living by crime or prostitution. The revolution broke out in France in February 1848 after the unprovoked firing by soldiers on a peaceful democratic demonstration.

The uprising against the French monarchy of Louis Philippe led the way in the great revolutionary tide that swept Europe in 1848. Uprisings occurred in Vienna against the Hapsburg monarchy, in Berlin against Frederick William IV, and in Milan, Venice, London, Belgium, and many smaller cities. Marx traveled first to France, where the provisional government gave him French citizenship and where he organized the secret return of hundreds of working-class cadre of the Communist League to Germany. In April and May Marx and Engels returned to Germany. In the ensuing revolutionary period in Germany, Marx and Engels opposed organizing the working class on the basis of its own demands before the bourgeois revolution was won.

Marxism was thus elaborated in a revolutionary environment to serve the interests of the urban working class, which was demanding higher wages, better working conditions, shorter hours, limits to child and female labor, and political representation. Yet there are contradictions between the conception of Marxism as a tool of combat or analysis and Marxism as a science, the basic principles of which are laid down for society and nature in the principles of dialectical materialism.

MARXISM VERSUS ANARCHISM

Wallerstein (1984) argues that the first great debate in the workers' movement was whether or not to organize at all. There was nothing obvious about long-term organizing. Throughout history oppressed groups have complained, demonstrated, and risen. But it was not until the nineteenth century that anyone took seriously the formation of formal organization that could mobilize and collect forces over a long period of time to achieve political objectives. Some thought that conspiratorial and rapid insurrection by a small elite was the correct strategy. Some thought that withdrawal into ideal communities based on the model of the utopian socialists was the right way. Some believed in terrorism via secret societies to disrupt corrupt societies and lay the ground for the re-establishment of optimal conditions for the flourishing of humanity. In contrast to these various versions of individual or small-group voluntarism, Marx believed that only the organized strength of the entire working class could defeat capitalism and create a socialist society.

The Paris Commune of 1871 was inspired more by the ideas of Mikhail Bakunin and Pierre-Joseph Proudhon (both anarchists) than by Marx, although

Marx hailed the commune.[22] Many workers were opposed to Marx's authoritarianism and centralist notions and to his proposals for nationalization of the means of production. They had greater regard for Proudhon's libertarian views, emphasis on the autonomy of small groups, and practical schemes for cheap credit and fair exchange for workers' products—ways of beating capitalism by peacefully constructing alternative economic institutions around it rather than by Marx's way of a head-on bloody political revolt against it.

Otto von Bismarck placed Loius Napoleon Bonaparte 's captured army at the disposal of Lous Adolph Thiers, and on May 21, 1871, it marched on Paris, taking the city in a week despite bitter resistance by the National Guard and the workers.[23] The hatred of the bourgeoisie for these uppity workers who had the nerve to seize power led them to slaughter fourteen thousand Communards and consign ten thousand others to prison or deportation. To justify these measures, the bourgeoisie of Europe attempted to interpret the Commune of Paris as a conspiracy by the International Workingman's Association (IWA).[24]

The outcome of the struggle in Paris made it impossible to hope for a new wave of democratic revolutions in Europe. Therefore, the General Council of the IWA called for the formation of legal working-class parties in each country. The followers of Louis Auguste Blanqui and Bakunin found this unacceptable.[25] The English trade unions were too weak to act as an independent force. Thus, the Paris Commune was the occasion of the final split between Bakunin and Marx at the Hague Congress of the First International in 1872, where is a struggle between the Marxists and Bakunin, who was expelled for setting up a parallel organization. The General Council moved to the United States following this congress, hoping that the vitality of the workers' movement in the United States and the distance from the petit bourgeois movements in Europe would help, but the IWA was formally dissolved in 1876.

After the dissolution of the IWA, international workers' conferences were held every few years from 1877 to 1888, although some sections of the workers' movement did not attend these meetings. In 1889 two competing conferences were held, one composed primarily of trade union leaders organized by the French Possibilists, and one attended by the major working-class parties organized by the Marxist followers of Jules Guesde.[26] The second conference initiated the reestablishment of the international.

Although the first congress was marked by the continuing conflict between Marxists and anarchists, by the time of the founding of the Second International in 1889, the Marxists had gained great ground on the anarchists (and syndicalists). The anarchists were subsequently excluded from the international and have remained a comparatively minor political force (except in some of the less-developed countries of southern Europe such as Spain). The greater challenge to revolutionary Marxism for most of the past century has been (and remains) reformist Marxism.

THE SECOND INTERNATIONAL AND REFORMIST MARXISM
One of the great contradictions that presented itself to the workers' movement was the contradiction between nationalism and internationalism. This was not

so much an ideological issue as a result of the ability of the major capitalist states to attract the support of sections of the working class for their imperialist ambitions. This loyalty was a result of the ability of these states to offer reforms and concessions to the workers.

The history of the Second International illuminates the rise of reformist Marxism. The twenty-five years that preceded World War I, when the Second International was in its prime, were characterized by renewed industrial prosperity. Production rose in all industrialized countries, and those where industrialization had barely begun were incorporated into the capitalist system.

The changing structure of world capitalism, or what Lenin described as the rise of monopoly capitalism and imperialism, was the context in which the parties of the Second International waged the class struggle. The improvement in workers' living standards and in their social security, however small, resulted from these class struggles.

The working-class organizations of this period grew very strong. According to some observers, this was a departure from the norms set by Marx and Engels in the IWA. Let's look for a minute at Ralph Miliband's (1977) observations about Marxist politics.

According to Miliband, Marx and Engels consistently dismissed the notion that there was a set of ideas that specifically defined revolutionary consciousness. In the *Communist Manifesto* they said that Communists "do not set up any sectarian principles of their own, by which to shape and mould the proletarian movement." In speaking of "alleged splits" in the First International, Marx and Engels noted that while the rules of the international gave its constituent societies a common object and program, that program was limited to outlining the major features of the proletarian movement, leaving the details of the theory to be worked out as inspired by the demands of the practical struggle and as growing out of the exchange of ideas among the sections, with an equal hearing given to all socialist views in their journals and congresses.

Miliband also emphasizes how Marx and Engels went to great lengths to stress their view that the emancipation of the working class must be the work of the working class itself. They adamantly opposed any view that the working class was too undereducated and first must be liberated from above by the philanthropic or petite bourgeoisie.

Yet by the time that Engels died in 1895, the Second International was in its prime and the prototypical party was the German Social Democratic Party, What is so impressive about the Second International and the German Party, in particular, is that it had become an authentic mass organization. By 1914 it had become a vast institution staffed by more than four thousand paid functionaries and eleven thousand salaried employees, had 20 million marks invested in business, and published more than four thousand periodicals. It also had substantial parliamentary representation and was a force in local and provincial government. To a greater or lesser extent, much the same was true of social democratic parties in other European countries (Miliband 1977:121).

Nothing demonstrates the maturation of the European working class in the socialist imaginary than this fact. Normally social democratic parties of this period were mass parties deeply involved in the political lives of their countries, though they were all loosely connected to the Second International. Perhaps corresponding to this status, although we should not accept this without further analysis, some would say that the corollary to the above-listed achievements was the notion that the transformation of capitalist society would occur as a strictly constitutional process, which must on no account be endangered by "an ill-conceived activism and adventurist policies" (Miliband 1977:121).

One must ask if the socialist movement of this period had a strategy built into a structural and historical analysis of the social world and the potential actors, rather than a one built on a voluntarist notion of revolution?

Miliband argues that the degree to which this was an accepted tenet of the European workers' movement was masked by the opposition evoked by Eduard Bernstein's explicit "revisionism."[27] Miliband discounts the rhetoric of the workers' movement of that period and suggests that revisionism was the characteristic perspective of that period for all but a very small segment of the *European* workers' movement. Thus, the "betrayal" of 1914 was a natural manifestation of it.

Miliband concludes that this view led to the exaltation of the party as the embodiment of the working class and the guardian against those whom would impress on the working class actions and policies that the party leadership deemed to be dangerous and irresponsible. Thus, the party leadership assumed the role of those who would drive the delicate machinery of the locomotive of socialism at safe speed through capitalist society.

Karl Kautsky (1854–1938) was one of the most influential theoreticians of this period. He taught the party to rely on the relentless march of history for the final overthrow of capitalism, while he continued to interpret Marxism in activist revolutionary terms. His views on economic determinism, however, persuaded the party that revolutionary action was not necessary so long as history was there to do the job.

Edward Bernstein (1961), a member of the German Social Democratic Party (SPD) who had been heavily influenced by the Fabian Socialists while in exile in England, claimed that economic, social, and political conditions had changed greatly since Marx's day. Wages were higher, democracy and universal suffrage were spreading, reforms were more likely than ever to favor the working classes, and trade union activity was encouraging. Capitalism was showing a new capacity to adapt to new conditions, remedy its excesses, and control itself. Bernstein concluded that a socialist party enrolling a major section of the electorate and linked with trade unions and cooperatives could achieve socialism by use of constitutional means. Although he favored socialism over capitalism, he urged his followers to forget ultimate aims and work on the means.

With the collapse of the Second International in August 1914, most Western European social democratic parties were faced by small minorities attempting to reinstate the principles of revolutionary Marxism. The war years saw numerous conferences of international socialists, but it was the October Revolution and the military defeat of the Axis powers in World War I that placed proletarian revolution on the agenda in Austria, Hungary, and particularly Germany. In

Germany the naval mutiny and the victory of the Munich workers in November 1918 led to a workers' rising in Berlin supported by the soldiers. Despite their resistance, the Majority Socialists and the trade unions were forced to accept this new situation. A coalition of Majority Socialists and independent socialists (which excluded Rosa Luxemburg and Karl Liebknecht) proclaimed the socialist republic.[28] The Majority Socialists and the trade union leaders formed a bloc with the established monarchial bureaucracy, the high command of the defeated army, and the industrialists.

The Left formed the Communist Party in late 1918, but the workers considered them to be a disruptive force. They were not heeded when they called for a permanent transfer of power to the workers' councils that had spontaneously sprung up throughout the country.

In this situation it was possible for the ruling class to reestablish itself in partnership with the Majority Socialists. To do this they were willing to make many concessions: the eight-hour day, unemployment assistance, and recognition of wage bargaining. What they really wanted, though, was for the Majority Socialists to take the rap for the war and the penalties of the peace treaty. They did not want to repeat the situation in Russia. With a strong foothold in the government, the ruling class mobilized the middle class against the Majority Socialists, who could once again be excluded from power. By the time the workers decided to implement their demands themselves, it was too late; they were attacked and defeated in one region after another.

Some point out that the October Revolution did spark the proletarian revolution that Marx had heralded, but the revolution was defeated throughout Western and Central Europe. Although these countries had to democratize their political institutions, they reestablished and strengthened their social institutions. Only in Scandinavia did the reformist working-class movement win a lasting influence over the state, although it did not threaten the structures of capitalist society. Thus we can say that the revolutionary movement in Europe saved the Russian Revolution from intervention but itself suffered defeat.

In March 1919 the founding congress of the Third International was held in Moscow. On the whole the groups at this congress were not representative of the mass workers' parties in their countries. Lenin's polemic against left-wing communism, directed against a group that split from the German Communist Party (KPD), convinced some of the larger working-class parties that the international rejected the utopianism of some of its followers in Western Europe. Thus, the Independent Social Democratic Party of Germany (USPD), and the French, Swiss, and Italian socialists decided to consider joining the Third International.

Lenin believed that World War I had opened an era of intensified class conflict and thus placed proletarian revolution on the agenda. He believed, therefore, that a new and very different organization from the previous one had to be created to bring together revolutionary parties of a type different from those that dominated the Second International. What this amounted to was placing what Miliband calls "insurrectionary politics" on the agenda on a world scale, not so much to prepare for immediate insurrection but to prepare for the possibility of the seizure of power in many advanced capitalist countries.

We can say in hindsight that Lenin's *Imperialism* exaggerated the revolutionary possibilities, misled by the revolutionary eruptions that occurred in Germany, Hungary, and Austria as well as the very radical temper that gripped large sections of the working class everywhere in 1918–1920 and led to great industrial strikes and social agitation. Lenin's views then represented very much the temper of the times. This was the context that fostered a class-first agenda among the revolutionaries of the Pan-European world.

If the movement was to respond effectively to the revolutionary situation that was upon them, it had to ensure that the organizational weapons at its disposal would enable it to win this showdown with capital. It is in this context that we come to understand the much-maligned twenty-one conditions of admission to the Communist International, the most important of which included (1) calls for the removal of reformists from all responsible posts in the labor movement, (2) the formation of illegal party apparatuses, (3) subordination of the parliamentary fractions of the parties to the party central committee, and (4) the binding of parties to the decisions of the Executive Committee of the Third International.

These twenty-one conditions virtually constituted a challenge to split the Western parties. Yet the USPD and the French Section of the Workers' International (SFIO) joined the international against the will of some of its top leaders. A minority of the Italian socialists around Antonio Gramsci and Amadeo Bordiga split off to form their own Communist Party.[29] By the beginning of 1921, the Communist International was a powerful force with legal mass parties in Germany, France, Italy, Norway, Bulgaria, and Czechoslovakia and legal or semilegal parties in Finland and Poland, both of which enjoyed considerable working-class support.

The Third International broke decisively with the Eurocentrism of the second. Active support for national liberation was mandatory. Yet when the German KPD attempted to lead the masses in revolution in March 1921, the party's weakness became evident. The determination of the party was no substitute for the lack of spontaneous militancy among the working class.

The insurrection in the West had ceased. What then was to be done with the international army that had been prepared for an assault on the citadels of world capitalism? The initial impulse was that it should prepare itself for the return of the revolutionary crisis, but in the meantime those members of the Communist International located in the core states became instruments for the defense of the socialist motherland.

Harry Braverman, a militant in the Trotskyist movement, argues persuasively that

> the long accruing changes in capitalism, changes which created an entirely new arena of analysis and struggle, cut the ground from under those Marxists who continued to repeat old slogans, and turned the familiar battle cries of Communism into futile incantation. . . .
>
> The entire monolithic edifice of Communism has been splintered, in part because it had been undermined politically and morally by a series

of disastrous events and policies, and in part because in the interim the whole historical epoch for which this movement had been shaped had passed it by. . . . The movement had come to the end of its path" (Braverman 1974:43).

Thus, it was not only that the revolution that Lenin anticipated after World War I did not come about but that the "socialist" parties now were explicitly parties of social reform, whose leaderships not only had no thought of revolution, but saw themselves as the defenders of the status quo. The Communist parties, in contrast, were formally dedicated to revolution but pursued opportunistic and "wayward" policies at the behest of the Comintern (Braverman 1974). Nowhere was an independent Marxist Left able to play any more than a marginal role outside of the two internationals. After recognizing the relative stability of the capitalist world economy in 1925, Stalin expounded in *Problems of Leninism* the doctrine of socialism in one country, dismissing the traditional view that it was not possible to create in Russia the political basis and economic foundation of socialism but that the collaboration of many industrialized countries was necessary for the establishment of socialism. If there was not to be a revolution in the West, then the Soviet leadership had a right to use the Western Communist parties as tools of Soviet foreign policy regardless of the interests of the workers in the industrialized countries.

What a dramatic shift in the story of the trajectory of the world socialist movement. How do we explain this? In his two-volume work on the Communist movement, Fernando Claudin (1975) argues that the causes are very complex but that one thing is incontestable; that is, the majority of the European working class, even where the crisis went furthest, as in Germany, continued to follow their traditional political and trade union organizations and not the new revolutionary party. Lenin and the Comintern leaders referred to this phenomenon as "the betrayal of the reformist leaders" but did not satisfactorily ascertain why the working class followed these "traitors" (Claudin 1975:56). Lenin's assumptions had always been that the working class would turn its back on these reformist leaders and be won to the side of the revolutionary party when the final struggle was at hand. Thus, he imagined that the process would unfold in much the same way it had in the Russian Revolution.

In Claudin's view, Lenin critically underestimated the depth of reformist politics and mentality among the Western working class. For Claudin the root of this error was in Lenin's concept of imperialism as the "eve of the socialist revolution" and as "moribund capitalism" (Claudin 1975:52, 59). In analyzing the contradictions of imperialism, Lenin made much of the destructive effects of these contradictions but did not sufficiently recognize the degree to which a restructuring process in the imperialist countries was also a result of these contradictions.

Lenin of course held that it was the phenomenon of colonial exploitation that led to reformism in the labor movement, but his understanding of the impact that this had in the core states was limited to the corruption of the labor aristocracy. Claudin, however, argues that reformism is also the result of structural transformations in capitalism connected with the development of the productive forces. Nor was Lenin able to appreciate the extent to which the Western working class was attached to national and democratic values. Claudin argues that the operation of the national principle was evident in the "betrayal" of the principle of internationalism by social democratic leaders (Claudin 1975:60).

However, I would argue that it is key to relate these values to the reformist strategies of the Western European ruling classes for whom the franchise, the welfare states, and the ideology of Pan-European racism were the basis of a compromise between labor and capital in the core, who then constituted a united front against the peoples of the colonial, semicolonial, and dependent areas of the capitalist periphery, and their internally colonized peripheries .

Where, then, is the revolutionary trajectory? We know today that the wrenching transformation of the workers' movement described above did not entail the end of the possibilities of transformation of world capitalism but the shift of the locus of revolutionary struggle from the Western proletariat to what Lenin had called the weak link of the capitalist system, but in such a manner that the full implications of this shift were not comprehended by the most influential parties in the world socialist movement.

Revolution in the East and the Challenge to the Eurocentrism of Class-First Strategies

Abdel-Malek (1981) explains that Lenin provided the link between classical European Marxism and the Orient, but Lenin remained to some extent wedded to Eurocentric notions and died too early to figure out the fuller implications of an anti-Eurocentric strategy in the world revolutionary struggle against capitalism and imperialism. Even Lenin was opposed by the Marxists of the Orient in the First and Second Congresses of the Comintern, however. In the Second, Third, and Fourth Congresses, ideological struggle was waged between Eurocentric Marxists and nationalistic Marxists from the Three Continents.[30] M. N. Roy, who represented the left wing of the national liberation movement, was closest to Lenin's position, but as early as the 1920s Sultan-Galiev was pointing out the difference between the situation of the proletariat of the Muslim (non-European) nations and that of the English and French proletariats. Galiev viewed the Muslim nations as proletarian nations.

Mir Sayit Sultan-Galiev was a member of the Tartar Muslim minority in the czarist empire. He was born the son of a schoolteacher in a village in Bashkiria in 1880. In 1917 he joined the Bolshevik Party, which was supported by an important section of the Tartar intelligentsia. Given the internationalist stance of the Bolsheviks, they hoped for a reversal of their fortunes under the czars, who fostered a system of Great Russian chauvinism. Sultan-Galiev rose to the leadership of the Central Muslim Commissariat, which was affiliated with the People's Commissariat for Nationalities, headed by the then little-known Bolshevik Joseph Stalin. Sultan-Galiev created a Muslim Communist Party, and despite the opposition of local Russian Communists, he was able to extract a commitment from the Central Government to form a large predominantly Muslim state, the Tartaro-Bachkir Republic. Sultan-Galiev viewed Muslim society as a unit that had been collectively oppressed under czarism and whose liberation should be a central objective of the socialist revolution since the prospects of socialist revolution were brightest in the colonial world. This position firmly opposed the Comintern's tendency to focus mainly on the Western proletariat. Since the socialist revolution was to begin in the East, who could bear the torch of socialism and culture into Asia better than the Bolshevik Muslims of the Russian Empire (Rodinson 1979)?

The Muslim Communist Party lost its autonomy when the idea of a lasting alliance between the petite bourgeoisie and the proletariat was rejected by the September 1920 Congress of Oriental People in Baku. It was proclaimed there that the national revolution had to be led by the proletariat, which of course meant the Western proletariat. The project of a Great Muslim state was dropped, forcing Sultan-Galiev into opposition to fight against what he termed Great Russian chauvinism. Though he was expelled from the party and arrested in 1923, he continued to organize clandestinely after being released from jail. He had concluded that the socialist revolution did not resolve the problem of inequality among peoples. Rather, the Bolshevik program had eliminated the oppression of the European bourgeoisie and replaced it with the oppression of the European proletariat.

This was of course inconceivable in the class-first framework that dominated the worldviews of radical Marxists in the Third International. Consequently, Sultan-Galiev called for the creation of a Communist Colonial International, which would be independent of the Third International. In November 1928 Sultan-Galiev was again arrested and sentenced to ten years hard labor. He was released in 1939 but executed in 1940 (Goble 2004).

Maxime Rodinson concludes that the socialism of the socialization of the means of production does not resolve all problems. Even Lenin had concurred before the seizure of power by the Bolsheviks, saying in 1916 that the fact the proletariat had carried out the social revolution would not turn it into a saint. This seems to imply that Lenin believed that one needed to be attentive to the continuation of power relations under any system. So for Rodinson, Sultan-Galiev's ideas are thought to be a precursor to Maoist communism, which concentrates on the immediate struggle for socialist revolution in the ex-colonies, but after the establishment of the socialist state, concentrated on the continuation of the class struggle in the socialist state.

Rodinson views the Afro-Asian bloc and the Chinese Communists as avatars of the Communist Colonial International advocated by Sultan-Galiev, who was the first prophet of the colonial struggle against white hegemony in socialism itself and the first to forecast a break between the Russians' European communism and colonial communism. He was also the first to proclaim the importance of Marxist nationalism in colonial countries and the international relevance for socialism of these national movements, which did not immediately envisage complete class warfare and socialization (Rodinson 1979:7).

Abdel-Malek also emphasizes the importance of the Chinese revolution as a turning point for the fortunes of the national movements. From 1927 through World War II, he points out, no socialist states were created on the three continents, thus perpetuating the primacy of Europe not only in the political and economic spheres but in the cultural and theoretical spheres as well. The revolutionaries of the periphery lived in the context of a dialogue with the Left in the core. There was no solidarity movement among the revolutionaries in the countries of the periphery unless they were geographically adjacent. The Chinese revolution was the first example of a socialist movement coming to power at the culmination of a very long and difficult war in a very large and significant country whose slogans, theoretical formulations, and lines were as autonomous as they were specific and thus very close to the political psychology of the people of the Orient. Abdel-Malek argues that this was the first alternative to both the "class against class" conception and the "national front" conception (Abdel-Malek 1981).

In this way the Chinese revolution became a model for revolutionary struggle in the periphery and semiperiphery of the world-system, but it also gained a large following in the core states, including the hegemonic power, the United States. In my 1999 book *We Are Not What We Seem* I argued that "during the 1970s the struggle against the war in Vietnam, the Black rebellions throughout the U.S., and the birth of oppositional movements of great variety severely undermined the legitimacy of the government, and indeed of U.S. civil society. The emergence of the Chinese Cultural Revolution within the process of socialist construction in China was fashioning an image of what the power of the people could do. Maoist ideas influenced the New Left throughout the United States, as in other core countries" (Bush 1999:209).

The Maoist movement that emerged from the New Left visualized reconnecting the revolutionaries to their revolutionary heritage in the Third International, through the prism of Mao Zedong thought. Maoism was envisioned to be a truly radical critique of reformism and revisionism, a means of continual social transformation through carrying out the class struggle under the dictatorship of the proletariat in the socialist countries, through the most superexploited sections of the working class in the core countries, and through the radical national liberation movements in the periphery. Some of these organizations envisioned the creation of a new international under the leadership of the Chinese Communist Party, although others thought such an international body would inevitably lead to the same situation of lack of national rootedness that the Communist Party of China (CPC) fought against in the Third International. Those who were skeptical about the formation of a new international often cited Mao's own contention that all movements had to develop their strategies according to their own conditions. Some of these organizations took the major significance of the Chinese Cultural Revolution to be the significance of proletarian socialism versus petit bourgeois socialism or liberal socialism (the socialism of the experts).

"While there was a considerable range of political sophistication in the movement, on one issue there was considerable unanimity: that through a voluntarist effort utilizing the correct line, revolutionary transformation could be undertaken. There was a great deal of variety among these organizations; some had exceptional strengths in some areas, and utilized the ideology in creative ways" (Bush 1999:210).

Cynthia Lucas Hewitt (2002) argued in a recent article that racial stratification in national labor markets is an aspect of the worldwide division of labor that the ruling strata used to grant and restrict access to the means of production. Specifically Hewitt argues, "Capital ownership and control is 1) cumulative at a geometric rate since the inception of the system in the sixteenth century, leading to centralization, and 2) this centralization is organized through ascriptive solidarity, that rests, ultimately, upon familial relations of marriage and inheritance." According to Hewitt, the key to this ascriptive solidarity is the European patriarchal family, and it is expressed most clearly in the concept of private property, which is then clearly expressed in white racial solidarity and endogeneity (Hewitt 2002:138).

Hewitt holds that the likelihood of employment correlates closely to one's social closeness to owners or controllers of productive capital. Social closeness is defined racially and enforced and reflected in marriage patterns. In contrast to scholars such as Dalton Conley, (1999) who make similar arguments pointing to the defining role of class in determining race relations, following Oliver Cromwell Cox (1950), Hewitt argues that "class is largely an artifact of racialized solidarity processes of expropriation and exclusion integral to the formation of modern nation-state structures" (Hewitt 2002:140). In this way Hewitt identifies what she feels to be a crucial measure of long-term intergenerational control of productive assets, which she argues is the distinguishing feature of capitalist accumulation.

Hewitt argues that one may very well view an oppressed minority as a group in the lower class but cautions that the theory of class focuses on a process of class differentiation based on individual or family choices and opportunities in a more or less open structure. This assumes sharing in any set of national borders as mandated by the imagined nation, but the reality for racist societies or nations is that racism assumes the exclusion of the group from the national identity.

Hewitt has been perhaps the strongest voice among the Black intelligentsia calling for a deepening of the analysis of the struggles of people of the African world. I attempt to expand on how this analysis applies to the wider world by looking at the evolution of George Padmore from an official of international communism to a Pan-African revolutionary.

George Padmore and the Pan-African Struggle

During the 1930s the class-first and race-first strains among Black radicals continued with some reshuffling of positions. Over the course of the postwar period Du Bois had moved from Fabian socialism to an increasingly radical race-first stance, deemed by Wilson Moses as an Afrocentric Marxism, as we saw in Chapter 2.

If Du Bois can be considered the father of Pan-Africanism, then George Padmore should surely be considered its ideologist. Padmore was born Malcolm Nurse. His father was a highly respected politically militant teacher who was friend and mentor to C.L.R. James's father.[31] At that time in the Caribbean, schoolmasters were considered to be the carriers of intellectual and social life, but Malcolm Nurse was on the lower rung of the Trinidadian color hierarchy of white, brown, and black. Since all groups accepted this color hierarchy as part of the natural order, C.LR. James feels that Nurse simply could not accept such restrictiveness and had to leave his native land for the United States in 1924 (James 1992:289).

C.L.R. James tells us that Malcolm Nurse went first to Fisk University in Nashville, Tennessee, and later to Howard University, the Black university in Washington, D.C. By the time he got to Howard, Malcolm Nurse had become a militant revolutionary.[32] James tells us that

> one day Esme Howard, the British Ambassador, was due to pay a visit to Howard University. In those days that was a great event and the black professors prepared a distinguished welcome for their visitor. Padmore, however, had had printed a set of leaflets which described in fierce terms the oppression of British imperialism in Africa. When the procession of dignitaries appeared, he suddenly stepped out from among the students and threw the leaflets in front of the British Ambassador, some say into his face. Padmore was not expelled as one would expect, but he abandoned his academic career and he next appeared as a paid functionary in the American Communist Party. (James 1992:289)

According to James,

> George adopted the Communist doctrine completely and became very expert in it. People who knew him then agree that he was a great militant—active, devoted and fearless. The complaint of George, and most of the other blacks in the Communist Party, was that the [white] leaders never understood that the Negro question had racial connotations which demanded special consideration by a political organization—however much this organization might aim to work for the equality of all mankind. This was the problem which formed the axis of George's career as a Marxist. Nevertheless, whatever the doubts were about George's strict Communist orthodoxy on the Negro question, by 1930 he was created head of the Negro department of the Profintern, with his headquarters in the Kremlin. He held that post until 1935, and if he had done nothing else his place in black history would still be safe. (James 1992:289)

By James's own estimate, Padmore was one of the greatest politicians of the twentieth century and had earned for himself the title of "Father of African emancipation" (Simmonds 2007:A10). What is the basis of such an estimate?

We find in Padmore's experience a story that underlines the story that I am telling about the autonomy of race as a component of the stratifying processes of historical capitalism. It was Du Bois and the New Negro radicals, such as Harrison and Garvey, who made us conscious of this social fact and made Blacks a social force to be reckoned with in world politics. It was Padmore who, according to James, took the next great step in the international organization and mobilization of Blacks.

Through his experience as a journalist at the *Trinidad Guardian*, at student newspapers at Fisk and Howard, and at the CPUSA paper *The Daily Worker* and as editor of *The Negro Champion* (later *Liberator*), Padmore accumulated a skill of immense value to the struggle for human emancipation. The leaders of international communism exercised uncommon judgment in 1929 when they selected Padmore for further study at the University of Toilers of the East in the Soviet Union and then in 1930 selected him to become the Communist International's expert on Negro affairs, secretary of the International Trade Union Council of Negro Workers, and editor of its paper, *The Negro Worker*. James argues that tens of thousands of Black workers in various parts of the world received their first political education through this paper, which provided information, advice, guidance, and ideas about Black struggles on every continent.

One of Padmore's early achievements was the international conference of revolutionary Black workers held in Hamburg in 1930. Padmore personally is said to have travelled over half the globe to help assemble the delegates to the conference. In *The Life and Struggles of Negro Toilers* he wrote,

> At this conference Negro delegates from different parts of Africa, the United States, West Indies and Latin America not only discussed trade union questions, but dealt with the most vital problems affecting their social and political conditions, as for example the expropriation of land by the imperialist robbers in Africa; the imposition of Head and Poll taxes; the enslaving of toilers through Pass laws and other anti-labour and racial legislation in Africa; lynching, peonage and segregation in the United States; as well as unemployment, which has thrown millions of these black toilers on the streets, faced with the spectre of starvation and death (Padmore 1971:6).

Not merely a token leader, during his years in the Comintern Padmore had become something of an institution. By the time he left the Comintern in 1935, he took with him a "carefully fostered 'net' of more than 4,000 connections throughout the colonial world" (Edwards 2003:248).

Edwards (2003) recalls some of the Padmore legend:

> There are whispers that he led a "gun-running expedition into the Belgian Congo to help native revolt there" and that he personally recruited sixty or more African radicals to study in Moscow, surreptitiously smuggling them into Europe. . . .

Padmore was said to be a master of disguises, entering colonial areas by pretending to be an anthropologist studying the life and customs of primitive peoples; entering South Africa by pretending to be the chauffer of a white juniour officer, who was actually his assistant; traveling to Gambia using his birth name (Malcolm Nurse) to help organize a general strike with one of the first trade unions in West Africa. (Edwards 2003:248–249)

During the late 1920s and early 1930s, the Comintern actively supported anticolonial movements including the Black Liberation movement in the United States. Padmore viewed the struggle for socialism as encompassing the struggle for African liberation. According to Edwards, under the influence of Francophone Blacks (especially Geran Kouyate, editor of *La Race negre*) Padmore moved to embrace a form of Black internationalism that called for the unity of Blacks from Africa, the United States, the West Indies, and other lands. Eventually the focus on discovering the most efficacious mode of Black anticolonialism (not necessarily under the leadership of the Comintern) clashed with the universalist pretensions of the Pan-European Communist movement as well as its vanguardist notions of leadership.

The French Communist Party was particularly sensitive on this issue, and there was collaboration between Kouyate, a Sudanese in the French Communist Party, and Padmore, a Comintern official, to undermine the limitations of the French party. Like the Black Communists in the United States, Kouyate came to consider the Third International not only as an natural ally but also as a means toward international Black unity. C.L.R. James argues that Padmore arrived at pretty much the same position. The Comintern was a means of doing the work of the emancipation of Black people everywhere (Edwards 2003:264).

In August 1933, as proceedings to expel Kouyate from the French Communist Party were initiated, Padmore learned that the International Trade Union Council of Negro Workers would be abandoned and the Comintern's work in the African colonies would be relinquished in a strategic move by the Soviet Union to focus on the danger of Fascism in Europe by aligning with the so-called democratic imperialist countries. Padmore immediately resigned from the Comintern (Edwards 2003:268). He pointed out that neither Germany nor Japan had colonies in Africa and that the United States was the most racially prejudiced country in the world.

While this period in Padmore's life needs closer examination, we do know that the break with the Comintern pushed Padmore in the direction of finding a source for Black internationalism outside of international communism and its relatively significant resources. In February 1934 he wrote a letter to W.E.B. Du Bois, whom from his position as a Comintern official he had criticized as a petit bourgeois reformer, a misleader, and an agent of international capital (Edwards 2003:246-247).

In the letter he told Du Bois of a conference with Francophone Blacks that was the most serious political discussion he had ever had with any group of Black folks. The conference was taking the initiative to convene a Negro World

Unity Congress for the purpose of hammering out a common program of action around which Black unity could be achieved. He requested Du Bois's assistance in creating a basis of unity among the Black populations of Africa, America, the West Indies, and other lands. Thus, at the end of his long struggle for Black internationalism using the resources of international communism, Padmore moved toward the inception of a relationship of mutual respect with Du Bois and thus toward the possibility of collaboration with Du Bois, which would be realized in the Fifth Pan-African Congress in Manchester in 1945 (James 1977:74–75).

In 1935 Padmore moved to London and reestablished ties with his boyhood friend C.L.R. James. There he joined James, Jomo Kenyatta, Amy Ashwood-Garvey, and J.B. Danquah in the International African Friends of Ethiopia to help organize opposition to Mussolini's invasion of Ethiopia.[33] When the Ethiopian question subsided, Padmore took over the International African Friends of Ethiopia and transformed it into the International African Service Bureau, which published a paper called *International African Opinion*. C.L.R. James was named the editor of that paper (Lewis 2002:49; James 1992:292).

James tells us that for some time after his appearance in London in 1935, Padmore had a very difficult time since the functionaries and militants of the Communist International persecuted and vilified him with great bitterness. Padmore was able to maintain his bearings, however, and emerged from this period with his reputation and his political standing intact. Soviet communism of this period was not able to shake the faith that Black people had in Padmore, though James holds that it shook the confidence of Black people in the Soviet communism of that period (James 1992:292).

From the founding of the International African Service Bureau in 1937 until his death in 1959, Padmore worked ceaselessly for the independence of Britain's African colonies. Although he worked with many white organizations and spoke at their conferences, he never attached the International African Service Bureau to any of them, although he did merge it into the Pan-African Federation in 1944 (Padmore 1972:127).

C.L.R. James had met Kwame Nkrumah as a student at Lincoln University.[34] In 1944, James, who was living in the United States, gave Nkrumah a letter of introduction to Padmore. When he traveled to London, where Padmore resided, to attend law school, Nkrumah met Padmore. They became fast friends, and Padmore became a mentor to Nkrumah. Padmore and Nkrumah worked together on the Fifth Pan-African Congress in Manchester in 1945, where the decision was made to organize and mobilize the African masses for independence. When the United Gold Coast Convention invited Nkrumah to return to Ghana, it was Padmore who persuaded him to accept the invitation (Lewis 2002:49).

Padmore's work as a revolutionary thinker, strategist, journalist, and union organizer aided him in his ability to summarize his thinking, experiences, and observations so as to benefit the movement and others who were interested. As we have seen, in 1931 he published *The Life and Struggles of Negro Toilers* to highlight the exploitation of Black labor throughout the world (Simmonds 2007:A10). In 1945 he published *The Voice of Coloured Labour (Speeches and*

Reports of Colonial Delegates to the World Trade Union Conference), which
provided colonial workers and workers of color their first opportunity to voice
their grievances and express their hopes and aspirations before a world audience
(Simmonds 2007:A10). He documented the Ethiopian crisis in *Africa and World
Peace* (1937). After World War II he wrote *Africa: Britain's Third Empire*(1949)
which triggered the move toward independence in the Gold Coast (Ghana) and
Kenya, though the colonial government in those countries banned his books
(Simmonds 2007:A10).

In addition to his books, Padmore's analysis of reality was often an accurate
guide to understanding the unfolding events in the social world. Hooker argues
that Padmore was the first to identify neocolonialism. James argues that Nkrumah lacked theoretical sophistication when he met Padmore in the forties, but
after a year of working with him he was writing the most sophsicated books on
imperialism in all the world. Padmore was very much involved in the tactics and
strategy of the revolutionary movement in Ghana under Nkrumah's leadership.
He traveled between Accra and London. He was in Ghana in 1951 to witness
Nkrumah's installation as leader of government business and the reopening of
the legislative council (Lewis 2002:50).

In August 1957 Padmore moved to newly independent Ghana, where President Nkrumah appointed him his personal adviser on African affairs. Hugh
Smythe described Padmore as the "silent hero of Ghana and a venerated and respected figure throughout Black Africa" (Lewis 2002:49).[35] He organized the first
meeting of independent heads of state in Accra and the first All-African People's
Congress (Lewis 2002:50).

Padmore's death in 1959 of course brought his involvement in the decolonizing project to an end, but ten years later more than forty African and Caribbean
countries had achieved their independence. Padmore is increasingly being celebrated by scholars as a leading pioneer in the great movement for the redemption
of Africa. Padmore himself concluded his presentation of Pan Africanism or
Communism with the following commentary: "In our struggle of national freedom, human dignity, and social redemption, Pan-Africanism offers an ideological alternative to Communism on the one side and Tribalism on the other. It re-
jects both white racialism and black chauvinism. It stands for racial co-existence
on the basis of absolute equality and respect for human personality" (Padmore
1972:355).

The Unfinished Business of Decolonization:
How Long Imperialism's Last Stage?

Since the publication of Kwame Nkrumah's 1965 book, *Neo-Colonialism: The
Last Stage of Imperialism*, not a few people have puzzled over just how long the
peoples of the Three Continents would have to contend with this "last stage."
By the 1970s there had developed something of a consensus within the world
Left that the locus of the main contradiction had shifted from the contradiction

beween capital and labor in the West, or between capitalism and socialism, to a contradiction between imperialism and the national liberation movements in the third world. The victory of national liberation movements in country after country since 1945 generated much optimism, though there was also a general consensus that the danger of neo-colonialism was an immediate danger to all of these movements as they came to power, thus achieving political independence.

But the post-Second World War order under U.S. hegemony was precisely one in which direct political over-rule was eschewed, for the economic integration of the world and the clarification of North/South dsparities in wealth. Imperial over-rule was deeply entrenced in the modern world-system as had been recognized by dependency theorists in Latin America (whose achievment of political independence from Spain had not helped very much with dealing with the control over their economic and political affairs by the United States, and being consigned to the U.S. backyard). African and West Indian intellectuals had also elaborated versions of dependency theory, which would eventually be elaborated into world-systems theory by intellectuals and militants from and working in Africa (including Samir Amin, Immanuel Wallerstein, Terence K. Hopkins, and Giovanni Arrighi). The 1949 victory of the Chinese Communist, the 1954 ouster of the French from Vietnam by the Viet-Minh, the stalemate in Korea in its war with the United States, the victory of forces of liberation in Algeria, and then Cuba, and then Vietnam, this time against the United States, the rise of the Black Power Movement in the United States which made common cause with these movements were all considered to be vindications of Nkrumah's claim that the national liberation movements would cut off the arms of the imperialist octopus, thus narrowing its options and room for maneuver, or of Lin Bao's notion that the countryside would surround the cities of the world placing a stranglehold on their power.

But the 1967–73 end of the postwar expansion of the world-economy curtailed the social democratization which much of the progress of the postwar world represented. It had to be admitted that global liberalism could not be spread to the entire world, and the people of the core states and of the third world had to dramatically reign in their expectations. Neoliberal globalization was the term given to the submission of all activity to the dictates of market rationality. Keynsianism which had been the orthodoxy of the postwar world was now a dead letter. The representatives of the national liberation movements in power now were forced to submit to the humiliation of structural adjustment.

Latin America, which had won its political independence from Spain in a different era, had been laboring under what some Latin Americans called the coloniality of power since that time. While African and African Diasporic intellectuals have also contributed signficantly to this concept, we might consider in this vein the work of Aime Cesaire, Frantz Fanon, Leopold Senghor, Richard Wright, W.E.B. Du Bois, John Henrik Clarke, George Padmore, C.L.R. James, Kwame Nkrumah, Sekou Touré, and others. But I would like to look at the work of some who are now calling for a decolonial option in Latin America.

Quijano argues that the formation of the Americas was constituted by two fundamental historical processes: (1) the codification of the differences between conquerors and conquered in the idea of "race," assumed to be a biological category that naturalized the hierarchical relationship between the conquerors and the conquered on the basis of the superiority of the conquerors and the inferiority of the conquered; and (2) the articulation of all known forms of labor control (slavery, serfdom, small commodity production, and reciprocity) on the basis of capital and the world market. The population of the new world and later the entire world was ordered along these axes. Terms which had heretofore referred to geographical designation such as European, Spanish, Portuguese now referred to a putative racial designation.

In Latin America the cultural repression and colonization of the people's imaginary was accompanied by a massive extermination of the indigenous people through harsh conditions of labor, the process of conquest, and diseases brought by Europeans. Within 50 years the European conquest had lead to the extermination of 65 million inhabitants in the Aztec, Maya, Caribbean, and Tawantinsuyana (or Inca) areas (Quijano 2007).

This cultural repression and massive genocide destroyed the high culture of America, turning them into illiterate peasant subcultures condemned to orality without their own pattern of formalized, objectivised, intellectual, and visual expression. The colonial relations of previous periods did not produce the same consequences because they were not the cornerstone of a global system of power relations.

In the Europe of the Enlightenment the categories of humanity did not extend to non-Western peoples, or only in a formal way. In accord with the organic image of reality Europe was the brain of the entire organism, and in every part of the world the "others" were the white man's burden. History was conceived as an evolutionary continuum from the primitive to the civilized; from the traditional to the modern; from the savage to the rational; from pre-capitalism to capitalism. And Europe thought of itself as the future to which all others aspired, the advanced form of the entire species.

In the Americas the idea of race was a way of granting legitimacy to the relations of domination imposed by the conquest. After the colonization of America, Quijano argues, the expansion of European colonialism to the rest of the world, and the subsequent constitution of Europe as a new identity required the elaboration of a Eurocentric perspective of knowledge, what Quijano views as "a theoretical perspective on the idea of race as a naturalization of colonial relations between Europeans and non-Europeans" (Quijano 2000:534-535).

Social domination was not new, but the use of the concept of race as a means of legitimizing this domination was indeed new, and has proven to be the most effective and long-lasting instrument of universal social domination. Race became the fundamental criterion for the distribution of the world population into ranks, places, and roles in the new society's structure of power.

This new structure of power included a new articulation of a variety of forms of labor control deliberately established to produce commodities for the world market. These forms of labor control included slavery, serfdom, petty commodity production, reciprocity, and wages. These forms of labor control were not mere extensions of their historical antecedents because of the manner in which they were tied and articulated under a system of commodity production for the world market.

In Anglo America the indigenous people were not colonized but were formally recognized as nations with formal international relations with international commercial and military relations. Colonial/racial relations only existed between blacks and whites. When the nation began to expand it dispossessed the native Americans of their land, and almost exterminated. The survivors were then imprisoned within North American society as a colonized race (Quijano 2000:560).

Quijano argues that the critique of the European paradigm of rationality/ modernity is urgent. For him it is indispensable that we extricate ourselves from the linkages between rationality/modernity and coloniality, from all power which is not freely chosen by free people. It is the instrumentation of the reasons for power, of colonial power which distorted paradigms of knowledge and spoiled the liberating promise of modernity.

He concludes that this calls for the destruction of the coloniality of world power, the first step of which is epistemological decolonization, as Decoloniality to clear the way for new intercultural communication. It is the very height of irrationality for some group to insist that its own cosmic vision should be taken as a universal rationality. This is nothing but an attempt to impose a provincialism as universalism. This is an attempt to liberate intercultural relations from the prison of coloniality so that people are free "to choose between various cultural orientations, and above all the freedom to produce, criticize, change, and exchange culture and society. This liberation is part of the process of liberation from all power organized as inequality, discrimination, exploitation, and as domination" (Quijano 2007:178).

Walter Mignolo agrees on the whole with Quijano, but also calls for the assertion of an "identity in politics" by internally colonized populations. He contends that Mignolo argues that Latin America is not a subcontinent naturally named by God, it is an invention of the Creole eleite of European descent in the nineteenth century with French imperial designs. Ethnicity in Latin America is thus a "site of struggle, the site of the coloniality of power, of knowledge, of being (Mignolo 2007:43). But rapports de force are rapidly shifting following the increased assertiveness of Indians and people of African descent who are "shifting the geography of knowledge and taking epistomology in their own hands" (Mignolo 2007:44). Mignolo distinguishes this process from what we now refer to (often dismissively) as identity politics, but as identity in politics which he feels is necessary "because the control of identity politics lies precisely in the construction of an identity that doesn't look as such but as the natural apperance of the world" which one finds in the white, heterosexual men. This hegemonic identity politics denounces opposing identities as fundamentalist and essentialist. One must speak form the identities that have been allocated in order to de-natualize the imperial and racial construction of identity in the modern world-system. Such constuctions have not expelled certain people from the system but has marked

them as exteriorities, as stigmatized beings by their superiors for purposes of
maintining the interior space which they inhabit.

For Mignolo the consequence of 300 years of direct colonial rule and 200
years of internal colonialism has been the growing force of nations within nations where in Latin America *metizaje* became the ideology of national homoge-
neity, while an Anglo-Protestant culture core into which others would assimilate
characterized the United States. But de-colonial thinking is the road to pluri-
versality as a universal project. This is posed in opposition to an abstract universalism whether of the liberal or the radical (Marxist) variety. For Mignolo the
defense of human sameness above human differences is always a claim made
from what he refers to as the "privileged position of identity politics in power"
(Mignolo 2007:55).

Mignolo argues that epistemic fractures are taking place around the world,
not just among indigenous communities in the Americas, New Zealand, and Aus-
tralia, but also among Afro-Andean, and Afro-Caribbean activists, and intellectuals, and among Islamic intellectuals and activists. Contrary to what might be
assumed, this process has lead to a retreat of nationalism, conceived as the identification of the state with one ethnicity and therefore to the fetishization of power.
If the state is identified with one ethnicity then there is no difference between the
power of the people and the power in the hands of people of that ethnicity who
represent the state. And the model of this form of organization is the Western
bourgeois state based upon the political theory from Plato and Aristotle to Ma-
chiavelli, Hobbes, and Locke. The de-colonial option came to the fore when Indigenous people around the world began to claim their own cosmology in the orga
nization of the economic and the social, of education and subjectivity, when
Afro-descendant groups in South America and the Caribbean follow the same
path, and will gain significant momentum when Islamic and Arab intellectuals
and activists follow the same path.

The U.S. American model of multiculturalism conceded "culture" while
maintaining "epistemology." Andean intellectuals introduced the term "intercu-
lurality" as a means of claiming epistemic rights (Mignolo 2007:62). For Mignolo
the struggle for epistemic rights because this struggle is what will determine the
"principles upon which the economy, politics, and education will be organized,
ruled, and enacted" (Mignolo 2007:65). These principles will allow many worlds
to co-exist and not be ruled out in the name of simplicity and the reproduction
of bianry opposition. This approach allows for the rise of a communal system
(different from the capitalist and socialist systems) in which power is not located
in the State or in the individual (or corporate) proprietor but in the community.

One might conclude from the work of Quijano and similar work by Mignolo, Grosfoguel, Madonado-Torres, Santiago-Valles, Boyce Davies, Wynter,
and Montes-Lao a body of work and praxis is accumulating which questions the
universalist pretensions not only of Western Liberalism, but also class-first socialists. For Quijano socialism is not at all state control of each and every sphere
of social existence. This is simply a form of despotism that appears to be a radical
redistribution of power in the minds of only the power holders. On the contrary,
socialism involves "the trajectory of a radical return of the control over labor/

resources/product, over sex/resources/products, over authorities/institutions/ violence, and over intersubjectivity/knowledge/communications to the daily life of the people" (573). The imposition of race to naturalize the relations between the conquerors and the conquered as the constituive act of the capitalist world-economy seems to require the decolonial option as suggested by Quijano and his comrades.

4

Black Feminism, Intersectionality, and the Critique of Masculinist Models of Liberation

While the significance of race and class within the Black liberation movement has been debated extensively, the issue of gender and the interplay of feminism and antiracism are not adequately theorized outside the Black feminist tradition. Black feminist or womanist thought, both implicit and explicit, contains a critique of racism, patriarchy, capitalism, and Eurocentrism. It also contains a powerful critique of patriarchal notions in Black nationalism while often offering a corrective Black feminist nationalism (or Afrocentrism), oriented not solely toward nation building per se but toward reconceptualizing race, class, and gender as interlocking systems of oppression. The power of the theoretical formulations in Black feminist thought, most powerfully articulated by Patricia Hill Collins, Barbara Smith, Angela Davis, Barbara Ransby, Frances Beal, Rose Brewer, bell hooks, Linda Burham and others, is that it transcends what might be called a counterhegemonic ideology, like that of more traditional Afrocentrism, to create a form of knowledge that is not simply oppositional but involves dialogue between partial perspectives where there is no need to decenter the experience of others (except for the dominant group, which by definition must be decentered). In this dialogue everyone has a voice, but everyone must listen and respond to others in order to remain in the community. Collins argues that sharing a common cause fosters dialogue and encourages groups to transcend their differences.

Rose Brewer (2003) has sought explicitly to breech the disjunction between Black radicalism's almost exclusive focus on the race-class dialectic by utilizing a gender critique. She knows that this will not be an easy task, because concern with race, white supremacy, and capitalist economic exploitation has been the driving force behind Black radical theory and practice despite the more complicated social world that this movement sought to transform, a world with a variety of forms of domination, including those of gender and sexuality. Black radical theory, Brewer argues, has long operated on the basis of a generic notion of African American life that renders the complexity and multiplicity of African American life nearly invisible with regard to gender and sexuality. It is therefore of great significance that alongside the emergence of a Black radical praxis concerned with race and class in the last few decades has been a Black feminist critique (Brewer 2003:112).

During slavery, Black women were constructed as producers and reproducers, as laborers in the production of wealth, and as women in the reproduction of material and social life. Brewer follows Bonnie Thornton Dill (1979) in asserting that these women resisted, defined themselves, and were probably the first Black feminists. They were certainly active in antislavery societies, which gave rise to the first wave of feminism in the United States. As Angela Davis (1983) points out, however, the suffragette movement of the first wave of feminism ultimately foundered on the conflict between women's rights and African American rights. Davis points out that this stance reflected long-standing structural and ideological contradictions in the United States, so it should not be a surprise that the underlying racism of the movement spearheaded by Susan B. Anthony and Elizabeth Cady Stanton continued during the second wave of feminism, in the 1960s and 1970s.

In both cases for Black women, the fight for African American rights took precedence over the fight for women's rights. While during the first wave of feminism, black women were ignored by the suffragettes, during the second wave of feminism, black women were faced with the choice of going forward in a women's movement that, once again, did not really include them, or supporting the rights of African Americans as a race without attending to the pressing gender issues that faced Black women. Davis does not equivocate that she feels that this was a very difficult choice. She clearly elucidates the failure of both waves of feminism to include all women and shows how necessary it is for women, regardless of race, to work together.

Given the prominence of white racial chauvinism among white men and white women, both the civil rights movement and the Black Power movement fell back on the race-first outlook until the late 1960s and early 1970s, when Black feminists began to stake out a voice among the women of the Student Nonviolent Coordinating Committee and among Black lesbian feminists who came together in the Combahee River Collective as well as the National Black Feminist Organization (Brewer 2003:113–114).

Barbara Ransby (2000) notes the loss of several Black feminist organizations over the course of the 1990s, including an organization that she founded with Deborah King and Elsa Barkley Brown, African-American Women in Defense of Ourselves, which mobilized sixteen hundred women in response to the Anita Hill–Clarence Thomas hearings, assembled a group of women who opposed the exclusionary policies of the Million Man March and the patriarchal outlook of its founder, and formed a Black feminist caucus in the Black Radical Congress in 1998.

There emerged in the Black Radical Congress a sometimes subterranean, sometimes open struggle about the status of feminist, gay, and lesbian themes in the Black Liberation movement. The Black Radical Congress was a unique organization in the history of Black Liberation in the prominence with which it dealt with the issues of feminism and sexuality. Antisexist and antihomophobic stances were among the points of unity that all must support in order to participate in the organization. While the leadership of the Black Radical Congress often posed this as a contradiction between themselves and Black Nationalists in the organization, the issue was much more complex. Left-wing antifeminism was widespread and by no means limited to Black Nationalists.

I would like to situate the reemergence of an explicit and dynamic Black feminism during the last forty years in relation not only to the dynamics of gender politics in the Black Liberation movement but also to the struggles in the larger society.

The Reassertion of Patriarchy and the Emergence of Black Feminism

The Black Pride movement of the 1960s got much of its impetus from the activity and praxis of the Black Muslim movement, which was organizationally anchored by the Nation of Islam. Much of the power of the Nation of Islam originated in the manner in which it linked traditional values to African American religious practices and used this blend as a source of communal strength. Central to the practice of the Nation of Islam was its call for a return to the patriarchal tradition that had flourished among Black people prior to their enslavement in the New World. Therefore, the Nation of Islam, and the Black Nationalist and Black Power movements more broadly, argued for the reassertion of the masculine power of Black men who had been pervasively emasculated over a period of centuries in the discourse and practice of American society. The Black Pride movement thus took many of the masculinist themes of the Nation of Islam and enshrined them in their ideology.

Ironically, one reaction to the assertion of Black Pride and resistance was the call for the reassertion of Black manhood, famously enshrined in Daniel Patrick Moynihan's 1965 report *The Negro Family: The Case for National Action*, commonly called the Moynihan Report. There is more here than a simple ideological convergence, however; we need to understand the debate around the Moynihan Report and the Black family in terms of the times in which this debate took place.

Family Values and the Conservative Backlash

The discourse on the underclass and family values so prominent since the 1980s emerged out of the 1960s debate about poverty and race, but the conservative turn in the debate cannot be understood outside of the impact of the Black insurgency on the social psychology of rebellion throughout society. The conservative backlash, however, did not simply line up against the enemy of the moment. By its very nature it sought to reassert the foundation of the social order by highlighting the relations of honor that put the most dishonored section of the population back in its place. It is not difficult to discern that the ideological discourse of the conservative backlash was part of a broad counterinsurgency designed to turn the nation away from a commitment to the general welfare and toward a focus on the survival of the fittest, defined as those who had earned their social positions because of their adherence to the work ethic, their cultural and family values, and so on. It is key that we pay close attention to the evolution of relations of force in this historical moment. My point is that the rise of the most dishonored sections of our population in itself leads inexorably to the elaboration of a variety of counterhegemonic discourses that constitute a fatal threat to centrist liberalism and the geoculture of the modern world-system. We cannot understand the conservative backlash of the post-1965 period without understanding the meaning of the postwar period for the world and the United States.

While the nineteenth-century workers' movement contained elements who were implacable foes of a capitalist system that they believed would increasingly undermine the very foundations of social life as it ground workers beneath the wheel of a heartless profit-making juggernaut, others hoped that workers' social struggles would result in humanizing the capitalist system. During the twentieth century social democratic movements springing from a variety of sources came to power throughout the countries of advanced capitalism, constituting a compromise that muted the ferocity of class warfare. Welfare states were established across Western Europe and in the settler colonies inhabited by the descendents of Western Europe.

In the United States this welfare state took the form of Franklin Delano Roosevelt's New Deal. However, the political strains in the New Deal coalition and continuing institutionalized racial disadvantage meant that the resultant policies made more substantial provisions for whites than for people of color. The social struggles mounted by people of color, combined with the geopolitical strategy of the United States as it rose to a preeminent position in the world-system, meant that the federal government could no longer ignore the grievances of an internal population of color that was relegated to second class-citizenship in a world in which decolonization resulted in the formation of many new states inhabited by people of color. If *decolonization* was the watchword of the emerging world order, the rise of the civil rights movement center stage in American society was a striking parallel for all the world to see. Dr. Martin Luther King's "I Have a Dream" speech at the 1963 March on Washington was a testament to the promise of the United States, but living out the true meaning of the United States' creed meant the elaboration of democracy in ways heretofore unimagined. While the civil rights movement sprang from a political culture that had been nourished in the centrist liberal establishment of the civil rights movement, the more radical faction had gained a significant following in the urban areas outside of the South, where civil rights were less of an issue and the more enduring problem was that of institutionalized or structural inequality and an ideological racism deeply embedded in the common sense of the nation. Malcolm

X was the most popular leader of this movement, and he saw not an American dream but an American nightmare. Those segments of the population had initiated their own form of rebellion starting in the early 1960s on the margins of the civil rights movement and moved to the urban areas of the northern, midwestern, and western states from 1964 onward. This upped the ante in a most dramatic fashion and ignited a fire in establishment circles to find a solution to the problems of racism and poverty in the United States. The search for solutions led to social policy debate in the administration of Lyndon Baines Johnson about solutions to the problems of poverty, race, and class that greatly expanded the horizons of our thinking about democracy, equality, and social justice. The egalitarian spirit of the civil rights movement took the country by storm as women, Mexican Americans, Puerto Ricans, and gays and lesbians reasserted their own grievances. Decolonization fostered an egalitarian spirit in the non-European world as well, giving rise to national liberation movements in various parts of the semicolonial and dependent nations of the third world. Lyndon Johnson, a master politician and a populist who saw his mission in life as the completion of the Great American Revolution, tried to improvise in the international arena by seeking to implement the notion that America's mission was to deliver democracy to other parts of the world where it was under threat. This position was both halfhearted and opportunist. Moreover, it was not that creative an idea, since it followed the line of the Truman Doctrine. Johnson was not able to deliver both guns and butter and was driven from office.

In the same year, King was assassinated as he moved closer to the politics of Malcolm X. After King's assassination, his followers and those of Malcolm X made common cause in mounting a challenge to the multiple forms of inequality both in U.S. society and between rich countries and poor countries (which included opposition to U.S. domination of poor countries). Viewing this as a threat not only to the bipartisan consensus on foreign policy but also to the geopolitical and geocultural order on which their power rested, the power elite of U.S. society launched a counterattack against those demanding equality by calling for a color-blind society, asserting that poverty was a consequence not of the structure of opportunity in society but of the lack of moral values among the poor, and launching military interventions in Nicaragua, Grenada, and Panama (all sites of a challenge to U.S. geopolitical domination of its backyard).

While centrist liberals have hastened to blame the excesses of the sixties insurgency for the conservative backlash, they have tended not to understand the sense in which the postwar social compact was precisely a compromise that placed limits on who was included in this compact. It was these limitations that gave rise to the civil rights movement in the first place, an attempt to get the United States to live the true meaning of its creed. What this movement did on the whole, though, was to clarify for many the limits of the so-called American dream and for some the extent to which universalism versus racism and sexism constituted what Immanuel Wallerstein came to refer to as the ideological tensions of capitalism.

Let us return to the 1960s and the line of argument presented by Moynihan in *The Negro Family: The Case for National Action*. Recall that by 1965 both the Civil Rights Bill and the Voting Rights Bill had become federal law. The civil rights movement had defeated Jim Crow (legalized segregation). According to the ideology of the civil rights movement and the white liberals with whom it was allied, the expectation was that Black people would rapidly assimilate into white society on the basis of equality.

The purpose of the Moynihan Report was precisely to refute any such expectation and to explain (from the point of view of the political and economic elite and the professional-managerial strata) why this would be the case. Although full recognition of Blacks finally had been won, the expectation by Blacks that they would achieve equality of results would not be fulfilled because of the crumbling of the family structure. Moynihan attributes this to three hundred years of almost unimaginable treatment (Moynihan 1967). For Moynihan the inability to assimilate the lower-class Negro was a social problem of monumental proportions to the United States because the integration of the lower-class Negro would finally complete the "Great Unfinished American Revolution" (Harding 1983:257; Levine 2003:16).

It is important to understand that Moynihan locates the Negro Revolution in the same landscape as India's struggle against British colonialism, the decolonization of Africa, and the increasing tensions between the white world and people of color the world over. It is in this broader geopolitical arena that Moynihan worries about the political culture of lower-class Negroes, specifically the Black Muslim doctrine, which was based on total alienation from the white world. He thus senses that the powerful influence of the Black Muslim doctrine in Negro America might also indicate the possibility of an attraction to Chinese communism. He argues that the course of world events would be profoundly affected by the success or failure of the Negro revolution in seeking peaceful assimilation of the races in the United States (Moynihan 1967:1).

Moynihan viewed the Negro revolution as a movement for equality as well as liberty. Although liberty and equality are the twin ideals of American democracy, they are not the same thing. Liberty has been more popular among the American middle class, and equality has enjoyed tolerance rather than acceptance. Moynihan is referring to equality of opportunity, but he then takes up Bayard Rustin's argument for the achievement of equality of results. If we do not achieve equality of results, Moynihan argues, there will be no social peace (Moynihan 1967:2–3).

Moynihan argues that at the heart of the deterioration of the fabric of Negro society is the deterioration of the family. For Moynihan the family is the basic social unit of American life and has been central in promoting the rapid progress of those immigrant groups that have been most successful in America. He tells us that the white family has achieved a high level of stability but that the family structure of lower-class Negroes is highly unstable and in many urban centers is approaching complete breakdown. He adduces the following propositions with statistical support to back up this claim: (1) nearly a quarter of urban Negro marriages are dissolved, compared to less than 8 percent of urban white marriages; (2) nearly one-quarter of Negro births are illegitimate, compared to 3 percent of white births; (3) almost one-fourth of Negro families are headed by females, compared to 9 percent of white families; (4) the breakdown of the Negro family has led to a startling increase in welfare dependency.

He views this breakdown as a consequence of the particularity of slavery in the United States and of the continued oppression of the Negro (particularly the male), both of which worked against the emergence of a strong father figure. Indeed, Moynihan argues that "segregation and the submissiveness it exacts, is surely more destructive to the male than to the female personality. Keeping the Negro 'in his place' can be translated as keeping the Negro male in his place: the female was not a threat to anyone" (Moynihan 1967:16). He relies on the African American sociologist E. Franklin Frazier to support his argument that at the time of emancipation, Negro women were already accustomed to playing the dominant role in family and marriage relations.

Just as urbanization produced the wild Irish slums of the nineteenth-century Northeast with their drunkenness, crime, corruption, discrimination, family disorganization, and juvenile delinquency, the sudden transition from country to city produced an analog in the Negro slums.

Moynihan is critical of the lack of attention given to the social impact of unemployment, for this is viewed as a central element in the weakness of the Negro family. Although Moynihan takes pains to note that it is a testament to the Negro people that they have survived the treatment accorded them in the United States, he points out that Negroes have paid a great price. The Negro community has been forced into a matriarchal structure, which, because it is so out of line with the rest of American society, seriously retards the progress of the group as a whole.

He tells us that ours is a society that presumes male leadership in private and public affairs, and a subculture in which this is not the pattern is placed at a distinct disadvantage. This matriarchal society is what Moynihan deems "the tangle of pathology." In contrast to the Negro family, the white family, despite many variants, remains a powerful agency, not only for transmitting property from one generation to the next but also for transmitting contacts in the world of education and work. "Three centuries of injustice have brought about deep-seated structural distortions in the life of the Negro American. At this point, the present tangle of pathology is capable of perpetuating itself without assistance from the white world. The cycle can be broken only if these distortions are set right . . . a national effort must be directed towards the question of family structure" (Moynihan 1967:47).

We should recall that The Negro Family was written during the most dramatic economic expansion in history. This expansion was the context of the social democratic strategy in the core states. During 1967–1973 the economy began to stagnate, and the ensuing profit squeeze was compounded by a geopolitical crisis in Vietnam and a crisis of governability because of the unruliness of the inner-city poor and their radical allies.

In line with the changes going on at that time, Moynihan's position would shift. He edited a volume titled On Understanding Poverty: Perspectives from the Social Science in which he argued in his introduction, titled "The Professors and the Poor," that the fashionable poverty ideology promoted by intellectuals in the poverty program was a disservice to the poor. He had nothing but contempt for these "white radicals" who gained positions of authority in the Office of Economic Opportunity and who perpetrated the notion that the poor are in poverty because the power structure deprived them of opportunity. He quotes Miller to make his point:

> Opportunity is not something that people are either inside or outside of. Americans may achieve widely varying degrees of success or failure in a thousand different spheres and in a thousand different ways. Beaming to lower status people the message that one can attain "success goals" by breaching, demolishing or otherwise forcing the "walls" that bar them from "opportunity" conveys a tragically oversimplified and misleading impression of the conditions and circumstances of success, in addition to fostering an imagery with potentially destructive consequences. (Moynihan 1968:32)

This language is strikingly different from the language he used in the 1965 report. Moynihan argues that the function of many community action programs was to raise among poor persons the level of perceived and validated discontent with the social system, without actually improving the conditions of life of the poor in anything like a comparable degree. For Moynihan, to blame the system is not an analysis, but its opposite.

In 1967 Moynihan delivered an address to the national board of the Americans for Democratic Action titled "The Politics of Stability." He attempted to understand the violence that the nation faced in the inner cities and in Vietnam as a consequence of liberal actions or caretaking.

> Liberals must see more clearly that their essential interest is in the stability of the social order; and given the present threats to that stability, they must seek out and make more effective alliances with political conservatives who share their interest and recognize that unyielding rigidity is just as great a threat to continuity of the social order as an anarchic desire for change. . . .
>
> Liberals must divest themselves of the notion that the nation— and especially the cities of the nation can be run from agencies in Washington. . . .
>
> Liberals must somehow overcome the curious condescension that takes the form of defending and explaining away anything, however outrageous, which Negroes, individually or collectively might do. (Moynihan 1974 :188, 191)

In the long trajectory of his political career, Moynihan started with an interest in transforming the Black family through race-, class-, and gender-conscious programs that provided preferential and compensatory programs for Black men. His longer-term objective was a patriarchal welfare state. He wanted to end the maternalist tradition in social welfare that enabled women to raise families without men. His early deliberations depicted the Black family in a manner intended to gain pity for poor Blacks (especially men) and thus promote the policies that he wished to pursue. Darryl Michael Scott argues that in February 1964, as the Johnson administration planned the War on Poverty, Moynihan argued that welfare had made poverty more endurable instead of providing an escape from it. As the War on Poverty progressed, Moynihan argued that welfare was a great achievement but must not be allowed to become the economic system of a permanent subculture. Men need jobs; families need fathers; communities need independence (Scott 1997:155).

Moynihan argued that the War on Poverty substituted the chimera of political empowerment (the citizen-participation stipulations of the Office of Economic Opportunity, known as the Community Action Program) for the time-tested process of social mobility. Scott argues that he wanted the state to assist the poor in their quest for social mobility, not to forge them into a self-conscious and politically active group.

The conflict between Moynihan's class-conscious liberals (who viewed the path of individual social mobility as the best road to social justice) and racial liberals would soon take a backseat to the conservative backlash, which emerged front and center after the Watts uprising. After Watts, the *Wall Street Journal*'s headline read, "Family Life Breakdown in Negro Slums Sows Seeds of Race Violence: Husbandless Homes Spawn Young Hoodlums, Impede Reforms, Sociologists Say." The *Wall Street Journal* relied on academic authorities who were decidedly outside of the group of racial liberals who had been most active in social policy making and deliberation in Johnson's Great Society Programs. Thus, the conservatives claimed the Moynihan Report as their own. William Ryan, author of *Blaming the Victim*, argued that Moynihan was no racist but that those who were upholding the report were engendering a new brand of racism in which white conservatives were "pleading guilty to the savagery and oppression against the Negro that happened 100 years ago, in order to escape being placed on trial for the crimes of today" (Scott 1997:158).

According to this new genteel racism, unemployment was a result of the breakdown of the Black family, poor education was a result of cultural deprivation among Negroes, and slum conditions were the result of the lack of acculturation among southern Negro migrants to the urban North.

The War on Poverty, short-lived though it was, is often blamed for the conditions in today's inner cities. While it is true that the War on Poverty did not really end poverty, it had a striking impact. The number of poor fell from 18 percent in 1960 to only 9 percent in 1972 (Quadagno 1994:175). This was a consequence of a substantial expansion of social welfare programs including Social Security, unemployment compensation, Medicare, food stamps, and public assistance. Child poverty rates declined from 27 percent in 1960 to 15 percent in 1974.

The percentage of Blacks enrolled in college increased from 13 percent in 1965 to 22.6 percent by 1975. Quadagno argues that if this trend had continued, Blacks would have established parity by 1983. Similarly, by 1989 the number of Blacks holding white-collar jobs had increased by 522 percent.

But poor Blacks did not fare nearly so well. Between the early 1970s and the late 1980s the percentage of two-parent Black families fell from 63.4 to 40.6 percent. The labor force participation rate of Black high school dropouts fell by

25 percent. Jobless rates for Black men rose from 4.7 to 13.6 percent, and the percentage of Black children born out of wedlock increased from 35.1 percent to 62.6 percent.

From 1970 to 1990 the rates of racial segregation, measured by the average level of racial concentration, remained basically the same. In 1970 the average was 84.5 percent; by 1990 it was slightly less, at 77.8 percent. Quadagno argues that segregation systematically builds deprivation into the residential structure of Black communities and increases the susceptibility of the neighborhoods to spirals of decline. A harsh environment also is said to create an oppositional culture that further separates ghetto residents from the majority of society.

When Reagan took office in 1981 he proceeded to roll back the welfare state. Funds for job training declined from more than $6 million in 1980 to less than $2.5 million in 1984. In 1981 federal aid to cities was reduced to 1968 levels. Support for low-income housing was reduced markedly from 183,000 starts in 1980 to 28,000 starts in 1985 (Quadagno 1994:178).

The position that elevates the role of the alleged lack of values among a racialized and gendered lower strata in the fomenting of social crisis seems to be called into question by some of the empirical research that I review above, but social policy analysis is determined as much by the ideological commitments of the political establishment as by the empirical findings of policy analysts.

In line with the 1970s declaration by Samuel Huntington about an excess of democracy that must be reigned in, by the 1980s many of these neoconservative intellectuals had come full circle from their radical youth to embrace the hard-line conservatism of the Reaganites. They sought to arrest the cascading demands for equality by the time-honored approach of blaming poverty on the vices of the poor. Thus, some advocates of the family values crusade argue that the absence of a biological father in the home has replaced race and class as the major cause of socioeconomic inequality and psychological disadvantage in America. Traditional conservatives, such as George Will, hold that what is called the race crisis is in reality a class problem arising from dysfunctional families and destructive behaviors.

The conservative contention that Blacks are lacking in family values does not square, however, with studies that show that traditional family ideology is as strong as or stronger among some Blacks than among whites, and indeed is quite strong among low-income Blacks as well. What, then, is the meaning of the attack on the Black family?

The defenders of historical capitalism have always blamed poverty on the poor rather than on the structural inequality that exists under the system. The attack on the Black family is nothing new in this regard. At this point in history it is the centerpiece of the capitalist attack on equality and any form of egalitarianism. It is an attempt to justify and rationalize the structural inequality that is inherent to capitalism and is driving billions worldwide, and millions in the center of world capitalism itself, the United States, to the very margins of social life. Spiraling poverty would discredit the system save for finding an explanation that is ideologically acceptable to large numbers of its supporters. This is precisely the role that racism plays. It is manifested in the attack on the Black family, the demonization of the underclass (read, dangerous class), and lately the incessant howl for law and order.

What does all of this mean? We must first move away from the conjunctural time in which we have situated counterinsurgency against the increased bargaining power of the working classes that won the social democratic compromise, and the granting of civil rights concessions to racial minorities and women. This is certainly important to the most powerful social forces in the United States, but the rebellions of the inner city threatened to breach the social reforms used to contain the potential of the rebellion of the lower strata. In the *longue durée*, these rebellions and the mobilizations with which they have been associated constituted a return of the dangerous classes, which frightened a section of the liberal elite into revising its liberalism and allying itself with conservatives against the radical thrust of the rebellion of the inner-city poor and its allied intellectuals.

The triumph of the Right in the 1980s was part of a global reversal of these trends, but this was not a sign of strength requiring another retreat of the Left. It should be no mystery that this movement aimed its fire at women, people of color, the underclass, and gays and lesbians. These are precisely the sites of greatest resistance and of those dreaming of a new society. Since this was also the period of the rise of women, it should not be surprising that Black feminists have argued most forcefully for a strategy based on race, class, gender, and sexuality as interlocking forms of oppression. This contribution by Patricia Hill Collins, Angela Davis, Rose Brewer, and others deepens the contribution of Black internationalism, which is an uncompromising break with the U.S.-centric perspective that the ruling class labored so hard to install across the political spectrum from the Right to the social democratic Left during the postwar period. It was Malcolm X's insight that most effectively demolished the power of that consensus when he argued that the Negro problem was not simply an American problem or a Black problem but an issue of the haves against the have-nots on a global scale—an issue not of civil rights but of human rights.

The elegant refrain in Malcolm X's call to the ramparts is not unfamiliar to most who lived through that time and to youth who came to intellectual maturity while listening to Malcolm's speeches and reading his autobiography and collections of his speeches. Malcolm's insights frequently resonate with an idea at the far reaches of our consciousness that was not previously clear but after his commentary provokes insights in those listening. Where do they go from there?

I have frequently encountered individuals who have argued that Black radical activists and intellectuals once had important insights that the rest of society should contemplate but that their heyday is long past because they exhausted their contributions in the 1960s and 1970s. While there is indeed an invigorating wind blowing from the rise of the new Black Power scholarship that I mentioned in Chapter 1, since the 1970s the most intellectually cogent social thought and praxis in the African American world has come from the ferment among Black feminists.

Black feminism is certainly not new, but I am less concerned here with indicating the depth and contribution of Black women to the Black Liberation movement than with reviewing an example of recent Black feminist interventions in the nation's intellectual and political arena.

Patricia Hill Collins holds that a striking focus in both the Moynihan report and the Bill Moyers documentary is their shared assumption that white economic advantage is due in large part to the superior attitudes and values of white Americans.[1] Self-discipline, motivation, and perseverance are said to be the essential ingredients of economic success, and poverty is the result of a failure of individual or group will. The two pieces argue that the "tangle of pathology" is capable of perpetuating itself without any assistance from the white world. Political and economic factors are either neglected or located in the distant past by both works. Racial comparisons are used to explain the economically disadvantageous social-class position of African Americans. Race and gender ideologies are thus, in Collins's view, used to justify social inequality.

Gender is also central to this construction because it is the attitudes and values of black men and women that account for the differences in economic status and family structure of blacks and whites. Neither subscribes to the dominant notions of masculinity and femininity. Black women are overly masculine and pass on these ideas to their children. Black men are too submissive to women and absent from their children's gender socialization. To lift themselves out of poverty, blacks must learn to think and act like whites.

To get back to the issue of intersectionality: Race and gender converge in these treatments to explain the social-class position of blacks. Racial difference is used to explain class disadvantage, and gender deviance is used to account for racial difference. In neither work is social class viewed as a causal variable that actively shapes the life chances of black people, their family life, or their attitudes and values.

Collins (1991:77) further argues that the image of the welfare mother provides ideological justifications for interlocking systems of gender, race, and class oppression. A network of controlling images converges at points defined by the conjunction of black and female, particularly in the context of poverty.

Bill Moyers's well-known film *The Vanishing Family: Crisis in Black America* broadcast to the entire world his sense that the world of the Black family is topsy-turvy, "a world turned upside down." Despite Moyers's best intentions, his film ended up producing a very upside-down analysis. It is important, perhaps poetic justice that Black feminist thought emerges at this time to give all of us greater coherence.

Collins on Racism, Nationalism, and Feminism

Patricia Hill Collins argues that African American women as a group may have experiences that provide them with a unique angle of vision but that expressing a collective, self-defined, Black feminist consciousness is problematic precisely because dominant groups have a vested interest in suppressing such thought. Those who control the schools, media, and other cultural institutions of society prevail in establishing their viewpoint as superior to those of others. Most of us are conscious of this social fact but do not always have the experience base to understand its manifestations in a wide variety of social and intellectual situations.

While for Collins this consciousness resides potentially in the experiences of individual African American women, regarding their shared point of view, Black feminist consciousness is in part a product of "aggregating and articulating these individual expressions of consciousness," giving rise to "a collective, focused group consciousness." This is not pedantic insistence on an intellectual position, in Collins's view. "Black women's ability to forge these individual, unarticulated, yet potentially powerful expressions of everyday consciousness into an articulated, self-defined, collective standpoint is *key to Black women's survival*" (my emphasis). Collins argues that a "fundamental feature of this struggle for a self-defined stand point involves tapping sources of everyday, unarticulated consciousness that have traditionally been denigrated in white, male-controlled institutions. For Black women, the struggle involves embracing a consciousness that is simultaneously Afrocentric and feminist" (Collins 1990:26).

In my view, Collins's understanding of Black feminist thought is important precisely because of its emphasis on knowledge, consciousness, and empowerment. We know that there are a number of Black women (not only women) who have achieved some prominence as intellectuals in the United States, but Collins cautions that

> one danger facing African American women intellectuals working in these new locations concerns the potential isolation from the types of experiences that stimulate an Afrocentric feminist consciousness—lack of access to other Black women and to a Black women's community. Another is the pressure to separate thought from action—particularly political activism—that typically accompanies training in standard academic disciplines. In spite of these hazards, contemporary Afrocentric feminist thought represents the creative energy flowing between these two focal points of history and literature, an unresolved tension that both emerges from and informs the experiences of African American women. (Collins 1990:31)

While there is always a vindicationist undertone in the discussion of the work of intellectuals who come from communities that are composed mostly of oppressed strata and whose voices have not heretofore been recognized, we should simply accept this and move on rather than making it the issue. Having said that, I could not agree more with Collins's contention that

> the potential significance of Black feminist thought as specialized thought goes far beyond demonstrating that African American women can be theorists. Like the Black women's activist tradition from which it grows and which it seeks to foster, Black feminist thought can create collective identity among African American women about the dimensions of a Black women's standpoint. Through the process of rearticulation, Black women intellectuals offer African American women a different view of themselves

and their world from that forwarded by the dominant group (Omi and Winant 1986:93). By taking the core themes of a Black women's standpoint and infusing them with new meaning, Black women intellectuals can stimulate a new consciousness that utilizes Black women's everyday, taken-for-granted knowledge. Rather than raising consciousness, Black feminist thought affirms and rearticulates a consciousness that already exists. More important, this rearticulated consciousness empowers African American women and stimulates resistance. (Collins 1990:31–32)

It is important for us to see that Black feminist thought is not an separatist endeavor but one that builds on the marginal position of Black women so that they can use what Collins refers to as their "outsider-within" stance as a position of strength to build effective coalitions and stimulate dialogue. Such dialogue and principled coalition create possibilities for new versions of truth (Collins 1990:36).

It is from this basic stance that we must assess the value of Patricia Hill Collins's new book, *From Black Power to Hip Hop: Racism, Nationalism, and Feminism*. This is a fresh perspective that opens the analysis of social movements like nothing that I can recall since the work of Marx and Engels themselves in their historic *Manifesto of the Communist Party*.

Here Collins deals not only with the variety of racisms, but also with the changing forms of racism over social time. She contextualizes the evolution of racism in larger social contexts but also the evolution of nationalisms, both that of the larger society and that of subordinate strata such as people of African descent. What she adds to this mix is a study of family and its role in the conception of the nation. This is one location where issues of gender equity are most obvious, but it also provides a context for extending the analysis of gender equity into the arena of the larger society.

Her efforts to elaborate visions of feminist nationalism are not entirely new, but in the context of the Black Liberation movement, they shift the center of the discussion of the movement in dramatic and unprecedented ways. Black feminism came to the fore in the 1970s and 1980s but was unable to sustain its radical potential in the face of the new racism. There is all too little attention given to the nature of the Black Liberation movement after the decline of the Black Power movement in the 1970s, though. While my last book, *We Are Not What We Seem* (Bush 1999), takes pains to avoid the narrative of decline that infects some other works and points to the vague possibilities in the hip-hop generation, there is much more talk about structure there than about agency. Robin D. G. Kelley's "Kickin' Reality, Kickin' Ballistics" (1996a) points to the future, but in general he provides an elegant scaffolding for further analysis.

Todd Boyd (2002) and Bakari Kitwana (2002) have recently made names for themselves as intellectuals who speak from the perspective of the hip-hop generation, without engaging the full power of the legacy that they seek to overthrow, narrowly described as the civil rights generation.

Collins's treatment is immensely rich and powerful in its potential. She tells us how the expressions of U.S. nationalism are affected by race, gender, and

class. Her focus on nationalism and feminism is important but has not been af-
forded adequate treatment among leftist intellectuals. Most leftists tend to view
nationalism as a backwards, essentialist ideology. At best they are tolerant of the
nationalism of the oppressed, but sometimes only barely. Collins views nationalism as a powerful set of ideas that can be used for a variety of purposes. Its
power lies, she argues, in its ability to annex expressive needs to political ends.

The cultural wars of the 1980s and 1990s should not be simply dismissed as
political gimmicks, for they are really about the meaning of American national
identity and the significance of America. Collins points out that notions of family are central to widely held notions of the meaning of American national identity. The Right's use of family values to define their notion of American national
identity has been extremely effective. Rather than denying the sincerity of the
Right's profession of the importance of family values in their own lives, the Left
should seek to draw some lessons from this political practice. There may indeed
be an element of truth in the manner in which the Right uses family values as a
political weapon; the Left critique of the very notion of family values, Collins
argues, is seriously out of focus.

She points out that American politicians, academics, and ordinary citizens
draw on family ideology to construct ideas about American national identity and
citizenship. Understandably, Western feminists have tended to view the family
much more as a site of women's oppression, since it consigns women to a domestic space, whereas male authority not only dominates the family but reigns supreme in the outside world, which James Brown reminds us is a man's world—a
world, however, that would be nothing without the soothing and loving support of
a woman or a girl. Listen to his song on that theme, written during the height of
the Black Power period, when he was also singing about being Black and proud.

Families play an important role in social reproduction and in socializing the
young. The family is thus crucial in conceptualizing the nation. Collins argues
that nationalism draws meaning from Western conceptions of family and race.

Feminist analysis of gender and nationalism has been very helpful in the
rethinking of ideas about the concepts of nation, nationalism, and national identity. In contrast to what one might have thought about nationalism as a patriarchal notion, Collins argues for a more sophisticated concept that views nationalism as deeply gendered but has women playing very specific roles: reproducing
the population in their role as mothers; keeping and transmitting the traditional
culture, and symbolizing the nation to be protected. Patriotism, of course, is the
purview of men, who use violence to protect their women, their families, and the
nation.

Collins notes the relationship of segregation to the predominance of Black
Nationalist themes among African Americans, a fact that many Black intellectuals have missed. One of the problems central to this intellectual dilemma is the
implications of practice for Black solidarity. Does Black solidarity require a lock-
step approach to strategy, or should strategy develop out of public debate and
contention? Black feminists, Black lesbian, bisexual, gay, and transgender people,
biracial people, and multiracial people have often been encouraged to subordinate
their interests to that of the larger group. However, Collins sees as worrisome

those who would suppress all group-based social action on the basis of enhancing the opportunities of individuals.

The temptation to subordinate the voices of some in the interests of a broader constituency should always provoke questioning. This is not to say that coordination is not needed in organizations or coalitions, but at the broad social level this practice has to be suspect. This kind of reasoning is not only reflective of vanguardism in all of its problematic and dogmatic forms; it is emblematic of false universalism, which is far more problematic than dogmatism.

Collins quotes Kobena Mercer, who argues that solidarity does not mean that everyone thinks the same way. People need to be able to disagree over issues of fundamental importance precisely because they care about constructing common ground.

While mainly defending Black Nationalism and Black ethnic politics, Collins also examines the paradigmatic weaknesses of Black Nationalism and Afrocentrism. The forms of Black cultural nationalism expressed through the Afrocentric movements that emerged in the 1980s and 1990s in the Black studies departments at white universities created an imagined culture that was different from the efforts of intellectuals such as Frantz Fanon and Amilcar Cabral in the 1950s and 1960s, who were inspired by actual and not imagined national liberation struggles. These intellectuals viewed culture as dynamic and changing, as a complex network of social practices that determine positions of domination, equality, and subordination.

The attempt to cull from selected African societies a set of values and norms that could be useful to a new nationalist project, however, tended to be more fundamentally connected to Western metaphysical dualism, which Michelle Wallace argues is the underpinning of racism and sexist domination (Collins 2006:103). Afrocentric emphasis on culture displaced to a distant and safe past, the argument that psychological freedom must precede political freedom, and the emphasis on the need for self-esteem and role models are all seen as problematic in Collins's view (Collins 2006:105). The focus of Afrocentric scholars has been an insistence that the main problem for Black people is internal. The problems are cultural, behavioral, and psychological rather than political, economic, or structural. An even more fundamental critique of Black cultural nationalism focuses on its patriarchal insistence that Black women play the proscribed roles of mothers and cultural bearers, making it profoundly gendered.

Despite these criticisms, Collins views Afrocentrism as a manifestation of the love ethic that Cornel West (1991) calls for as the center of a politics of conversion. In a climate of institutionalized racism that valorizes whiteness, Afrocentrism offers a love ethic directed toward Black people, thus reaching out to ordinary Black men and women in a manner that is not available to the best academic antiracist, feminist, Marxist, or postmodern social theories. Collins holds that while sociology provides knowledge and postmodernism stresses tools of critique, Afrocentrism offers hope (Collins 2006:119–120).

Collins argues for a resource-mobilization approach to power relations rather than a power-as-domination approach. The latter holds that power relations are negotiated in a zero-sum setting where the dispossessed plead their case to those in power and if successful are granted concessions. If the powerful refuse to hear grievances, this could result in rebellion or revolution. In the resource-mobilization approach, power struggles occur in the micropolitics of everyday life, the challenge of everyday norms, and so on.

Black women's political activity is complicated by the necessity to grapple with intersecting systems of oppression. Insisting on fidelity to the complexity of social reality rather than acting upon a reified notion of social reality means that Black women are positioned between often competing politics of nationalism and feminism. Thus, Black women have united with Black men around race and class issues (employment, education, health, and education) but have often separated from them around issues of domestic violence, sexual violence, and homophobia. Since Black women's community work has been the arena in which they have elaborated their political understandings, they have had a stronger commitment to social justice grounded in fighting for the rights of an oppressed community than has the more individualist-oriented Western feminist movement.

This does not mean that Black women should eschew feminism, however. Indeed, Collins calls for Black women's political activism to be more, not less feminist. Black women often wind up sacrificing their needs as women to their central role in Black community work. Collins points out that Black women who were involved in the Student Nonviolent Coordination Committee during the civil rights movement experienced a growth in feminist consciousness as a result of the organization's gender politics (as we saw in Chapter 1). This tendency that emerged out of Black women's community work should continue. Black women should continue to insist—and more aggressively insist—on placing issues of gender more squarely at the center of the African American freedom struggle, where neither race nor gender can gain primacy without harming political efficacy. Collins argues that a clear implication of the social dynamic that leads to the increasing incarceration of Black men and the increase in female-headed households is the need for gender to be at the center of Black political agendas. This should require that Black men place fighting against gender inequities at the center of their political activity.

In the hip-hop generation, Black women's political stance includes an insistence on a personal, unique, individual identity unencumbered by someone else's standards. These women have been most conscious of the manner in which the idea of Black solidarity at all costs promotes a paradigm of individual sacrifice that borders on exploitation. Collins cites Joan Morgan, who in responding to questions about her commitment to Black feminism argued,

> Since my sexual preference could not be of any relevance to you, whatcha really wanna know is how I feel about brothas. It's simple. I love Black men like I love no other. And I am not talking about sex or aesthetics, I'm talking about loving ya'll enough to be down for the drama—stomping anything that threatens your existence. Now only a fool loves that hard without asking the same in return. So yeah, I demand that Black men fight sexism with the same passion that they battle racism. I want you to annihilate anything that endangers sistas' welfare—including

violence against women—because my survival walks hand in hand with yours. (Quoted in Collins 2006:149)

Collins holds that if one accepts the subtlety of Black feminist methodology then antiracist, group-based political struggles should respect individual rights and human rights, should be based on a global analysis, and should be informed by the best of feminism and nationalism and not their most troubling elements. The failure of many African American women and girls to engage in personal advocacy on their own behalf, according to Collins, stems from the absence of sustained debate of feminist ideas in African American communities. The continued segregation of African American communities means that the majority of African American women and girls lack access to the types of educational experiences that give them access to feminism. Their work and family responsibilities make it very difficult for them to engage in grassroots political activism of any sort, especially multiracial feminist coalitions. Thus, prevailing Black Nationalist traditions persist among Black women and men, including those with explicitly sexist themes.

Taken by themselves, Western feminist and Black Nationalist perspectives hold partial perspectives on Black women's community work generally and on Black feminist Nationalism or Black Nationalist feminism in particular. Rather than viewing feminism as primarily a criticism of nationalism and vice versa, feminism and nationalism may reinforce each other (Collins 2006:151–152). "When it comes to Black women's political resistance, where you stand, what you can see from that vantage point, and what you may stand for matters greatly. Versions of the political put forward by any group can offer only a partial perspective on definitions of feminism, nationalism, or any form of Black women's politics. No matter how significant any view may be, elevating one version of women's political activism over other forms and declaring it the 'best' or most 'authentic' approach redefines a partial perspective as a universal truth" (Collins 2006:160).

Collins finishes with Anna Julia Cooper's refrain: "When and where Black girls enter into freedom, there, too, will others also find hope for the future." (Collins 2006:26). If indeed the success of social transformation requires that we create a new commonsense, then such a project is not possible if we do not recognize the central role of women.

2

Radical Social Movements

5

The Civil Rights Movement and the Continuing Struggle for the Redemption of America

W hen some staff members of the Southern Christian Leadership Conference, including Jesse Jackson, resisted the proposal of Dr. Martin Luther King, Jr., to go to Memphis in support of the striking sanitation workers, Dr. King was incensed. Some staff members, concerned with their own more-favored projects, argued that this new project would spread them too thin. Dr. King issued a strong rebuke to their narrowing of the horizons of the movement and argued that he thought that this country was in critical condition and that they all had to work together to "redeem the soul of America" (Frady 1996:225). Dr. Martin Luther King was a man with a transcendent vision, but in stating these prescient sentiments he stood on the shoulders of giants. This is too often forgotten in treatments of the civil rights movement. I try in this chapter to understand the role of the civil rights movement in the context of its larger role as a force for the democratization of U.S. society as a whole, both internally and in its international relations.

Such transformative movements not only change the relations of force between mobilized oppressed strata and those who seek to occupy a privileged position in the body politic but also powerfully transform our collective understanding of social reality. We come to see the oppressed strata with new eyes, and they see themselves with new eyes. We reach for a new collective understanding of our social world as a consequence of such transformative social struggles. The rise of the lower strata in the civil rights period and throughout the postwar world stimulated new understandings of the social world.

This chapter originally appeared as Rod Bush, "The Civil Rights Movement and the Continuing Struggle for the Redemption of America," *Social Justice* 30, no. 1 (Winter 2003).

While liberals and leftists have tended to disregard FBI director J. Edgar Hoover's fear of subversion in the civil rights movement as either a disingenuous cover for his own racism or the paranoid fantasy of an anti-Communist psychosis, I argue that Hoover's fears were well-founded within the context of his own premise: that the civil rights movement posed a fundamental threat to the power arrangements of the American social order that he was sworn to defend. I have long felt that the lack of a serious appraisal of J. Edgar Hoover among liberals stemmed from a fear of confronting the contradictions in liberalism itself, partly revealed in its bastard offspring, neoconservatism. American liberalism is particularly torn between its egalitarian principles (vis-à-vis the New Deal and Great Society traditions) and its desire for stability and social order (stemming both from its social position as the hegemonic power in the capitalist world-economy and from its propagation of one of the founding principles of the capitalist world, the myth of Pan-European supremacy).

Martin Luther King understood well these contradictions. His statement in his "Letter from a Birmingham Jail" could apply to liberals as well as to moderates:

> I must confess that over the last few years I have been gravely disappointed with the white moderate. I have almost reached the regrettable conclusion that the Negro's greatest stumbling block in the stride toward freedom is not the White Citizen's Councilor or the Ku Klux Klanner, but the white moderate who is more devoted to "order" than to justice, who prefers a negative peace which is the absence of tension to a positive peace which is the presence of justice. . . . We will have to repent in this generation not merely the vitriolic words and actions of the bad people, but for the appalling silence of the good people. (King 1986:295–296)

While broad segments of white America speak with pride of their support of the civil rights tradition of Martin Luther King (at least up to the 1963–1965 period), there were some who had serious reservations. Despite the accolades given today to Martin Luther King's dream, there were a good many liberals who shared J. Edgar Hoover's fears about the civil rights movement: that it would ratchet up general dissatisfaction with America, leading others not only to support the demands of the Negro but to seek redress of their own grievances, causing an exponential growth in dissatisfaction with the American social order and the alleged Euro-American cultural foundation of humanity's greatest achievements.

One can sense this ambivalence in the public pronouncement of Daniel Patrick Moynihan, one public figure who has consistently supported redistributive programs on behalf of the disadvantaged. Moynihan decried America's inaction in the face of the increasing crises and consequent alienation of the Negro inner city. While Moynihan's concern that the Nation of Islam and other Black militants might soon follow the model of the Chinese Communists may today seem totally outside the bounds of scholarly discussion, it makes perfect sense given Moynihan's clear combination of support for redistributive programs and opposition to programs that enhanced the social and political power of the poor because they gave them the wrong message about how one should pursue success in America. Moynihan perfectly reflects the neoconservative dilemma without committing himself to the neoconservative movement.

Studies of the civil rights and Black Power movements of the 1960s have provided us with rich and powerful analyses of the sources of the struggle; the resources that enabled people to struggle effectively; and the intelligence, creativity, and vision of the women and men who committed their lives to the struggle for justice, equality, and democracy in America. Yet despite their status as second-class citizens, often occupying segregated ghettos away from the American mainstream, Black people and their struggles have been remarkably central to the story of American democracy and will continue to be central to the task of completing the great American revolution.

The story of the civil rights movement in its broad outlines is familiar to many readers; I do not repeat it here. I present here an intellectual history that focuses on the interaction of the ideas put forward by the civil rights and Black Power movements, the evolution of ideas and strategies in the liberal center, and the rise of a counterrevolutionary ideology fashioned in opposition to the radical threat posed by the rise of an increasingly large cadre of revolutionary ideologues and their location in an increasingly insurrectionary inner-city poor, the corollary of the nineteenth-century dangerous classes.

The Black freedom struggle assumed a variety of organizational forms in its attempts to articulate the increasingly assertive, militant, and radical sentiments of people in America's inner cities. Some of the pivotal organizations of the 1960s radical awakening were the Nation of Islam, the Student Nonviolent Coordinating Committee (SNCC), the Revolutionary Action Movement, the Organization of Afro-American Unity, the Black Panther Party, and the Students for a Democratic Society (SDS). While these organizations constituted much of the core of the mid-1960s Black Power militancy, they ultimately gave way to attempts to transcend the limitations of the civil rights, Black Power, and New Left movements.

The histories of these organizations provide us with spectacular stories of heroism, creativity, and vision. Yet despite the boldness and creativity of the individual and organizational leadership that came to the fore in the 1960s, the level of challenge that they mounted could not be normalized. It depended on the continued mobilization of an insurrectionary community. Once the insurrection subsided, the forces of repression moved to eliminate the threat to the social order. The revolutionary militants who came to the fore during this period returned to the drawing boards to figure out the way forward.

Instead of seeking to deepen their understanding of the complex relationship between the action of the masses and the thinking of leaders, intellectuals, and organizations, they overemphasized the role of organization and leadership and their failure to give sufficient leadership to the spontaneous rebellion of the masses. The militants thus concluded that they had failed as revolutionaries and looked for a revolutionary model that would enable them to organize their communities for a protracted struggle for power and social transformation. Most scholars of social movements have simply dismissed this period as the thrashings of a wounded beast going through its final death throes, descending predictably into a swamp of sectarianism, bickering, and utopian groups far removed from the concerns of their former inner-city bases. I believe that the evolution was far more complex and is thus worthy of much closer study. While these scholars lament the shattering of the Left-liberal consensus of the 1960s and attribute it to the extremism of the militants, I argue that the shattering of the Left-liberal consensus was both inevitable and over the long run liberating. In contrast to those who attribute the fracturing of the coalition to the extremism of the New Left, I argue that it was the liberal center that imploded the coalition by its collusion with the Right in the brutal repression of the popular Left (Malcolm X, Martin Luther King, the SNCC, the SDS) and its acceptance of the presumptions of American power as a force for good in the world.

The strategy of armed self-defense used by some of the Black Power militants was not a strategy for urban guerrilla warfare. While the notion of urban guerrilla warfare had some currency during the earlier cadre-development period among the forces associated with the Revolutionary Action Movement, it did not by and large survive the mass-mobilization period of the later sixties, when the Black Panther Party and others articulated the notion of the long march. The concept regained currency among some only after the murderous assault on the movement's leaders, including Malcolm X, Martin Luther King, and many leaders of the Black Panther Party. Both the Black Panther Party and the Nation of Islam advocated a policy of self-defense, which clearly incited the animosity of federal and local law enforcement agencies, whose command of a counterinsurgency state allowed them to plot the wanton murder of popular Black leaders. These law enforcement agencies pursued the suppression of the militants with reckless glee and cold-blooded ruthlessness.

This was a shattering dose of reality. It absolutely crushed any illusions about the liberal-democratic nature of the United States for those who were members of the opposition. It led to a search for an approach that did not result in the kind of vulnerability that allowed the late-1960s Black Power militants to be so easily targeted and eliminated. The New Left as a social force had come to the fore in opposition to the alleged collusion and betrayal of the Old Left, both social democratic and Communist. This hostility toward the Old Left meant that the members of the New Left were not only unlikely to form working relationships with the Old Left, but also unlikely to engage in a careful study of their experience. Those who had relative trust in the liberal-democratic nature of U.S. society attempted to consolidate their forces. The New American Movement merged with the Democratic Socialist Organizing Committee to become the multitendency Democratic Socialists of America.

Those who were most influenced by the struggles of the excluded minorities tended to focus on the exclusionary rather than the democratic aspects of U.S. society and thus searched for a model capable of withstanding the extremes of repression likely to be used in a revolutionary situation. These militants were attracted to the model of professional revolutionaries developed by the Third

International when they formed the leadership of the resistance movement against Fascism. Among these militants some followed not only the organizational form of the Third International but also the Marxist-Leninist theoretical framework, which they felt allowed for the development of a truly revolutionary unity of theory and practice. Some Black, Latino, Asian, and Native American militants adopted the organizational forms of the Third International but clung to a theoretical framework more revolutionary-nationalist in content and, like most of these forces, deeply influenced by Maoism.

While the paramilitary organizational forms used by these movements often fostered dogmatism in their ranks, the spirit of Maoism was deeply democratic, in line with the democratic critique of the New Left overall. It was precisely this democratic spirit that led to the spreading of the revolutionary spirit to so many different sectors of the population, and it was this democratic contagion that J. Edgar Hoover wanted to stop. Gil Scott-Heron made precisely this point about the Reagan phenomenon in his epic poem-song, "B-Movie." Scott-Heron tells us of the challenge to U.S. world hegemony during the 1970s. He argues that America no longer had John Wayne to come in and rescue America at the last minute like in a B movie, so we settled for Ronald Reagan. "Go give those liberals hell, that was the message to the new Captain Bly on the new ship of fools . . . Civil Rights, Women's Rights, Gay Rights. It's all wrong. Call in the cavalry to stop this perception of freedom run wild. Damn it, first one want freedom, and then the whole damn world wants freedom."[1]

While we cannot begin to analyze the histories of these organizations in this chapter, I simply allude to them here as a pervasive force and influence on the *rapports de force*. This book is part of a larger project that will involve a more detailed study of a broad range of organizations such as the Revolutionary Action Movement, the Black Panther Party, the League of Revolutionary Black Workers, the Black Workers Congress, the Congress of African People, the Malcolm X Liberation University, Peoples College, the Student Organization for Black Unity / Youth Organization of Black Unity, the Revolutionary Workers League, the Patrice Lumumba Coalition, the Harlem Fightback Organization, the Revolutionary Union, the Progressive Labor Party, Students for a Democratic Society, the Weather Underground Organization, the Sojourner Truth Organization, the Communist Labor Party, the Communist Workers Party, the Revolutionary Communist League, the Worker's Viewpoint Organization, the October League, the Puerto Rican Revolutionary Workers Organization, the August Twenty-Ninth Movement, the Prairie Fire Organizing Committee, the All African People's Revolutionary Party, the African Peoples Party, the African People's Socialist Party, the Black Workers for Justice, the Third World Women's Alliance, Line of March, the Communist Party USA, the Black Liberation Army, and the Black Guerilla Family.

Simply listing these organizations seems to be a stark counterpoint to the relative moderation of some of the Black public intellectuals who came to define the Black Left in the 1980s and 1990s and the conservative Black Nationalists who were associated in the public mind with Black radicalism. Just who were these "bad and militant children of the sixties" (Marable 1981:93)? Were they simply a product of that particular time, or do they have antecedents and descendents that would help us understand the contradictions and difficulties of our history?

What does social movement theory tell us about this history? Can the revolutionary musings and hopes of this generation of Black youth be seen as simply a negation of what Malcolm X identified as an American nightmare, or were they an expression of frustration about being excluded from the American dream of which Martin Luther King spoke so eloquently? Maybe there was nothing as grand and eloquent as I and its participants imagined, just the age-old drama of hopes frustrated and opportunities found.

I have developed a theme about the relation of the Black Liberation movement to the American dream that I use in public presentations designed for recruitment, celebrations, memorials, and the like. Gradually I began to wonder if slain civil rights leaders Malcolm X and Dr. Martin Luther King could effectively be used as the vehicles for mounting a critique of the hypocrisy of the American dream? Once I moved beyond a popular approach, I became aware of how difficult it was to separate these two towering figures from their social location in the American century despite the enormous international influences on their thought and action. Thus, despite the various labels attached to these imposing figures of the twentieth-century world, they were both quintessential products of the American century, and they spoke most eloquently across the color line and across national borders about the possibilities of a better world, a world that is substantively democratic, egalitarian, and just. These two leaders were steeped in the respective African American traditions of field-Negro revolt and Talented Tenth radicalism, which they intertwined with the most advanced thinking in both the U.S. and world arenas. The synthesis that each of these men made was based on the work of the giants who had come before them: John Brown, Frederick Douglass, W.E.B. Du Bois, Marcus Garvey, Paul Robeson, Ida Wells Barnett, Cyril Briggs, and so on.

The 1960s Rebellion

The 1960s was a period of considerable social unrest throughout the world-system. The 1950s dream of a white middle-class American utopia safely tucked away in a suburban haven was challenged by the realities of a larger world more racially and ethnically diverse, much less well-to-do, and residing across a wide geographic expanse far beyond the idyllic world of the 1950s American century. While the 1960s is viewed by most as a tumultuous period in U.S. history, only a few writers have seen clearly that it was comparable to the civil war of the 1860s. That this period is sometimes referred to as the Second Reconstruction by radical intellectuals and activists is only a partial recognition of its historical significance.

In the United States the revolt was spearheaded by the rebellion of the African American people. The intensity of the Black revolt surprised not only the U.S. Left but also intellectuals and revolutionaries throughout the world-system, for it did not accord with the analytic frameworks in which most operated. The Chinese, Cuban, and African revolutionaries were among the first of the mid-century revolutionary generation to view the African American revolt as part of the worldwide revolt against white Western domination. Mao Zedong argued that the evil system of imperialism began with the enslavement of the Negro people and would surely come to an end with the complete liberation of the Black people. Malcolm X's meteoric rise to revolutionary status after his split with the Nation of Islam was not in any way a product of Maoist dogma but the elaboration of a much older revolutionary tradition related by a similar but historically independent relationship to the larger social world. Malcolm X drew from the long tradition of field-Negro revolt that partook of an independent assessment of world anticolonial, socialist, and revolutionary forces over the course of the twentieth century.[2]

Anticolonial agitation was far from new to African Americans, who frequently made common cause with victims of colonial oppression, often seeing their own situation as parallel in some ways. From the turn-of-the-century attack on the humanity of African people, an anticolonial, anti-imperialist mentality took shape in the African diaspora. From the Ethiopian defeat of the Italian invaders in 1897 to the Pan African Congress of 1900, to Hubert Harrison's Race First Movement, to the identification with Japan's 1905 victory over Russia, to Cyril Briggs and the African Blood Brotherhood, to Garvey's Universal Negro Improvement Association, to the massive movement against Benito Mussolini's invasion of Ethiopia, to the efforts of Du Bois, Robeson, and Shirley Graham in the Council on African Affairs we see the growth and maturation of a radical anticolonial mentality among African American activists and intellectuals.[3] The modern civil rights movement was a product of the post–World War II world. In the international arena, movements for national liberation were prominent in every part of the formerly colonized world, that is, Indochina, India, China, and Africa. Thus, the civil rights movement was born during a period of worldwide decolonization. In this period, the British, French, and Dutch empires collapsed and new nations emerged composed of people of color. To be able to influence these new nations, the United States had to eliminate its official sanction of segregation and adopt a posture of support for civil rights. African Americans were aware of the decolonization movements in the third world, and many came to interpret these events as a sign of the increasing vulnerability of white power, not only in the wider world, but at home.

The collapse of the European empires seemed a vindication of the notion of the inevitable rise of the dark world, which was a part of the folklore of the Black working-class communities from which Malcolm had come. So during this time of the flowering of the civil rights movement, Malcolm X said that we had arrived at the end of white world supremacy. While the civil rights movement drew inspiration from the challenge to the white world, it did not develop a position so frankly oppositional as Malcolm X and the Black nationalists had. The civil rights leaders such as Dr. King and others hoped that their movement might lead to the redemption of America.

The major campaigns of the civil rights movement, from the Montgomery Bus Boycott to the voter registration drives of 1963 and 1964, were aimed at forcing the U.S. social system to live up to its own ideology of equality for all under the law. The overall goal of the movement was the integration of Blacks into the existing system, the destruction of caste barriers, and the affording of basic civil rights to all Americans. Initially the movement did not question the structure and goals of the system itself. It was during this period that the movement enjoyed the greatest support of whites in terms of money, the media, personnel, and the government. This is the period of the classical civil rights movement, which simply called on the United States to live up to its ideology.

In the period after 1965, equal employment, access to trade unions, affirmative action, and fair housing became the goals of the civil rights movement. These goals called for a redistribution of wealth and services, changes in the functioning of institutions, and changes in the North as well. It was during this period that much white liberal support was withdrawn. There were fundamental challenges to American society concerning its values, its violent history, its hypocritical self-image, its role in world affairs, and its economic structure, which was said to generate exploitation at home and dependence abroad.

During this period Dr. King's views came increasingly to resemble those of Malcolm X. Malcolm was arguing for a coalition of the radicals in the civil rights movement, Black nationalists in the United States, and revolutionaries in the Three Continents (Asia, Africa, and Latin America). As Malcolm moved actively and aggressively to create such coalitions, he was assassinated by forces in league with the conservative leadership of the Nation of Islam, the Federal Bureau of Investigation, and the Central Intelligence Agency.

To understand the reasoning behind the U.S. government's extreme measures against Malcolm X, and later Dr. Martin Luther King and the Black Panther Party, we should review some other aspects of the geopolitical situation in which the civil rights movement came to the fore.

The Bolshevik Revolution of World War I had installed a regime in power that had been a decisive factor in the defeat of the Fascists and whose military sphere had expanded into central Europe as a result of the war. This was an element in a larger issue, the rise of a world Communist movement. European Communist parties had played important roles in the resistance to Fascism throughout Europe. While this had been the basis of the ability of Communist parties to come to power in some Eastern European countries (with more or less help from the Red Army), strong Communist parties now existed in some Western European countries and appeared to be in a position to challenge the capitalist parties.

While the Soviet Union was viewed as the center of a world socialist movement organizing for a worldwide proletarian uprising, it also proclaimed itself the natural ally of the national liberation movements. This claim flowed from its socialist and anti-imperialist ideology, but its more solid grounding was that the Soviet bloc consisted primarily of semiperipheral states who had been victims of semicolonial or neocolonial domination. It was thus a combination of fears that drove the United States in this period. There was the possible ideological appeal to a rebellious working class, to a left and cosmopolitan intelligentsia, and to the left-outs, some of whom identified with allied forces in the third world, which America was attempting to win to its side in the cold war with the Soviet Union.

So when Malcolm X argued that the Black freedom struggle was a component of the world struggle against capitalism and imperialism, it was J. Edgar Hoover's and the U.S. ruling establishment's worse nightmare. When Malcolm X successfully drew Martin Luther King into an alliance with him, this all but signed a death warrant for both of them.

While Black leaders had long criticized U.S. foreign policy, since its role in the cold war brought it in opposition to the aspirations of people of color in Africa and elsewhere, over time many Black leaders muted their criticism, especially in view of McCarthyism. Paul Robeson, W.E.B. Du Bois, and Shirley Graham were among the few who consistently opposed U.S. foreign policy at great price. All these leaders were both prosocialist and anti-imperialist. After the Battle of Dien Bien Phu in 1954, in which the poorly armed Vietnamese decisively defeated the French army, Paul Robeson published an article titled "Ho Chi Minh: The Toussaint L'Overture of Indochina." In this article Robeson not only compared Ho Chi Minh to the famous leader of the Haitian slave revolt but also warned of Eisenhower's threat to send Americans to Vietnam to protect the tin, rubber, and tungsten of Southeast Asia for the "free world."

Du Bois criticized the alleged anticolonial role of the United States as a new type of colonialism. In 1950 Du Bois ran for the U.S. Senate in New York on the American Labor Party ticket. In his campaign he was very critical of the anti-Communist policies of both the Republican and Democratic parties. On February 8, 1951, the Truman administration indicted Du Bois for allegedly being an agent of a foreign power in his work with the Peace Information Center in New York. The eighty-two-year-old Du Bois was handcuffed and fingerprinted and treated like a common criminal in the press. In November 1951 a federal judge dismissed the case because the federal government did not submit one shred of evidence to substantiate its claim.

In addition to being subjected to legal and paralegal harassment, both men had their passports revoked and were ostracized by the centrist leadership of the civil rights movement. Benjamin Davis and Henry Winston, Black leaders of the Communist Party of the USA, went to prison.

While traditional Black criticism of U.S. foreign policy waned during this repressive period, the black protest leaders used the United States' sensitivity about its image as the leader of the free world to put pressure on the United States to make certain concessions to Blacks. This had been precisely the tack of the early 1940s March on Washington Movement led by A. Philip Randolph.

In this sense the March on Washington Movement was the model for the modern civil rights movement. From 1944 to 1950, Black initiatives led to several concessions by the executive and judicial branches of the federal government. The white primaries were struck down in the courts, President Truman formed the first presidential civil rights commission, segregation in interstate bus travel was legally denied, segregation in the army was attacked, literacy tests

for voting were declared unconstitutional, border states began the token desegregation of the graduate schools, dining cars were desegregated, and so on.

This was the context in which the NAACP initiated a full-fledged attack on
the basic principle of separate but equal. Black leaders paid a price for these
gains, however, either by soft-pedaling their opposition to U.S. foreign policy or
by outright opposing those such as Robeson, Graham, and Du Bois, who stood
up for the indivisibility of the anticolonial struggles in the third world and the
black struggle for freedom, justice, and equality in the United States.

The scourge of McCarthyism was to nearly wipe the memory of these central characters from African American and American life more broadly. But
Malcolm X was to revive their vision—more vividly and closer to the grass roots.
Malcolm's contentions that people of color were not a minority but a majority of
the have-nots in the world and that their struggle should be for their God-given
human rights instead of civil rights, which Uncle Sam could grant or deny at his
discretion, are examples of how he illuminated the landscapes of an entire generation of intellectuals, activists, and people at the grass roots. Quickly the recognition began to sink in at the highest levels of the U.S. government. Moynihan
compared the Black revolt to the Chinese Communists, noting that the Black
Muslim movement indicated the near-total alienation of segments of the African American population from the United States. Others of the U.S. elite compared the Black revolt to the National Liberation Front in Vietnam.

But FBI director J. Edgar Hoover had decided in 1963 that the civil rights
movement was the leading edge of a social revolution in the United States and he
set out to destroy it. Hoover often used the danger of violence to justify his hunt-
ing for Communists in the civil rights movement, and his concern about Communist influence as an excuse for his surveillance of Dr. Martin Luther King and
other civil rights leaders. His 1963 decision to destroy the civil rights movement,
however, preceded any of the major urban rebellions that rocked the nation's cities from 1964 to 1971.

Hoover and the elites he represented were concerned about violence, but this
violence was not a product of the activity of the civil rights movement per se; they
were both a part of the zeitgeist. Hoover feared that the democratic and egalitarian spirit of the civil rights movement would become contagious, pushing other
groups to make similar claims. This would overwhelm the ruling consensus,
which was based on the acceptance of the justification of inequality, claiming
inferiority, lack of initiative, and lack of human capital among groups who were
culturally different from those who occupied the social, political, and economic
mainstream. Violence was not the issue; it was a symptom of a loss of control
and a nearly total lack of legitimacy.

While Hoover called for all attempts to prevent the rise of a messiah who could
unify the Black Nationalist "hate groups," his intent was to prevent the unifica-
tion of the disparate members of excluded groups with sympathetic members of
the white mainstream. This could create a volatile mix that might be interested
in pursuing an egalitarian agenda vis-à-vis the elites of the American race-class
system.

A major component of the restructuring of the capitalist world-system during the period 1945–1990 was the transnational expansion of U.S. capital. The capital migration of this period was a response to the class and social conflicts of the 1960s and 1970s, which further strengthened the bargaining power of the U.S. labor force, which was established as a consequence of the militant labor struggles of the 1930s.[4]

In the 1970s, the deepening economic crisis intensified competition among the various segments of the labor force, but during the unprecedented expansion of the 1960s, there seemed to be room to bring more and more people into the labor force. In this situation, concessions could be made to the African American population, which had mounted a ferocious attack on the citadels of power, including militant protest and violent rebellion. During this period Blacks were admitted to sections of the labor force that had previously been closed to them. Black people's history as a labor force in the United States had lent a certain intensity to their perception of social relations in the world of work, however. They thus made demands for treatment that others thought extreme or touchy. Militant caucuses and radical worker organizations were formed all over the country.

Given that this new group of militant and radical workers entered the labor force at a time of rapid expansion, their militancy was underscored by a tight labor market. The outcome of this combination of labor market factors led, in capital's view, to an alarming lack of labor discipline. As the profitability of capitalist enterprises began to be squeezed, they sought cheaper and more malleable workforces outside of the core zones. They also manipulated immigration laws to allow for an influx of immigrant laborers who were not citizens, some of whom were not documented. At the same time, they sustained an intense ideological attack on the labor force, targeting their unreliability, lack of discipline, and lack of a work ethic in comparison with the leaner work forces of the periphery. This ideological campaign against a "fat-cat working class" was complemented by a subterranean campaign designed to justify the wholesale dismissal of the militant Black and Latino working class from the workforce altogether. A third—the most intense—component of this ideological attack focused on the marginal sections of the working class who were subjected to long-term or structural unemployment but who were entitled to the dregs of the welfare state, such as Aid to Families with Dependent Children. This moral critique against the poor became the center of the conservatives' southern strategy, a mean-spirited, cold-blooded, and cynical strategy of color-blind racism designed to undercut any sense of human solidarity with the most disadvantaged segments of the population.

In addition, given the gains of the civil rights movement, room had been created for a significantly enlarged Black middle class, which formed both the basis for a move to the right among the major civil rights organizations and the establishment of a conservative segment of the Black body politic to the right of the liberal civil rights establishment. The new Black and Latino conservatives would play a useful role in the class warfare waged against the poor by those seeking to recapture the white republic of old, but this time with a large number of honorary whites, a groveling and morally debased group who capitulated to the victim-blaming and self-righteous moral poverty of the white conservatives.

We should not lose focus on the larger framework that enclosed this drama—that overall the central theme of this era was the crisis of U.S. hegemony represented by the military and political challenge in Vietnam and spearheaded by the increasing competitiveness of Japanese and German enterprises vis-à-vis U.S. enterprises. The global liberalism of the post–World War II era was no longer adequate; the political and economic elite sought a way to reverse the declining fortunes of the United States. The backlash started in the 1970s.

The conservatism of the Reagan-Bush years was a reaction to the challenges of the 1960s and 1970s and fundamentally a reaction to the revolution of 1968. Too often this period is viewed as simply a society-wide revulsion for the extremes of the New Left. But the extremes of the New left reflected the real polarization in the world-system, in which subaltern groups allied with the American hegemon all over the world were under challenge. What was truly remarkable about this period was the depth of support in the United States for these movements in opposition to U.S. hegemony and the rule of its subaltern allies. This kind of internationalism had been a regular feature of large sections of the Black freedom struggle and the world socialist movement. But now it was the dominant position of large sections of the population, with a majority of young blacks and a significant number of white college students arguing that a revolution was necessary in the United States.

In the United States, the prototypical organizations of the New Left included SDS, the Revolutionary Action Movement, and the Black Panther Party. Yet the New Left was much more complicated than just those three groups would indicate. Robert Williams and Malcolm X were public figures who most clearly represented this trend.[5] The stories of this period generally link the decline of the New Left with the decline of the Black Panther Party and Students for a Democratic Society, but actually the decline of these two organizations led to the proliferation of a number of organizations that defined themselves as operating in the tradition started by these organizations but that had learned from their errors.

If the New Left organizations brandished the weapon of ungovernability, the Left Leninists and the revolutionary nationalists who took up the banner of these organizations represented an unprecedented crisis of legitimacy. This stratum of activists entered the culture of the professional revolutionaries who had emerged during the antisystemic movements of around the time of the advent of Leninism in the Soviet Union. They then emerged throughout the revolutionary movements of the capitalist world. These revolutionaries were preparing for the long march—a protracted struggle to defeat capitalism. Many knew that they would not personally live to see the victory of the people but that they would through their struggle contribute to an alteration in the relations of force that would eventually cumulate to such an extent that the people would finally be able to overthrow the rule of capital. This had nothing to do with violent revolution and everything to do with the power of the people being organized materially and morally into an irresistible force.

There is a profound historical gap in our scholarship on this period, reflecting perhaps an even more profound historical amnesia. Max Elbaum has provided a service of immeasurable value with the comprehensive analytical history of this period in his recent book, *Revolution in the Air* (2002). Elbaum tells us a story of a world full of possibilities, when millions of youth sided with the barefoot people of the world as Dr. King preached during the last year of his life. For Elbaum, the revolutionary fervor of this period stemmed in part from the all-important recognition "that the power of the oppressed was on the rise and the strength of the status quo was on the wane" (Elbaum 2002:2). During this period there was a growing sense among those protesting against social injustice that their ranks were growing and that the ranks of the aggrieved everywhere were not only growing but that they were being joined by increasing numbers of people everywhere. The decline in the strength and prestige of the defenders of the status quo were of course visible everywhere. Things were indeed changing because of the actions of the people, deepening the sense of those protesting against social injustice that their actions could bring about social change. Though it is today surprising, during the 1970s no one would be shocked that in early 1971, polls reported that upward of 3 million people thought a revolution was necessary in the United States (Elbaum, 2002:2). Forty years of an hegemonic conservative backlash have erased or rewritten the public memory of those halcyon days.

The very idea of a cadre of professional revolutionaries seems like an astonishing departure from reality, but the world of the 1970s was still a part of the era of 1968, when revolution seemed to be on the agenda everywhere. The emergence of a generation of professional revolutionaries in the heart of world capitalism, building on the legacies of Malcolm X, Martin Luther King, and the Black Panther Party, was no laughing matter. The extremes of state violence that were visited on these predecessors were an accurate gauge of the state's reaction.

Let us attempt here to carefully trace this period in U.S. history, which I will argue is of far greater import than is usually acknowledged. This history has itself become a victim of the struggle between the forces of movement, democracy, and equality on the one hand and reaction and the maintenance of an imperial, Pan-European status quo on the other. Put simply, we might follow Malcolm X's insight that we were witnessing the end of white world supremacy.

American Dream or American Nightmare

While some have sensed in Martin Luther King's "I Have a Dream" Speech at the 1963 March on Washington the most eloquent testimony to the American dream, others regard Malcolm X's description of an American nightmare as America's most fundamental challenge. Yet, no matter how bitter some have been about the hypocrisy of the American dream, there can be little doubt that these two larger than life figures of the twentieth century precisely because their lives and actions were shaped by and helped to influence the countours of the American century. The historical trajectory of the American century gave them their stage, but it also elevated their voices to a global stage because of their location in it. I have argued elsewhere that Dr. Martin Luther King's "I Have a

Dream" speech represented the high point of U.S. world hegemony or what some call the American century (Bush 1999). While some were skeptical of Dr. King's dream from the outset, the momentum of the forces of progress seemed to overwhelm the forces of reaction so dramatically that people's sense of optimism was heightened beyond what seems now to be possible. These people had every confidence that the determined and the virtuous could bring about a fundamental democratic transformation of American society, in part by doing the same in the larger world. America would finally live up to its creed and would loosen its grip on countries around the world where their subaltern allies were holding down "their own people" in the interests of U.S. elites.

While most based their pessimism on what they felt to be the prospects of the inner-city poor outside of the South, the victory over Jim Crow gave to the civil rights movement a level of moral authority and momentum that might have created a political movement that could lead to the kind of transformation reflected in King's dream. Many activists and scholars felt that the failure of the dream was simply a lesson that needed to be learned, if not by the middle-class leadership of the civil rights movement, then certainly by its predominantly working-class base. The sense was that Malcolm X had always had it right and that King too would learn this lesson.

The reification of Malcolm X and King into polar opposites, however, imposed a framework that hindered the militants' ability to understand the subtle evolution of American society and the social forces within it at that time. We all know that Malcolm X's critique caught on like wildfire subsequent to Martin Luther King's hopeful pleading and that King himself was soon to follow Malcolm's lead and say that his dream had turned into a nightmare. For Dr. King, the revolution in the streets of the Black and Brown ghettos and in the jungles of Vietnam had exposed the cold-blooded and ruthless nature of the American social system. To understand King's despair and his seeming transformation into an advocate of global revolution, we should pay careful attention to this historical period.

In this sense J. Edgar Hoover is much more careful in his analysis of these times than many activists and scholars who supported the democratic and egalitarian ideals of the civil rights movement. Hoover understood the social psychology of rebellion. It was at this time that he argued that the civil rights movement was the leading edge of a social revolution in the United States and thus had to be destroyed. Hoover could see the power of the connections that linked the increasingly radical Black freedom struggles, radical nationalist movements in the third world, and an emerging rainbow coalition carrying a radical message to the increasingly impatient tenants of the inner city and a broad section of labor, youth, women, and liberal intellectuals and activists. Hoover understood well the social psychology of rebellion; he had studied closely the history of rebellion in the United States.[6]

The rise of the United States to hegemonic status in the post–World War II world called for a social psychology altogether different from that of the era of contention for hegemony. The late 1940s established the centrality of anticommunism to the repression of popular democracy and the construction of an atmosphere of repressive tolerance, where ideas of individual freedom coexisted with the harshest repression of political difference. An utterly white world emerged in the suburban havens, concerned with consumer goods, family life, and obeisance to God and country. God had blessed America (or rather white America), leading *Time* magazine editor Henry Luce to declare it the American century. The liberal and radical intelligentsia and the social movements with which they were affiliated might have opposed such a program had they not been locked in mortal internal conflict between the so called revolutionaries and the so-called reformists in the Left and between the anti-Stalinist Left and those who were aligned with or open to the Communist Party and its popular fronts. One of the major instruments of this counterinsurgency was the CIA-funded Congress of Cultural Freedom, which won an important segment of the anti-Stalinist Left to side with liberal and reactionary anticommunism as a mechanism for developing a patriotic center-left force that eschewed the traditional cosmopolitan internationalism of Left and liberal intellectuals, thus severely constraining opposition to the great American celebration. The combination of carrot and stick was an effective tool for the suppression of dissent, but the evolution of worldview of U.S. activists was more complex. It was a matter of not just CIA manipulation but the establishment of an atmosphere that effectively allowed for a stance that accepted American hegemony as a positive force in a world menaced by the Communist danger. It was in this context that a segment of the radical and liberal intelligentsia adopted the status quo orientation of the conservatives vis-à-vis the American presumption of leadership in world affairs.

The Communists had been an important force in an increasingly strong and volatile interwar workers' movement and in the struggle for racial justice as well. This is not to say that the Communists built these movements but that they lent important energy and resources to them, and in the case of the struggle for racial justice, they did so like no other predominantly white organization of that time. What made the Communists such a dangerous force in the eyes of the guardians of the status quo was the role that they played in connecting a great number of social forces. The United States' declaring that the Communists were agents of a foreign power was much more a strategy for legitimizing the repression of dissent than for protecting America's national security against the Soviet Union. During the 1930s and 1940s, intellectuals and activists associated with the popular front came to articulate a form of American patriotism that was democratic, cosmopolitan, and egalitarian and that eschewed the racist strains of Pan-European supremacy and world hegemony.[7]

Those sectors of the U.S. Left that did not succumb to the American celebration were either associated with the popular front or were oriented toward the revolutionaries of the Three Continents (Africa, Asia, and Latin America)—what in African American parlance was known as the dark world. That these categories of social forces frequently overlapped is a testimony to their common causes and should not be surprising or perceived as evidence of a sinister conspiracy. It was a credit to the Communist movement that it recognized the transformative potential in the Black freedom struggle, although the relationships formed during this period were never smooth and trouble free. The rise of radical nationalist movements in the third world revitalized the Black third world within, which had itself been repressed with the attacks on Du Bois, Robeson, Alphaeus Hunton, and others in the Council of African Affairs and the Peace Information Center.[8]

In the context of this brutal repression, the modern civil rights movement came to the fore wrapped in the blanket of anticommunism. Nonetheless, the March on Washington Movement of the early 1940s had firmly established an appreciation of the importance of international events in the strategizing of what was to become the Black liberal leadership. But the Black intellectual tradition had long been a deeply internationalist, radical tradition. The struggle during the 1940s and 1950s was to bring the Black radical tradition under liberal hegemony. So the 1960s movement did not create something new; it reconnected with the long-standing Black radical tradition. What was new was the conjuncture in which it took place, which provided this moment with particular significance, but which also enables us to recontextualize occurrences of Black radicalism in previous eras. In the 1960s and 1970s, Malcolm X, Dr. King, and the Black Panther Party moved to the forefront of a new American revolution that would take place in solidarity with the exploited and oppressed of the larger world-system.

The civil rights movement centered in the South and the Black Nationalist movements outside the South emerged during the 1950s and 1960s as the main challenge to the American celebration since they represented the largest segment of a status group that had been explicitly excluded from the spectacular postwar economic prosperity. Women too had been largely left out or had been contradictorily incorporated as the celebrated housewives of the 1950s ideal nuclear families. This was an exceedingly cruel embrace in most cases, but many women increasingly defected from the cast as even the radical men of the white New Left and the third world within took up their own versions of manhood rights.

Black society had functioned under the myth that the problem with Black society, notoriously repeated in the controversial Moynihan Report on the Negro family, was that the women ran the show, castrated Black men, and so on. In the meantime, women played exemplary, though largely unrecognized, roles as leaders of the Black freedom struggle. Easily recognized names here include SNCC founder Ella Baker, SNCC leader Fannie Lou Hamer, Third World Women's Alliance leader Fran Beal, Montgomery NAACP leader Rosa Parks. But there were debates taking place in many of the revolutionary organizations and many examples of strong female leadership such as in the New York City–based December 12 Movement who have been central actors in the Black activist movement in the city, and who have built a powerful social justice movement in Bedford-Stuyvessant Brooklyn. New York readers may be familiar with Sista's Place a project started by some of the leadership of the December 12 Movement.

The civil rights movement and the more radical forces in the inner cities outside the South provoked a society-wide debate about the nature of racism, power, poverty, equality, and democracy. These debates and the overall circumstances of the era led to the elaboration of social policy based on vastly expanded notions of equality and social justice. The notion of institutional racism propounded by the Black Power militants, for example, was the foundation for the development of relatively radical attacks on the racial division of labor via policies such as affirmative action. In contrast to this great flowering of opportunity for populations within the boundaries of the United States, the demands of an imperial state were to undermine this debate and polarize America in ways not seen since the Civil War. The defenders of the status quo mounted a counterinsurgency unprecedented in U.S. history that led to the assassinations of Malcolm X, Dr. King, Fred Hampton, Bunchy Carter, George Jackson, among others, and to the imprisonment of many others. These assassinations were devastating to the young radical forces and fundamentally altered the terms of the struggle. Leaders such as these are a rarity. While the secular Left is often critical of what they call the cult of personality, all revolutionary movements have leaders whose skills and charisma are important components of the revolutionary process. While the deepening of the revolution beyond the mobilization for state power requires a democratization of leadership, the very extraordinariness of revolution itself requires exceptional leadership.

I have attempted to argue here that Dr. King and Malcolm X did not create this moment. During what some call the American century, a mature global liberalism held sway, promising the spread of the good and then the great society to all Americans and eventually to all in the world who followed their example and direction. Dr. King pushed this idea as far as possible, but Malcolm X was skeptical. The youthful rebels of SDS argued for a radical democratization of U.S. society. But the rebellion against U.S. hegemony manifested in the struggles in Vietnam, Algeria, Cuba, China, Ghana, Guinea, and other parts of the three continents undermined the largesse of the liberal state. One of the central themes of the twentieth-century Black freedom struggle was the rise of the dark world, which now seemed at hand. The *rapports de force* had shifted decisively in favor of the colonized, semicolonized, dependent zones of the world economy, and Malcolm X, SNCC, SDS, the Congress of Racial Equality, and finally Dr. King and a host of others called not only for solidarity with the revolutionaries of the three continents but also for their followers to become a part of this elemental rebellion against the way things were. The world revolutionary trend was global in scope, despite the global power of U.S. hegemony, or perhaps because of the global power of the U.S. hegemon.

I now refocus the lens to see how the seizure of center stage by the wretched of the earth affected the nature of the debates among social scientists and others concerned with social policy, poverty, race, and social inequality. Scholarly debate is not simply about scholarly taste for ideas; it is in addition a response to action in the streets, and thus, at its best, a manifestation of the human agency of the oppressed.[9]

Scholars Debate Poverty, Race, and Class Formation

While the term *culture of poverty* originated in the work of Oscar Lewis (1959), the concept that it purports to describe derives at least from the early period of capitalism, when pauperism was the fate of large sections of the proletarianized masses in the core of the capitalist world economy. While Michael B. Katz (1989) argues that terms such as *culture of poverty* and *underclass* are simply modern terms for the very old concept of the *undeserving poor*, I argue for a broader definition of the concept, rooted in the central stratifying processes of the capitalist world economy.

Lewis's use of the term *culture of poverty*, like Marx's use of the term *lumpen proletariat*, reflected a concern about the degradation of the lower rungs of the working population by the conditions of their existence in the capitalist system. Lewis, like Marx, felt that this condition reflected the fact that some sections of the population (for Marx, the lower rung of the reserve army of labor) were completely demoralized and declassed by their experiences at the very bottom of the economic ladder.

For both Lewis and Marx, the terms *culture of poverty* and *lumpen proletariat* corresponded to the level of perceived class consciousness and political organization among the lowest rung of the working class. To some extent, both men used these terms to call attention to the degradations of the capitalist system, although their overall frameworks differed. Similarly, Michael Harrington and Moynihan used similar approaches (although different concepts) to appeal to the political and economic elite, intellectuals, and the middle class to support reforms that would alleviate the wretched conditions of the "other America" and the black family, respectively.[10]

Although there were differences in the views of the authors cited above, they all can be said to be on the left of the political spectrum.[11] The differences in conceptual elaboration between the revolutionary (Marxist) Left and the reformist Left (i.e., Moynihan) were polarized by the social practice of the lower strata itself, leading to a significant breakthrough in understanding of the ideological underpinnings of the capitalist world economy on the revolutionary Left (e.g., the critique of universalism by Samir Amin and Immanuel Wallerstein)[12] and to the cooptation of sections of the reformist Left by the conservative elites of the capitalist system (Moynihan in particular, but the neoconservatives in general).[13]

By the mid- and late 1960s, the notion of a culture of poverty or of the predominant demoralization of the lower strata became increasingly untenable, as this sector of the population rose in revolt all around the world and thus began to speak for itself. In doing this it was supported by left-wing and organic intellectuals and political leaders such as Frantz Fanon, Mao Zedong, Malcolm X, Andre Gunder Frank, and Samir Amin.[14] In the face of the Algerian Revolution, the great proletarian Cultural Revolution in China, the Black Power movement, the Vietnam liberation movement, and the generalized world revolution of 1968, the idea of a culture of poverty seemed to lack grounding in reality.

While in the 1960s, liberal intellectuals used the term *culture of poverty* to support their appeals for an interventionist approach to the problems of poverty, by the 1970s the term had become a tool of conservative reaction and the Left had began to articulate the more radical notion of a "culture of resistance." There is in Lewis's work a distinct notion that when lower-class people organize themselves in trade unions or socialist parties, that is, when they became class conscious, then they are no longer a part of the culture of poverty. This notion is quite similar to the notion of a culture of resistance.

The idea of a culture of resistance was popularized by the anthropologist Mina Davis Caulfield (1969, 1974). She adapted it from Robert Blauner, who described a process of culture building as central to the cultural activities of the African slaves in North America. For Caulfield this process developed as both an adaptation to and a protest against the social experience of the colonial situation. She argues that this process could be discerned in the group lives of most, if not all, "culturally exploited people."[15]

Caulfield argued "we must look not only at the way in which the colonizer acts to break down family solidarity, but also the ways in which the colonized— women, men, and children—act to *maintain, consolidate, and build anew* the basic units in which children can grow and be enculturated in the values and relationships that are independent of and in opposition to imperial culture" (Caulfield 1974:72–73).[16]

In contrast to the theory of a culture of poverty, Caulfield argued that the main characteristics of the culture of resistance are resourcefulness, flexibility, and creativity, rather than fatalism, passivity, and dependence. In contrast to Lee Rainwater, she argued that cultures of resistance are not simple adaptive mechanisms, but alternative means of organizing "production, reproduction, and value systems critical of those of the oppressor" (Caulfield 1974:84).[17]

The term *culture of resistance* acquired broad usage throughout the Left, particularly in the context of the world revolution of 1968.[18] Wallerstein argued in 1980 that the world economy is a complex of cultures, however, not a haphazard one. For Wallerstein there existed a *"Weltanschauung* of Imperium, albeit, one with many variants," and "cultures of resistance to this Imperium" (Wallerstein 1984:13-26).[19]

For Wallerstein, the deepening of the capitalist division of labor, the need to facilitate its operation through the allocation of workforces, and the justification of inequality led to the use of an ideology of racism that became the central organizing theme of the world bourgeoisie. Equally central was the ideology of universalism that held that there existed a universal culture to which the cadres of the world division of labor were assimilated.

Wallerstein defined culture as the "the idea-system" of the capitalist world economy (Wallerstein 1991:166). In this sense he viewed culture as the outcome of our collective historical attempts to come to grips with the contradictions, ambiguities, and sociopolitical complexities of the capitalist world. Seen in this way, then, Wallerstein concludes, the very construction of culture is the key ideological battleground of the opposing interests in the capitalist system.

Why, then, is racism the central organizing cultural theme of the world bourgeoisie? There is general agreement that capitalism is by definition an inegalitarian system, but how does this fact square with the ideology of equality of opportunity?

The argument is that reward is based on merit, and that all—even the children of the poor—if they are talented, have the opportunity to obtain high reward.

But since there is so little upward social mobility, how is it that the notion of equality of opportunity is not declared a sham?

The justification, according to Wallerstein, is precisely racism:

> It provides the only acceptable legitimation of the reality of large-scale collective inequalities within the ideological constraints of the capitalist world-economy. It makes such inequalities legitimate because it provides theoretically for their transitory nature while in practice postponing real change for the Greek calends. . . . The hinge of the argument is that those who have low ethnic status (and consequently low occupational position for the most part) find themselves in this position because of an unfortunate but theoretically eradicable cultural heritage. They come from a group which is somehow less oriented to rational thinking, less disciplined in its work ethic, less desirous of educational and/or earned achievement. Because we no longer claim these presumed differential aptitudes are genetic but merely cultural we congratulate ourselves on having overcome the crudities of racism. . . . We tend to forget that if a cultural heritage differs from a biological one in that it is historically changeable, it is also true that, if the word "culture" means anything here, it indicates a phenomenon that is slow to change, and is slow to change precisely because it has become part of the superegos of most members of the group in question (Wallerstein 1988).[20]

In this way the oppressed are told that their position in the world can be transformed provided they are educated in the skills necessary to act in certain ways, which are said to be the means by which the currently high-ranking groups obtained their positions. It is precisely the slowness of change that makes racism so central to the functioning of the capitalist world economy.

Wallerstein also argues that ethnic consciousness both enables a group to struggle politically for its rights and socializes the young to a realistic perception of social polarization and thus to occupational expectations. So, racism keeps people in while their labor is needed, it is able to put them on hold when their labor is not needed, and it can bring them back in when conditions permit. This means, according to Wallerstein, that such groups are eager and willing to be brought back in and thus can rightly be considered a "reserve army" in a literal sense (Wallerstein 1988:13-14).

There may be less reserve than meets the eye, though. While racism may impede one's entry into the formal economy, we must know something about the operation of the informal economy before we can speak with relatively certainty of someone's willingness to be "brought back in." So if there come to be better opportunities in the so-called informal economy—criminal employment, drug dealing, and the like—will some members opt for this more lucrative opportunity than for the marginal jobs normally available to them, even in good times?

Why not? Any teenager can tell you that the attraction of the drug economy is the quick buck. What is there in the cultural values of the dominant culture that entreats us not to go after the quick buck? Certainly there exist value systems among the population (religious values, Black Nationalist values, etc.) that alternatives to the dominant value system. Despite all the hype one hears about the need for positive role models in the inner city, we seem as a society quite disappointed in the propensity of some inner-city denizens to follow the bottom-line thinking of the corporate elite.

Where does that leave us? We must understand the idea of a culture of resistance as a product of a period of popular mobilization among the peripheral and peripheralized populations of the capitalist world economy. During periods of demobilization, this culture of resistance takes an individual form and today is referred to by some scholars as a culture of opposition, sometimes viewed simply as negative or nihilistic (Anderson 1999:316; West 1994:17-31).[21] Lewis argues that one of the things that distinguish groups that we think of as having a culture is that they are self-conscious. Thus, to the extent that the urban poor are not a self-conscious (or class-conscious) group, but atomized individuals, Lewis argues, a culture of poverty can be said to exist (Lewis (1970:74).

Who could disagree with the sentiment expressed here? Lewis is impressed by his observations of revolutionary Cuba (O. Lewis, R. Lewis, and S. Rigdon 1977a, 1977b) but does this lament about the presumed lack of class consciousness among the inner-city poor in the United States point us in the right direction? I think not. We must resist the magic aura that these words hold and recognize the impact of multiple stratifying processes which give rise to interlocking forms of oppression *and* exploitation, not just that of class. Here again we see the hegemonic class first lense that we reviewed in Chapter 3.

Max Weber viewed classes in relationship to one another as simply objective categories, but not ones that implied any form of consciousness or capacity for collective action. He argued that immediate class interests were given by market position and hence were theoretically indeterminate so far as collective action was concerned. For collective action to take place, something in addition to class interests had to be introduced (Weber (1978:926-939).

In contrast, status groups are by definition groups that act collectively in relation to one another and are endowed with the will to collective action. For Weber, political communities entail by construction "value systems," which provide the parameters in which groups have more or less legitimacy and prestige in comparison with one another, and with reference to which they have more or less pride, solidarity, or capacity to act collectively in relation to one another.

Thus a status-group-structured distribution of power provides a natural or logical context for the collective action of status groups. In contrast, a class-structured distribution of power does not provide its constituent classes with any necessary solidarity in their relations with one another and hence no capacity for collective action, because the market principle eliminates all considerations of honor or is constrained in its working by such considerations.

For Giovanni Arrighi, Terence K. Hopkins, and Immanuel Wallerstein (1989), this calls for an extension of Weber, which presupposes that by definition "status groups are constituents of and thereby carriers of a moral order. . . . Classes are not: if they become so, it is in virtue of processes fundamentally different from, and not entailed in, those that constitute them as classes in relation to one an-other" (Arrighi, Hopkins, Wallerstein (1989:3–28).

Arrighi, Hopkins, and Wallerstein counsel us to resist the intellectual pres-sure to reify groups, to presume their permanence and longevity, although they realize that it is difficult to resist such pressure. They point out that while groups that are self-conscious seem to act collectively in significant ways and seem very solid and resilient, we tend to lose sight of the extent to which this solidarity is a consequence of the group's actions in relationship to others. Following this line of reasoning, we would conclude that class consciousness and other forms of group consciousness (or cultures) are derivative. They derive from the social practice of the groups involved. That is why the term *culture of poverty* fell into disuse during the high tide of political and social mobilization among the lower strata worldwide and why it returned to favor during a period when these strata became the objec-tive of a withering economic, political, and ideological offensive and were rendered politically and socially subordinate.

While there are many who have viewed the phenomenon of ethnic proletari-anization as a dilemma reflecting particular national situations such as those in the United States and South Africa, Wallerstein argues, in opposition to Gunnar Myrdal (1944), that racism and underdevelopment are not dilemmas, but consti-tutive of the capitalist world economy as a historical system. Indeed, according to Wallerstein, racism and underdevelopment are the "primary conditions and essential manifestations of the unequal distribution of surplus value. They make possible the ceaseless accumulation of capital. They organize the process occu-pationally and legitimate it politically" (Wallerstein, 1988:17).

We are not captives of these structural restraints. Just as the political and military defeat of the 1960s–1970s insurgency provided the condition for the reassertion of such regressive formulations as the *culture of poverty* and the *un-derclass*, it may well be that there will not be a resurgence of large-scale sympa-thetic study of the lower strata until they reassert themselves as a social and political force. In the meantime, some who are more closely aligned with these strata may set out the questions that seem most in need of investigation in terms of the system of structural and ideological constraints that so profoundly restrict the human potential of the most disadvantaged members of our social world. We should be particularly attuned to those issues that will assist particular sections of the lower strata in getting a grip on their situations so that they can take effi-cacious action as the opportunity presents itself.

In *We Are Not What We Seem*, I attempted to use these formulations to ana-lyze the trajectory of the Black freedom struggle during the American century. It seemed clear to me that the universalism-versus-racism-and-sexism (Balibar and Wallerstein 1991) ideological tension was key to understanding the different modalities of the Black freedom struggle.[22] It helped me to understand that from the viewpoint of certain strata in the ruling class, the civil rights movement was part of the mature global liberalism of the American century. It was not so much that the civil rights movement itself was the program of the liberal ruling class, but that they had their own civil rights agenda to which they were able to co-opt some in the Black liberal establishment. Talented Tenth radicalism remained the most powerful component of the civil rights movement, however, and when articulated with the worldview of the Black working class (I neglected to emphasize Black women), the Black radical tradition remains the most powerful pole of antisystemic thought in American society. What is the worldview of the Black working class? I held that since the Black working class continued to be a victim of racism, which was intensified during the post–civil rights period, various forms of Black Nationalism would continue to resonate with this class. While the Black working class might someday transcend this nationalism, thus far revolutionary nationalism had been the most powerful component of the Black radical tradition (e.g., the work of Hubert Harrison, Cyril Briggs, W.E.B. Du Bois, Paul Robeson, Malcolm X, Huey Newton, and Queen Mother Moore).[23]

Despite the seeming permanence of racism as an ideological feature of historical capitalism, we should pay close attention to emerging groups generated by the changing shape and forms of the capitalist world economy. Perhaps these groups will combine in unforeseen ways and the centers of social action will shift at given times. We should not forget the constant refrain of the civil rights movement to keep our eyes on the prize.

6

Black Power, the American Dream, and the Spirit of Bandung: Malcolm X and Dr. Martin Luther King, Jr., in the Age of World Revolution

"The specter of a storm is haunting the Western world," wrote the Black Power poet Askia Muhammad Touré in 1965. "The Great Storm, the coming Black Revolution, is rolling like a tornado; roaring from the East; shaking the moorings of the earth as it passes through countries ruled by oppressive regimes. . . . Yes, all over this sullen planet, the multi-colored 'hordes' of undernourished millions are on the move like never before in human history." Touré was pondering the appeal of "the East" to African-American youth in the aftermath of the 1955 Bandung conference. There President Sukarno of Indonesia had told the representatives of 29 African and Asian nations that they were united "by a common detestation of colonialism in whatever form it appears. We are united by a common detestation of racialism." Those were the days when Malcolm X met with Fidel Castro at the famed Teresa Hotel in Harlem, and when Malcolm, from his perspective of "Islamic internationalism," came to understand the civil rights movement as an instance of the struggle against imperialism, seeing the Vietnam war and the Mau Mau rebellion in Kenya as uprisings of the "darker races" and, like the African-American struggle, part of the "tidal wave" against Western imperialism (Aidi 2003).

If the civil rights movement was a noble enterprise to redeem the soul of America, a challenge to the United States that it live out the true meaning of its creed, in what relation does the Black Power movement stand to the true meaning of the U.S. creed? While there is a popular narrative engaged across the spectrum of U.S. politics about the society-wide consensus (outside the white South) about the elimination of Jim Crow, can we say that the victory over Jim Crow has made the American dream a reality for all U.S. citizens?

Since the Black Power movement as articulated by Stokely Carmichael and the members of the Student Nonviolent Coordinating Committee (SNCC) is a product of the post–civil rights world, the obvious verdict is that proponents of Black Power did not think so, but there was obviously no consensus outside the ranks of Black Power proponents. The Black political scientist Michael C. Dawson (1996) argues that Black Power was a slogan that energized a generation of Black youths, troubled their elders, including Martin Luther King, Jr. (who agreed with many of the goals but saw the slogan itself as divisive), and appalled the great majority of whites. Dawson points out tellingly that as much as the Black Power slogan divided Blacks, the intraracial gap was small compared to the interracial gap. According to Aberbach and Walker (1970), 49.6 percent of Blacks had an unfavorable opinion of the slogan, whereas 80.7 percent of whites had an unfavorable opinion. Whereas many Blacks saw Black Power as fairness (19.6 percent) or Black unity (22.6 percent) for a 42.2% favorable total, whites viewed it as replacing white supremacy with Black supremacy (80.7%).

The differing interpretations of the slogan should not be surprising given the tenor of race relations in the United States. But a question that is seldom asked is: How did the proponents of Black Power view it in relationship to the American dream or as a potentially society-wide project with implications for all Americans and even for those beyond our borders? Was Black Power a form of Black Nationalism or Black internationalism?

We often forget that Malcolm X's 1963 declaration that we had arrived at the end of white world supremacy was part of a speech made in the aftermath of the assassination of John F. Kennedy, for which he was expelled from the Nation of Islam for violation of Elijah Muhammad's prohibition about speaking out about Kennedy's assassination, saying that it was a case of the "chickens coming home to roost." As I argued in the introduction, Malcolm X shone light on the handwriting on the wall; in historical hindsight we can gauge the significance of his discourse. For the leadership of the Nation of Islam, this was an unforgivable transgression, a ratcheting up of agitation by the national spokesperson, which could bring the organization under the scrutiny of federal, state, and local security forces. Part and parcel of this threat to the Nation of Islam's project stemmed not merely from provocation from ill-considered remarks but on a much deeper level from the wider implications of a violation of the Nation of Islam's prohibition against involvement in the "white devil's" political system. While the members of the Nation of Islam's inner circles had long been concerned about Malcolm's venture into the secular arena of world politics, Muhammad had defended Malcolm because he had been largely responsible for the spectacular growth of the organization since his rise to a top leadership position during the 1950s. It was Malcolm X's position in the secular arena of world politics that gave the organization such standing, but it also attracted the attention of law enforcement and surveillance authorities.

It was not so much that African American social movements had eschewed the arena of world politics but that the repression of the Left during the onset of the American century consisted especially of the repression of the Black Left, which had been central to a cosmopolitan U.S. Left and which had played a key role in the rise of an internationalist Left in the United States during the post–World War I period, a process that continued during both the interwar period and during and after World War II.

Chapter 2 details the early development of Black internationalism through the life and times of W.E.B. Du Bois, and Chapter 3 details the evolution of the New Negro radicals and what I have elsewhere deemed the Blackening and intensification of U.S. radicalism (Bush 1999, Chapter 4). While I do not detail the Black popular front of the 1930s and 1940s here, it is an important link not only to the Black Power movement of the 1950s and 1960s but also to the civil rights movement, as described in Chapter 5.

Thinking about the Black Power Sixties in the Age of Neoliberal Globalization and Color Blindness

The Black Power concept seemed to soar into the public imagination in the United States during the late 1960s. The concept reflected in part the increasing polarization of U.S. society during a period when residents of the nation's inner cities were involved in insurrections against the routine abuses to which they had long been subject; there was no longer a sense of resignation to the way things were. The very promise of the civil rights victories from 1954 to 1965 had raised the hopes of the nation's long-oppressed African American population in an unprecedented manner. In 1964 Barry Goldwater, the most conservative candidate for president in the nation's history, had been vanquished by Lyndon Baines Johnson. During the 1963 March on Washington, King had challenged the nation to live out the true meaning of its creed. The Civil Rights Act of 1964 had been enacted, following the march, and the Voting Rights Act was passed the following year.

As indicated in Chapter 5, the nation had reached the height of its glory during the early and mid-1960s as the civil rights movement rode the crest of an exceedingly confident national consensus determined to rid the nation of the disgraceful images of the Jim Crow South. Despite the common roots of the subordinate social status of Black people in the South and Black people outside the South, the inability of the attack on Jim Crow to address the more deeply rooted problems of the urban ghettos outside the South could understandably increase people's frustration with the routine abuses of power that underlined the slow pace of change in the inner cities of the northeastern, midwestern, and western United States.

It was, of course, not so simple. Black agency outside the South had more often than not taken the form of an ideological stance much closer to that of Black Power than that of the southern movement.[1] As we saw in Chapter 5, on civil rights, and Chapter 3, on the class-first, race-first debate, Black movements outside the South were close observers of the southern movement, were involved in a great number of supportive actions of the southern movement, and were organizing to deal with their own problems as well.

Nonetheless, with the national spotlight on the events in the southern states, scholars and the general public can be forgiven for adhering to a schema that sensed in Martin Luther King's "I Have a Dream" speech at the 1963 March on Washington the high point of U.S. democracy and in Malcolm X's nightmare its most fundamental challenge. I argue in this chapter, on the contrary, that we miss the larger significance the Black freedom struggle against a common set of problems when we envision that they can be so easily separated. I argue that both the civil rights movement and the Black Power movement of the twentieth century (from W.E.B. Du Bois, Marcus Garvey, Cyril Briggs, and Paul Robeson to Malcolm X, Dr. Martin Luther King, Jr., Ella Baker, Fannie Lou Hamer, Huey Newton, Angela Davis) represent the transcendence of the American dream by articulating notions of social justice that refused to be confined by our national borders and that reached out to a variety of social actors outside of our borders in a manner that is eminently sensible and would be consonant with our common sense if powerful forces did not exist that constrict so many people's views along the lines of a U.S. hegemonic nationalist vision, which severely constricts not only their vision but also their options. The world workers' movements of the nineteenth and twentieth centuries called for the workers of the world to unite, but when revolutionaries called for the formation of a new international after the members of the European workers' movement organized in the Second International, all supported their ruling classes during World War I, the "civilized world" was shocked and incredulous that anyone would have the nerve to call for such "sedition."

As we have seen throughout this book, the social strata of which the people of African descent in the United States are composed occupied a social location that made them much less susceptible than most to these kinds of U.S. nationalist appeals. After all, they had lived in a state where they had lacked citizenship rights for centuries. What might surprise anyone looking in from outside the United States' racialized social system is that they harbored such feelings of patriotism. This is emphatically not an issue of identity, as is so often assumed, but an issue of the structuring of power and socioeconomic position. The castelike location of the Black population as a whole in the United States has led some to view them as an internally colonized group or members of a third world in the United States. Such strata exist in all of the core states of the world-system and are often viewed as marginal to the socioeconomic mainstream to the extent that they are viewed as a third world within. In the United States this includes people of African descent centered in the African American population, Native Americans, Mexican Americans, Puerto Ricans, and Filipinos.

While there are many who argue that the collapse of the Second International at the time of World War I was an indication of the taming of the dangerous classes in the centers of the capitalist world and the subsequent consignment of such dangerous social strata to the more safe and remote periphery of the world-system, I argue that the capitalist centers still contain some elements of the dangerous classes, specifically those who are located in what some call the third world within (or the so-called colonized minorities). These groups occupy a distinct subordinate and marginal position in all of the societies in which they live, though some of them also are members of the professional-managerial strata of the host society. Because of their marginal status, they are likely to be viewed as outsiders despite their sometimes long residence in these societies. Groups of significant size and long residence often consciously constitute themselves as fundamentally threatening of the system of inequality, exclusion, and injustice not only of their societies but of the capitalist-colonial world as a whole.

Despite the ability of movements based in these populations to force concessions from the defenders of the system to the benefit of some of their number, the bottom layers of these populations have continued as victims of the most obscene oppression, victimization, and subjugation. What makes these populations so volatile is precisely their length of time in low rank and their location in large ghettoized communities, which facilitate a sense of social solidarity among both the lower strata and the members of their group who occupy a higher class position. These aspects of their social situation and social organization contribute to the sense that they constitute an internal colony, which of course has the advantage of proximity to the centers of power and wealth and thus the potential to use its potential to disrupt the status quo in ways that can increase its spaces for operation and maneuver.

What I do in this chapter, as in the rest of this book, is use a long time frame, which allows us to view what is happening in our inner cities and the potential for the future in ways that are different from those of more mainstream scholars, who are not part of the communities that are the objects of their commentary and or research.

During the past twenty-five or thirty years, the bottom layers of the populations of the core states have been devastated by policies of neoliberal globalization that have reversed the social regimes of the post–World War II period. This withering social warfare has been accompanied by an ideological assault, a veritable scorched-earth strategy so overwhelming in scope and power that when combined with the racist common sense (the assumptions about the inferiority of these very lower strata of the population) that has been with us for the last five hundred years, most of the public have entirely lost their bearings and simply cannot see beyond the parameters that have been so insistently and relentlessly locked into the public imagination.

For those of us who lived through what we now see as a golden age, the enormity of the changes in the relations of force is hardly conceivable. There is and has been a widespread sense that the social crisis of our inner cities is beyond repair. With one out of three young black men under thirty under the jurisdiction of the criminal justice system, with the majority of black children living in homes without fathers, and with a zero-tolerance mentality among the police and much of the general public, there is little optimism in the land regarding our racial dilemmas and therefore the civic peace. While the law-and-order rhetoric of the 1960s and 1970s was concerned more with social disorder than with crime, by the 1990s people's concern about street crime was a reflection of the state of civil unrest in our society (including a sometimes insurrectionary oppositional mentality, induced at the level of individuals and in forms of social organization that prevail in these communities and articulated through the medium of hip-hop culture). The sense of social crisis is a reflection of the deep bifurcation in our society, the borders of which are often roughly associated with the people of color of the inner cities and their middle-class spokespeople and allies, and the whites who occupy a decidedly different and separate turf. Whatever one might think of his poor tortured soul, Tupac Shakur offers important insight on the resulting societal tensions on the track "Keep Your Head Up":

> Last night my buddy lost his whole family
> It's gonna take the man in me to conquer this insanity
> It seems tha rain'll never let up
> I try to keep my head up, and still keep from gettin wet up
> You know it's funny when it rains it pours
> They got money for wars, but can't feed the poor
> Say there ain't no hope for the youth and the truth is
> it ain't no hope for tha future
> And then they wonder why we crazy
> I blame my mother, for turning my brother into a crack baby
> We ain't meant to survive, cause it's a setup
> And even though you're fed up
> Huh, ya got to keep your head up.

Many have long conceptualized these troubled times as predominantly a crisis of our inner cities, an aberration in an otherwise healthy and thriving society. The 1980s were viewed as a period of renewal for the United States, when we stood tall with the confidence brought to us by President Reagan's reassertion of our national pride and world position, including finally the victory over Soviet communism. The 1980s were also considered to be the beginning of the post–civil rights period, the end of an era of easy progress for African Americans, who were no longer the objects of racial discrimination and could take their place alongside all the other hardworking people in the country. This too was a part of societal renewal, since the United States would no longer have a privileged and spoiled section of the population looking for special privileges and handouts. This meant that as a society America could insist on a common standard of behavior and values around issues of family values, discipline, hard work, and thrift. Everyone could carry their own weight, and society did not have to pay the burden of uplift for those who were not committed to the country's national values.

What we saw, then, in the inner cities was a crisis of the inner-city poor, who were spoiled by a liberal culture and liberal social policies that acted as disincentives for people most in need of the habits of discipline, hard work, and thrift, which enable them to lift themselves up by their bootstraps. These values are all that is needed for success in the United States, as we can see that even new immigrants want only a chance to work at whatever wage they are able to obtain.

I argue against the grain of our emerging common sense that the crisis of the inner-city poor is the depths of a larger and deeper crisis, which includes a crisis of the American dream. The withdrawal of the state from the inner cities is part of a modern nightmare that Malcolm X thought was approaching its endpoint in 1963, since he thought then that we had arrived at the end of white world supremacy. Malcolm had assumed that the imminent rise of a decolonized African America would combine with the decolonization of the rest of the world so that U.S. imperialism and the system of white world supremacy would simply implode. While today this may seem a fantastic scenario, during the 1960s not a few people believed in it.

The possibility of such a scenario was not only the source of the spread of liberation ideology within the borders of U.S. society that we saw during the 1960s; it was also the source of an authoritarian, ultranationalist, xenophobic ideology that came from the right. It is in this context that we see the emerging dominance of a U.S. political culture with a level of depraved indifference toward the plight of the inner-city poor that is simply unfathomable. Such indifference not only deflects criticism from the more powerful and the more privileged; it also serves to camouflage the true nature of our contemporary crisis, now more than ever! Racism is deeply embedded in the common sense of our society, so much so that many do not notice how it serves to camouflage other social relationships, especially class relations and the social relations of capitalism.

The social struggles of the 1960s were not fortuitous, as some now imply. They were indeed quite consequential, which explains the price that some are now paying. The brief window of the golden age that some glimpsed during that period is not an impossible dream but the contours of a struggle that is still going on. It was not new even then. From the early twentieth century, U.S. elites and intellectuals feared the collapse of capitalism and white world supremacy, as we saw in the introduction. They feared that Bolshevism would spread to the United States, especially via the retuning Black GIs. It was for this reason that they took such pains to repress the Garvey movement and other sections of the New Negro movement in the 1920s and 1930s. But in the 1950s and 1960s, they faced a bloc of socialist states and radical nationalist states and movements in the third world. With significant internal populations joining or making common cause with the challenge posed by these radical states and movements, those with foresight took this evolution of events very seriously.

All of this is very difficult to understand if one looks only at the surface of these times. The intense passions seem oversized, exaggerated, and lacking in perspective. Surely I must overstate. But take the time to review the scope of this history, which I summarize in the remainder of this chapter, and you will see something far more powerful and serious than the myths and misrepresentations that have been spread by the corporate media, the defenders of white privilege, and many ordinary people whose sense of proportion and status were offended by the rebels.

The Intellectual Framework for Black Power

While we can clearly trace an intellectual framework for the Black Power movement of the 1960s to any number of prominent Black intellectuals of the last one hundred years, I would like to examine the work of a prominent sociologist whose intellectual and political work in the 1930s and 1940s directly contradicted the centrist liberal premises of the National Association for the Advancement of Colored People (NAACP) leadership of the 1950s and 1960s. Howard University sociologist E. Franklin Frazier had been a member of the Black popular front during the 1930s and 1940s and had assumed that the wartime struggles for racial and economic justice would be continued in the postwar period. He was one of a few prominent intellectuals who refused to repudiate his association with the Left. During the 1950s he waged an unrelenting war of words with the political conformity and anti-Communist hysteria that characterized U.S. political culture and with the banality and materialism of its cultural life, now slavishly imitated by the emerging Black bourgeoisie (actually the Black middle class).

While there is some reservation about Frazier among the Left intelligentsia because of his association with the intellectual discourse about Daniel Patrick Moynihan's report *The Negro Family: The Case for National Action*, this discourse is a dramatic mismeasure of Frazier's intellectual stance. Frazier's stubborn adherence to the Left anticolonialism of the 1930s and 1940s provided a militant language of critique for the Left intellectuals who would come to the fore in the 1950s and 1960s—intellectuals such as Lorraine Hansberry, Malcolm X, and LeRoi Jones (Amiri Baraka).

Perhaps more important, it was Frazier who not only questioned the facile notion that assimilation was the best option for people of African descent in the United States but also argued that such assimilation would be tantamount to losing their souls. Frazier warned against the country's cultural hegemony over the consciousness of its Black subject peoples. He was one of a cadre of intellectuals of African descent (including George Lamming, Aimé Césaire, and Frantz Fanon) who pushed in the 1950s for a revolutionary decolonization of Pan-European cultural hegemony over the people of African descent and over colonized people everywhere.

These intellectuals sought to challenge colonial and civilizational hierarchies that denied the historical agency of people of African descent and that viewed modernity as the sole province of the Pan-European world. Furthermore, they challenged the assumption that Westernized people of African descent should be in the vanguard of the Pan-African movement. They thus posited an intellectual anticolonialism designed, in the view of Kevin Gaines, to create new possibilities and new structures of feeling among formerly colonized peoples toward a revolutionary decolonization of Western culture (Gaines 2005:508).

"The truth of the matter is that for most Negro intellectuals, the integration of the Negro means . . . the emptying of his life of meaningful content and ridding him of all Negro identification. For them, integration and eventual assimilation means the annihilation of the Negro—physically, culturally and spiritually" (Frazier 1998). Frazier viewed integration as a limited option for Black people in the United States, incapable of addressing the nation's deeply entrenched social inequalities. For Frazier this was a departure from the more organic social relationships that defined African Americans during the war: an alliance between organized labor and civil rights and solidarity with African anticolonial movements. It meant as well that African Americans would forfeit their group consciousness, subordinating it to the imperatives of the U.S. nation.

Likewise, Julian Mayfield balked at the notion that Black writers would enter the mainstream as political and social integration advanced. For Mayfield, the more important issue was that what was called the mainstream was a hegemonic political culture defined by U.S. nationalism and imperialism. While Mayfield favored full and equal citizenship rights, he rejected full identification with the American image—that great-power face that the world knows and that the Negro knows better (Gaines 2005:514).

Skeptical of the establishment posture of the civil rights movement, Mayfield settled in Ghana in 1961, a few steps ahead of federal authorities, who were seeking him for his involvement with Robert Williams and the Monroe, North Carolina, NAACP, who were advocating armed defense against Ku Klux Klan terror.

At the Conference of the American Society of African Culture (AMSAC), Lorraine Hansberry pointed out that time was running out for a misguided worldwide minority because "the universal solidarity of the colored people of the world" had arrived. The issue that Hansberry, Mayfield, Frazier, and Du Bois confronted most squarely is that integration into a materialistic and repressive cold war U.S. society would be a threat to African American cultural traditions, including a history of democratic struggles.

Frazier's legacy, found in his last article, "The Failure of the Negro Intellectual," is that he raised the key question of whom and what African Americans were becoming in relation to modern political change in the United States and Africa. Could it be that they would simply become unhyphenated Americans? Or would full citizenship bring them into a unique social situation among Americans, one that would forge a transnational U.S. citizenship in solidarity with African peoples and democratize the United States? Would this have a profound impact on the relationship of the United States to the nations of the dark world (Gaines 2005:527)?

Frazier thinks that the distinction between integration and assimilation is an important one. He argues here that the integration of the Negro into American society is only the first stage of dealing with the problems of Negroes in American society. A more important issue for Frazier is the assimilation of Negroes into American society, which implies not a whitening of the Negro in her/his place (low social class position on the margins of the U.S. American mainstream, but the fusing of the Black stripe into the social, economic, cultural, and political domains of U.S. society.

Integration means the acceptance of Negroes as individuals into the social and economic mainstream of American society. This would imply the gradual dissolution of the Black community and the decline of its associations, institutions, and other forms of associated life that have historically constituted the Black community in the United States. So integration involves more than just individuals; it involves the organizational and institutional life of the Black community.

Moreover, assimilation involves integration in the most intimate phases of the organized social life of a country and thus leads to complete identification with the people and culture of the community in which the social heritages of different people become merged and fused.

The Black community has the disadvantage of a conformist and supplicant intellectual class who simply wants the approval of whites. They therefore do not provide leadership, nor do the institutional leaders in the community, which is the reason for the popularity of the Black Muslims, according to Frazier. Black youth were in rebellion against the traditional leadership, who had usually acted as mediators between the Black and white communities.

Since these leaders seek only to integrate and assimilate into American society as it is, they have little grasp of the necessity to address the economic and social organization of American life. The use of the Gandhian philosophy of nonviolence is an example of the attempt of the Negro intellectual to escape from the Negro heritage. Langston Hughes is named as an exception to this tendency. They have written no novels or plays about Denmark Vesey or Harriett Tubman; even today they run from Robeson and Du Bois.

Frazier holds that there is no parallel in human history where people have been subjected to such mutilation of body and soul. While African intellectuals realize the impact of colonialism and see their most important tasks as the mental, moral, and spiritual rehabilitation of the African, African American intellectuals are seduced by dreams of final assimilation and cannot for the most part see beyond these aspirations.

Negro intellectuals have failed to dig down deeply into the experience of the Negro and provide a transvaluation of that experience so that the Negro can have a new self-image or a new conception of her- or himself.

"It was the responsibility of the Negro intellectual to provide a positive identification through history, literature, art, music, and the drama. . . ." (Frazier 1998:65). He feared the spiritual, cultural, and physical annihilation of the Negro who viewed their place in a Eurocentered world from the standpoint of what Sekou Toure, Frantz Fanon , and Leopold Senghor referred to as the complex of the colonized.

Thus Frazier calls on Negro intellectuals to cease being obsessed with assimilation. They must come to realize that integration does not mean annihilation, self-effacement, and an escape from identification with the Negro race.

Frazier seeks to emphasize a point made elsewhere that the American Negro has little to contribute of Africa, as had previously been argued by Black Nationalists, but that Africa in achieving freedom could possibly save the souls of Negro Americans by providing them with a new self-image and a new sense of personal dignity (Frazier 1998:66).

Black Internationalism and the Political
Origins of Black Power

Most observers of African American history can trace the development of institutionalized Black Power to the late-eighteenth-century formation of the Free
African Society and the African Methodist Episcopal Church. Most readers are
familiar with Komozi Woodard's contention that the ideas of modern Black
Power were crystallized in the National Negro Convention Movement from
1830 to 1861. In Chapters 2 and 3 we discussed the role of Du Bois and the New
Negro radicals in the story of Black internationalism. I would like to turn now to
the interwar Black movement and the origins of Black Power.

George Padmore describes Du Bois as the father of Pan-Africanism, who
differed from Garvey in the sense that his Pan-Africanism was viewed as an
aid in the promotion of national self-determination among Africans under
African leadership, for the benefit of Africans, whereas Garvey envisioned
Africa as a place for colonization by Western Negroes who would be under
his personal domination. However, Padmore readily saw, as did Du Bois, that
the Garvey movement was a people's movement rather than a movement of
intellectuals.

Padmore holds that the Soviet interest in Black people is based on their belief that Black people are "revolutionary expendables" in the global struggle of
communism against Western capitalism. They are courted to tag along with the
white proletariat and thus swell the revolutionary ranks against the imperialist
enemies of the Soviet fatherland (Padmore 1972:268–269).

If this sounds like Crusean-style anticommunism, it might make sense to at
least see how Padmore supports this argument.[2] It goes to the very crux of his
framing of the political question of Pan-Africanism or communism. We touched
on this issue in Chapter 3, on race first versus class first.

Padmore points out that the urban working class in czarist Russia was a
small part of a Russian Empire that stretched from central Europe to the Pacific
and from the Black Sea to the Baltic Sea, an empire that was overwhelmingly
peasant and a culture partly European and partly Asiatic.

The heterogeneity of the Russian population inspired the formation of a political program that promised land and freedom from usury to the peasants and
the right of self-determination to the subject nationalities and racial minorities
living under czarist rule (Padmore 1972:269–270). Padmore points out that Lenin
had argued for these positions against the other left-wing organizations in the
Russian Empire and against considerable opposition among his Bolshevik comrades as well. On the European side of the empire, this offer was accepted: the
Finns, the Poles, the Letts, and the Lithuanians. On the Asiatic side the subject
nationalities were reorganized into so-called independent federated and autonomous territories, the Union of Soviet Socialist Republics.

Padmore points out that the offer of self-determination to the non-Russian
nationalities had a tremendous psychological impact, inspiring confidence
in the Bolsheviks at a time when the enemies of the new regime were waging
war to restore the czarist empire. The newly emancipated colored people thus

supported the Soviet power against the white guard aristocrats, who were receiving financial assistance from Britain and France (Padmore 1972:271).

Padmore's analysis of the Bolsheviks' turn toward Asia is based not only on geopolitical strategy but also on a cultural affinity or perhaps a geocultural strategy. Here Padmore quotes the scholar Upton Close (1927), author of *The Revolt of Asia: The End of the White Man's World Dominance*:

> The Russian peasant and even the proletarian city dweller exists on much the same standard as the Asiatic. The mujik with his "shirt tails out" is a cultural kinsman to the Chinese in the coolie coast. Both live on a dirt floor, break the ground with a wooden plough, and eat cabbage and grain. The Chinese keeps his fire under the raised portion of the floor, and the Russian puts his in the wall. The Chinese has much more of civilization behind him and of the code of the gentleman in him, but both have kindly humour, hospitality and the cruelty that comes out of squalor when aroused. . . . Thus Russia followed her destiny towards Asia—not under the banner of the old imperialism but that of the new idealism. Or, if that word in connection with the Soviet system seems inadmissible, one may call it "enlightened imperialism" (Padmore 1972:278).

In the meantime the Communist movement in the United States had recruited Black cadres during the period of the emergence of the African Blood Brotherhood. As we saw in Chapter 3, the major movement of African Americans by far was Marcus Garvey's Universal Negro Improvement Association. Padmore argues that the Communist movement learned from their analysis of the Garvey movement that a key issue would be the brandishing of the right of self-determination to the African American people, but in the form of Stalin's formula, which located the African American nation in the Black Belt South. Padmore attributes this theory to a former Finnish university professor of Marxist sociology, Dr. Otto Kussinin, at the time one of the secretaries of the Comintern.

This was a disastrous policy from Padmore's perspective, but more important it was an indication of lack of principle among the Communists, which was expressed over the 1930s and 1940s in a series of twists and turns that alienated them from many activists in the African American communities.

Padmore himself resigned from the Comintern when it disbanded the International Trade Union Congress of Negro Workers, of which he was secretary. Upon learning of the decision in August 1933, Padmore immediately resigned his position, but there was no public reaction to his resignation until the following April. Padmore had argued that he had been called on to endorse the new diplomatic policy of the Soviet government to put a brake on anti-imperialist work against British, French, and U.S. imperialism in favor of the united front against Fascism. Padmore argued that Britain and France were the main imperialist countries in Africa and that the United States was the most racist country in the world. This new policy meant the sacrifice of the young national liberation movements in Asia and Africa; he therefore had no choice but to resign from the Communist International (Lewis 2002:49).

After the break with the Comintern, Padmore moved to London, where his childhood friend C.L.R. James resided. In 1937 members of the International Friends of Abyssinia met in London to form the International African Service Bureau, the forerunner of the Pan-African Federation. Principal officers included Padmore, the West African trade unionist Wallace Johnson, Chris Jones of Barbados, C.L.R. James, Jomo Kenyatta, and T. R. Makonnen (Padmore 1972: 124).[3] The International African Service Bureau organized meetings, conferences, and protests and wrote letters to advance the cause of African independence (Lewis 2002:49).

In 1944 C.L.R. James gave Kwame Nkrumah a letter of introduction to Padmore, with whom Nkrumah became fast friends. Over this last period Padmore had been observed to be more cynical about the role of the working class and of anti-imperialists in the imperialist countries and began to argue that the liberation of the colonized people would be the work of the colonized people themselves. Early in 1945 Padmore suggested that it was time for another Pan-African Congress. This would bring together Padmore, Nkrumah, Du Bois, Jomo Kenyatta, and Jaja Wachuku of Nigeria.[4]

The Fifth Pan African Congress was distinguished from the previous congresses in the words of Kwame Nkrumah, who suggested that the congress participants "were practical men and women of action and not, as was the case at the four previous conferences, merely idealists contenting themselves with writing theses but quite unable or unwilling to take any active part in dealing with the African problem. Like Garveyism, the first four conferences were not born of indigenous African consciousness. Garvey's ideology was concerned with black nationalism as opposed to African nationalism" (Tunteng 1974:37).

What finally emerged in Africa was neither Pan-Africanism nor communism. Communism was never a powerful force in Africa, and despite the formation of the Organization of African Unity, it was much more a federation of sovereign states cooperating in matters of mutual interests than any kind of movement for a United States of Africa, as Nkrumah called for in *Africa Must Unite* and as Padmore calls for briefly at the end of *Pan- Africanism or Communism* (Padmore 1972:356).

When Leopold Senghor, Gatson Monnerville, and Aimé Césaire addressed the president of France and others on April 27, 1948, the one hundredth anniversary of the abolition of slavery in France, all three used the memory of slavery, revolution, and emancipation to oppose then-current colonial practices, despite the official posture of French tolerance and benevolence.[5] Monnerville and Senghor wanted the government to honor the tradition of abolition by using the same principles in the present. Césaire, in contrast, viewed plantation slavery, colonial violence, and anti-Black racism as part and parcel of the modern French political order, inscribed in its social relations (Wilder 2004:32). Racism was part of the rationality of the French social order, not an irrational aberration. Césaire did not view 1848 as the victory of enlightened republicanism over colonial backwardness; the radical currents to the republican tradition had fallen victim to the revolution's dominant bourgeois-colonial elements.

During the 1920s a heterogeneous community of Antillean and African intellectuals, professionals, and labor organizers consolidated in Paris. They debated one another and produced journals and associations out of which would
emerge the Negritude movement in the late 1930s. Césaire was a member of
these groups, who sought to join demands for political equality with demands
for cultural recognition. Césaire sought to reconcile humanism and nativism.
After the liberation of Martinique, Césaire became an advocate of political assimilation and was one of the architects of the 1946 law transforming Martinique, Guadeloupe, Guiana, and Teunion into formal French *départements*. Frantz
Fanon, who had worked on Césaire's successful campaign to become a member
of the French National Assembly, would later become Césaire's student. Césaire
was paradoxically an unrelenting critic of the colonial order and a French political official. A new generation of Antillean activists therefore both celebrated him
and criticized him. This, of course, was not unlike the position of some members
of the U.S. Black Power generation after some of their political successes.

Bandung and the Historical Grounding of Black Liberation in the Postwar Era

Between 1947, when India won independence, and 1963, when Kenya and Zanzibar won independence, virtually the entirety of the dark world were able to
free themselves from the bonds of colonialism. This was a time, one might say,
when the specter of national liberation haunted the imperialist powers. Con-
cretely this process was facilitated by the weakening of the imperialist nations in
Europe, which made resistance to imperialist power possible. Though the threat
of a united front against the colonial and neocolonial powers brandished by the
Bandung Conference of 1955 did not materialize, the decolonizing process that
did materialize represented the rise of the dark world that had been the coin in
trade of a number of African American leaders, from Du Bois and Garvey to
Elijah Muhammad and Malcolm X (Wolfenstein 1981:234).

In 1947 Du Bois petitioned the newly formed United Nations Commission on
Human Rights arguing that prolonged policies of segregation and discrimination
had involuntarily welded the mass of Black people almost into a nation within a
nation. Blacks lived in a state of extreme segregation with their s own schools,
churches, hospitals, newspapers, and many business enterprises. The United
States, of course, denied the reality asserted by Du Bois, but with the location of
the United Nations in New York City, the problem of the African American people
had become internationalized.

In the decade prior to the April 1955 meeting of twenty-nine nations in Bandung, Indonesia, millions of people emerged from the shadow of European colonialism through the pursuit of anticolonial social struggles. India, Burma, Indonesia, Egypt, and China were among those who achieved independence during this
period. The twenty-nine countries meeting in Bandung represented more than
half of the world's population at that time, 1.4 billion people (Layton 2000:70).

Richard Wright (living in exile in Paris), Adam Clayton Powell, and Carl Rowan were prominent African Americans who attended the conference. Neither Robeson nor Du Bois was able to attend because of travel restrictions imposed by the U.S. State Department. Mainstream coverage of the conference in the United States was limited and negative in tone. The January 1, 1955 issue of *Newsweek* magazine characterized the conference as "an Afro-Asian combination turned by communists against the West." (Wright 1956:74). The U.S. Black media commentary on the conference was celebratory. The meeting in Bandung was deemed the most important international meeting in the history of the world, with incalculable implications for Blacks in the United States and throughout the African diaspora and for colored people everywhere (Layton 2000:71).

Richard Wright, the African American writer and author of the well-known novel *Native Son*, attended the 1955 conference and went on to write a book about it.

> The despised, the insulted, the hurt, the dispossessed—in short, the underdogs of the human race were meeting. . . . Here were class and racial and religious consciousness on a global scale. Who had thought of organising such a meeting? And what had these nations in common? Nothing, it seemed to me, but what their past relationship to the Western world had made them feel. This meeting of the rejected was in itself a kind of judgment upon the Western world! (Wright 1956:10)

Many of us will recall a few years back the flourishing of intellectual and political activity around the fiftieth anniversary of the April 1955 meeting of African and Asian nations in Bandung, Indonesia. The editors of the special edition of *Radical History Review* commemorating this event (Antoinette Burton, Augusto Espiritu, and Fanon Che Wilkins) tell us that when they submitted a proposal for a panel on the fate of nationalism in the age of Bandung to the program committee of the American Historical Association (the largest professional organization for historians in the United States) for the 2005 annual meeting, they were told that no one on the committee had ever heard of it.

Burton, Espritu, and Wilkins note that in "1963 Malcolm X had offered the Bandung meeting as an organizational model for African Americans searching for political allies in the Third World at home and abroad" (Burton, Espritu, and Wilkins 2006). They note also that throughout what they refer to as the long 1960s, Black freedom movement activists frequently referenced Bandung, since this was a period in which Afro-Asian solidarity efforts reached a fever pitch in the U.S. New Left. Sadly this history is not widely known outside of those who were involved at the time. If North Americans know about it at all today, it is most likely through the account of Richard Wright, whose 1956 book, *The Color Curtain*, captured the epic meanings of Bandung for peoples of color around the world as indicated above. Wright, a former member of the CPUSA, one of the most politically sophisticated intellectuls of his time, argued that this was a kind of meeting that no anthropologist, sociologist, or political scientist could ever dream of staging. ". . . it was too simple, too elementary, cutting through the outer layers of disparate social and political and cultural facts down to the bare brute residues of human existence. . . . Only brown, black, and yellow men who had long been made agonizingly self-conscious, under the rigours of colonial rule, of their race and their religion could have felt the need for such a meeting. . . . The agenda and subject matter had been written for centuries in the blood and bones of the participants." The political ideologies of Left and Right mattered much less than that fact that they lived in Asia and Africa (Wright 1956: 11–12).

Wright's excitement is palpable here, as it must have been at the conference itself, when Sukarno of Indonesia opened the proceedings with the declaration, "This is the first international conference of colored peoples in the history of mankind!"(Quoted in Wright 1956:117).

Sukarno continued,

All of us, I am certain, are united by more important things than those which superficially divide us. We are united, for instance, by a common detestation of colonialism in whatever form it appears. We are united by a common detestation of racialism. And we are united by a common determination to preserve and stabilise peace in the world. . . .

We are often told "Colonialism is dead." Let us not be deceived or even soothed by that. 1 say to you, colonialism is not yet dead. How can we say it is dead, so long as vast areas of Asia and Africa are unfree?

And, I beg of you do not think of colonialism only in the classic form which we of Indonesia, and our brothers in different parts of Asia and Africa, knew. Colonialism has also its modern dress, in the form of economic control, intellectual control, and actual physical control by a small but alien community within a nation. It is a skilful and determined enemy, and it appears in many guises. It does not give up its loot easily. Wherever, whenever and however it appears, colonialism is an evil thing, and one which must be eradicated from the earth. (Africa-Asia Speaks from Bandung 1955).

Senghor argued that Bandung represented the death of the inferiority complex of colonial peoples (Furedi 1998:208). For Burton, Espritu, and Wilkins, appreciating the ongoing significance of the spirit of Bandung for post- and anticolonial politics would be an important task for intellectuals, activists, and supporters of the struggles of the people of the third world and the third worlds within. There is little doubt that Bandung represents a watershed moment in world history and that a fuller history of that fateful week in April could and should be written

What Burton, Espritu, and Wilkins seek to do in this project is to offer a rereading of Bandung from the perspective of third world nationalisms as they echoed through a variety of metropolitan spaces, the United States prime among them.

Cary Fraser (2003) argues that the Bandung Conference ushered in a new era of international relations since it marked the determination of nations of color to end colonial rule in the non-European world and its corollary of white world supremacy. Fraser holds that the creation of the nonaligned movement at Bandung was discomforting to the United States since it subjected its domestic practices vis-à-vis citizens of color within their own borders to the scrutiny of a world public. It also brought to public attention Washington's colonial designs in the Caribbean and the Pacific, as well as its willingness to underwrite European imperial designs.

As the United States rose to the commanding position in the world-system, the rise of Bandung complicated the U.S. effort to manage an international system that was increasingly shaped by the politics of race and anticolonialism. As Malcolm X would argue throughout this period, this was noplace more the case than within the borders of the United States itself. There can be little doubt that the politics of race and Bandung imposed limits on the capacity of the United States to influence the evolution of the international order. One need only mention some of the more important personalities in the movement to get a sense of this: Gamal Abdel Nasser of Egypt, Kwame Nkrumah of Ghana, Jawaharlal Nehru of India, Sukarno of Indonesia, Marshall Tito of Yugoslavia, and Chou En-lai of China.

Wallerstein explains that the 1956 First World Congress of Black Writers and Artists in Paris was a watershed event in closing the gap that had existed between the various circuits of Pan-Africanism: the British colonial subject in Africa and the Caribbean, the French colonial subjects in Africa and the Caribbean, and the subjects (?) of African descent in the United States. Alioune Diop, editor of *Présence Africaine*, called for unity among those convened, whether one believed in God or was an atheist, "whether Christians, Muslims, or Communists" (Wallerstein 1967:15). Aime Césaire, a member of the French Communist Party from Martinique, added to Diop's frame that "there are two ways to lose oneself: by segregation within the walls of the particular or by dilution in the 'universal'" (Wallerstein 1967:15). For Césaire the universal is one that is "rich with the particular, rich with all the particulars, a deepening and a coexistence of the particulars" (Wallerstein 1967:15).

This was a time when nationalist movements were taking root everywhere. Wallerstein points out that the independence of the Indian subcontinent had had profound consequences for English-speaking Africa. For French-speaking Africa the struggle in Indochina was a formative experience that transformed the realm of the politically possible. The Bandung Conference of April 1955 was an assertion of strength and identity vis-à-vis European colonialism. It transformed the sense of solidarity among the colonized into the Afro-Asian concept that Wallerstein argues would play a role for ten years to come.

In Africa this new sense of solidarity brought together North African and Sub-Saharan African states, as well as French-speaking and English-speaking Africans.

The U.S. Black Power Movement and the Spirit of Bandung

Nikhil Singh points out that at the first Congress of Black Artists and Writers in Paris in 1956, Césaire generated considerable controversy among the African American delegation when he argued that "even our American brothers, as a result of racial discrimination, find themselves within a great modern nation in an artificial situation that can only be understood in reference to colonialism." Césaire's definition included colonial, semicolonial, and paracolonial situations, which encompassed independent nations such as Haiti, racial minority populations such as U.S. Blacks, and people suffering under colonial rule (Singh 2004:174).

As I indicated above Du Bois and Robeson had been unable to attend the congress because the State Department would not allow them to travel. But Dr. Du Bois refused to be silenced and sent a letter to the Congress about why he could not attend and cautioned that "any Negro-American who travels abroad today must either not discuss race conditions in the United States or say the sort of thing which our State Department wishes the world to believe" (Singh 2004:175).

So there was furious debate about the conditions of African Americans, the degree of racial progress in the United States, and so forth, with the U.S. delegates pretty much taking up the positions that Du Bois had predicted. Richard Wright was an exception. He was silent on the colonialism issue in the United States but unleashed a ferocious attack on African culture as backward and primitive.

Césaire argued against the valorization of European culture, saying that he had a different idea of the universal, a universal that is rich with all that is particular. He articulated a critique of the false universalism of the Western world that Wright himself would later reflect in White Man, Listen! But even then Wright claimed to be a man of the West. But the moment that Césaire sought had not yet arrived, nor is it merely a moment. The concept of a postcolonial era assumes that the dismantling of the official apparatus of colonialism is the same as the abolition of colonialism, or as others would say the "coloniality of power."

Colonialism required a discourse in which everything that is good, advanced, and civilized is measured in European terms. The project of colonial conquest requires not only the physical subjection of a population, but the naturalization of that conquest through the imposition of a Eurocentric framework on knowledge. As Mignolog (2007) argues, this hegemonic identity politics, seizing the mantle of universalism by conquest denounces opposing identities as fundamentalist and essentialist. As I indicated in Chapoter 3, Mignolo argues in much the same way that Césaire argued over 50 years ago, that one must speak from the identities that have been allocated in order to de-naturalize the imperial and racial construction identity in the modern world-system.

Bernard Magubane points out that the post–World War II period saw the rise of a collision between the historical treatment of Blacks in the United States and the attitude that the United States would have toward an independent Africa and the Black world as a whole.[6] One cannot understand the relationship

of African Americans to Africans, however, without understanding the historical development of that relationship.

Magubane argues that Blacks could not have a sense of security in a world
that degraded and rejected them. Given the negative political psychology that
pervaded much of the upper strata of African American society (such as it was),
attitudes toward Africa reflected this degradation. So Blacks initially expressed
their interests in Africa in terms of their duty to regenerate Africa and Africans.
For Magubane, Ethiopianism, Pan-Africanism, and Garveyism all include sentiments that can be explained only in terms of the nature of white hegemony over
African Americans.

This, I would argue, is true of what Wilson Moses refers to as the classical
age of Black Nationalism, which ends with the demise of the Garvey movement.
However, the race-first radicals in the New Negro Movement would eventually
set African America on a new course. By the 1920s the impact of those intellectuals profoundly affected by Du Bois had in turn transformed the doctor in
ways that moved him far beyond the Fabian socialism (social imperialism) of his
turn-of-the-century persona.

By the 1960s Black radicals, represented most ably by Malcolm X, had come
a long way. Magubane interrogates how Malcolm X views two opposing strategies for African American advancement and the implications for a changing
sense of identity. Though Malcolm was the individual most capable of grabbing
the spotlight, he was not alone in this issue.

In 1959 Hansberry told CBS News correspondent Mike Wallace "that the
sweep of national independence movements globally was inextricably linked to
the political initiatives of black Americans engaged in similar, and sometimes
overlapping, struggles for freedom, full citizenship, and self-determination"
(Wilkins 2006:192). According to Fanon Che Wilkins, this stance dates from
the early period of the civil rights movement. In this way Wilkins shows that the
cold war did not obliterate the Black Left but fostered a split with centrist liberals in the NAACP. Wilkins does not accept the assertions of Gerald Horne,
Brenda Gayle Plummer, and Penny Von Eschen that the unanimity of anticolonial opinion among African Americans during the early 1940s was shattered by
the cold war, resulting in the cutting off of 1960s activists in the SNCC and the
Black Panther Party from an older generation of Black radicals who had been
engaged in anticapitalist and anti-imperialist critiques of U.S. and European
imperialism.[7] Wilkins argues, as do Ian Rocksborough Smith and others, that a
significant presence of Black Left figures from the 1940s facilitated an intergenerational exchange of ideas and practices that built on the legacy of Black internationalism.[8] Hansberry was part of that contingent during the 1950s until her
death in 1965. During this period that preceded the SNCC's assumption of the
Black Power stance, Hansberry "remained committed to an anticolonial/ anti-
imperialist political project that challenged the supremacy of American capitalism and advocated for some variant of socialist development at the height of
McCarthyism and beyond" (Wilkins 2006:192).

While Hansberry, like her contemporary Frantz Fanon, anticipated the dangers of neocolonialism that would confront the newly decolonized states of Africa

and Asia, her views were reflective of the radical spirit of the 1955 Bandung Conference. Malcolm's position was slightly different, however, since he anticipated that the decolonization of African America would shatter the power of the U.S. hegemon and in concert would bring about the end of white world supremacy.

It is for this reason that Malcolm's logic seems unassailable to just about anyone who really listens to him. He argues with absolute certainty and humility (quite a combination) that those who believe in civil rights spend most of their time trying to prove that they are Americans, confining themselves to domestic issues in the United States, viewed from the perspective of a minority. When these people look on the American stage they see a white stage. This manner of framing African American identity simply reinforces the minority perspective, which is the perspective of an underdog who is impelled toward a begging, hat-in-hand, compromising approach (Magubane 1987:187).

For Malcolm X, Black Nationalists are more interested in human rights than in civil rights. They do not look upon themselves as Americans. "They look upon themselves as a part of dark humankind. They see the whole struggle not within the confines of the American stage, but they look upon the struggle on the world stage. And in the world context, they see that the dark man outnumbers the white man. On the world stage the white man is just a microscopic minority" (Magubane 1987:187).

Magubane also cites Harold Isaacs, who argued, "The downfall of white supremacy system in the rest of the world made the survival of it in the United States suddenly and painfully complicated. It became our most exposed feature and in the swift unfolding of world affairs, our most vulnerable weakness. When hundreds of millions of people all around look in our direction it seemed to be all that they could see" (Magubane 1987:188).

Finally, Magubane quotes Nehru speaking at a private meeting with Black and white civil rights leaders, at the behest of Ralph Bunche and Walter White: "Whenever I warn against acceptance of Soviet promises of equality because they are so frequently broken, I am answered quite often by questions about America's attitude toward dark skinned people. The people of Asia don't like colonialism or racial prejudices. They resent condescension. When Americans talk to them about equality and freedom, they remember stories about lynchings. They are becoming increasingly aware that colonialism is largely based on color—and for the first time in the lives of many of them they realize that they are colored" (Emerson and Kilson 1965:1059; Magubane 1987:189).

What Magubane has done is to reframe our gaze on the impact of the U.S. system of white supremacy on African Americans and on their relations with the entire dark world. He also points out that the African American espousal of Black Nationalism is the heart of the revolt against white world supremacy. Magubane then argues that the "Ethiopianism, Garveyism, and Pan-Africanism of the early twentieth century may have been poor efforts—small fissures in the dry crust of white hegemony—but they revealed an abyss. Beneath the apparently solid surface of world domination by whites they showed oceans of liquid matter only needing expansion to rend into fragments the hold of white supremacy" (Magubane 1987:193).

It was Malcolm X more than any other leader or intellectual of that period who was a tireless supporter of what has been called the spirit of Bandung. He popularized this notion on the Black street. He pointed out,

> It has been since the Bandung Conference that all dark people on the earth have been striding toward freedom . . . but there are 20 million Blacks here in America yet suffering the worst form of enslavement . . . mental bondage, mentally blinded by the white man, unable now to see that America is the citadel of white colonialism, the bulwark of white imperialism . . . the slave master of slave masters. . . .
>
> At Bandung they had to agree that as long as they remained divided a handful of whites would continue to rule them. But once our African [and] Asian Brothers put their religious and political differences into the background, their unity has had sufficient force to break the bonds of colonialism, imperialism, Europeanism . . . which are all only diplomatic terms for the same thing, WHITE SUPREMACY (Carson 1991:174–175).

Malcolm continued his presentation, indicating that 20 million Blacks in the United States are also kept divided and ruled by the very same white man, but Blacks in Harlem are so riven by petty differences that they cannot come together to confront the common enemy. Blacks in Harlem, Malcolm X argued, should hold their own Bandung Conference.

Like Malcolm X, the Revolutionary Action Movement (RAM) emphasized the spirit of Bandung in its analysis and theorizing. RAM argued that the major contradiction in the world was between Western imperialism and the revolutionary people of color, the Bandung world. It held that Black people in the United States were part of that Bandung world. This included all people of color from Asia, Africa, Latin America, Central America, the Caribbean, North America, the Indian subcontinent, and the Pacific Islands (Ahmad 2006:271). The structure of power within these coordinates gave a clear international dimension to the social conflicts and social struggles in this world. It is noteworthy that RAM shares the language of Malcolm X in its analysis of this situation, calling for unity against the common enemy. Indeed, Ahmad points out that RAM derived this position from Malcolm X.

During its early years, RAM representatives wrote a letter in support of the Vietnamese National Liberation Front, declaring RAM's solidarity with their struggle and proclaimed the organization's independence from the foreign policy of the United States. They viewed their closest international allies as the revolutionaries in China, Zanzibar, Cuba, Vietnam, Indonesia, and Algeria. They viewed their approach as a revision of traditional or Western Marxism, which they deemed Bandung Humanism. They would later drop this term and use *Black internationalism* or *revolutionary Black internationalism* instead. After 1966, Ahmad points out, the documents of the movement focused more on domestic struggles.

It was at this point that RAM emphasized its standpoint as one of revolutionary Black Nationalism in contrast to both the bourgeois reformism of the early Du Bois and the bourgeois nationalism of Marcus Garvey and Booker T. Washington. RAM leaders declared themselves the vanguard of the Black underclass. They supported the Black Pride component of bourgeois Black Nationalism but opposed the emphasis on Black capitalism. RAM argued that nationalism was the natural doctrine of the Black working class and that their advocacy of revolutionary Black Nationalism would rouse the anger of the Black working class to destroy the bourgeoisie (Ahmad 2006:274).

Ahmad traces the development of the Black radical movements of the 1960s and 1970s to Ella Baker, who from the late 1930s served of the staff of the NAACP and the Southern Christian Leadership Conference and was the organizer of the SNCC; Queen Mother Moore, who was a member of Garvey's Universal Negro Improvement Association and the Communist Party of the USA and who worked with Richard Moore and the National Coalition of Blacks for Reparations in America; James and Grace Boggs; and Malcolm X.[9]

Ahmad identifies three periods in the development of Malcolm's political thought. From 1952 to 1962, Malcolm was a leading member of the Nation of Islam and adhered closely to its version of Black Nationalism. During this first period, Malcolm X slowly returned to aspects of the Black Nationalism of his childhood, when his parents were members of Garvey's Universal Negro Improvement Association. In 1962 Malcolm X evolved toward a secular form of Black Nationalism, and during that time he began to subtly differentiate himself from the theology of the Nation of Islam. This period reached its highest development in the spring of 1964, but with his trip to the Middle East and Africa in April and May 1964, he began his evolution toward Pan-African internationalism.

Ahmad provides important insight into the evolution of Malcolm X by telling the story of Malcolm's political growth while in prison. While Malcolm's autobiography emphasizes the influence of Elijah Muhammad and the Nation of Islam, Ahmad tells how the imprisoned Malcolm X was influenced by the activities of Paul Robeson, who addressed a meeting of the Civil Rights Congress at Madison Square Garden attended by ten thousand people at which he called on Black people to resist the draft and not fight against their Asian brothers in the Korean War. Malcolm wrote a letter from prison to President Truman indicating his support for Robeson. Ahmad points out that Malcolm also supported and embraced the efforts of Paul Robeson and William Patterson (chairman of the Civil Rights Congress) to petition the United Nations to charge the United States for genocide against African Americans (Ahmad 2007:24).

There is, of course, a much longer legacy here that we have already discussed in previous chapters. Malcolm X did not emerge from the head of Elijah Muhammad and the Nation of Islam but was the product of a profound culture of opposition that had long caused unease in the citadels of power in U.S. society. More immediately, the source of the Black Power movement came from the interrelationship of the northern movement, in which Malcolm X was central, and the southern movement, in which the SNCC commanded the largest share of the foot soldiers.

In 1964, according to Ahmad, the SNCC still believed that freedom could be achieved through nonviolent, peaceful change in the capitalist system. This was the logic of the Mississippi Freedom Democratic Party, which challenged the Dixiecrats at the Democratic National Convention in 1964. By 1964 Malcolm X had transcended the Black Muslim theology of the period 1952–1962 and argued that African Americans were oppressed because their oppression served the interest of the white capitalist ruling class. Furthermore, the freedom struggle could not be limited to one tactic. Tactical flexibility was required to deal with any eventuality.

Kwame Ture (formerly Stokeley Carmichael) relates the story of Freedom Riders who traveled to Monroe, North Carolina (home of the local NAACP, headed by Robert Williams), to show white support for the demands of Monroe Blacks. The Freedom Riders, who were experienced in nonviolent protest, along with local youth had set up a picket line, which was set upon by an angry white mob.

> Bill Mahoney later told us: " I just knew we were dead. Man, we were completely surrounded by angry white folk. People started jumping out of the crowd to take swings at us. . . . People were bleeding. The threats got louder. . . . It was only a matter of time before they swarmed over us. . . ."
>
> I had been watching this old, old toothless man in overalls getting hysterical. His face was all red and convulsed. He kept screaming, "Kill the niggahs. Goddamn, kill 'em. Go on kill the nigguhs. . . ."
>
> Then I saw the old man's face suddenly change. He started pointing over my head. "Gawddammit," he cried. "Them niggahs got guns. Them goddamn niggahs got guns." The old cracker started jumping up and down, pointing and weeping, and shaking with rage. "Gawddamn," he wailed. "Them niggahs got guns." (Carmichael 2003:225–226)

During 1964, SNCC members John Lewis and Donald Harris traveled to Africa, where Malcolm X was on tour meeting with a variety of people. Everywhere they went they were asked where they stood in relation to Malcolm. Malcolm had established a position that dramatically altered the image of African American freedom fighters in the eyes of Africans (Ahmad 2007:26). In Nairobi the SNCC delegation crossed paths with Malcolm, and they sat down together to discuss the issues. Malcolm impressed on the SNCC delegation that it was important to view the U.S. Black freedom struggle in its human rights dimension and to recognize the role that Africa could play in supporting the African American struggle for human rights. William Sales points out that Lewis and Harris recommended that the organization reevaluate its position with regard to Malcolm's movement, and Lewis would later say that Malcolm, "more than any other single personality,[he had been] able to articulate the aspirations, bitterness, and frustrations of the Negro people [forming] a living link between Africa and the civil rights movement in this country" (Sales 1994:129).

Ahmad points out that the Nation of Islam had been the center of Black Nationalist activity during the late 1950s and early 1960s. In 1962–1963, several independent Black student formations emerged outside of the South, all closely related to the Nation of Islam (Ahmad 2007:26). In Detroit there was Uhuru; in Chicago, the National Organization of African Americans; in Oakland, California, the African American Association; in Cleveland, the African American Institute; in New York, Umbra; and in Philadelphia, the Revolutionary Action Movement. As the traveling representative of the Nation of Islam, Malcolm was in contact with all of these organizations (Ahmad 2007:26).

Muhammad Ahmad argues, as have others, that Malcolm's break with the Nation of Islam started in 1962, when Elijah Muhammad ordered him not to retaliate for a police raid on a Los Angeles temple that killed a member of the temple (a close friend of Malcolm's) and wounded several others.

According to Ahmad, by 1963 a group of young Muslims left the Nation of Islam and formed the National Liberation Front. This group left the Nation of Islam prior to Malcolm's departure and adhered to a revolutionary nationalist position. When Malcolm left the Nation of Islam early in 1964, members of the National Liberation Front met with him and asked him if he wished to be the leader of their organization. Malcolm X accepted, and this organization became the core of Muslim Mosque Incorporated (Ahmad 2007:27).

There was a nationalist wing close to Malcolm X in the southern student movement as well, composed of people inside and outside of the SNCC. Its center was in the Afro-American Student Movement at Fisk University in Nashville, Tennessee. At the urging of the National Liberation Movement, the Afro-American Student Movement organized the first national Black student conference.

Following Harold Cruse's brilliant article "Revolutionary Nationalism and the Afro-American" RAM militants viewed African America as a de facto member of the nonaligned nations, as part of the Bandung world. In November 1964, the Second Conference of the Afro-American Student Movement was held in Nashville with the theme "The Black Revolution's Relationship to the Bandung World." In a 1965 article in the RAM journal Black America ("The Relationship of Revolutionary Afro-American Movement to the Bandung Revolution") RAM argued that the central contradiction in the capitalist world was not the struggle between capital and labor but the struggle between Western imperialism and the third world. The goal of the Black American revolution was said to be "the international eradication of 'Yanqui' (U.S. & NATO) imperialism, not integration into this decadent imperialist framework" (RAM 1965b:11).

The article continued with a call for a revolutionary revision of Western Marxism. It argued that the failure of Marxism to revolutionize Western Europe and the United States during the 1930s Depression has forced African American revolutionists to advocate Bandung humanism or revolutionary Black internationalism.

An earlier unsigned article in the same issue, "The African American War of National Liberation" (RAM 1965a) notes that "The bourgeois revolution of the West was founded . . . maintained . . . on . . . national and international color injustice." It further argued that the nature of capitalist development and expansion was developed on the superexploitation of dark-skinned peoples. As previous revolutions began to degenerate, the article argued, the world revolution took on more of a racial character, whether people of color liked it or not.

During the previous one hundred years, the majority of workers in the imperialist countries had been cut in on a share of the surpluses wrung from the labor of the exploited races and therefore had a stake in maintaining this system of exploitation (RAM 1965a:4).

The historical reality, the article concluded, was that the subproletariat, not the proletariat, had become the vanguard of the revolution. African Americans were primarily located in the ranks of the subproletariat, although they lived in the belly of the beast, which created certain contradictions and a form of duality that cut against the grain of revolutionary potential and also enhanced the possibilities of revolution. By 1965 this movement had reached what many felt to be an unprecedented level of political sophistication. In May 1964, *Monthly Review* published a special issue titled "The Colonial War at Home," giving its readers among the U.S. and international Left a sense of the new radical forces emerging out of the African American movement. The issue featured an interview with Malcolm X by A. B. Spellman and excerpts from Max Stanford's "Towards Revolutionary Action Movement Manifesto."

The *Monthly Review* issue was a key document in making connections between Black radicals and the broader U.S. Left, but a year or so later, after Black inner rebellions had dramatically transformed the relations of force between dominated Blacks and the larger society, a series of exposes in *Life* magazine and *Esquire* identified RAM as one of the leading extremist groups "plotting a War on Whitey" (Kelley and Esch 1999:20). "The 'Peking-backed' group was considered not only armed and dangerous but 'impressively well read in revolutionary literature—from Marat and Lenin to Mao, Che Guevara and Frantz Fanon'"(Kelley and Esch 1999:20).

These highly publicized articles were followed by police raids of the homes of RAM members in Philadelphia and New York City, and RAM members were charged with conspiracy to instigate a riot, poison police officers with potassium cyanide, and assassinate Roy Wilkins and Whitney Young.[10]

By 1969 RAM as an organization had essentially dissolved, but RAM was significant beyond its organizational structure; it was its network of members, people in its orbit, allies, and sympathizers. The names I have indicated above make up a very short list of individuals. There were many, many more.

This social force saw African Americans in the United States as part of Lin Biao's global countryside.[11] Some readers will recall that in "Long Live the Victory of Peoples War!" Lin Biao had argued that the world revolution would begin in the global countryside and that it would spread and surround the global cities. Kwame Nkrumah had also argued that as members of the revolutionary third world liberated their territories from the yoke of capitalism and imperialism, revolutionary conditions would come to exist in the capitalist metropole, even in the belly of the beast, the fabled jewel of liberal capitalist civilization, the United States of America. Both these notions still make considerable sense, and indeed we see something like this happening, although not in such a linear fashion. The main problem with the notion as propounded in the 1960s and 1970s is that the time frame did not take into consideration the plurality of social times noted by Fernand Braudel, and with the subsiding of the mass mobilizations during this revolutionary period, the cadres drew conclusions that their expectations and their tactics had been excessive, that their practice was characterized by a form of revolutionary romanticism that had led them to make mistakes in their estimate of the possible.[12]

The demise of RAM did not end this period, though. Out of the network of revolutionary activists that had been spawned by RAM, Malcolm X, the Nation of Islam, and the radicals of this period rose the Black Panther Party, with which most readers have some familiarity. While some have commented that the membership of the Black Panther Party did not have the same level of theoretical sophistication as the militants associated with RAM, Black Panther Party members, as good Maoists, placed their emphasis on practice—not in the revolutionary underground but in the public arena. They were masters of revolutionary theater, which Molefi Asante (1999) argues is a key element of strategy in a modern information society.

By 1970 this network of revolutionary-minded youth, combined with other segments, of U.S. American activists had produced a complex network of individuals, organizations, and movements who manifested an oppositional spirit similar in density to that of the revolutionaries of the 1930s but more intense in its projection. Nixon's brutal invasion of Cambodia in May 1970 led to the largest explosion of protest on U.S. college campuses in the nation's history. By then a seemingly unbeleivable four out of ten college students, nearly 3 million people, thought that a revolution was necessary in the United States. *Business Week* lamented, that the governments's blunders in Cambodia and its clumsy repression of student protesters in such places as Kent State University in Ohio had more and more turned "the academic community against the war, against business, and against government." The Business Week editors held this to be a most "dangerous situation," a threat to "the whole economic and social structure of the nation" (Elbaum 2002:18–19).

The New Left, in search of a more adequate ideology, turned to third world Marxism, as SDS split into more radical forces such as Weatherman and the Revolutionary Youth movements (RYM). Within the Puerto Rican Left, the Young Lords, El Comite, and the Puerto Rican Socialist Party won tens of thousands to revolutionary politics in the 1970s (Elbaum 2002:78), making Leninism the dominant perspective on the Puerto Rican Left. While third world liberation movements had a powerful influence on all left-moving youth, for those with powerful Communist movements in their homelands, community formation itself was linked to the deepening of a radical sensibility. The third world strikes at San Francisco State and Berkeley were crucial in the evolution of Asian American radicalism. While cultural nationalism was a strong feature of Hispanic organizations such as the Brown Berets, Marxism was the dominant perspective in the Center for Autonomous Social Action (CASA), which did not distinguish between Mexicans born north of the border and those born south of the border. Marxist ideas also were established in the Native American movement. Of course the story of Black radicals is by now familiar, as most people know some of the histories of the Black Panther Party, the League of Black Revolutionary Workers, and the SNCC.

Left organizations composed primarily of persons of color include the Communist League (later the Communist Labor Party, and now the League of Revolutionaries for a New America), I Wor Kuen, the August Twenty-Ninth Movement, and the Revolutionary Communist League (formerly the Congress of African People), which eventually merged to form the U.S. League of Revolutionary Struggle. The Black Workers Congress split into a number of smaller groups. The Revolutionary Workers League, which stemmed from the merger of People's College, Malcolm X Liberation University, and the Youth Organization for Black Unity, would later establish powerful links with the Young Lords Party offshoot the Puerto Rican Revolutionary Workers Organization to form the short-lived Revolutionary Wing. The Workers Viewpoint Organization, which stemmed from the Asian Study Group, became the Communist Workers Party, which incorporated a significant number of cadres from the Revolutionary Workers League. The Union of Democratic Filipinos united with members of the Third World Women's Alliance and the Northern California Alliance to form Line of March.

The details of the U.S. Third World Left is a story that I will tell elsewhere. I would like to turn to the story of interaction between the Chinese American Red Guard Party and the Black Panther Party to illustrate the manner in which this period constituted what Omi and Winant (1994) term a great transformation of racial meanings and practices.

Grace Lee Boggs says that prior to the late 1960s, the term *Asian American* did not exist. It was created by students and young adults of Asian descent who began to view the rebellion of African Americans as an inspiration for them to embrace a new radical identity for themselves (Boggs 1998:1). Before that time, Asian Americans were identified in terms of national descent: Chinese Americans, Japanese Americans, and Filipino Americans were the main groups. They were not regarded as a force because of their small number and because of their reluctance to challenge U.S. institutions. "Just study hard, and don't rock the boat" was the advice of Boggs's parents, voicing the accommodationist rhetoric of the great African American leader Booker T. Washington.

But the Black Power movement was part of a global rising of oppressed strata that coincided with reforms such as the Civil Rights Act of 1964, the Voting Rights Act of 1965, and the Hart-Celler Immigration Act of 1965. According to Boggs (2005), the Hart-Celler Immigration Act opened the way for a significant influx of immigrants from China, the Philippines, Korea, India and south Asia, and Southeast Asia—approximately 7 million between 1970 and 2000.

On January 22, 1969, an organization called the Third World Liberation Front began a student strike at the University of California, Berkeley, demanding an autonomous third world college; eventually they won a compromise Ethnic Studies Division. The strike ended March 14. This event is often cited as the beginning of the militant stance among Asian American students. Two weeks later a group of young Chinese Americans calling themselves the Red Guard Party held a rally in San Francisco's Chinatown to announce their ten-point program, modeled on the ten-point program of the Black Panther Party. Daryl Maeda argued that the Red Guard Party's style, language, and dress strongly resembled that of the Black Panther Party, which had exerted significant influence in the formation of the Red Guard Party (Maeda 2006:117).

Maeda tells us that the Red Guard Party was among the first radicals to arise from Asian American communities. The group would later become I Wor Kuen, one of the main Maoist organizations of what I call the post-1968 Left. The Red Guard Party built community programs, organized Asian American workers, fought for better living conditions in Asian American communities, protested against the U.S. war in Vietnam, and was a leading organization of the post-1968 New Left (Maeda 2006:118).

Maeda argues that the Red Guard Party exemplified an ideology that was key in the construction of Asian American identity: third world internationalist radicalism. While this form of radicalism exercised brief hegemony over large segments of the U.S. Left during the late 1960s and early 1970s, it was practically definitive of the African American Left of this period. The Black Panther Party was the most well-known exponent, but other proponents included RAM, the Freedom Now Party, the SNCC after Black Power, the Congress of African People, the African Liberation Support Committee, the Youth Organization for Black Unity, the National Association of Black Students, Malcolm X Liberation University, and People's College. Many of these groups merged with the offshoot of the Asian Study Group (later the Workers Viewpoint Organization to form the Communist Workers Party). Among Latinos were the Young Lords Party and the August Twenty-Ninth Movement, which would later unite with I Wor Kuen and remnants of the Congress of African People to form the U.S. League for Revolutionary Struggle (Bush 1999:211).

Maeda argues that the cultural issues raised regarding the relationship between Asian American identity and Blackness in Frank Chin's play *Chickencoop Chinaman*, are similar to the domestic cultural nationalism of the Black Pride movement of that same period. While Maeda agreed that in Chin's play the "performance of Blackness catalyzed the formation of Asian American identity," it was "not mere mimicking as Chin leveled at the Red Guard Party." It "involved a process of racial positioning through the contemplation of Blackness, which enabled Asian Americans to form a racial identity rather than an ethnic or national identity" (Maeda 2006:119). Maeda and others utilize Omi and Winant's (1994) conception of racial formation to explain the process that took place during this period. As many scholars argue, race itself is a social construction, so consciousness of the process avoids any puerile debates about the authenticity of Asian Americans as a race. Maeda also avoids the stark contrast between third world internationalism and domestic cultural nationalism that so plagued the relationship between the Black Panther Party and the US organization during the late 1960s and early 1970s, of which there are some echoes in the debates about Afrocentrism on the Left today.[13]

The more important implication for both approaches is a resistance to assimilation into whiteness. At the initial rally organized by the Red Guard Party, David Hilliard, chairman of the Black Panther Party, admonished the audience for the alleged lack of militancy of Chinese Americans. He also argued that it was important for them to relate to revolutionary China (the People's Republic of

China). At the moment when Asian American assimilation seemed possible for the first time, the Black Panther Party urged them to reject assimilation, and the Red Guard Party accepted this admonition.

It is important to understand that the Black Power movement was a moment of racial formation for Blacks as well. In their elaboration of the Black Power concept, Carmichael and Hamilton (1967) called for Blacks to redefine themselves, reclaim their history and their culture, and create their own sense of community and togetherness. Maeda points out that they deemed "assimilated" and "integrated" Blacks to be co-opted by whites and hence ineligible to participate in creating this new Black community and identity (Maeda 2006:121–122).

Unlike prior assimilationist groups, such as the Japanese Americans Citizen League, Maeda argues that the Asian American activists of this period viewed racism as systemic rather than an aberrant feature of U.S. society. They believed that the racial oppression of Asian Americans served to justify their economic exploitation, and thus they sought to build autonomous Asian American power and culture, free of white approval. Instead of inserting themselves into the mainstream, they sought to strengthen Chinatown's community institutions.

Maeda points out that the political theater of rallies, marches, proclamations, and social programs—along with literary and cultural productions—produced a novel form of Asian American subjectivity by highlighting parallels between the common racialization affecting African Americans and Asian Americans of various ethnicities. The Asian American Political Alliance, founded in 1968 by Richard Aoki, a Japanese American who had been a member of the Black Panther Party, hoisted posters with "Free Huey" inscribed in Mandarin, Japanese, Tagalog, and English. Overall, this process is seen as having assisted in the construction of Asian American identity as a new form of subjectivity that rejected assimilation and consolidated multiple Asian ethnicities under the rubric of race.

The importance of political theater should not be diminished. These posters in a variety of languages were carried by a group whose primary language was almost assuredly English. The Red Guard Party itself consisted of disaffected American-born Chinatown youth drawn from a community agency called Legitimate Ways (or Leeways), which provided alternatives to street life and petty crime to youth who were faced with substandard housing, poor schools, overcrowding, and endemic poverty (Maeda 2006:126).

The Critique of Identity Politics

One can hardly mention the term *Black Power* or *Black nationalism* without encountering what seems like an obligatory lecture from most intellectuals educated in the Pan-European world about the dangers of identity politics, racial essentialism, and narrow nationalism. Some years back I heard that Robin D. G. Kelley and Todd Gitlin squared off over this issue at a conference at Columbia University. Afterward, Kelley was heard ruminating about the neo-enlightenment Left. It seemed puzzling that the reflections of those who expressed so much regret about the "twilight of our common dreams" (Gitlin 1995) seemed so unaware or uninterested in the critique of the Eurocentrism of the dominant knowledge in the Pan-European world.

Frances Fox Piven and Richard Cloward (1997) point out that Marx's great insight was that capitalism would lead increasingly to the concentration of wealth at one pole and the accumulation of poverty and misery at the other, thus uniting the working class, eliminating ancient differences, and paving the way for the emergence of a universal workers' movement. They argue further that this idea lent a certain élan to the world socialist movement, which emboldened its members and strengthened them for the long haul.

But the transformations of the last thirty years have undone this sense of international mission and universalism of the world's working classes. Instead we seem bombarded by particularisms, identity politics, and fractiousness, leading in some cases to genocidal conflicts along these lines of division.

Piven and Cloward caution that this manner of presentation may be misleading because there have always been elements of identity politics in the workers' movement and because identity politics could be liberating as it binds people together in a sense of their common grievances against a common enemy.

An example of the progressive role of identity politics can be seen in the United States in the post–World War II Black movement and the feminist movements. These two movements are pointed out as examples of emancipatory constructions and assertions of group identity. But some observers also note that these assertions provoked alarm among those groups whose sense of identity depended on the subordination of Blacks and women. The social and political tension around conflicting assertions of identity then became fodder used by political elites, who capitalized on the politics of backlash to oppose the expansion of the maneuvering space for Blacks and women to be fully included in the American social compact. Republican Party operatives and others made the politics of backlash central to their appeals. This, of course, was the logic of the Republican Party's southern strategy, including the so-called Moral Majority and the Christian Coalition.

Piven and Cloward contend that racism and patriarchy are the twin appeals of this conservative coalition. Here the critique of identity politics is based on a fairly well-established discourse that seeks to evade the divide-and-conquer strategy of the ruling classes. There is also a concern in the larger arena of political discourse in that these particularisms seem to be leading to a rising tide of destructiveness in the contemporary world. This involves the weakening and collapse of nation-states, the accelerating migration of peoples, and the intensifying competition for scarce resources.

Piven and Cloward think it important to demystify what is actually happening in the contemporary world. While the dominant discourse points out that ancient animosities arise whenever central government can no longer hold them in check, they do not deal adequately with the sociostructural basis of increased competition among social groups based on the social policies of dominant economic strata and institutions. The eastern European revolution is more about the right to shop than about the right to vote.

How, then, does one interpret the intensification of ethnonationalism following the collapse of the socialist and social democratic projects? Do these events confirm or undermine Marx's projection that the promise of the labor movement is that class solidarity would override state patriotism? This indeed was the case when successful use of the strike weapon demanded it. But organized labor has lost ground from 30 percent of the private labor force in 1952 to 11 percent of the private labor force in 1980. The declining power of the labor movement is only one factor undermining the bargaining power of the working class; the constraints that globalization is said to place on the state are also construed to be constraints on democratic publics.

The capitalist class has launched a withering ideological offensive about an increasingly globalized world operating according to natural law, penetrating national economies to their core and beyond the reach of politics. This is said to be the way of the future, a great force for progress, the hope of humankind. The workers' movement is no longer the moral force of old and is often in disarray, claiming, as Vaclav Havel says, that when people can no longer depend on rational knowledge, they cling to the ancient certainties of the tribe.[14] The logic of the increased competitiveness among social groups in the current period of neoliberal globalization seems to clinch any argument in opposition to identity politics and to auger for a stance that is perilously close to a need to accept the logic of neoliberal globalization because there is no alternative, as was argued by the great prophets Margaret Thatcher and Ronald Reagan, who restored the majesty and confidence of the (white) Western world.

While Piven and Cloward's reservations about the critique of identity politics are salutary, I would like to review two other kinds of response to the critique of identity politics, one a direct critique, the other a response to the implied critique.

Linda Alcoff argues that the critique of identity involves three major issues. First, strongly held cultural identities are held to lead to conflicting loyalties in the context of ethnic groups in a single nation-state.[15] She refers to Schlesinger's notion of the "cult of ethnicity," which exaggerates differences, intensifies resentments and antagonisms, and deepens the wedge between various ethnic groups (Alcoff 2006:16–18).[16] Second, identity politics is also said to reify group identities, which lead to conformity based on a constructed model of authenticity, intolerance of differences in the group, and patriarchal norms. Third, identity politics makes rational deliberation in the larger society impossible since the group's mandates will always prioritize the possible rather than rational deliberation (Alcoff 2006).

Alcoff does not accept the manner in which identity groups are defined by their critics as the only definition possible. She cites an alternative definition by Manuel Castells, who views identity as a generative source of meaning, necessarily collective rather than wholly individual, and useful as a source of agency as well as a meaningful narrative (Castells 1997:7).

She acknowledges that one source of reservation about the role that identity groups play in social organization is the fear that identities are really imposed on subordinate groups by the more powerful. She argues, however, that the identities that are imposed on the less powerful by those higher in status tend to reflect more an ascription than an identity that must resonate with and unify lived experience. For Alcoff, then, identity is not simply constructed from air; it makes epistemic difference. It is "a way of inhabiting, interpreting, and working through both collectively and individually, an objective social location and group history" (Alcoff 2006:22).

Alcoff concludes insightfully, in my view, that this means that when one is identified, one's horizon of agency is also identified. Social identity consequently is related to epistemic judgment, not so much because identity determines judgment but because they draw on a collective pool that impacts a horizon of perception relevant to the formation of knowledge claims or theoretical analysis.

Given the universal claims of European phenomenology, an Africana phenomenology could be discovered or revealed only through pulling apart the imperial geography and its exclusive relationship between reason and European culture. Paget Henry argues that the dialectical logic of Georg Wilhelm Friedrich Hegel's phenomenology was an attempt to retain the explanatory agency of spirit in light of the rise of the natural sciences.[17] Edmund Husserl's call for self-reflection related to the crisis produced by the positivistically reduced notions of rationality and humanity that accompanied the rise of mathematics and science. Jurgen Habermas formulated this reduction in terms of the colonization of the Western life-world by its systems of technical and instrumental rationality. Henry cites Jean-Paul Sartre's contention that the need for self-reflection derives more insistently than a mere intellectual exercise from the capacity of Western thought to mobilize reason in the service of unreason and untruth.

Du Bois's concept of double consciousness is the key to penetrating the veil of European phenomenology. Double consciousness, of course, is a product of the racialization of the Africana subject.

> For Du Bois, this racialization of identities and supporting institutional orders were not leftovers from the traditional past but integral parts of the modern world order of European capitalism. It was as integral as the processes of commodification, colonization, rationalization, and secularization that Marx, Weber and Durkheim thought were so central to the rise Western capitalism. The growth of processes of racialization throughout the formative and mature periods of Western capitalism is evident in its expanding discourses on the hierarchies of races and the increasingly global reach of its institutions of white supremacy" (Henry 2006:7).

Du Bois calls for Black folks to stand above the loud tumult produced by the contradictions of Black life in the European world, but he realizes that this takes a special effort, which he describes as a fiercely sunny disposition, one quite unlike the disposition of some Black people filled with bitterness and silent hatred of everything white, whose lives have been wasted in despair about the hopelessness of their situations. What is needed is for Black folks to make use of their gift of second sight.

In Du Bois, our first glimpses of such critiques are to be found in his early short story, "A Vacation Unique." In this story, Du Bois's hero, Cuffy, invites his Harvard classmate to disguise himself as a "negro" and to come and see the world from this point of view. Cuffy says to his classmate: "outside of mind you may study mind, and outside of matter by reason of the fourth dimension of color you may have a striking view of the intestines of the fourth great civilization. . . ." In other words, what the classmate will get is an intestinal view of American civilization, of the hunger that drives it to dominate and racialize. This intestinal view of the white imperial self is repeated in *Darkwater*, in another of Du Bois's classic statements of what I have called potentiated second sight. In the chapter, "The Souls of White Folks," he writes: "of them I am singularly clairvoyant. I see in and through them. I view them from unusual points of vantage. Not as foreigner do I come, for I am native, not foreign, bone of their thought and flesh of their language. . . . Rather I see these souls undressed and from the back and side. I see the workings of their entrails. I know their thoughts and they know that I know" (Du Bois 1999:17; Henry 2006:10).

Jane Gordon (2006) takes up the issue of double consciousness in a manner similar to that of Paget Henry (2006).[18] She maintains that the need to establish a Black or Africana viewpoint stems from the need to be able to assess the issue of legitimacy from modernity's underside, that is, from the perspective of peoples in tension with the social order whose standard of universality is precisely that which is hostile to these dominated peoples. Such people literally live in a society that does not have room for them. Gordon argues that they are perpetual outsiders evaluated by insider norms. The classic statement about this situation stems from W.E.B. Du Bois's writings and commentary on double consciousness.

Gordon credits Du Bois with the insistence that racialized and racializing identities and the institutional orders that buttress and are buttressed by them are not remnants of earlier social and political forms but integral to the modern world-system in the same way as commodification, rationalization, and secularization (Gordon 2006:1). She argues that it is important to note that Du Boisian double consciousness is not simply having to live for the sake of another's consciousness but having to exist for the sake of a self-consciousness that racialized itself as white, a process that is derived from the racialization of the Africana subject as Black (Gordon 2006:3).

Du Bois's generation and subsequent generations had their own weapon readily at hand. In his *Darkwater* essay, "The Souls of White Folk," Du Bois wrote,

High in the tower, where I sit above the loud complaining of the human sea, I know many souls that toss and whirl and pass, but none there are that intrigue me more than the Souls of White Folk. Of them I am singularly clairvoyant. I see in and through them. I view them from unusual points of vantage. Not as a foreigner do I come, for I am native, not foreign, bone of their thought and flesh of their language. . . .

Mine is not the knowledge of the traveler or the colonial composite of dear memories, words and wonder. Nor yet is my knowledge that which servants have of masters, or mass of class, or capitalist of artisan. Rather I see these souls undressed and from the back and side. I see the working of their entrails. (Du Bois 1999:17)

Du Bois asserts that he knows their thoughts and that they know that he knows them, which alternatively makes them embarrassed and furious. This special access to the dehumanizing will to power of the European imperial subject is a form of social power that undercuts the legitimacy of the ruling race and class in a fundamental manner. For it is this special insight of the Black life-world that makes it such a threat to the white life-world's claims of universalism. It is the insider status of the former slaves that performs such a debilitating function, one that the white life-world cannot escape and that therefore must be silenced at all costs. It is for this reason that U.S. society has sought to deal with the Negro question for so long and, failing to assimilate this troublesome presence, has sought to pronounce the presence null and void via the society's announcement that it is color blind.

In closing this chapter I would like to point out how the spirit of Bandung and the significance of Black Power as Black internationalism are captured by the image of Malcolm X in Africa. For Malcolm X, the importance of the Organization of Afro-American Unity was that it sought to elevate the Black freedom struggle above the domestic level of civil rights and to internationalize it by placing it at the level of human rights (Tyner 2006:134). In July 1964 Malcolm had submitted a brief on behalf of the Organization of Afro-American Unity at a Cairo meeting of the Organization of African Unity explaining that he represented 22 million Afro-Americans whose human rights were being violated daily by U.S. imperialists. Since these 22 million Afro-Americans were not in the United States by choice, he held that African problems are also Afro-American problems and Afro-American problems are African problems. He called for the Organization of African Unity to assist the Organization of Afro-American Unity in bringing their problems before the United Nations.

Malcolm strategically stepped outside of the confines of the United States. He refused to go to the criminal and ask the criminal for civil rights when what the Blacks in the United States really needed was to hold the criminal accountable in the court of world opinion for the violation of the God-given human rights of the African American people. Malcolm's association between African Americans and the dark world is hailed by James Tyner as a strategic move that presented a new balance sheet of power. While the civil rights discourse limited Blacks to a position as minorities seeking integration and acceptance in U.S. society, declaring solidarity with the dark world repositioned them as part of the majority in the larger world-system (Tyner 2006:135–136).

On the basis of this repositioning, Tyner then argues that the issue of African American colonization is essentially a creature of the minority-majority reversal. Critics of the concept have argued on the basis of its impractical nature. Classically colonized people can eject the colonial power from their territories and send them home, but this is said not to be an option for African Americans, who are a minority in U.S. society. In this case Malcolm viewed African American liberation as part of the worldwide struggle against white supremacy.

Arthur Schlesinger, Jr., argues that the militants of ethnicity are promoting a separatism which, "nourishes prejudice, magnifies differences and stirs antagonisms" (Schlesinger 1991:17). This cult of ethnicity has come to represent a significant threat to what he views as the defining ethos of American nationhood. Some may see in Schlesinger's claims an echo of the post-Reconstruction era attacks on Blacks to achieve national reconciliation. Coincidental? Let us look further. Schlesinger holds that Americans are a new race of men, the best hope of all humanity, drawing on J. Hector St. John Crevecoeur's *Letters from an American Farmer* (1788). Schlesinger neglects to say, however, that Crevecoeur's "universal man" was either a European or a descendant of a European (Singh 2004:34).

Black intellectuals and activists who have challenged the false universalism of the U.S. intelligentsia and public discourse have suffered exile, repression, ostracism, and assassination (Singh 2004:42).

Black particularity, much disparaged in a range of U.S. social thought, has often been a search for a wider struggle for social justice, and while drawing on values of the Euro-American canon such as liberalism and Christianity, it has also reached beyond the boundaries of the U.S. political imagination to Islam, international socialism, Black nationalism, third world Marxism, and the like (Singh 2004:42).

Black folks' claim to worldliness (à la Richard Wright) has challenged not only particularism masquerading as universalism but also a universalism whose vicious opposition to Black humanity has revealed its true nature.

Thus, Black antiracism discourse and communal identity are not about and cannot be reduced to integration into U.S. society. Rather, they represent the counterstatements of political subjects who have struggled to widen the circle of humanity (Singh 2004:44). This may be more difficult for some to see in the rhetoric of the Black internationalism of the Black Power militants, but I argue that this attempt to widen the circle of we was the dominant framework not only of the explicit Black Power radicals but of the civil rights radicals as well. It's expressed nowhere as clearly as in the 1960s trajectory of Dr. Martin Luther King, Jr., and the older civil rights radicals, who moved from a desire to simply be included in the U.S. mainstream, to a critique of U.S. society from the perspective of the larger world.

The Trajectory of Dr. Martin Luther King, Jr.

In 1963 Dr. Martin Luther King, Jr., articulated his vision of the future as 250,000 demonstrators marched on Washington:

> I say to you today, my friends, that in spite of the difficulties and frustrations of the moment, I still have a dream. It is a dream deeply rooted in the American dream.

I have a dream that one day this nation will rise up and live out the true meaning of its creed: we hold these truths to be self-evident: that all men are created equal.

I have a dream that one day on the red hills of Georgia the sons of former slaves and the sons of former slave owners will be able to sit down together at the table of brotherhood.

I have a dream that my four children will one day live in a nation where they will be judged not by the color of their skin but by the content of their character.

I have a dream today.

I have a dream that one day down in Alabama, with its vicious racists, with its governor having his lips dripping with the words of interposition and nullification that one day, right here in Alabama, little black boys and black girls will be able to join hands with little white boys and white girls as sisters and brothers." (Washington 1986:219)

This was King's hope. He called for freedom to ring throughout the land. Then he concluded,

When we let freedom ring, when we let it ring from every village and every hamlet, from every state and every city, we will be able to speed up that day when all God's children, Black men and white men, Jews and Gentiles, Protestants and Catholics, will be able to join hands and sing in the words of the old Negro spiritual, free at last! Free at last! Thank God almighty, we are free at last! (Washington 1986:220)

Dr. King's dream was a testament to the American dream. It was a revival and a deepening of the American dream. One might say that it called for the completion of the great unfinished American revolution. The audacious optimism in King's remarks reflects the anticipation of victory in battle. While King did not fear to appropriate the American dream as the legitimate right of black people, he did not hesitate to chastise America for failing to deliver on its promise.

Within a year or so after the 1963 March on Washington, legislation had been passed that broke the back of Jim Crow and de jure segregation. The civil rights revolution had overcome the reactionary caste system of the Old South.

But what of those outside the South, where a segregated and marginalized urban proletariat lived in squalid conditions despite their access to formal citizenship rights? Some social scientists, historians, journalists, and political leaders readily conceded that the sentiments of this segment of the Black population have been more accurately expressed by Malcolm X, who argued that black people should have no illusions about being included in the American dream. Rather, the reality of Black people in America was an American nightmare. He said just because kittens are born in an oven, you don't call them biscuits. You can't sit at the table and throw us a few crumbs from the table and call us Americans. Malcolm X said you could not go to the criminal and ask for civil rights; you had to take the criminal to the world court and sue for denial of your human rights. Malcolm was involved in a process of rearticulating the American dream, or perhaps he sought to abolish the American dream.

In 1964 Dr. Martin Luther King was awarded the Nobel Peace Prize. He most certainly deserved it, but Martin Luther King and the movement he led most emphatically refused to abide by an unjust peace and massively abridged that peace, over and over again. Now, clearly the Nobel committee had another kind of peace in mind, namely the peaceful settlement of the collective grievances of America's former slaves in their quest for full citizenship. America's liberal establishment had long tolerated the second-class status of its Black population, however, and considered civil rights agitation disruptive to the ruling coalition and harmful to the cause of Black people themselves. Dr. Martin Luther King's "Letter from a Birmingham Jail" applied to a much larger group than the southern white moderates.

For some in the Black community, there is a clear logic to the Nobel committee's decision to award the world's most prestigious peace prize to a man who led so many demonstrations, which made it impossible to do business as usual. When Malcolm X was considered as an alternative, Dr. King, for all of his troublemaking, seemed a more desirable alternative.

After the emergence of Malcolm X and the Nation of Islam into the nation's public life, Dr. Martin Luther King's ideas and person were cynically juxtaposed to Malcolm's, while Malcolm's views were parodied. After King's death, those who hated him in life cynically twisted his message to their own ends. Consider the following.

Some years ago, on Dr. Martin Luther King, Jr.'s, birthday, the Reverend Al Sharpton attempted to lead a march across the Brooklyn Bridge., New York City Mayor Giuliani condemned the march as as a violation of the spirit of Dr. Martin Luther King, Jr. It was an abridgement of the peace. And then they intoned with the most cynical hypocrisy imaginable that Martin Luther King, Jr., was an apostle of peace.

I am reminded of the comments of the poet Carl Wendell Himes, Jr.:

> Now that he is safely dead
> Let us praise him
>   Build monuments to his glory
>   sing hosannas to his name.
>   Dead men make
> Such convenient heroes: they
>   Cannot rise
>   to challenge the images
>   We would fashion from their lives
>   and besides,
>   it is easier to build monuments
>   than to make a better world.
>   So, now that he is safely dead
> We, with eased consciences
>   Will teach our children

> *that he was a great man . . . knowing*
> *that the cause for which he lived*
> *Is still a cause*
> *and the dream for which he died*
> *Is still a dream,*
> *a dead man's dream." (Harding 1996:3–4)*

What is perhaps most ironic is that the institutionalization of King as a national hero was overseen by some of his most vicious opponents (President Ronald Reagan and George Bush) and in the midst of the most ferocious assaults on the dream in modern times. For these people the bottom line was unequivocal; they desired passivity in the face of this ferocious assault. You might say, let them eat holidays.

For King nonviolence was a means to protest injustice without bitterness and hatred, but it was not about keeping the peace in an unjust or unfair situation. King's focus was on ending racial injustice or white racism, but he also fought to end economic injustice and the bullying of small countries by large ones. He said that when he died he did not want people to say that he had won a Nobel Prize, nor to mention where he went to school. He said he wanted people to say that Dr. Martin Luther King, Jr., tried to give his life serving others. He wanted them to know that he tried to love somebody. He wanted people to know that he tried to feed the hungry and clothe the naked. He wanted people to know that Dr. Martin Luther King, Jr., was a drum major for justice, a drum major for peace, a drum major for righteousness.

King wanted to be viewed as a drum major for peace, but he did not believe there could be peace if there was no justice. He did not believe that any people should peacefully accept injustice. The fight for justice was the most important thing, but the fight should be done with love and without bitterness. The legacy of Dr. Martin Luther King, Jr., and of the civil rights movement that he led was not peace and harmony, but no justice, no peace.[19]

The 1963 March on Washington was an attempt to draw the attention of the people of the United States and the people of the world to the sorry situation of black people in the United States, subject to unjust laws that discriminate against them. Dr. Martin Luther King accused the United States of having written the Negro people a bad check, one that had come back marked "insufficient funds." Yes, King had a dream, but the realization of this dream was not imminent.

Indeed, on Christmas Eve 1967, he told his congregation at Ebenezer Baptist Church that "not long after the speech in Washington, D.C., he saw his dream turn into a *nightmare*! The revolution in the streets of the black ghettos and in the jungles of Vietnam exposed the ruthless and cold-blooded nature of the U.S. social system." Dr. King was challenged by Malcolm X and by the youthful foot soldiers of the Student Nonviolent Coordinating Committee. He learned from them and synthesized the lessons of this history.

While in Ghana, Malcolm also solidified his ties with representatives of radical third world nations such as China, Cuba, and Algeria. The Algerian ambassador Taher Kaid was a Muslim and a revolutionary but would have been classified as a white man in the United States. When Malcolm argued that he followed the social, political, and economic philosophy of Black Nationalism in the United States and Africa, Taher Kaid asked where that left him.

Malcolm began to think about how one related to the nonblack revolutionaries from the Three Continents (Africa, Asia, and Latin America). From that time, he began to understand the contradictions of nationalism. He told an OAAU audience "we nationalists used to think we were militant. We were just dogmatic" (Breitman 1965:213).

This did not mean that he became an integrationist. Indeed, Malcolm's contribution consisted of his internationalization of the struggle. He convinced a whole generation of youth, both black and nonblack, to see themselves as part of the majority of the world's people struggling against an imperialist white ruling class and their privileged white populations in the United States and Western Europe. Malcolm's revolutionary legacy led to a fundamental transformation of the consciousness of an entire generation of black, Latino, Asian, Native American, and white youth, and also of older activists. Dr. Martin Luther King was a part of this transformation. Malcolm X did seek to ally with the radicals in the civil rights movement, and through them was able to effect an alliance with Martin Luther King himself.

Toward the end of his life Martin Luther King, Jr. began to sound more like Malcolm. He called for a movement that "would cripple the operations of an oppressive society until it was ready to listen to the cries and see the real fires of the poor" (Harding, 1996:18). In addition, he argued, "The dispossessed of this nation—the poor, both white and Negro—live in a cruelly unjust society. They must organize a revolution against that injustice" (Harding 1996:18).

Rather than depending on a friendly federal government, in this new period Martin Luther King held that "Negroes must, therefore, not only formulate a program; they must fashion new tactics which do not count on government good will, but serve instead, to compel unwilling authorities to yield to the mandates of justice" (Harding 1996:19).

Martin Luther King held that "the Negro revolt is evolving into more than a quest for desegregation and equality. . . . Black freedom struggle was actually exposing the evils that are deeply rooted in the whole structure of our society. It reveals systemic rather than superficial flaws and suggests that radical reconstruction of society itself is the real issue to be faced" (Harding 1996:20). Finally, he predicted, "The storm is rising against the privileged minority of the earth, from which there is no shelter in isolation or armaments. The storm will not abate until a just redistribution of the fruits of the earth enables men everywhere to live in dignity and human decency. The American Negro . . . may be the vanguard of a prolonged struggle that may change the shape of the world, as billions of deprived shake and transform the earth in the quest for life, freedom, and justice" (Harding 1996:21). With these words one can almost hear the assassin put a round of ammunition in the chamber of the gun. Could the servants of the ruling strata in the nation's security apparatus allow such a man to live?

These words may have constituted Dr. King's death warrant. He had gone beyond the pale. But the U.S. Federal Bureau of Investigation had already reached the conclusion that Dr. King could not be allowed to continue as a black leader. Indeed, in 1963 J. Edgar Hoover said he intended to destroy the civil rights movement because it was the leading edge of a social revolution in the United States. Hoover had Dr. Martin Luther King in mind but quickly saw the potential of Malcolm X and sided with Elijah Muhammad, Louis Farrakhan, and others in the Nation of Islam to remove Malcolm from the scene.

Malcolm was the preeminent revolutionary leader of this century. He had developed alliances with revolutionaries throughout the three continents. He had established relations with the radicals in the civil rights movement, in the SNCC, RAM, the Southern Christian Leadership Conference, and the Congress of Racial Equality. Dr. Martin Luther King's lawyer had met with Malcolm to form a coalition in which Dr. Martin Luther King would continue to lead those forces in the South where he had established a powerful force, and Malcolm would lead those forces outside of the South. Dr. Martin Luther King agreed to support Malcolm in his efforts to take the United States before the United Nations for the violation of the human rights of the African American people.

It was the joining together of these two trajectories at last that seemed to point the way to the future, though the Counterintelligence Program labored mightily to disrupt the possibility of these two strands coming together. What is clearer now than it was then is that it is precisely this attempt to widen the "circle of the we" that was so adamantly opposed because it poses questions that the concept of citizenship elides but that it is supposed to address. The notorious exceptionality of the Black populations was the focus of a concerted effort to turn the clock back in the manner of the Ku Klux Klan march from Atlanta to Selma, symbolically turning the clock back on the gains of the civil rights movement, but also in this case abandoning the responsibility for the general welfare that should be the responsibility of any civilized society.

The liberal Eurocentrism of the Enlightenment had been the cultural foundation of the period of social democratic compromise in the core states of the world-system and to some extent of the radical semiperipheral states of the Pan-European world as well. In hindsight, many now view this period as the golden age of historical capitalism, but it is also brought us to the limits of the system because this compromise could not be extended to the rest of the world without exhausting the limits of the profit-maximizing logic of historical capitalism on a world scale. The ruling classes of the hegemonic power in its twilight are searching for an alternative strategy but are terrified that the preemptive warriors of the Far Right are the only plausible answer to the this crisis of U.S. hegemony, which is accompanied by a crisis of white world supremacy, and finally by a structural crisis of historical capitalism.

The golden age of capitalism enabled subaltern strata in the "belly of the beast" and in its periphery to glimpse larger possibilities for social transformation and to attempt to realize them. In the meantime, the harsh rhetoric against those subaltern strata has been ratcheted up. Civil tensions in the United States are at an unprecedented level, giving rise to a dramatic expansion of the carceral state and what Steve Martinot (2003) refers to as the parastate.[20] It is not merely ironic that this be juxtaposed to the historic moment of Barack Obama's run for president of the United States, and his final victory over Hilary Clinton in the Democractic Party primary, and over John McCain and Sarah Palin in the Presidential Election.

Barack Obama and the End of White World Supremacy

The foundation of the Barack Obama's successful presidential bid is the historical strength of Black solidarity against systemic racism in the United States *and* of its internationalist stance in the larger world-system. The Black Freedom Struggle with its foundation in large sections of the lower strata of U.S. society is a large bloc of any Left within U.S. society. It is also important to note its very conscious self-conception of itself as a *segment* of oppressed strata within the United States *and* within the larger world-system. Note should be taken of gender dynamics as well for the manner in which Black women have been so central to that struggle, and in contesting the notion of manhood rights.

I have argued here that systemic racism is the foundation of the new world formed with the European conquest of the Americas, the destruction of the Amerindian civilizations, and the capture of Africans to serve as slave labor in the colonial societies. It was at this time that the concept of race was introduced into scientific and public discourse as a means of naturalizing the relationship between the conquerors and the conquered, and was generalized to the entire world-economy during the subsequent European conquest of the rest of the world

As I argue throughout this book, the enslaved Africans, unlike the indigenous populations, were a part of the newly formed United States of America, and were living contradictions to the "land of the free" rhetoric of the nation's propagandists. Their incorporation into U.S. American society, even as second class citizens would remain the achilles heel, not only to U.S. pretensions of freedom and democracy, but would also constitute the foundation of its internally colonized periphery, or "third world within." The growth of this racialized populations disproportionately concentrated in the lowest social classes is a very unstable mix. Melanie Bush and I will explore this at length in our forthcoming *Tensions in the American Dream* (Temple University Press, 2010), but I would like to highlight how these tensions illuminate where we stand at this historical moment.

Black particularity has long haunted the imaginary of the U.S. American elite and large segments of the pan-European population, as well, because their relative privileges and their relatively higher social status rested on the racial foundation provided by people of African descent and other people of color. Needless to say this creates substantial social tension between the groups and a sense of defensiveness when Blacks and other people of color raise questions about a naturalized system meant precisely to be invisible (Bush 2004, McIntosh 2008, Bonilla-Silva 2003).

As we have seen Black solidarity and Black internationalism within the United States has taken a variety of political forms. This includes the liberal nationalism and anti-colonialism of the Pan-African Conference and Dr. Du

Bois at the turn of the century, the militant and assertive Black solidarity of the Niagara Movement of 1905, and the Race First radicals of the New Negro movement whose leaders included Marcus Garvey, Hubert Harrison, Cyril Briggs, Richard Moore, W.A. Domingo, and Claude McKay. Even the Class First radicals of the New Negro movement (A. Philip Randolph and Chandler Owen) were firm practitioners of Black solidarity and Black internationalism. In the 1920s and 1930s W.E.B. Du Bois forcefully challenged the false universalism of both the Center and the Left within the U.S. American and Pan-European body politic while building alliances with radical nationalist movements and independent governments in the dark world, and beginning a dialogue with revolutionaries in the Soviet Union who were not quite white by the standards of that time. In the 1930s and 1940s many of these forces (Du Bois, Paul Robeson, Richard Wright, Ralph Ellison, C.L.R. James, Angelo Herndon, Oliver Cromwell Cox, E. Franklin Frazier, Ralph Bunche, Abram Harris, George Padmore, Shirley Graham, Claude Lightfoot, John Henrik Clarke) constituted a Black popular front which stood in the forefront of the struggle for defining the Black freedom struggle as one against racism *and* imperialism, and for U.S. involvement in the construction of Henry Wallace's Century of the Common Man (as opposed to the imperialist project of an American century). During the 1950s and early 1960s the continuing influence of the race first radicals influenced the move to the Left within the Nation of Islam under the leadership of Malcolm X, Muhammad Ahmed, and others. During this same period remnants of the Black popular front connected with Dr. King and the civil rights movement (including young militants in both SNCC and the Nation of Islam).

It could not have escaped the attention of American elites that the Black population in the United States has constituted the most consistent base and leadership of the U.S. Left since the time of the Great Migration (1910–1920). What is surprising is that the Clintons thought that Hilary Clinton could so easily win the formerly solid South, since whites left the Democratic Party in such large numbers after the civil rights legislation of 1964 and 1965. After all why is it that the Republicans use a Southern strategy? But the Southern strategy is dead, has been dead since at least the 2000 election, when voter suppression was used to win elections and to give the voting public a sense of its infallibility. So McCain/Palin's attempt to utilize the Southern strategy, but with echoes of the KKK carried little currency with most of the voting public. They clearly had not seen the handwriting on the wall. After all what is the logic of attempting to connect the Southern strategy with anti-immigrant hysteria? Any thought given to the votes of the Latino population in key states in the Southwest?

When Barack Obama entered onto the national stage he struck me as something of a synthesis of the Black sociologist William Julius Wilson and Jesse Jackson during his Rainbow Coalition phase. Wilson argued in the late 1970s that race had declined in significance in determining the life chances of Black people (Wilson 1978). In the late 1980s he argued that universal programs which addressed the structural roots of oppression were more important and more politically viable than race specific programs like affirmative action (Wilson 1987). The subtext was quite straightforward in my view. If you talk about racism to most whites it ends the conversation, and becomes a wedge issue used by Republicans. It is better to emphasize class so one can construct a progressive political coalition that can address the roots of the problems of social subordination, of which racism is only a sympton. This summarizes a great deal of very sophisticated research, but there is not space for a more elaborate presentation. This was confirmed for me sometime later when I learned that Reverend Jeremiah Wright had said that Obama was beginning to sound like Wilson (who by the way had spent many years on the faculty of the University of Chicago).

Part of the strategy that the elites turned to in the 1970s was a policy of benign neglect which Daniel Patrick Moynihan explicitly recommended to President Nixon. It was a policy of taking the issue of racial oppression off the table. Whenever people of color raised the issue they were accused of playing the race card. In 1986 when the issue of racism was given a high profile by the mob which chased a Black youth to his death in Howard Beach Queens, the issue of justice and equality for Black people regained the high profile it had enjoyed for much of the postwar period. One group of organizers called for a boycott of white businesses. But Jesse Jackson argued that such tactics did not attack the real source of the problems. He asserted that we needed to move away from the racial battleground to the economic common ground, and that "the boardrooms of the New York Times, ABC, CBS, and NBC . . . were more segregated than Howard Beach" (Horne 1987).

Obama seemed to differ from Jackson because he was more careful than Jackson to avoid being labeled as simply a Black politician. He also moved strategically to capture a significant section of the political center, unlike the Rainbow Coalition which was much more Left in its stance. To do so he played the "race neutral card" with deliberateness and consistency in an environment where accusation of playing the race card would be used by the "color blind racists" of the Republican Party to neutralize one's ability to appeal to the white electorate.

And of course there are some who want to use Obama's success as an indication that the nation is overcoming its racial divisions. This is of course nonsense. Racism is systemic, it is the foundation of the modern-world-system, of historical capitalism. And it is part of our commonsense, structured into our superegoes. But I do think that the Southern strategy is dead. Has been dying since 2000, but voter suppression has been used effectively to give us a sense that it is still in power. People of color are becoming too large a demographic to simply dismiss by demonizing Blacks and Latinos, especially when Samuel Huntington has been fanning the flames of apocalyptic cultural clashes with long academic tomes about the Hispanic threat, the Muslim threat, and the Chinese threat. Who has forgotten his 1970s declaration that the U.S. and the world suffer from too much democracy. The pushback against white world supremacy has been integral to the rise of oppressed strata throughout the twentieth century. It is not separate from the increased power of working people, women, and increased opposition (or at least a relaxation of) hetero-normativity. The relations of force between the dominant forces and the subordinate forces within the world-system have been altered in favor of subordinate forces over the longue duree of the world-system.

It consists of a need for decolonization of the U.S. Empire both internally and externally.[21] This thrust will continue, whatever Obama does. But his election is a consequence of the slow change in relations of force both internally as people of color increase their numbers within U.S. society, and their strength within the world-system.

While there is great concern among some Leftist intellectuals and activists about what Obama will do, the people that I met while doing GOTV in North Philadelphia on November 4 were very clear that this election represented a potential change in the country that would require continued struggle by the people themselves to advance the agenda toward the change that we need.

Notes

INTRODUCTION: "THE HANDWRITING ON THE WALL"

1. Both Bell (1992) and Asante argue that racism is an intractable problem in U.S. society. See my summary of Asante's position in Chapter 6, "Afrocentrism and Multiculturalism as Strategies for Black Liberation."

2. The term *hegemon* is short for *hegemonic power*, which refers to a state that holds unchallenged dominance in the world economy; there have been three in the five-hundred-year history of world capitalism: the United Provinces, the United Kingdom, and the United States.

3. Fernand Braudel (1902–1985) was the leading exponent of the "Annales" school of history, which emphasizes total history over long historical periods and large geographical space. Braudel argued that time is a social creation and thus that it is of the utmost importance to understand the multiple forms of social time. First we have the short term which is the time of the event. The short term is the tempo of individuals, of our illusions and rapid judgments. It is the chronicler's and journalist's time. It is the most capricious and deceptive form of time. Second, we have the middle run (cyclical or conjunctural time) (10, 25, 50 yrs). It is the narrative of the conjuncture or cycle. We might think here of the long economic cycles of expansion and stagnation in the economy. Third, there is the long term (or longue durée). It is here that "structure" becomes key. The word structure for observers of social life implies organization, coherence, and fairly stable relationships between social realities and people over historical or long periods of time.

Works:

Civilization and Capitalism 15th-18th Century (Three Volumes): *The Structures of Everyday Life; The Wheels of Commerce;* and *The Perspective of the World.*
The Mediterranean And the Mediterranean World in the Age of Philip II
A History of Civilizations
Material Life and Civilization

4. Sekou Toure is the first president of Guinea, 1958–1984. In 1945–6 he became a leader of the trade union movement in French West Africa, founding the Confederation Generale da Travail (CGT), which he led for 12 years. He was alos a founder of the Parti Democatique Africain (PDG), and A member of the Guinean Section of the Rassemblement Democratique Africain (RDA), and in 1952 took over its leadership. See Wallerstein (1962) and Wallerstein (1966).

5. Melanie E. L Bush writes about everyday forms of whiteness in *Breaking the Code of Good Intentions: Everyday Forms of Whiteness* (Bush 2004). Many readers may be familiar with how Peggy McIntosh writes about how whites are carefully taught not to recognize white privelege in her classic essay "White privilege: Unpacking the White Knapsack (McIntosh 1988).

6. Omi and Winant (1994) explain the concept of the rearticulation of racial discourse in *Racial Formation in the United States: From the 1960s to the 1990s.*

7. Historical capitalism is an historical social system, which means that it operates in a systematic manner across the historical long term or longue durre. The form that it takes is that of a capitalist world-economy. World-economy refers to a large economy with an axial division of labor and integrated production processes, but with multiple states and multiple cultures. This is different from a world-empire which has one state. What this means is that the economic processes always cross state borders and cannot be controlled by one state, no matter how powerful. The axial division of labor in this concept refers to the invisible axis which holds the capitalist economy intact binding together core-like processes and peripheral processes. This is what makes for the systemness of the world-economy. It does not necessarily mean world scale, but a social world, a self-enclosed entity. See Wallerstein (2004).

8. See also Scott (1993), Von Eschen (1997), and Plummer (1996).

9. As we shall see later in the book the meeting of representatives from 29 Asian and African countries at Bandung, Indonesia in 1955 had enormous geopolitical impact in their assertion of independence from the colonial powers whose colonies were now declaring or fighting for their independence. This was an important meeting at this time when the people of the dark world were asserting their independence.

10. This excerpt is from a speech made in 1963 after the assassination of President John F. Kennedy.

11. The employee mentality is one which does what is minimally required to keep the job. One takes no initiative because one does not have a sense of ownership.

12. See also Von Eschen (1997) and Plummer (1996).

13. Primitive Accumulation was the concept used by Marx to explain the "original" accumulation which laid the foundations for the emergence of capitalism. See *Capital: The Critique of Political Economy*, Volume 1, Chapter 17.

14. Also in *The Poverty of Philosophy* (Marx 1963: 111–112).

15. See Marx (1963:188–189).

16. See the chapter by I. K. Sundiata (1984) in the same volume.

17. Critiques of modernization theory, which is often the ideological and analytical root of such assumptions, have been provided by Wallerstein (1979), Frank (1984), and Amin (1976).

18. See also Griffler (1993), Hawkins (2000), and Winston James (1998).

19. The Crusader was started by Cyril Briggs, and became the journal of the African Blood Brotherhood.

20. The Communist International determined that Negroes in the United States were said to constitute a nation in the Black Belt South in a large number of contiguous

counties with majority Black populations that stretched from areas of Maryland through Virginia, North Carolina, South Carolina, Georgia, Alabama, Tennessee, Mississippi, Arkansas, Louisiana, and Texas. McKay was connected to raising this issue.

21. See Cruse (1967, 1968) and Drake (1970) for an elaboration of this approach.

22. Gilkes (1996) argues that Du Bois was an exception.

23. See Newton (1972).

CHAPTER 1: THE PECULIAR INTERNATIONALISM OF BLACK NATIONALISM

1. Robert Williams was accused of kidnapping a white couple who wandered into his neighborhood in Monroe, North Carolina during a tense period when they might have been at risk. He took them inside. For this he was accused of kidnapping them. He fled because he thought that law enforcement authorities were after him because of his stance against KKK aggression.

2. Casey Hayden was a SNCC staff member who was also a member of the National Executive Committee of the Students for a Democratic Society (SDS). With Mary King she co-wrote the 1964 position paper from the Waveland Retreat calling for SNCC to confront the issue of sexual discrimination within the organization. The paper called for the SNCC to force the rest of the movement to stop such discrimination and recognize "that this is no more a man's world than it is a white world" (Carson 1981:147–148). A year later Hayden and King (1966) would address the issue of women's rights to the wider peace and freedom movement in the pages of *Liberation*.

3. Gwen Patton was a youth leader for the Montgomery Improvement Association and the Southern Christian Leadership Conference (SCLC). While at Tuskegge Institute she was an activist and antiwar organizer. She was a founding member of the Student mobilization Committee Against the War in Vietnam (SMC) and the national Black anti-War, Anti-Draft Union (NBAWADU). While a SNCC organizer, she chaired its Black Women's Liberation Committee. She was the founder of the National Association of Black Students (Joseph 2006).

Willie Ricks and Cleve Sellers were important leaders of the Student Nonviolent Coordinating Committee (SNCC) who became especially important within the leadership of the organization during the Black Power period.

4. Samora Machel was a leader of FRELIMO, the leading national liberation organization in Mozambique.

5. Max Elbaum was a leader of the New Communist Movement during the late 1960s through the 1980s. Author of *Revolution in the Air: Sixties Radicals Turn to Lenin, Mao and Che*. New York: Verson, 2002.

6. Patricia Hill Collins is the author of the pathbreaking class *Black Feminist Thought: Knowledge, Consciousness, and the Politics of Empowerment* and more recently of *From Black Power to Hip Hop: Racism, Nationalism, and Feminism*. She is presently chair of the American Sociological Association. See Chapter 4 for more on Collins.

CHAPTER 2: THE SOCIOLOGY OF THE COLOR LINE: W.E.B. DU BOIS AND THE END OF WHITE WORLD SUPREMACY

1. I am indebted to Terence K. Hopkins for the term *relations of rule*.

2. These comments reflect the popularity of the natural selection arguments of the predominant social Darwinist outlook of the time.

3. This interpretation is shared by both Meier (1971:104) and Marable (1986:41–43).

4. The Carnegie Foundation was founded by Andrew Carnegie in 1905 and chartered in 1906 by an act of Congress. The Carnegie Foundation for the Advancement of Teaching has a long and distinguished history. It is an independent policy and research center, whose primary activities of research and writing have resulted in published reports on every level of education. Eight presidents have guided the Foundation through its history, each bringing unique shape to its work.

The Rockefeller Foundation (RF) was established in 1913 by John D. Rockefeller, Sr., who amassed a vast fortune as the founder and developer of the Standard Oil Company. According to the Foundation's current President, Gordon Conway, "Mr. Rockefeller gave us a broad mandate to further the "well-being of mankind throughout the world."

5. The details of Du Bois's criticism are spelled out in Du Bois 1961:42–54.

6. In his famous "Of Mr. Booker T. Washington and Others" (Du Bois 1961:42–54), this is not really spelled out clearly, although it is certainly intimated.

7. T. Thomas Fortune was a journalist and editor. He founded *The Globe*, which later became the *The Freeman*, and then *The New York Age*. Fortune was viewed as an agitator. He is known for coining the term Afro-American and for arguing that class conflict was the foundation of race conflict in the post civil war United States. During his years as an agitator he called upon Blacks to arm themselves or retaliate with force. He defended interracial marriage, and was founder of the Afro-American League in 1898 in Rochester, NY.

William Monroe Trotter was the editor of the *Boston Guardian*, and co-founder with W.E.B. Du Bois of the Niagara Movement, an all-Black civil rights organization who opposed the accommodationist approach of Booker T. Washington. Trotter is considered one of the most militant among the Black leaders of this period.

8. This story is told in Marable 1986:45–51.

9. See the Niagara Movement's Declaration of Principles in Grant 1968:206–209.

10. Mary White Ovington was a Brooklyn born white settlment worker from an abolitionist family. William Lloyd Garrison had been a personal friend of her grandfather. She met Du Bois in 1903–1904. While a fellow in social work at Greenwich House in Manhattan she began the study of housing and employment prolems in Black Manhattan. She worked on the precursor to the Urban League and in 1903 joined the Socialist Party. She wrote for Oswald Garrison Villard's New York Post where she covered Booker T. Washington's National Negro League and the Niagara movement. After the race riot in Springfield, Illinois in 1908 she called upon Villard and Walling to organize a national conference on racial justice.

Dr. Henry Moscowitz was a Jewish civil rights activist, a physician, and a socialist. Walling brought him to meet with Mary White Ovington to discuss the call for the conference. In 1917, he was the Commissioner of Public Markets in New York City and associate leader of the Society for Ethical Culture of New York (Ovington 1996).

Oswald Garrison Villard was a progressive, a newspaper publisher (*The New York Post*) and the grandson of the reknowned abolitionist William Lloyd Garrison (Franklin and Moss1998:318). He issued the call for the National Conference on Racial Justice at the behest of Mary Ovington White and William English Walling.

11. See the selection from Du Bois's summary, "The Amenia Conference: An Historic Negro Gathering," in Meier, Rudwick, and Broderick 1971:73–74, summarized in Broderick 1969:371–372.

12. Kantilya is the fictitious Indian Princess in *Dark Princess*. Matthew is the fictitious African American character in *Dark Princess*.

13. Harry Haywood was a member of the African Blood Brotherhood and an early recruit to the Communist Party USA. He is generally said to be responsible for the CPUSA position on the Afro-American national question established in the late 1920s. He is author of *Black Bolshevik:The Autobiography of an Afro-American Communist* and of *Toward Negro Liberation*.

14. Kelly Miller was a Dean at Howard University. He was considered to be much more conservative than most of the Afro-American intellectuals of that period. Miller is known for his leadership of the Negro Sanhedrin, an All Race Assembly led by the NAACP and the National Equal Rights League.

15. I thank Carolyn Moon for bringing this concept to my attention.

CHAPTER 3: THE CLASS-FIRST, RACE-FIRST DEBATE

1. Friederich Engels is co-author with Karl Marx of the *Manifesto of the Communist Party*, and worked closely with Marx on research and theory about capitalism, political economy, the working class, communism, and scientific socialism.

2. The *Messenger* is a magazine published by African American socialists A. Philip Randolph and Chandler Owen. The intellectual group around the *Messenger* is informally referred to as the *Messenger* Group.

3. Claude McKay is a key literary figure in the Harlem Renaissance. He is author of *Home to Harlem*, *The Negro in America*, and a *Long Way From Home*. Many know him for his poem, "If We Must Die."

4. The Lusk Committee was a joint legislative committee to investigate seditious activities formed in 1919 by the New York State legislature. It gathered information about suspected radical organizations by raiding offices and examining documents, infiltrating meetings, assisting in the arrest of radicals, and subpoenaing witnesses for committee hearings. Viewed by some as part of a nationwide "Red Scare" when it occurred throughout the United States after World War I.

5. *The Crusader* was founded by Cyril Briggs, who also put out a call for people to join the African Blood Brotherhood. *The Crusader* became the jouranl of the ABB.

6. The Workers Party was the "above ground" legal arm of the U.S. Communists who had been driven underground during the Palmer Raids of January 1920. See Draper (1986:20-21).

7. Although this article is attributed to Randolph and Owen in the section heading of the book, a footnote indicates that it was an unsigned editorial and their names were listed because they are editors. Winston James has noted that Domingo was the author of some of the key Bolshevik-supporting articles in *The Messenger* (James 1998: 163).

8. Recall that the Workers Party was the above ground, legal arm of the CPUSA which had been driven underground by the Palmer Raids.

9. Leon Trotsky was a leading member of the Bolshevik Party and of the Communist International before Lenin's death in 1924, after which he conflicted with Stalin's strategy of "socialism in one country" and was expelled from the Soviet Union in 1929. Trotsky inspired a "Left Opposition" to Stalinism until he was assassinated in Mexico in 1940.

10. Even after becoming a member of the CPUSA, Briggs continued to refer to himself in terms indicating that his primary affiliation was with the Communist International

and that he was simply assigned to the CPUSA as a resident of the United States. See, for example, his statement about the CPUSA's correct application of the line of the Communist International in a June 1931 article in *The Communist* titled "The Decline of the Garvey Movement," 547–552.

11. Otto Hall was one of the Black cadres of the CPUSA who met with Stalin in 1925 to discuss the Negro Question. He was the older brother of Harry Haywood, but strongly disagreed with Harry about the Negro nation formulation.

12. Abram Harris was a professor at Howard University, an economist. He emphasized the role of class in the subordination of Blacks. He worked with Frazier and Ralph Bunche at Howard.

13. Lovett Fort-Whiteman was one of the earliest Black recruits to the CPUSA. Fort-Whiteman had been a professional Shakespearian actor, and became a drama critic for *The Messenger* from his interaction with the Black socialists on the streets of Harlem. Fort-Whiteman became the top ranking Black member of the CPUSA, responsible for recruiting Blacks into the party (Hutchinson 1995, Draper 1986).

14. M. Sultan-Galiev was a leader of the Moslem Communist Party in the USSR following the Bolshevik Revolution. He sought unsuccessfully to extend its autonomy vis-à-vis the Russian Communist Party from which he was expelled in 1923. I will spell out what I feel to be the significance of the Sultan-Galiev experience later in the chapter.

15. James Allen was the CPUSA's leading theoretician of Negro Liberation during the early 1930s. His actual name was Sol Auerbach. Allen is author of *The Negro Question in the United States* (1936).

16. Here chauvinism refers to expressions of nationalist consciousness or cultural self-assertion by Black people. Such assertions were deemed to be bourgeois and opposed to the working class unity needed for revolutionary struggle within the United States.

17. M.N. Roy was the founder of the Indian Communist Party who while living in Mexico and founding the Mexican Communist Party, elaborated an analysis of the relationship between national liberation and socialist revolution which was very influential within the Communist International. Roy was also a leading member of the Communist International.

18. Heywood Hall is Harry Haywood's real name.

19. See Michael Lewis (1970) for an extensive treatment that indicates that Garveyism was not such a divergence from the U.S. mainstream and was therefore more attractive than more radical approaches, such as that of the Nation of Islam.

20. Jean-Jacques Rousseau was an influential Enlightenment philosopher who argued that human beings are good by nature, but are corrupted by their experience in society.

21. Marx and Engels argued that the struggle for legislation limiting the working day started in England as early as the late eighteenth century and spread by 1830. The Ten Hour Bill limited the maximum number of hours of work per week for all workers to 58 hours. Lord Ashley, a Tory philanthropist led support for the Ten Hour Bill. It was only applicable to children and did not pass until 1847.

22. Mikhail Bakunin was a Russian anarchist, a contemporary of Marx and Engels who had numerous disputes with them within the First International. Pierre-Joseph Proudhon was a French socialist-anarchist. Proudhon wrote a book entitled *What is Property?* (answer: it is theft). He was a printer by trade, whose anarchism envisioned a society of independent, self-employed artisans. According to Bakunin, Proudhon was the first person to call himself an anarchist

23. Otto von Bismarck was Chancellor of Germany from 1862–1890. He is known for designing the world's first old age insurance, and for the strategy of cooptation rather

than repression of the struggles of the working class. He also initiated laws about medical insurance (1883); accident insurance and old-age benefits (1884); and retirement at age 60 (1889) (Beaud 2001). Louis Napoleon Bonaparte, or Napoleon III was the nephew of Napoleon I, and President of the Second Republic (1848–51) during the period when revolutionary struggles emerged all across Europe. Later he became Emperor of the French (1852–1870). Louis Adolphe Thiers (1797–1877) was a French historian and statesman. He was Prime Minister in 1836 and 1840. In the Second Republic he was deputy to the Constituent and Legislative Assemblies. He was President of the Third Republic from 1871–73, and is referred to by Marx as the "hangman of the Paris Commune (Marx 1963:161).

24. The Paris Commune was the first workers government created from the 1871 rebellion of the Parisian working class.

25. Louis Auguste Blanqui was a French revolutionary and utopian Communist. He advocated conspiratorial methods and secret soceieties. He was an organizer of the revolt of May 12, 1839 and during the Revolution of 1848, according to Marx (1963:152), stood on the extreme Left wing of the democratic and proletarian movement in France. He was frequently sentenced to jail terms in France.

26. Jules Guesde was a journalist who founded a socialist weekly *L'Egalite*. In 1880 he joined with Marx's son-in-law Paul Lafarge to form the Workers party and in 1893 was elected to the Chamber of Deputies. In response to their claim to be Marxists, Marx said that if they are marxists, then he is not a Marxist. He was critical that they denied the value of reformist struggles.

27. Eduard Bernstein was a member of the German SPD (a social democratic party) who argued explicitly for an evolutionary rather than a revolutionary parth to socialism. See Bernstein (1961).

28. Polish-born Rosa Luxemburg was one of the leaders of the 1919 Spartacist Revolution in Germany that ended with her murder while in the custody of the German army. She had been the founder of the Polish Social Democratic Party and headed the left wing of the German Social Democratic Party. She was a critic both of Bernsteinian revisionism and of Lenin's centralism. Karl Liebknecht was the son of Wilhelm Liebknecht, one of the founders of the SPD. As a lawyer he defended many Social Democrats in political trials. As a deputy in the Reichstag he was one of the first SPD representatives to break party discipline and vote against war credits in December 1914. He became a figurehead for the struggle against the war. His opposition was so successful that his parliamentary immunity was removed and he was imprisoned.

Freed by the November revolution he immediately threw himself into the struggle and became with Rosa Luxemburg one of the founders of the new Communist Party (KPD). Along with Luxemburg he was murdered by military officers with the tacit approval of the leaders of the SPD after the suppression of the so-called "Spartacist Uprising" in January 1919.

29. Antonio Gramsci (1891–1937) was a leading Italian Marxist. He was an intellectual, a journalist and a major theorist who spent his last eleven years in Mussolini's prisons. During this time, he completed 32 notebooks. The central and guiding theme of the Notebooks was the development of a new Marxist theory applicable to the conditions of advanced capitalism. He emphasized the role of ideology in maintaining the rule of the bourgeoisie in modern societies. His books include *The Modern Prince* and the *Prison Notebooks*. Amadeo Bordiga (13 June 1889–23 July 1970) was an Italian Marxist, a contributor to Communist theory, the founder of the Communist Party of Italy. Bordiga was born at Resina, in the province of Naples. Like other youths in his socialist

cohort he was outraged by the Libyan war and aligned with the revolutionary intransigent group contributing several articles to *La Soffitta* in 1912. Following the October Revolution, Bordiga rallied to the Communist movement and formed the Communist Abstentionist faction within the Socialist Party. Abstentionist in that it opposed participation in "bourgeois elections", the group would form, with the addition of the former L'Ordine Nuovo grouping in Turin around Antonio Gramsci, the backbone of the Communist Party of Italy (PCd'I,Partito Comunista d'Italia)—founded at Livorno in January 1921. This came after a long internal struggle in the PSI: it had voted as early as 1919 to affiliate to the Comintern, but had refused to purge its reformist wing. In the course of the conflict, Bordiga had attended the 2nd Comintern Congress in 1920, where he had added 2 points to the 19 conditions of membership proposed by Vladimir Lenin. Nevertheless, he was criticised by Lenin in his work *Left-Wing Communism: An Infantile Disorder*.

30. The term "Three Continents" is used by some intellectuals from the Arab world to designate what is called the Third World in the West. It is always capitalized. It refers to Asia, Africa, and Latin America (and the Caribbean)

31. C.L.R. James was a Trinidadian intellectual and revolutionary known around the world in radical intellectual and activist circles. He is the author of numerous books, including *The Black Jacobins, The History of Pan-African Revolt, Nkrumah and the Ghana Revolution*, and *Notes on Dialectics*.

32. Malcolm Nurse adopted the cover name George Padmore by 1928 to use when he engaged in business related to the Communist party USA which he joined in mid-1927, according to Hooke (1967:6).

33. Jomo Kenyatta at this time was an outspoken Kenyan nationalist who demanded Kenyan self-government and independence from Great Britain. He helped organize the Fifth Pan-African Congress in Manchester in 1945. He was president of the Kenyan African Union, and later a leader of the Kenyan African National Union which lead Kenya to independence in 1964. Kenyatta was named its first president. Amy Ashwood Garvey was co-founder with Marcus Garvey of the Universal Negro Improvement Association (UNIA) in July 1914. She was the secretary of the organization. She married Marcus Garvey in 1919, and divorced him in 1922. J.B. Danquah was from a prominent family in the Gold Coast (now Ghana), held a doctorate in law, and was an early Gold Coast nationalist. He was a founder of the United Gold Coast Convention in 1946.

34. Kwame Nkrumah was the leader of the independence movement in the Gold Coast, the first president of Ghana, and is considered the most effective advocate of Pan-African unity. He is author of numerous books, including *Africa Must Unite; Neo-Colonialism: The Last Stage of Imperialism*; and *Class Struggle in Africa*.

35. During the 1940s Hugh Smythe worked with W.E.B. Du Bois on special NAACP projects. Later he was a faculty member in the Department of Sociology at Brooklyn College of the City University of New York. He was the first African American to serve as an ambassador in the Middle East (Syria). He was appointed by Lyndon Johnson.

CHAPTER 4: BLACK FEMINISM, INTERSECTIONALITY, AND THE CRITIQUE OF MASCULINIST MODELS OF LIBERATION

1. "The Vanishing Family: Crisis in Black America" (1986). This is a Bill Moyers documentary considered an update on the Moynihan Report. Takes place in Newark, NJ

where Moyers follows a number of young Black women and men in their stories about having children in one-parent (female-headed) families.

CHAPTER 5: THE CIVIL RIGHTS MOVEMENT AND THE CONTINUING STRUGGLE FOR THE REDEMPTION OF AMERICA

1. See Gil Scott-Heron. 1981. "B-Movie," on *Reflections*. Arista Records.

2. Cedric Robinson (2000) has elaborated most eloquently on this notion.

3. Shirley Graham was a well-known writer and activist who married W.E.B. Du Bois in 1951.

4. See Arrighi and Silver (1984).

5. Robert Williams was the president of the Monroe, North Carolina NAACP. He called for Blacks to arm themselves for defense against KKK attacks. He fled to Cuba when law enforcement officials attempted to arrest him for kidnapping a white couple who had wandered into his neighborhood during a tense moment.

6. I present this argument at some length in Bush (1999), building upon the literature on COINTELPRO in O'Reilly (1989); Churchill and Vander Wall (1990); Churchill and Vander Wall (1988).

7. This point is presented in Melanie Bush, *Breaking the Code of Good Intentions: Everyday Forms of Whiteness*. Lanham, MD: Rowman and Littlefield, 2004.

8. Alpheus Hunton was a member of the Communist Party USA and a leader of the Council on African Affairs with Paul Robeson, and W.E.B. Du Bois.

9. See Melanie Bush (2004) for an extended formulation of this idea.

10. Michael Harrington is the author of the landmark book *The Other America* which exposed the poverty that exists in the midst of an affluent United States. The book is often credited with influencing President John F. Kennedy to undertake a federal fight against poverty.

11. Here the term "spectrum" is used deliberately in contradistinction to the word "continuum" which implies too much continuity in views.

12. Samir Amin is an Egyptian economist and lifelong political militant. He was an early exponent of dependency theory and world-systems analysis. He is the author of many books including *Accumulation on a World Scale; Unequal Development: the Social Formations of Perihpheral Capitalism; Capitalism in the Age of Globalization; The Arab World;* and *Beyond U.S. Hegemony*.

13. Howard Winant's description of the evolution of some liberals into neo-conservatives is very insightful. See Howard Winant (1990).

14. Organic intellectuals are intellectuals without formal credentials but who become intellectuals by virtue of their work in organizations of subaltern strata such as trade unions, civil rights movements, women's rights movements, etc. The term is commonly attributed to Antonio Gramsci, a leader of the Italian Communist Party who elaborated a notion of the role of organic intellectuals making common cause with traditional intellectuals to create a new commonsense.

15. Mina Davis Caulfield (1969:202).

16. Mina Davis Caulfield (1974b:72–73).

17. Lee Rainwater is a noted social scientist who has written extensively on the issues of poverty and inequality within the United States. He is author of *The Moynihan Report and the Politics of Controversy*.

18. Here I follow the analysis of Giovanni Arrighi, Terence K. Hopkins, and Immanuel Wallerstein (1989b, 97–115).

19. Immanuel Wallerstein (1984:13–26).

20. Immanuel Wallerstein (1988).

21. See Elijah Anderson (1999:316) and Cornel West (1994:17–31). Anderson differs from West in that he recognizes a strong sense of group consciousness that generates opposition.

22. See Immanuel Wallerstein, "The Ideological Tensions of Capitalism: Universalism versus Racism and Sexism" in Balibar and Wallerstein (1991). I had intended to deal with the issue of sexism later in the book, but did not do so.

23. Queen Mother Audley Moore was a member of the Universal Negro Improvement Association and the Communist Party USA. During the 1960s she became a mentor to many during the Black Pride/Black Power period, including Robert William, Malcolm X, and the Revolutionary Action Movement (Ahmad 2008:7–13)

CHAPTER 6: BLACK POWER, THE AMERICAN DREAM, AND THE SPIRIT OF BANDUNG

1. The Southern Movement refers to the struggle against Jim Crow and related practices in the U.S. American South from the anti-lynching movement of the nineteenth century to the Scottsboro Boys of the 1930s to the Southern Negro Youth Congress (1937–1949), to the Civil Rights Movement of the 1950s and 1960s.

2. Harold Cruse, author of *The Crisis of the Negro Intellectual* and *Rebellion or Revolution* is a former member of the Communist Party USA known among the Black Power generation for his theorization of the concept of domestic colonialism as it applied to Negro Americans, and his assessment that African Americans are a part of the Third World revolt against white world supremacy and U.S. imperialism. The CPUSA and its diaspora viewed Cruse's criticisms in *Crisis* as anti-communist attacks against popular Black intellectuals such as Paul Robeson and W.E.B. Du Bois. People were also concerned by his attack on Caribbean intellectuals as integrationists (wanting to be like whites).

3. T.R. Makonnen is Guyanian, and a founder of the International African Service Bureau. He was very close to George Padmore and a major figure in the Pan-African movement. Like Padmore, he was close to Nkrumah and went to Ghana in 1956 to settle there just before independence. He was imprisoned for several months after the overthrow of the Nkrumah government. He was freed at the behest of Kenyatta, and moved to Kenya where he became a citizen (Makonnen 1973).

4. Jaja Anucha Wachuku (1918–1996), was a Pan-Africanist at heart and action; and a distinguished Nigerian statesman, lawyer, politician, diplomat and humanitarian. He was the first Speaker of the Nigerian House of Representatives, as well as first Nigerian ambassador and Permanent Representative to the United Nations.

5. Leopold Senghor (1906–2001), president of Senegal (1960–1981), and an internationally respected poet, philosopher, and theoretician. A French-speaking African intellectual, Senghor defended and promoted the cultural heritage of Africans, developing the idea of négritude. He led the movement for Senegal's independence and was elected the nation's first president.

Gaston Monnerville (1897–1991) was a French politician and lawyer. The grandson of a slave, he grew up in French Guiana and went to Toulouse to complete his studies.

He became a lawyer in 1918 and worked with César Campinchi, a lawyer who later became an influential politician. He joined the Radical Party and was elected Deputy from French Guiana in 1932. He was Undersecretary of State for the Colonies in the Chautemps government of 1937–1938, becoming the first black man to hold a senior position in the French government.

6. Bernard Magubane is a South African anthropologist who spent much of his academic career at the University of Connecticut at Storrs. He is a member of the African national congress who returned to South Africa after the end of the apartheid regime.

7. Gerald Horne is a prominent scholar activist and a leading authority on the cold war. He is author of *Black Liberation/Red Scare; Race Woman: The Lives of Shirley Graham Du Bois; Class Struggle in Hollywood; Race War: White Supremacy and the Japanese Attack on the British Empire; Black and Red: W.E.B. Du Bois and the Afro-American Response to the Cold War, 1944–1963.*

Brenda Gayle Plummer is author of *Rising Wind: Black Americans and U.S. Foreing Affairs, 1935–1960.*

Penny Von Eschen is author of *Race Against Empire: Black Americans and Anticolonialism, 1937–1957.*

8. Ian Rocksborough-Smith has written about intergenerational connections between the 1940s Left and the civil rights movement of the 1950s and 1960s.

9. James and Grace Lee Boggs were activist intellectuals working in Detroit. James Boggs had been an autoworker and is author of the 1960s classic, *Racism and the Class Struggle.* Grace Lee Boggs is Chinese American and held a Ph.D. in philosophy but worked in the movement all of her adult life. They worked with C.L.R. James, Marty Glaberman, and Raya Dunayevskaya in the 1940s in the Johnson-Forrest Tendency within the Workers Party. They later worked with rhe Revolutionary Action Movement in the 1960s, and later formed their own organization, the National Organization for an American Revolution. They are auhors of *Revolution and Evolution in the Twentieth Century* and *Conversations in Maine.* Grace Lee Boggs is recently author of *Living For Change: An Autobiography.*

10. Roy Wilkins was the Executive Secretary of the NAACP during the 1960s, and had been a member of the leadership of the organiztion since the 1930s. He was hostile to the Left within and outside of the NAACP during the 1940s, and to the Black Power Movement in the 1960s.

Whitney Young was the leader of the Urban League from 1960 to 1971. He influenced President Lyndon Baines Johnson through his advocacy of a domestic Marshall Plan, but broke with Johnson over the Vietnam War in 1969 which he argued was diverting funds from domestic programs needed by the poor. Many Black Power militants viewed Young as an accommodationist leader in the mould of Booker T. Washington.

11. Lin Biao was the second ranking member of the Communist Party of China during the Great Proletarian Cultural Revolution. He was author of an important pamphlet which applied Mao Zedong's theory of Peoples War to a theory of world revolution. He was commander of the People's Liberation Army.

12. Fernand Braudel (1902–1985) was the leading exponent of the "Annales" school of history, which emphasizes total history over long historical periods and large geographical space. Braudel argued that time is a social creation and thus that it is of the utmost importance to understand the multiple forms of social time. First we have the short term which is the time of the event. The short term is the tempo of individuals, of our illusions and rapid judgments. It is the chronicler's and journalist's time. It is the most capricious and deceptive form of time. Second, we have the middle run (cyclical or conjunctural

time—10, 25, 50 years). It is the narrative of the conjuncture or cycle. We might think here of the long economic cycles of expansion and stagnation in the economy. Third, there is the long term (or longue durée). It is here that "structure" becomes key. The word structure for observers of social life implies organization, coherence and fairly stable relationships between social realities and people over historical or long periods of time.

13. The US Organization was founded by Maulana Karenga based on what is now known as the Nguzu Saba, but which in the 1970s was called the Black Value system. As cultural nationalists, the US Organization emphasizes the elaboration of culture, or a cultural revolution as the precondition for the kind of community building and social solidarity necessary to build true power within the social world.

14. Vaclav Havel is a former president of Czechoslovakia and of the Czech Republic. He is also a playwrite and writer.

15. Linda Alcoff is a professor of Philosophy, Women's Studies, and Political Science at Syracuse University. She is the author of *Visible Identities: Race, Gender, And The Self.*

16. Arthur Schlesinger is the author of *The Disuniting of America: Reflections on a Multicultural Society.*

17. Paget Henry is Professor of Sociology and Africana Studies. His specializations are Dependency Theory, Caribbean Political Economy, Sociology of Religion, Sociology of Art and Literature, Africana Philosophy and Religion, Race and Ethnic Relations, Poststructuralism, and Critical Theory. He has served on the faculties of SUNY Stony Brook, University of the West Indies (Antigua), and the University of Virginia. He is the author of *Caliban's Reason: Introducing Afro-Caribbean Philosophy* (Routledge, 2000), *Peripheral Capitalism and Underdevelopment in Antigua* (Transaction Books, 1985), and co editor of *C.L.R. James's Caribbean* (Duke UP, 1992) and *New Caribbean: Decolonization, Democracy, and Development* (Institute for the Study of Human Issues, 1983).

18. Jane Anna Gordon teaches in the Department of Political Science at Temple University, where she also is Associate Director of the Institute for the Study of Race and Social Thought and the Center for Afro-Jewish Studies. She is the author of *Why They Couldn't Wait: A Critique of the Black-Jewish Conflict Over Community Control in Ocean-Hill Brownsville, 1967–1971* (Routledge, 2001), which was listed by The Gotham Gazette as one of the four best books recently published on Civil Rights, and editor of "Radical Philosophies of Education," a special issue of *Radical Philosophy Review*. She also is co-editor of *A Companion to African-American Studies* (Blackwell's, 2006) and *Not Only the Master's Tools* (Paradigm Publishers, 2005). Her current work focuses on problems of legitimacy in democratic societies.

19. The slogan used by New York City mayor David Dinkins during periods of interracial and interethnic strife between Blacks and Koreans and between Blacks and Jews. The slogan used by the militants in New York City, including Sharpton, C. Vernon Mason, and Alton Maddox and the more radical December 12th Movement. When Rev. Al Sharpton claims the mantle of Dr. Martin Luther King, Jr., he is certainly speaking in good faith.

20. Steve Martinot is a union and community organizer, a cultural studies lecturer at San Francisco State, and author of *The Rules of Racialization: Class, Identity, Governance.*

21. See Ramón Grosfoguel, "Latinos and the Decolonization of the U.S. Empire in the 21st Century," *Social Science Information*, 47:4, 605–622.

Bibliography

Abdel-Malek, Anouar. 1981. *Social Dialectics: Nation and Revolution.* Albany: State University of New York Press.

———. 2000. "The Civilizational Orientation in the Making of the New World." *Festschrift for Immanuel Wallerstein,* Part 2. Special issue, *Journal of World-Systems Research* 6, no. 3, Fall–Winter, pp. 564–579.

Abendroth, Wolfgang. 1972. *A Short History of the European Working Class.* New York: Monthly Review.

Aberbach, Joel D., and Jack L. Walker. 1970. "The Meaning of Black Power: A Comparison of White and Black Interpretations of a Political Slogan." *American Political Science Review* 64, pp. 367–388.

Adeleke, Tunde. 1998. *Unafrican Americans: Nineteenth-Century Black Nationalists and the Civilizing Mission.* Lexington, KY: University Press of Kentucky.

Africa-Asia Speaks from Bandong. 1955. "President Sukarno of Indonesia: Speech at the Opening of the Bandung Conference, April 18 1955," *Modern History Sourcebook:* Djakarta: Indonesian Ministry of Foreign Affairs, pp. 19–29.

Ahmad, Akbar Muhammad. 1978. "On the Black Student Movement, 1960–70." *Black Scholar* 9:8–9 (May-June), 2–11.

———. [1980?] "History of RAM—Revolutionary Action Movement." Self-Published pamphlet.

———. 2006. "RAM: The Revolutionary Action Movement." In Judson L. Jeffries, ed., *Black Power in the Belly of the Beast.* Urbana: University of Illinois Press, 252–280.

———. 2007. *We Will Return in the Whirlwind: Black Radical Organizations, 1960–1975.* Chicago: Charles H. Kerr Publishing.

Aidi, Hisham. 2003. "Let Us Be Moors: Islam, Race and "Connected Histories," *Middle East Reports,* (Winter): http://www.merip.org/mer/mer229/229_aidi.html.

Alcoff, Linda Martin. 2006. *Visible Identities: Race, Gender, and The Self.* New York: Oxford University Press.

Alkalimat, Abdul. 1973. *Introduction to Afro-American Studies: A Peoples College Primer.* Chicago, IL: Twenty-First Century Books.

———. 1974. "Imperialism and Black Liberation: A Proposal to Black Intellectuals to Serve the Black Liberation Movement Through a Year of Study and Struggle, 1974–1975, The Year to Pull the Covers Off Imperialism." Unpublished document.

———. 1981. "Search for a Vanguard: A Series of 10 Documentary Anthologies Covering the Revolutionary Aspects of the Black Liberation Movement in the 1970s." Unpublished document.

———. 1990. *Malcolm X for Beginners.* New York: Writers and Readers Publishers.

Allen, Robert. 1970. *Black Awakening in Capitalist America.* Garden City, NY: Anchor Books.

Amin, Samir. 1976. *Unequal Development: An Essay on the Social Formations of Peripheral Capitalism.* New York: Monthly Review Press.

Anderson, Elijah. 1999. *Code of the Street: Decency, Violence, and the Moral Life of the Inner City.* New York: W. W. Norton.

Arrighi, Giovanni, and Beverly Silver. 1984. "Labor Movements and Capital Migration." In Charles Bergquist, ed., *Labor in the Capitalist World-Economy.* Beverly Hills, CA: Sage Publications, pp. 183–216.

Arrighi, Giovanni, Terence Hopkins, and Immanuel Wallerstein. 1989a. *Antisystemic Movements.* New York: Verso.

———. 1989b. "1968: The Great Rehearsal." In Giovanni Arrighi, Terence Hopkins, and Immanuel Wallerstein, eds., *Antisystemic Movements.* New York: Verso, pp. 97–115.

———. 1989c. "Rethinking the Concepts of Class and Status-Group in a World-Systems Perspective." In Giovanni Arrighi, Terence Hopkins, and Immanuel Wallerstein, eds., *Antisystemic Movements.* New York: Verso, pp. 3–28.

Asante, Molefi Kete. 1999. "Systematic Nationalism: A Legitimate Strategy for National Selfhood." In James Conyers and Alva Barnett, eds., *African American Sociology.* Chicago: Nelson Hall, pp. 3–14.

Badiou, Alain. 2005a. "The Cultural Revolution: The Last Revolution." *Positions* 13, no. 3, pp. 481–514.

———. 2005b. "The Triumphant Restoration." *Positions* 13, no. 3, pp. 659–662.

Baldwin, Kate. 2002. *Beyond the Color Line and the Iron Curtain: Reading Encounters between Black and Red, 1922–1963.* Durham, NC: Duke University Press.

Balibar, Etienne, and Immanuel Wallerstein. 1991. *Race, Nation, Class: Ambiguous Identities.* New York: Verso.

Basch, Linda, Nina Glick Schiller, and Cristina Szanton Blanc. 1994. *Nations Unbound: Transnational Projects, Postcolonial Predicaments, and Deterritorialized Nation-States.* Langhorne, PA: Gordon and Breach.

Beale, Frances M. 1995. "Double Jeopardy: To Be Female and Black." In Beverly Guy-Sheftall, ed., *Words of Fire: An Anthology of Black Feminist Thought.* New York: New Press. Originally published in Toni Cade, ed., *The Black Woman.* New York: Signet, 1970.

Beaud, Michel. 2001. *A History of Capitalism, 1500–2000.* New York: Monthly Review Press.

Bell, Derrick. 1992. *Faces at the Bottom of the Well: The Permanence of Racism.* New York: Basic Books.

Belvin, Brent. 2004. "Malcolm X Liberation University: An Experiment in Independent Black Education." Master's thesis, North Carolina State University.

Bermanzohn, Sally Avery. 2003. *Through Survivors' Eyes: From the Sixties to the Greensboro Massacre*. Nashville, TN: Vanderbilt University Press.

Bernstein, Eduard. 1961. *Evolutionary Socialism: A Criticism and Affirmation*. New York: Schocken Books.

Blair, Thomas. 1977. *Retreat to the Ghetto: The End of a Dream?* New York: Hill and Wang.

Bloom, Jack. 1987. *Class, Race, and the Civil Rights Movement*. Bloomington: University of Indiana Press.

Boggs, Grace Lee. 1998. *Living For Change: An Autobiography*. Minneapolis: University of Minnesota.

———. 2005. "Living for Change: Asian Americans Face New Challenges." *Michigan Citizen* 28, no. 37, July 31–August 6, p. B8.

Bourne, Randolph. 1992. *The Radical Will: Selected Writings, 1911–1918*. Edited and with an introduction by Olaf Hansen. Preface by Christopher Lasch. Berkeley: University of California Press.

Bowser, Benjamin P. 2003. "A Meaning of 9/11: Failure of Race Relations at Home Has Led to a Failed U.S. Foreign Policy Overseas." *Sage Race Relations Abstracts* 28, nos. 3–4, pp. 19–24.

Boyd, Todd. 1997. *Am I Black Enough for You: Popular Culture from the 'Hood and Beyond*. Bloomington: University of Indiana Press.

———. 2002. *The New H.N.I.C.: The Death of Civil Rights and the Reign of Hip Hop*. New York: New York University Press.

———. 2003. *Young, Black, Rich and Famous: The Rise of the NBA, the Hip Hop Invasion, and the Transformation of American Culture*. New York: Doubleday.

Bracey, John, August Meier, and Elliott Rudwick, eds. 1970. *Black Nationalism in America*. Indianapolis, IN: Bobbs-Merrill.

Branch, Taylor. 1988. *Parting the Waters: America in the King Years 1954–63*. New York: Simon and Schuster.

———. 1998. *Pillar of Fire: America in the King Years 1963–65*. New York: Simon and Schuster.

Braudel, Fernand. 1972. "History and the Social Sciences: The Longue Duree," in Peter Burke, ed., *Economy and Society in Early Modern Europe*. London: Routlege and Kegan Paul, pp. 11–42.

Braverman, Harry. 1974. *Labor and Monopoly Capital: The Degradation of Work in the Twentieth Century*. New York: Monthly Review Press.

Breitman, George. 1965. *Malcolm X Speaks: Selected Speeches and Statements*. New York: Grove Press.

Brewer, Rose M. 1993. "Theorizing Race, Class and Gender: The New Scholarship of Black Feminist Intellectuals and Black Women's Labor." In Stanlie M. James and Abena P.A. Busia, eds., *Theorizing Black Feminisms: The Visionary Pragmatism of Black Women*. New York: Routledge. Reprinted in Rosemary Hennessy and Chrys Ingraham, eds., *Materialist Feminism: A Reader in Class, Difference, and Women's Lives*. New York: Routledge, 1997.

———. 2003. "Black Radical Theory and Practice: Gender, Race and Class." *Socialism and Democracy* 17, no. 1, Winter–Spring, pp. 109–122.

Briggs, Cyril V. 1929. "Our Negro Work," in *American Communism and Black Americans: A Documentary History, 1919–1929*. Philadelphia: Temple University Press, pp. 245–219.

————. 2005. "The Salvation of the Negro," in *Look for Me All Around You: Anglophone Caribbean Immigrants in the Harlem Renaissance*, Louis J. Parascandola, ed. Detroit: Wayne State University Press, pp. 208–211.

Broderick, Francis L. 1969. "W.E.B. Du Bois: Entente with White Liberals, 1910–1920." In Melvin Drimmer, ed., *Black History: A Reappraisal*. Garden City, NY: Doubleday.

Brown, Elsa Barkley. 1992. "'What Happened Here?' The Politics of Difference in Women's History and Feminist Politics." *Feminist Studies* 18, Summer, pp. 295–312.

Bunche, Ralph J. 1936. "A Critique of New Deal Social Planning as It Affects Negroes." *Journal of Negro Education* 5, no. 1, January, pp. 59–65.

Burnham, Linda. 2001. "The Wellspring of Black Feminist Theory." Working Paper Series, no. 1. Women of Color Resource Center. Memphis, TN.

Burton, Antoinette, Augusto Espiritu, and Fanon Che Wilkins. 2006. "Introduction: The Fate of Nationalisms in the Age of Bandung," *Radical History Review* 95: pp. 145–148.

Bush, Melanie E. L. 2002. "American Identity and the Mechanisms of Everyday Whiteness." *Socialism and Democracy*, Victor Wallis, ed. New York: Research Group on Socialism and Democracy.

————. 2004. *Breaking the Code of Good Intentions: Everyday Forms of Whiteness*. Lanham, MD: Rowman and Littlefield Publishers.

Bush, Roderick. 1999. *We Are Not What We Seem: Black Nationalism and Class Struggle in the American Century*. New York: New York University Press.

————. 2004. "'When the Revolution Came.' Review of Max Elbaum's Revolution in the Air: Sixties Radicals Turn to Lenin, Mao, and Che." *Radical History Review*, no. 90, Fall, pp. 102–111.

————. 2006. "Acting for a Good Society: Racism and Black Liberation in the Longue Duree." In Hernan Vera and Joe Feagin, eds., *Handbook on the Sociology of Racial and Ethnic Minorities*. New York: Springer Publishing.

Carmichael, Stokely (Kwame Ture), and Charles V. Hamilton. 1967. *Black Power: The Politics of Liberation in America*. New York: Random House.

Carmichael, Stokely, with Ekwume Michael Thelwell. 2003. *Ready for Revolution: The Life and Struggles of Stokely Carmichael (Kwame Ture)*. New York: Scribner.

Carson, Clayborne. 1981. *In Struggle: SNCC and the Black Awakening of the 1960s*. Cambridge, MA: Harvard University Press.

————. 1991. *Malcolm X: The FBI File*. New York: Carroll and Graf Publishers.

Castells, Manuel. 1997. *The Power of Identity. Vol. 2 of The Information Age: Economy, Society, and Culture*, Oxford: Blackwell.

Caulfield, Mina Davis. 1974a. "Culture and Imperialism: Proposing a New Dynamic." In Dell Hymes, ed., *Reinventing Anthropology*. New York: Random House.

————. 1974b. "Imperialism, the Family, and Cultures of Resistance." *Socialist Revolution* 4, no. 2, October, pp. 67–85.

Chang, Jeff. 2001. "Where Do We Stand? With Deft Skill and Moral Uncertainty, Asian American Studies Stumbles into the 21st Century." *Colorlines* 4, no. 3, October 31, p. 38.

Churchill, Ward, and Jam Vander Wall. 1988. *Agents of Repression: The FBI's Secret Wars against the Black Panther Party and the American Indian Movement*. Boston: South End Press.

————. 1990. *The COINTELPRO Papers: Documents from the FBI's Secret Wars against Dissent in America*. Boston: South End Press.

Clarke, John Henrik. 1987. "Why Africana History?" John Henrik Clarke Virtual Museum. http://www.nbufront.org/html/MastersMuseums/JHClarke/ArticlesEssays/WhyAfricanaHistory.html.

Clarke, John Henrik. 1994. "Education for a New Reality in the African World." http://www.africawithin.com/clarke/part4of10.htm

Clarke, John Henrik. 1996. *A Great and Mighty Walk*. Directed by St. Clair Bourne, 90 min.

Claudin, Fernando. 1975. *The Communist Movement: From Comintern to Cominform*. New York: Monthly Review Press.

Clegg, Claude Andrew, III. 1997. *An Original Man: The Life and Times of Elijah Muhammad*. New York: St. Martin's Press.

Close, Upton. 1927. *The Revolt of Asia: The End of the White Man's World Dominance*. New York: G. P. Putnam's Sons.

Cobb, William Jelani. 2006. *Antidote to Revolution: African American Anticommunism and the Struggle for Civil Rights, 1931–1954*. New York: Columbia University Press.

Collins, Patricia Hill. 1986. "Learning from the Outsider Within: The Sociological Significance of Black Feminist Thought." *Social Problems* 33, no. 6, pp. 14–32. Reprinted in Joan Hartman and Ellen Messer-Davidow, eds., *(En)Gendering Knowledge: Feminists in Academe*. Chicago: University of Chicago Press, 1991.

———. 1989. "A Comparison of Two Works on Black Family Life." *Signs: Journal of Women in Culture and Society* 14, no. 4, pp. 875–884.

———. 1991. *Black Feminist Thought: Knowledge, Consciousness, and the Politics of Empowerment*. New York: Routledge.

———. 1998. *Fighting Words: Black Women and the Search for Justice*. Minneapolis: University of Minnesota Press.

———. 2004. *Black Sexual Politics: African Americans, Gender, and the New Racism*. New York: Routledge.

———. 2006. *From Black Power to Hip Hop: Racism, Nationalism, and Feminism*. Philadelphia, PA: Temple University Press.

Combahee River Collective. 1981. "A Black Feminist Statement." In Cherrie Moraga and Gloria Anzaldua, ed., *This Bridge Called My Back: Writings by Radical Women of Color*. Watertown, MA: Persephone Press. Originally published in Zillah Eisenstein, ed. *Capitalist Patriarchy and the Case for Socialist Feminism*. New York: Monthly Review Press, 1978.

———. 1986. *The Combahee River Collective Statement: Black Feminist Organizing in the 1970s and 1980s*. Lanham, NY: Kitchen Table, Women of Color Press.

Cone, James. 1991. *Martin and Malcolm and America: A Dream or a Nightmare*. Maryknoll, NY: Orbis Books.

Cox, Oliver. 1950. "Leadership among Negroes in the United States." In Alvin Gouldner, ed., *Studies in Leadership: Leadership and Democratic Action*. New York: Harper and Row, pp. 228–271.

Cruse, Harold. 1962. "Revolutionary Nationalism and the Afro-American," *Studies on the Left*. 2:3.

———. 1967. *The Crisis of the Negro Intellectual*. New York: Morrow.

———. 1968. *Rebellion or Revolution*. New York: Morrow.

Davis, Angela. 1983. *Women, Race, and Class*. New York: Random House.

———. 1990. *Women, Culture and Politics*. New York: Random House.

————. 1998a. "Meditations on the Legacy of Malcolm X," in *The Angela Y. Davis Reader,* Joy James, ed. Malden, MA: Blackwell, pp. 279–288.

————. 1998b. "Black Nationalism: The Sixties and the Nineties," in *The Angela Y. Davis Reader.* Joy James, ed. Malden, MA: Blackwell, pp. 289–293.

Davis, Horace B. 1967. *Nationalism and Socialism: Marxist and Labor Theories of Nationalism to 1917.* New York: Monthly Review Press.

Davis, John P. 1936. "A Survey of the Problems of the Negro under the New Deal." *Journal of Negro Education* 5, no. 1, January, pp. 3–12.

Dawson, Michael C. 1996. "Black Power in 1996 and the Demonization of African Americans." *PS, Political Science and Politics* 29, no. 3, September, pp. 456–461.

Dill, Bonnie Thornton. 1988. "Dialectics of Black Womanhood." In Micheline R. Malson, Elisabeth Mudimbe-Boyi, Jean F. O'Barr, Mary Wyer, eds., *Black Women in America: Social Science Perspectives.* Chicago: University of Chicago Press.

Dorsey, Emmett E. 1936. "The Negro and Social Planning." *Journal of Negro Education* 5, no. 1, January, pp. 105–109.

Drake, St. Clair. 1970. *The Redemption of Africa and Black Religion.* Chicago: Third World Press.

————. 1984. "Black Studies and Global Perspectives: An Essay." *Journal of Negro Education* 53, no. 3, pp. 226–242.

Draper, Theodore. 1986. *American Communism and Soviet Russia.* New York: Viking Press.

Du Bois, W.E.B. 1919. "I.W.W." *Crisis* 18, June, p. 60.

————. 1936. "Social Planning for the Negro, Past and Present." *Journal of Negro Education* 5, no. 1, January, pp. 110–125.

————. 1950. *Russia and America: An Interpretation.* Unpublished manuscript.

————. 1961. *The Souls of Black Folk.* Greenwich, CT: Fawcett Publications.

————. 1968. *The Autobiography of W.E.B. Du Bois.* New York: International Publishers.

————. 1970. *Dusk of Dawn: An Essay toward an Autobiography of a Race Concept.* New York: Schocken Books.

————. 1971. "The Amenia Conference: An Historic Negro Gathering," in *Black Protest Thought in the Twentieth Century,* Meier, August, and Elliott Rudwick, eds. Indianapolis: Bobbs-Merrill, pp. 73–74.

————. 1973. "Marxism and the Negro Problem." In Theodore Vincent, ed., *Voices of a Black Nation: Political Journalism in the Harlem Renaissance.* San Francisco: Ramparts Press, pp. 210–216.

————. 1975. *The Negro.* New York: Henry Holt.

————. 1979. *Black Reconstruction in America: An Essay toward a History of the Part Which Black Folk Played in the Attempt to Reconstruct Democracy in America, 1860–1880.* New York: Atheneum.

————. 1995. *Dark Princess: A Romance.* Jackson: University Press of Mississippi.

————. 1999. *Darkwater: Voices from within the Veil.* Mineola, NY: Dover Publications.

Edsall, Thomas Byrne, and Mary Edsall. 1992. *Chain Reaction: The Impact of Race, Rights, and Taxes on American Politics.* New York: W. W. Norton.

Edwards, Brent Hayes. 2003. *The Practice of Diaspora: Literature, Translation, and the Rise of Black Internationalism.* Cambridge, MA: Harvard University Press.

Elbaum, Max. 2002. *Revolution in the Air: Sixties Radicals Turn to Lenin, Mao, and Che.* New York: Verso.

Emerson, Rupert, and Martin Kilson. 1965. "The American Dilemma in a Changing World: The Rise of Africa and the American Negro." *Daedalus* 94:4 (Fall), pp. 1055–1084.

Essien-Udom, E. U. 1964. *Black Nationalism: A Search for Identity in America.* New York: Dell Publishing.

Evanzz, Karl. 1992. *The Judas Factor: The Plot to Kill Malcolm X.* New York: Thunder's Mouth Press.

Ex-PL Cadre. 1979. "Two Chapters from Progressive Labor Party History." *Theoretical Review,* no. 13, pp. 23–29.

Ford, James W. 1936. "The Communist's Way Out for the Negro." *Journal of Negro Education* 5, no. 1, January, pp. 88–95.

Frady, Marshall. 1996. *Jesse: The Life and Pilgrimage of Jesse Jackson.* New York: Random House.

Frank, Andre Gunder. 1984. "The Unequal and Uneven Historical Development of the World Economy." *Contemporary Marxism* 9, Fall, pp. 71–95.

Fraser, Cary. 2003. "An American Dilemma: Race and Realpolitik in the American Response to the Bandung Conference, 1955." In Brenda Gayle Plummer, ed., *Window on Freedom: Race, Civil Rights, and Foreign Affairs, 1945–1988.* Chapel Hill, NC: The University of North Carolina Press, pp. 115–140.

Frazier, E. Franklin. 1935–1936. "The Du Bois Program in the Present Crisis." *Race* 1, Winter, pp. 11–13.

———. 1998. "The Failure of the Negro Intellectual." In Joyce Ladner, ed., *The Death of White Sociology.* New York: Random House.

Freeman, Don. 1964. "Black Youth and Afro-American Liberation." *Black America,* Fall, pp. 15–16.

Furedi, Frank. 1998. *The Silent War: Imperialism and the Changing Perception of Race.* New Brunswick, NJ: Rutgers University Press.

Gaines, Kevin. 2005. "E. Franklin Frazier's Revenge: Anticolonialism, Nonalignment, and Black Intellectuals' Critiques of Western Culture." *American Literary History* 17, no. 3, pp. 506–529.

Gardell, Mattias. 1996. *In the Name of Elijah Muhammad: Louis Farrakhan and the Nation of Islam.* Durham, NC: Duke University Press.

Garrow, David. 1988. *Bearing the Cross: Martin Luther King, Jr. and the Southern Christian Leadership Conference.* New York: Random House.

Gilkes, Cheryl Townsend. 1996. "The Margin as the Center of a Theory of History: African-American Women, Social Change, and the Sociology of W.E.B. Du Bois." In Bernard W. Bell, Emily R. Grosholz, James B. Stewart, eds., *W. E. B. Du Bois on Race and Culture: Philosophy, Politics, and Poetics.* New York: Routledge.

Gilroy, Paul. 2000. *Against Race: Imagining Political Culture beyond the Color Line.* Cambridge, MA: Harvard University Press.

Gitlin, Todd. 1995. *The Twilight of Our Common Dreams: Why America is Wracked by Culture Wars.* New York: Henry Holt.

Glaude, Eddie S., Jr. 2000. *Exodus! Religion, Race, and Nation in Early Nineteenth-Century Black America.* Chicago: University of Chicago Press.

Goble, Paul. 2004. "Putin and the Dream of Sultan-Galiev." *Chechen Times,* November 25.

Goldman, Peter. 1979. *The Death and Life of Malcolm X.* Bloomington: Indiana University Press.

Gordon, Jane Anna. 2006. "Legitimacy from Modernity's Underside: Potentiated Double Consciousness." *Worlds and Knowledges Otherwise,* Fall, pp. 1–21.

Grant, Joanne. 1968. *Black Protest: History, Documents, Analyses, from 1619 to the Present.* Greenwich, CT: Fawcett Publications.

Grant, Madison. 1920. *The Passing of the Great Race or the Racial Basis of European History*. New York: Charles Scribner and Sons.

Griffler, Keith. 1993. "The Black Radical Intellectual and the Black Worker: The Emergence of a Program for Black Labor, 1918–1938." PhD diss., Ohio State University.

Grosfoguel, Ramon, and Ana Margarita Cervantes-Rodriguez, eds. 2002. *The Modern/Colonial/Capitalist World-System in the Twentieth Century: Global Processes, Antisystemic Movements, and the Geopolitics of Knowledge*. Westport, CT: Praeger Publishers.

Gurley, John. 1982. *Challengers to Communism*. Stanford, CA: Stanford Alumni Association.

Haley, Alex. 1964. *The Autobiography of Malcolm X*. New York: Grove Press.

Hanchard, Michael. 1990. "Identity, Meaning and the African-American." *Social Text* 8:24, pp. 31–42.

Hanchard, Michael. 1999. "Afro-Modernity: Temporality, Politics, and the African Diaspora." *Public Culture* 11:1, pp. 245–268.

Harding, Vincent. 1983. *There is a River: The Black Struggle for Freedom in America*. New York: Random House.

———. 1996. *Martin Luther King: The Inconvenient Hero*. Maryknoll, NY: Orbis Books.

Harrison, Hubert Henry. 1997. *When Africa Awakes*. Baltimore, MD: Black Classics Press.

Hasty, Olga Peters. 2006. "*Beyond the Color Line and the Iron Curtain: Reading Encounters Between Black and Red, 1922–1963* (review)," *Comparative Literature Studies* 43, nos. 1–2, pp. 174–175.

Hawkins, Clifton C. 2000. "'Race First versus Class First': An Intellectual History of Afro-American Radicalism, 1911–1928." PhD diss., University Of California, Davis.

Hayden, Sandra, and Mary King. 1966. "Sex and Caste," *Liberation* (April), pp. 35–36.

Haywood, Harry. 1978. *Black Bolshevik: Autobiography of an Afro-American Communist*. Chicago: Liberator Press.

Henry, Paget. 2006. "Africana Phenomenology: Its Philosophical Implications," *Worlds & Knowledges Otherwise* Fall, pp. 1–23.

Herskovits, Melville. 1958. *The Myth of the Negro Past*. Boston: Beacon.

Hewitt, Cynthia Lucas. 2002. "Racial Accumulation on a World-Scale: Racial Inequality and Employment." *Review* 25, no. 2, pp. 137–171.

Hill, Robert. 1987. *The Crusader*. Vols. 1–3. Los Angeles: UCLA Press, 1987.

Holloway, Jonathan Scott. 2002. *Confronting the Veil: Abram Harris Jr., E. Franklin Frazier, and Ralph Bunche, 1919–1941*. Chapel Hill: University of North Carolina Press.

Holloway, Joseph, ed. 1990. *Africanisms in American Culture*. Bloomington, IN: University of Indiana Press.

Hooker, James. 1967. *Black Revolutionary: George Padmore's Path from Communism to Pan-Africanism*. New York: Praeger Publishers.

Hopkins, Terence, and Immanuel Wallerstein with John Casparis, Georgi Derlugian, Satoshi Ikeda, Richard Lee, Sheila Pelizzon, Thomas Reifer, Jamie Sudler, Faruk Tabak. 1996. *The Age of Transition: Trajectory of the World-System 1945–2025*. London: Zed Press.

Horne, Gerald. 1986. *Black and Red: W.E.B. Du Bois and the Afro-American Response to the Cold War, 1944–1963*. Albany: State University of New York Press.

———. 1987. "Jackson Points to the Classic Issue. *City Sun*, February 4.

———. 1999. "Race from Power: U.S. Foreign Policy and the General Crisis of White Supremacy," *Diplomatic History* 23, no. 3, Summer, pp. 437–461.

Hughes, Langston. 1968. "The Founding of the NAACP." In Joanne Grant, ed., *Black Protest: History, Documents, Analyses, from 1619 to the Present*. Greenwich, CT: Fawcett Publications, pp. 210–214.

Huntington, Samuel P. 2005. *Who Are We: The Challenges to America's National Identity*. New York: Simon and Schuster.

Hutchinson, Earl Ofari. 1995. *Blacks and Reds: Race and Class in Conflict, 1919–1990*. East Lansing: Michigan State University Press.

Isserman, Maurice, and Michael Kazin. 2000. *America Divided: The Civil War of the 1960s*. New York: Oxford University Press.

Jacques-Garvey, Amy, ed. 1968. *Philosophy and Opinions of Marcus Garvey*. Vols. 1 and 2. New York: Atheneum.

James, C.L.R. 1977. *Nkrumah and the Ghana Revolution*. London: Allison and Busby.

———. 1992. "Notes on the Life of George Padmore." In Ann Grimshaw, ed., *The C.L.R. James Reader*. New York: Blackwell Publishers, pp. 288–295.

———. 1993. *World Revolution 1917–1936: The Rise and Fall of the Communist International*. Atlantic Highlands, NJ: Humanities Press.

James, Winston. 1998. *Holding Aloft the Banner of Ethiopia: Caribbean Radicalism in Early Twentieth-Century America*. New York: Verso.

Johnson, Cedric. 2003. "From Popular Anti-Imperialism to Sectarianism: The African Liberation Support Committee and Black Power Radicals." *New Political Science* 25, no. 4, December, pp. 477–507.

Jones, Charles, ed. 1998. *The Black Panther Party Reconsidered*. Baltimore, MD: Black Classics Press.

Joseph, Peniel. 2006. *Waiting 'til the Midnight Hour: A Narrative History of Black Power in America*. New York: Henry Holt.

Kelley, Robin D. G. 1994. *Race Rebels: Culture, Politics, and the Black Working Class*.

———. 1996a. "Kickin' Reality, Kickin' Ballistics: Gangsta Rap and Post-Industrial Los Angeles." In William Eric Perkins, ed., *Droppin' Science: Critical Essays on Rap Music and Hip Hop Culture*. Philadelphia: Temple University Press.

———. 1996b. "The World the Diaspora Made: C.L.R. James and the Politics of History." In Grant Farred, ed., *Rethinking C.L.R. James*. New York: Blackwell Publishers.

Kelley, Robin D. G., and Betsy Esch. 1999. "Black Like Mao: Red China and Black Revolution." *Souls* 1, no. 4, Fall, pp. 6–41.

King, Martin Luther, Jr. 1968. "On Honoring Dr. Du Bois: A Speech." Delivered at Freedomways' Celebration of Dr. W. E. B. Du Bois's 100th Birthday, Carnegie Hall, February 23.

———. 1986a. "Letter from a Birmingham Jail." In James M. Washington, ed., *A Testament of Hope: The Essential Writings and Speeches of Martin Luther King, Jr*. New York: HarperCollins, pp. 289–302.

———. 1986b. "A Time to Break Silence." In James M. Washington, ed., *A Testament of Hope: The Essential Writings and Speeches of Martin Luther King, Jr*. New York: HarperCollins.

Kirby, John B. 1974. "Ralph J. Bunche and Black Radical Thought in the 1930s." *Phylon* 30, no. 2, pp. 129–141.

Kitwana, Bakari. 2002. *The Hip Hop Generation: Young Blacks and the Crisis in African-American Culture*. New York: Basic Books.

Kondo, Baba Zak A. 1993. *Conspiracys: Unraveling the Assassination of Malcolm X*. Washington, DC: Nubia Press.

Krauthammer, Charles. 1990. "The Black Rejectionists," *Time*, 136:4.

Kuumba, M. Bahati. 2002. "You've Struck a Rock": Comparing Gender, Social Move-
    ments, and Transformations in the United States and South Africa." *Gender and
    Society* 16, pp. 504–523.
Layton, Azza Salama. 2000. *International Politics and Civil Rights Policies in the United
    States, 1941–1960.* New York: Cambridge University Press.
Lemelle, Sidney, and Robin D. G. Kelley, eds. 1994. *Imagining Home: Class, Culture and
    Nationalism in the African Diaspora.* New York: Verso.
Levine, Robert S., ed. 2003. *Martin R. Delany: A Documentary Reader.* Chapel Hill, NC:
    University of North Carolina Press.
Lewis, David Levering, ed. 1995. *W.E.B. Du Bois: A Reader.* New York: Henry Holt.
———. 2000. *W.E.B. Du Bois: The Fight for Equality and the American Century, 1919–
    1963.* New York: Henry Holt.
Lewis, Lester. 2002. "George Padmore—The Forgotten Man of History." *New African,*
    June, pp. 48–50.
Lewis, Michael. 1970. "The Negro Protest Movement in Urban America," in *Protest,
    Reform, and Revolt,* Joseph Gusfield, ed. New York: John Wiley & Sons, Inc., pp.
    149–190.
Lewis, Oscar. 1970. "A Culture of Poverty." In *Anthropological Essays.* New York: Ran-
    dom House, pp. 67–80.
Lewis, Oscar, Ruth Lewis, and Susan Rigdon. 1977a. *Four Men: Living the Revolution,
    an Oral History of Contemporary Cuba.* Urbana: University of Illinois Press.
———. 1977b. *Four Women: Living the Revolution, an Oral History of Contemporary
    Cuba.* Urbana: University of Illinois Press.
Lin Biao. 1965. *Long Live the Victory of People's War!* Beijing: Foreign Language Press.
Lincoln, C. Eric. 1973. *The Black Muslims in America.* Boston, MA: Beacon Press.
Lomax, Louis. 1963. *When the Word Is Given: A Report on Elijah Muhammad, Malcolm
    X, and the Black Muslim World.* New York: Signet.
———. 1968. *To Kill a Black Man.* Los Angeles: Holloway House.
Maeda, Daryl. 2006. "Black Panthers, Red Guards and Chinamen: Constructing Asian
    American Identity Through Performing Blackness, 1969–1972." *Works and Days*
    47/48, 24, nos. 1–2., pp. 117–140.
Magubane, Bernard. 1984. "The Political Economy of the Black World—Origins of the
    Present Crisis." In James Turner, ed., *The Next Decade: Theoretical and Research
    Issues in Africana Studies.* Ithaca, NY: Africana Studies and Research Center, Cor-
    nell University, pp. 281–298.
———. 1987. *The Ties that Bind: African-American Consciousness of Africa.* Trenton,
    NJ: Africa World Press.
Makonnen, Ras. 1973. *Pan-Africanism from Within.* New York: Oxford University Press.
Malcolm X. 1965. *The Autobiography of Malcolm X.* New York: Grove Press.
———. 1966. *Malcolm X Speaks.* New York: Pathfinder.
———. 1971. *The End of White World Supremacy: Four Speeches.* New York: Merlin Press.
———. 1992. *The Final Speeches: February 1965.* New York: Pathfinder.
Makalani, Minkah. 2004. *For the Liberation of Black People Everywhere:The African
    Blood Brotherhood, Black Radicalism, and Pan-African Liberation in the New Negro
    Movement, 1917–1936.* PhD. Diss., University of Illinois at Urbana-Champaign.
Mao Zedong. 1967. "On Practice." *Selected Works of Mao Tse-tung.* Vol. 1. Peking: For-
    eign Language Press, p. 308.
Marable, Manning. 1981. *Blackwater: Historical Studies in Race, Class Consciousness
    and Revolution.* Dayton, OH: Black Praxis Press.

———. 1985. *Race, Reform and Rebellion: The Second Reconstruction in Black America, 1945–1982.* Jackson: University of Mississippi Press.

———. 1986. *W.E.B. Du Bois: Black Radical Democrat.* Boston: Twayne Publishers.

Martin, Tony. 1976. *Race First: The Ideological and Organizational Struggles of Marcus Garvey and the Universal Negro Improvement Association.* Dover, MA: Majority Press.

Martinez, Elizabeth. 2003. "Don't Call This Country 'America': How the Name Was Hijacked and Why It Matters Today More Than Ever." *Z Magazine*, July–August, pp. 69–72.

Martinot, Steve. 2007. "Dual-State Character of U.S. Coloniality: Notes toward Decolonization." *Human Architecture: Journal of the Sociology of Self* 5, special double issue, Summer, pp. 371–382.

Marx, Karl. 1963a. *The Poverty of Philosophy.* New York: International Publishers.

Marx, Karl. 1963b. *The Eighteenth Brumaire of Louis Bonaparte.* New York: International Publishers.

McKay, Claude. 1979. *The Negroes in America.* Port Washington, NY: Kennikat Press.

McKinney, Ernest Rice. 1936. "The Workers Party's Way Out for the Negro." *Journal of Negro Education* 5, no. 1, January, pp. 96–99.

Meier, August. 1962. "Negro Class Structure and Ideology in the Age of Booker T. Washington." *Phylon* 23, pp. 258–266.

———. 1971. *Negro Thought in America, 1880–1915.* Ann Arbor: University of Michigan Press.

Meier, August, and Elliott Rudwick. 1976. *From Plantation to Ghetto.* 3rd ed. New York: Hill and Wang.

Mignolo, Walter. 2007. "The Decolonial Option and the Meaning of Identity in Politics," *Anales* 9:10, pp. 43–72.

Miliband, Ralph. 1977. *Marxism and Politics.* New York: Oxford University Press.

Mintz, Sidney. 1974. *Caribbean Transformations.* New York: Columbia University Press.

Mintz, Sidney, and Richard Price. 1992. *The Birth of African-American Culture: An Anthropological Perspective.* Boston: Beacon Press.

Monteiro, Anthony. 2000. "Being and African in the World: The Du Boisian Epistemology." *Annals of the American Academy of Political and Social Science* 568, March, pp. 220–234.

Monthly Review Editors. 1964. "The Colonial War at Home." *Monthly Review* 16, no. 1, May, pp. 1–13.

Moses, Wilson Jeremiah. 1978. *The Golden Age of Black Nationalism, 1850–1925.* New York: Oxford University Press.

———. 1996. *Classical Black Nationalism: From the American Revolution to Marcus Garvey.* New York: New York University Press.

———. 1998. *Afrotopia: The Roots of African American Popular History.* New York: Cambridge University Press.

Moynihan, Daniel Patrick. 1967. "The Negro Family: A Case for National Action", in *The Moynihan Report And The Politics Of Controversy*, Lee Rainwater and W.L. Yancey, eds. Cambridge, MA: M.I.T. Press.

———. 1968. "The Professors and the Poor," in *On Understanding Poverty: Perspectives from the Social Sciences*, Daniel Patrick Moynihan, ed. New York: Basic Books, pp. 3–35.

———. 1974. "The Politics of Stability" in *Coping: On the Practice of Government.* New York: Vintage.

Mullen, Bill V. 2003. "Du Bois, *Dark Princess*, and the Afro-Asian International," *positions*, 11:1 (Spring), pp. 217–240.

Mullen, Bill V. 2004. *Afro-Orientalism*. Minneapolis, MN: University of Minnesota Press.

Myrdal, Gunnar. 1944. *An American Dilemma*. 2 vols. New York: McGraw-Hill.

Newton, Huey. 1972. *To Die for the People*. New York: Random House.

Omi, Michael, and Howard Winant. 1986. *Racial Formation in the United States: From the 1960s to the 1980s*. New York: Routledge and Kegan Paul.

Omi, Michael, and Howard Winant. 1994. *Racial Formation in America: From the 1960s to the 1990s, Second Edition*. New York: Routledge.

O'Reilly, Kenneth. 1989. *Racial Matters: The FBI's Secret File on Black America, 1960–1972*. New York: Free Press.

Owen, Robert. 1827. *Second Discourse On A New System Of Society*.

Padmore, George. 1971. *The Life and Struggles of Negro Toilers*. Hollywood: Sun Dance Press.

———. 1972. *Pan-Africanism or Communism*. Garden City, NY: Doubleday Anchor Books.

Painter, Nell Irvin. 1976. *Exodusters: Black Migration to Kansas after Reconstruction*. New York: Alfred Knopf.

Parker, George Wells. 1981. *The Children of the Sun*. Baltimore, MD: Black Classics Press.

Patterson, Tiffany R., and Robin D. G. Kelley. 2000. "Unfinished Migrations: Reflections on the African Diaspora and the Making of the Modern World." *African Studies Review* 43, no. 1, pp. 11–46.

Perry, Jeffrey. 2001. *A Hubert Harrison Reader*. Middletown, CT: Wesleyan University Press.

Pinderhughes, Charles. 2006. "The Continuing Relevance of Internal Colonialism Theory." Paper read at the 36th Annual Meeting of the Association of Black Sociologists, Montreal, Quebec, Canada, August 8–11.

Piven, Frances Fox, and Richard A. Cloward. 1997. *The Breaking of the American Social Compact*. New York: The New Press.

Platt, Anthony M. 1991. *E. Franklin Frazier Reconsidered*. New Brunswick, NJ: Rutgers University Press.

Plummer, Brenda Gayle. 1996. *Rising Wind: Black Americans and U.S. Foreign Policy*. Chapel Hill: University of North Carolina Press.

Price, Richard. 1996. *Maroon Societies: Rebel Slave Communities in the Americas, Third Edition*. Baltimore, MD: The John Hopkins University Press.

Quadagno, Jill. 1994. *The Color of Welfare: How Racism Undermined the War on Poverty*. New York: Oxford University Press.

Quijano, Anibal. 2000. "The Coloniality of Power, Eurocentrism and Latin America. *Nepantla: Views from the South* 1, no. 3, pp. 533–580.

———. 2000. "The Coloniality of Power and Social Classification." Originally published as "Coloniadad del poder y clasificacion social." *Festschrift for Immanuel Wallerstein*, Part 1. Special issue, *Journal of World-Systems Research* 6, no. 3, Fall–Winter 2000, pp. 342–386.

RAM. 1965a. "The African American War of National-Liberation." *Black America*, Summer–Fall, pp. 3–4, 12, 18–19.

———. 1965b. "The Relationship of Revolutionary Afro-American Movement to the Bandung Revolution." *Black America*, Summer–Fall, p. 11.

Randolph, A. Philip. 1936. "The Trade Union Movement and the Negro." *Journal of Negro Education* 5, no. 1, January, pp. 54–58.

Ransby, Barbara. 1989. "Abortion Is a Race and Class Issue." *The Guardian*, October 25, p. 1.

———. 2000. "Black Feminism at Twenty-one: Reflections on the Evolution of a National Community." *Signs: Journal of Women in Culture and Society* 25, no. 4, Summer, pp. 1215–1221.

———. 2003. *Ella Baker and the Black Freedom Movement: A Radical Democratic Vision.* Chapel Hill: University of North Carolina Press.

Reed, Adolph, Jr. 1997. *W.E.B. Du Bois and American Political Thought: Fabianism and the Color Line.* New York: Oxford University Press.

Reed, Adolph, and Julian Bond. 1991. "Equality: Why We Can't Wait." *The Nation* 253, no. 20, December 9, pp. 733–737.

Rhea, Joseph Tilden. 1997. *Race Pride and the American Identity.* Cambridge, MA: Harvard University Press.

Robinson, Cedric. 1983. *Black Marxism: The Making of the Black Radical Tradition.* London: Zed Press.

———. 1997. *Black Movements in America.* New York: Routledge.

Rocksborough-Smith, Ian. 2007. "Filling the Gap: Intergenerational Black Radicalism and the Popular Front ideals of Freedomways Magazine's Early Years (1961–1965)." *Afro-Americans in New York Life and History,* 31:1 (January), pp. 7–42.

Rodinson, Maxime. 1979. "Sultan Galiev—A Forgotten Precursor." In Maxine Rodinson, ed., *Marxism and the Muslim World.* London: Zed Press, 1979.

Rose, Tricia. 1994. *Black Noise: Rap Music and Black Culture in Contemporary America.* Hanover, NH: Wesleyan University Press.

Rosenthal, A. M. 1995. "On My Mind: Farrakhan Owned the Day," *New York Times,* October 17.

Rossanda, Rossana. 1971. "Mao's Marxism." *Socialist Register,* pp. 53–80.

Ryan, William. 1971. *Blaming the Victim.* New York: Vintage Books.

Sales, Williams W., Jr. 1994. *From Civil Rights to Black Liberation: Malcolm X and the Organization of African American Unity.* Boston: South End Press.

Saxton, Alexander. 1990. *The Rise and Fall of the White Republic: Class Politics and Mass Culture in Nineteenth-Century America.* New York: Verso.

Schlesinger, Arthur M., Jr. 1991. *The Disuniting of America: Reflections on a Multicultural Society.* New York: W.W. Norton.

Scott, Daryl Michael. 1997. *Contempt and Pity: Social Policy and the Image of the Damaged Black Psyche, 1880–1996.* Chapel Hill, NC: University of North Carolina Press.

Scott, William R. 1993. *The Sons of Sheba's Race: African-Americans and the Italo-Ethiopian War, 1935–1941.* Bloomington: University of Indiana Press.

Simmonds, Yussuf J. 2007. "George Padmore: Revolutionary, Scholar, and Father of Pan Africanism." *Los Angeles Sentinel,* July 5–11, p. A10.

Singh, Nikhil Pal. 2004. *Black Is a Country: Race and the Unfinished Struggle for Democracy.* Cambridge, MA: Harvard University Press.

Sleeper, Jim. 1991. "Blacks and Jews," *The Nation,* September 9, pp. 252–253.

Smith, Barbara. 1979. "Notes from Yet Another Paper on Black Feminism, Or Will the Real Enemy Please Stand Up." *Conditions Five* 2, no. 1, pp. 123–127.

———. 1985. "Some Home Truths on the Contemporary Black Feminist Movement." In Beverly Guy-Sheftall, ed., *Words of Fire: An Anthology of African-American Feminist Thought.* New York: New Press, 1995.

————. 1998a. *The Truth That Never Hurts: Writings on Race, Gender, and Freedom*. New Brunswick, NJ: Rutgers University Press.

————. 1998b. "'We Refuse to Be Bought Off': An Open Letter from Barbara Smith." *Women's Forum*, June, p. 8.

Stanford, Maxwell C., Jr. 2003. "We Will Return in the Whirlwind: Black Radical Organizations 1960–1975." PhD diss., Union Institute and University.

Steinberg, Stephen. 1993. *Turning Back: The Retreat from Racial Justice in Thought and Policy*. Boston: Beacon Press.

Stephens, Michelle. 1998. "Black Transnationalism and the Politics of National Identity: West Indian Intellectuals in Harlem in the Age of War and Revolution." *American Quarterly* 50, no. 3, pp. 592–608.

————. 1999. "Black Empire: The Making of Black Transnationalism by West Indians in the United States." PhD diss., Yale University.

————. 2005. *Black Empire: The Masculine Global Imaginary of Caribbean Intellectuals in the United States, 1914–1962*. Durham, NC: Duke University Press.

Stoddard, Lothrop. 1921. *The Rising Tide of Color against White World-Supremacy*. New York: Charles Scribner and Sons.

Stuckey, Sterling. 1972. *The Ideological Origins of Black Nationalism*. Boston, MA: Beacon Press.

————. 1975. "History of the Black Peoples of America." In *The World Encyclopedia of Black People*. Vol. 1. St. Clair Shores, MI: Scholarly Press, pp. 221–240.

————. 1987. *Slave Culture: Nationalist Theory and the Foundations of Black America*. New York: Oxford University Press.

Sultan-Galiev, M. 1982. "The Social Revolution in the East." *Review* 4, no. 1, Summer, pp. 3–11.

Sundiata, I. K. 1984. "Africa's Contribution: African History in World Context." In James Turner, ed., *The Next Decade: Theoretical and Research Issues in Africana Studies*. Ithaca, NY: Africana Studies and Research Center, Cornell University, pp. 95–106.

Takaki, Ronald. 1993. *A Different Mirror: A History of Multicultural America*. Boston: Little, Brown.

Thomas, Darryl. 2001. *The Theory and Practice of Third World Solidarity*. Westport, CT: Praeger.

Thomas, Norman. 1936. "The Socialist's Way Out for the Negro." *Journal of Negro Education* 5, no. 1, January, pp. 100–104.

Touré, Askia. Nd. "Askia Touré Talks To *Konch*." Ishmael Reed's *Konch Magazine*. http://www.ishmaelreedpub.com/articles/toure.html.

Touré, Sekou. 1959. *Toward Full Re-Africanisation; Policy and Principles of the Guinea Democratic Party*. Paris: Presence Africaine.

Touré, Sekou. 1972. "The African Elite in the Anti-Colonial Struggle," *The Black Scholar*, 3:5 (January), 211.

Tunteng, P. Kiven. 1974. "George Padmore's Impact on Africa: A Critical Appraisal." *Phylon* 35, no. 1, pp. 33–44.

Tyner, James. 2006. *The Geography of Malcolm X: Black Radicalism and the Remaking of American Space*. New York: Routledge.

Tyson, Timothy. 1999. *Radio Free Dixie: Robert F. Williams and the Roots of Black Power*. Chapel Hill, NC: University of North Carolina Press.

Van Deburg, William L. 1997. *Modern Black Nationalism: From Marcus Garvey to Louis Farrakhan*. New York: New York University Press.

Von Eschen, Penny. 1997. *Race against Empire: Black Americans and Anticolonialism, 1937–1957*. Ithaca, NY: Cornell University Press.

Waller, Signe. 2002. *Love and Revolution: A Political Memoir: People's History of the Greensboro Massacre, Its Setting and Aftermath*. Lanham, MD: Rowman and Littlefield.

Wallerstein, Immanuel. 1962. "The Political Ideology of the P.D.G.," *Présence africaine*, Eng. ed., 12 (1st Quarter 1962), pp. 30–41.

———. 1966. "The Comparative Study of the Radicalization of Nationalist Movements in Black Africa," *Transactions of the Sixth World Congress of Sociology, Evian, 4–11 September 1966*.

———. 1967. *Africa: The Politics of Unity*. New York: Random House.

———. 1979. *The Capitalist World-Economy*. New York: Cambridge University Press.

———. 1984. *The Politics of the World-Economy*. New York: Cambridge University Press.

———. 1988. "The Myrdal Legacy: Racism and Underdevelopment as Dilemmas." Lecture at University of Stockholm, Faculty of Social Sciences, November 10.

———. 1991a. "Antisystemic Movements: History and Dilemmas." In Samir Amin Giovanni Arrighi, Andre Gunder Frank, Immanuel Wallerstein eds., *Transforming the Revolution: Social Movements in the World System*. New York: Monthly Review Press.

———. 1991b. *Geopolitics and Geoculture: Essays on the Changing World-System*. New York: Cambridge University Press.

———. 1998. *Utopistics: Or Historical Choices of the Twenty-first Century*. New York: New Press.

———. 1999. *The End of the World As We Know It: Social Science in the Twenty-first Century*. Minneapolis: University of Minnesota Press.

———. 2000. "The Twentieth Century: Darkness at Noon?" Keynote address at PEWS 24, "The Modern World-System in the Twentieth Century." Boston College, March 24.

———. 2004. *World-Systems Analysis: An Introduction*. Durham, NC: Duke University Press.

Wallerstein, Immanuel, and Paul Starr, eds. 1971. *The University Crisis Reader: The Liberal University under Attack*. Vol. 1. New York: Random House.

Washington, Booker T. 1965. *Up from Slavery*. New York: Avon Books.

———. 1971. "The Atlanta Exposition Address—September 1895." In August Meier, Elliott Rudwick, and Francis Broderick, eds., *Black Protest Thought in the Twentieth Century*. New York: Bobbs-Merrill.

Washington, Booker T., and Robert E. Park. 1913. *The Man Farthest Down: A Record of Observation and Study in Europe*. Garden City, NY: Doubleday Page.

Washington, James M., ed. 1986. *A Testament of Hope: The Essential Writings and Speeches of Martin Luther King, Jr.* New York: HarperCollins.

Weber, Max. 1978. *Economy and Society: An Outline of Interpretive Sociology*. Vol. 2. Berkeley: University of California Press.

Weinbaum, Alys Eve. 2001. "Reproducing Racial Globality: W.E.B. DuBois and the Sexual Politics of Black Nationalism," *Social Text* 19:2 (Summer), pp. 15–41.

West, Cornel. 1991. "Nihilism in Black America: A Danger that Corrodes from Within," *Dissent*, Spring 1991, pp. 221–226.

———. 1994. *Race Matters*. New York: Random House.

White, Stephen. 1974. "Communism and the East: The Baku Congress, 1920." *Slavic Review* 33, no. 3, September, pp. 492–514.

Wilder, Gary. 2004. "Race, Reason, Impasse: Cesaire, Fanon, and the Legacy of Emancipation." *Radical History Review*, no. 90, Fall, pp. 31–61.

Wilkins, Fanon Che. 2001. "'In the Belly of the Beast': Black Power, Anti-Imperialism, and the African Liberation Solidarity Movement 1968–1975." PhD diss., New York University.

———. 2006. "Beyond Bandung: The Critical Nationalism of Lorraine Hansberry, 1950–1965." *Radical History Review*, no. 95, Spring, pp. 191–210.

Wilson, Edmund. 1972. *To the Finland Station: A Study in the Writing and Acting of History*. New York: Farrar, Straus, and Giroux.

Winant, Howard. 1990. "Postmodern Racial Politics in the United States: Differences and Inequality." *Socialist Review* 20, no. 1, January–March, pp. 121–147.

Wolfenstein, Eugene Victor. 1981. *The Victims of Democracy: Malcolm X and the Black Revolution*. Berkeley: University of California Press.

Wood, Joe, ed. 1992. *Malcolm X in Our Own Image*. New York: St. Martin's Press.

Woodard, Komozi. 1999. *A Nation within a Nation: Amiri Baraka (LeRoi Jones) and Black Power Politics*. Chapel Hill: University of North Carolina Press.

Wright, Richard. 1956. *The Color Curtain: A Report on the Bandung Conference*. London: Dennis Dobson.

INDEX